Mathematics

Sadlier School

Cover: *Series Design:* Studio Montage;
Title design: Quarasan, Inc.

Photo Credits: Cover: age fotostock/Keith Levit: *bottom left;* Rainer Martini: *right.* Getty Images/Jupiterimages: *top left;* Siede Preis: *bottom left.* Used under license from Shutterstock.com/RoboLab: *background.* Interior: age fotostock/Justus de Cuveland/im: 225; Sonderegger Christof: 39. Alamy/caia images/Moretti/Viant: 8 *top.* Blend Images/Corbis: 38 *top;* GM Visuals: 224 *top;* John Lund/Sam Diephuis: 132 *top.* Corbis/Reuters/ISSEI KATO: 9. Dreamstime.com/Steve Allen: vi *bottom left;* Njnightsky: vi *top right.* Getty Images/Jupiterimages: vi *center.* Masterfile/Royalty Free: 302 *top.* Used under license from Shutterstock.com/Ilya Akinshin: vi *bottom right;* Jana Guothova: 8 *bottom,* 38 *bottom,* 132 *bottom,* 224 *bottom,* 302 *bottom;* koosen: vi *top left;* RoboLab: 1, vi *background;* Ivan Ryabokon: vi *top left.* SuperStock/age fotostock/Steven Bernard: 133; Cusp: 303.

Illustrator Credit: Dave Titus

For additional online resources, go to sadlierconnect.com.

William H. Sadlier, Inc.
9 Pine Street
New York, NY 10005-4700

Printed in the United States of America.
ISBN: 978-1-4217-3355-5
1 2 3 4 5 6 7 8 9 WEBC 17 16 15 14 13

Contents

NEW YORK COMMON CORE LEARNING STANDARDS

		Page	CCLS
Welcome!		vi	
Unit 1	**Focus on Operations and Algebraic Thinking**		
	Progress Check/Home Connect	7	
	Essential Question	9	
Lesson 1	Use Grouping Symbols and Evaluate Numerical Expressions	10	5.OA.1; 5.OA.2
Lesson 2	Write and Interpret Numerical Expressions	18	5.OA.2
Lesson 3	Analyze Numerical Patterns	26	5.OA.3
	Common Core Review	34	
	Performance Task	ONLINE	
Unit 2	**Focus on Number and Operations in Base Ten**		
	Progress Check/Home Connect	37	
	Essential Question	39	
Lesson 4	Understand Place Value	40	5.NBT.1
Lesson 5	Powers of 10: Use Patterns and Whole-Number Exponents	48	5.NBT.2
Lesson 6	Read and Write Decimals to Thousandths	56	5.NBT.3a
Lesson 7	Compare Decimals to Thousandths	64	5.NBT.3b
Lesson 8	Round Decimals: Use Place Value	72	5.NBT.4
Lesson 9	Multiply Fluently with Multi-Digit Numbers	80	5.NBT.5
Lesson 10	Divide Whole Numbers: Use Place Value Strategies	88	5.NBT.6
Lesson 11	Divide Whole Numbers: Use Properties of Operations	96	5.NBT.6
Lesson 12	Add and Subtract Decimals to Hundredths	104	5.NBT.7
Lesson 13	Multiply Decimals to Hundredths	112	5.NBT.7
Lesson 14	Divide Decimals to Hundredths	120	5.NBT.7
	Common Core Review	128	
	Performance Task	ONLINE	

NEW YORK COMMON CORE LEARNING STANDARDS

CCLS

Unit 3 Focus on Number and Operations–Fractions

		Page	CCLS
Progress Check/Home Connect		131	
Essential Question		133	
Lesson 15	Add and Subtract Fractions with Unlike Denominators	134	5.NF.1
Lesson 16	Problem Solving: Add and Subtract Fractions	142	5.NF.2
Lesson 17	Interpret Fractions as Division	150	5.NF.3
Lesson 18	Interpret Products of Fractions	158	5.NF.4a
Lesson 19	Find Areas of Rectangles: Tile and Multiply	166	5.NF.4b
Lesson 20	Interpret Multiplication of Fractions as Scaling	174	5.NF.5a; 5.NF.5b
Lesson 21	Problem Solving: Multiply Fractions and Mixed Numbers	182	5.NF.6
Lesson 22	Divide Unit Fractions by Whole Numbers	190	5.NF.7a
Lesson 23	Divide Whole Numbers by Unit Fractions	198	5.NF.7b
Lesson 24	Problem Solving: Divide Unit Fractions and Whole Numbers	206	5.NF.7c
Common Core Review		214	
Performance Task		ONLINE	

Unit 4 Focus on Measurement and Data

		Page	CCLS
Progress Check/Home Connect		223	
Essential Question		225	
Lesson 25	Convert Customary Measurement Units	226	5.MD.1
Lesson 26	Convert Metric Measurement Units	234	5.MD.1
Lesson 27	Problem Solving: Use Line Plots	242	5.MD.2
Lesson 28	Understand Concepts of Volume Measurement	250	5.MD.3a; 5.MD.3b
Lesson 29	Measure Volume	258	5.MD.4
Lesson 30	Find Volume: Relate Packing of Unit Cubes to Multiplying	266	5.MD.5a
Lesson 31	Find Volume: Use the Associative Property	274	5.MD.5a

continued next page

NEW YORK COMMON CORE LEARNING STANDARDS

		Page	CCLS
Lesson 32	Problem Solving: Apply Volume Formulas for Prisms	282	5.MD.5b
Lesson 33	Problem Solving: Decompose Figures to Find Volume	290	5.MD.5c
Common Core Review		298	
Performance Task		ONLINE	

Unit 5 Focus on Geometry

		Page	CCLS
Progress Check/Home Connect		301	
Essential Question		303	
Lesson 34	Understand Points on the Coordinate Plane	304	5.G.1
Lesson 35	Graph Points to Represent Problem Situations	312	5.G.2
Lesson 36	Analyze Properties to Classify Two-Dimensional Figures	320	5.G.3; 5.G.4
Common Core Review		328	
Performance Task		ONLINE	

Performance Task 1	217
Performance Task 2	331
Foundational Skills Handbook	337
Problem-Solving Model	343
Common Core State Standards for Mathematical Practice	346
Glossary	347
Index	351

Welcome

You have an exciting year ahead of you. You will be learning more about mathematics and the tools you will need to solve everyday problems.

Did you know that you solve problems and use math all the time? Think about your day. When you play sports after school, shop at your favorite store, cook delicious food, build something awesome like a tree house, or travel in a car, bus or train, you are using math and applying that understanding to make sense of the world around you.

Common Core Progress will help you improve problem-solving skills while becoming more confident in mathematics. That's why it's called *progress*.

Have a great year!

UNIT 1

Look at how the Common Core standards you have learned and will learn connect.

It is very important for you to understand the standards from the prior grade level so that you will be able to develop an understanding of operations and algebraic thinking in this unit and be prepared for next year. To practice your skills, go to sadlierconnect.com.

GRADE 4 I Can...	Before Unit 1	GRADE 5 Can I ?	After Unit 1	GRADE 6 I Will...
4.OA.1 Interpret a multiplication equation as a comparison Write multiplication equations to represent multiplicative comparisons	☐	**5.OA.1** Write and evaluate expressions that use parentheses, brackets, or braces	☐	**6.EE.1** Write repeated multiplication expressions as exponential expressions Evaluate numerical expressions involving exponents
4.OA.2 Solve word problems involving multiplicative comparisons by multiplying or dividing	☐ ☐	**5.OA.2** Write simple expressions that record calculations with numbers Interpret numerical expressions without evaluating them	☐ ☐	**6.EE.2** Write expressions that use numbers and letters standing for numbers Evaluate expressions for given values of their variables
4.OA.5 Generate a pattern of numbers or shapes that follows a given rule Explore and explain features of patterns generated from given rules	☐	**5.OA.3** Generate two numerical patterns using two given rules, and explore how the two patterns are related	☐	**6.EE.3** Generate equivalent expressions **6.EE.6** Use variables and expressions when solving a real-world or mathematical problem

HOME ✦ CONNECT...

Your child has used the Order of Operations to evaluate numerical expressions. This year they will be asked to interpret a real-world problem and find its solution by writing a numerical expression or equation. These problems will involve more than one operation, which often requires your child to use more than one grouping symbol.

You can help your child by recalling the purpose of the Order of Operations and its definition: a set of a rules that is used to evaluate mathematical expressions given more than one operation.

The Order of Operations:

- Evaluate inside grouping symbols.

  parentheses ( )

  brackets [ ]

  braces { }
- Multiply or divide from left to right.
- Add or subtract from left to right.

On the Go: The next time you and your child have extra time, challenge him or her to write numerical expressions for ones you say aloud. For example, you could say: "add six and nine, and then double the sum" or ask "What is two less than the quotient of fifteen and three?"

In this unit your child will:

- Use grouping symbols and evaluate numerical expressions.
- Write and interpret numerical expressions.
- Analyze numerical patterns.

NOTE: All of these learning goals for your child are based on the Grade 5 Common Core State Standards for Mathematics.

Ways to Help Your Child

As your child's math lessons become more challenging, be sure to avoid making negative comments such as "I was never good at math," or "I don't like math." A positive attitude is important to your child's academic success. And if your child is learning math in ways that are new to you, learn together.

ONLINE

For more Home Connect activities, continue online at sadlierconnect.com

Focus on Operations and Algebraic Thinking

UNIT 1

Essential Question:
How can you apply the properties of operations to represent, interpret, and evaluate numerical expressions?

Lesson 1

Use Grouping Symbols and Evaluate Numerical Expressions

Essential Question:
How do grouping symbols affect the values of numerical expressions?

5.OA.1, 5.OA.2

Words to Know:
- numerical expression
- parentheses
- grouping symbols
- evaluate
- brackets
- braces

Guided Instruction

In this lesson you will write and evaluate expressions that have parentheses and other grouping symbols.

Understand: Order of Operations and parentheses

Mr. Jay's class wins 10 books for its library. 3 books are nonfiction, 5 books are fiction, and the remaining books are reference books. Write and evaluate an expression to find the number of reference books.

To find the number of reference books, you add to find the total number of nonfiction and fiction books, and then subtract the sum from the total number of books. Write a numerical expression to model this.

A numerical expression is a mathematical phrase containing only numbers and one or more operation symbols.

Use parentheses, ( ), to show that the addition is done before the subtraction. Parentheses are grouping symbols. They group part of an expression together to show that it should be evaluated first.

total number of books the class wins		number of nonfiction books		number of fiction books
↓		↓		↓
10	−	(3	+	5)

Now, evaluate, or find the value of, the expression to find the number of reference books. Do the calculations inside parentheses first.

$10 - (3 + 5)$ ← Numerical expression.
$10 - 8$ ← Add inside parentheses.
2 ← Subtract.

Remember!
Order of Operations:
- Evaluate inside grouping symbols.
- Multiply or divide from left to right.
- Add or subtract from left to right.

➡ Two of the books the class wins are reference books.

Zak wrote the expression $10 - 3 + 5$ to represent the problem. Explain why the expression Zak wrote is not correct.

Guided Instruction

Understand: Using more than one set of grouping symbols

A baking company makes 634 loaves of bread each day. They sell 350 loaves to supermarkets and 275 loaves to restaurants. They donate the rest to a local shelter. Write and evaluate an expression to find the number of loaves the company donates over a 5-day workweek.

Step 1

Write an expression for the number of loaves the company sells each day.

350	+	275
loaves sold to supermarkets		loaves sold to restaurants

Step 2

Subtract that sum from 634 to represent the number of loaves the company donates each day.

Use parentheses to show that the addition is done first.

634	−	(350 + 275)
loaves made each day		loaves sold each day

Step 3

Multiply the expression from Step 2 by 5 to represent the number of loaves the company donates in 5 days. You need to use another set of grouping symbols to show that the expression in Step 2 is evaluated *before* the multiplication. When you need to put one set of grouping symbols inside another, use brackets, [ ], for the outside set.

[634 − (350 + 275)]	×	5
loaves donated each day		Number of days

Step 4

Evaluate the expression. When there is more than one set of grouping symbols in an expression, work from the inside out.

$[634 - (350 + 275)] \times 5$ ← Numerical expression.
$[634 - 625] \times 5$ ← Add inside the parentheses.
9×5 ← Subtract inside the brackets.
45 ← Multiply.

➡ The baking company donates 45 loaves of bread during a 5-day workweek.

Guided Instruction

Connect: What you know about grouping symbols and evaluating expressions

Evaluate: $\{\frac{2}{6} + [4 \times (\frac{5}{6} + \frac{2}{6})]\} \div 5$

The expression $\{\frac{2}{6} + [4 \times (\frac{5}{6} + \frac{2}{6})]\} \div 5$ contains three sets of grouping symbols: parentheses, brackets, and braces { }.

To evaluate an expression with more than one set of grouping symbols, work from the inside set of grouping symbols (the parentheses) out.

$\{\frac{2}{6} + [4 \times (\frac{5}{6} + \frac{2}{6})]\} \div 5$ ← Numerical expression.

$\{\frac{2}{6} + [4 \times \frac{7}{6}]\} \div 5$ ← Add inside the parentheses.

$\{\frac{2}{6} + \frac{28}{6}\} \div 5$ ← Multiply inside the brackets.

$\frac{30}{6} \div 5$ ← Add inside the braces.

$5 \div 5 = 1$ ← Divide.

➡ The value of $\{\frac{2}{6} + [4 \times (\frac{5}{6} + \frac{2}{6})]\} \div 5$ is 1.

Sam and Raj wrote expressions for the following problem:

Olivia's grandfather gave her $10 for mowing his lawn. She spent $6 of her earnings on a movie and added the rest to $32 she already had saved. How much in total has she saved?

Sam wrote $(10 - 6) + 32$, and Raj wrote $10 - 6 + 32$. Explain why both expressions are correct.

Guided Practice

Complete the operations within the grouping symbols first to evaluate each expression.

1. [1,225 − (568 − 203)] × 10

[1,225 − ______] × 10

______ × 10

______

2. $\frac{2}{5} + (4\frac{4}{5} - 3)$

$\frac{2}{5}$ + ____

____

Solve the problem.

3. Amy has twenty $1 bills and twelve $10 bills. Kevin has forty-two $1 bills and eighteen $5 bills. How much more money than Kevin does Amy have?

a. Insert grouping symbols to write a numerical expression that models this problem.

Amy: Kevin:
20 × 1 + 12 × 10 − 42 × 1 + 18 × 5

b. Evaluate the expression and answer the question.

Think • Pair • Share

MP7 **4.** Compare expressions a–d. Then evaluate each and tell which two expressions are equivalent. Explain your reasoning.

a. 36 − {[15 + (3 × 10)] ÷ 5}

b. 36 − [15 + (3 × 10 ÷ 5)]

c. 36 − [(15 + 3) × (10 ÷ 5)]

d. 36 − 15 + 3 × 10 ÷ 5

Independent Practice

Evaluate each expression.

1. $15 - (7 + 6)$

   $15 -$ ____

   ____

2. $(24 - 10) \div (2 + 5)$

   ____ $\div$ ____

   ____

3. $[100 - (58 + 16)] \times 91$

   $[100 -$ ____ $] \times 91$

   ____ $\times 91$

   ____

4. $\frac{3}{8} - [(1 + 1\frac{1}{8}) - \frac{7}{8} \times 2]$

   $\frac{3}{8} - [$ ____ $- \frac{7}{8} \times 2]$

   $\frac{3}{8} - [$ ____ $-$ ____ $]$

   $\frac{3}{8} -$ ____

   0

List the operations in the order they should be performed.

5. $160 - [9 \div (12 \times 4) + 6]$

   multiplication

   ____

   ____

   ____

6. $\{[(18 - 3) \div 3] + 2\} \times 7$

   ____

   division

   ____

   ____

7. Which expression is equivalent to $[8 + (2 \times 7) + 12] \div 2$?

   a. $8 + 2 \times 7 + 12 \div 2$

   b. $[8 + (2 \times 7 + 12) \div 2]$

   c. $(8 + 2 \times 7 + 12) \div 2$

   d. $(8 + 2) \times 7 + 12 \div 2$

MP2 8. Interpret the two expressions below without evaluating them.
$19 - (6 + 6)$ and $19 - 6 + 6$

Independent Practice

Evaluate each expression. Show your work.

9. $(4 + 11) \times 9$

10. $52 \div (\frac{1}{2} + 3\frac{1}{2})$

11. $(9 + 7) \times 10 + 145$

12. $[(5\frac{4}{8} - 5\frac{3}{8}) \times (19 - 11)] \times 16$

13. $205 \div [14 \times (2 + 1) - 37]$

14. $2 \times [5\frac{1}{6} - (3\frac{1}{6} + 1\frac{5}{6})$

For exercises 15–17, circle the correct answer.

15. A bouquet of flowers contains 4 carnations, 3 roses, and 5 tulips. Which expression represents how many flowers are in 10 bouquets?

a. $10 \times (4 + 3 + 5)$

b. $10 \times 4 + 3 + 5$

c. $(10 \times 4) + 3 + 5$

d. $4 + 3 + 5 \times 10$

16. Don has 45 yards of fabric. He uses $5\frac{3}{4}$ yards to make a blanket and $1\frac{1}{4}$ yards to make a pillow. If Don makes 4 blankets and pillows, which expression represents how many yards of fabric will he have left?

a. $45 - 5\frac{3}{4} + 1\frac{1}{4} \times 4$

b. $4 \times (5\frac{3}{4} + 1\frac{1}{4}) - 45$

c. $45 - [(5\frac{3}{4} + 1\frac{1}{4}) \times 4]$

d. $(45 - 4) \times (5\frac{3}{4} + 1\frac{1}{4})$

17. Lucia and Matteo want to buy a basketball that costs $17 and a backboard that costs $85. Lucia babysat for 5 hours last week and earned $6 per hour. Matteo babysat for 7 hours and earned $5 per hour. If they combine their babysitting money, which expression represents how much more money will they need to buy the basketball and backboard?

a. $(5 \times 6 + 7 \times 5) - (17 + 85)$

b. $[(17 + 85) - 5 \times 6 + 7]$

c. $5 \times [6 + (7 \times 5)] - (17 + 85)$

d. $(17 + 85) - (5 \times 6 + 7 \times 5)$

Independent Practice

MP2 **18.** Look at the expression below. Without evaluating, tell whether the value of the expression would be the same or different without parentheses. Explain.
$(5 \times 1) + (3 \times 5) + (2 \times 10)$

MP3 **19.** Ari has 4 boxes of pencils. Each box has 6 red pencils and 8 blue pencils. He wants to divide all the pencils equally between his 2 sisters. Ari wrote the expression $(4 \times 6 + 8) \div 2$ and plans to give each sister 16 pencils. Is he correct? Explain.

MP1 **20.** Which expression below has the greater value?

a. $\{1340 - [15 \times (4 + 16)]\} + 18$

b. $1340 - \{[(15 \times 4) + 16] + 18\}$

Show your work.

Answer ______________________________

MP2 **21.** Rewrite the expression below inserting parentheses so that the value of the expression is 144.

$12 - 9 + 45 \times 3$

Show your work.

Answer ______________________________

Independent Practice

MP3 **22.** Joseph says that $[(5 + 12) \times 2] - (9 + 7)$ is the same as $5 + 12 \times 2 - 9 + 7$. What is his error?

Show your work.

Answer ____________________

____

Write and evaluate an expression to solve the problem.

MP2 **23.** Leila uses $1\frac{1}{4}$ cups of orange juice, $2\frac{3}{4}$ cups of cranberry juice, and 3 cups of seltzer to make punch. If Leila wants to serve the punch to 7 people, how many cups of punch will each person get?

Show your work.

Answer ____________________

MP2 **24.** Ralf is packing 180 books. He has 3 large boxes, and each box holds 25 books. He has 2 medium boxes, and each box holds 18 books. He has 5 small boxes, and each box holds 12 books. Can Ralf pack all 180 books with the boxes he has? Explain.

Show your work.

Answer ____________________

Lesson 2

Write and Interpret Numerical Expressions

Essential Question:
How do you write and interpret numerical expressions?
5.OA.2

Guided Instruction

In this lesson you will write expressions to represent calculations with numbers. You will also interpret numerical expressions without evaluating them.

Understand: How to write numerical expressions

Write a numerical expression to represent each of the following phrases.
"twice the sum of five and seven"
"three times the result of subtracting four from nine"
"two less than the result of dividing fifteen by three"
"one more than five groups of two-fifths"

To write a numerical expression for each phrase, think about what the words mean. Identify the operations, and use numbers, symbols, and parentheses.

- "*twice* the *sum* of five and seven"
  $(5 + 7) \times 2$
- "three *times* the result of *subtracting* four from nine"
  $3 \times (9 - 4)$
- "two *less than* the result of *dividing* fifteen by three"
  $15 \div 3 - 2$
- "one *more than* five *groups of* two-fifths"
  $5 \times \frac{2}{5} + 1$

Remember!
When necessary, use parentheses to group the operation that needs to be performed first.

➡ The numerical expressions for the phrases:
$(5 + 7) \times 2$
$3 \times (9 - 4)$
$15 \div 3 - 2$
$5 \times \frac{2}{5} + 1$

Parentheses are not needed in the last two expressions because multiplication and division are done before addition and subtraction.

✏ What is another way to write "one more than five groups of two-fifths" in words?

Understand: How to interpret numerical expressions

Andrea writes the expression $3 \times (235 + 62)$ to represent the inventory in her store. Jacob writes the expression $235 + 62$ to represent the inventory at his store. How does Andrea's inventory compare to Jacob's inventory.

To compare the values of Andrea and Jacob's expressions without evaluating them, interpret the numbers, operations, and the placement of the parentheses.

Both expressions contain $235 + 62$, or the *sum* of 235 and 62. Andrea's expression $3 \times (235 + 62)$, *multiplies* $235 + 62$ by 3, or *triples* that sum.

The value of Andrea's expression $3 \times (235 + 62)$ is 3 times as much as the value of Jacob's expression $235 + 62$.

➡ Andrea has 3 times as many items in inventory at her store as Jacob has at his store.

There are many ways to compare expressions using words.

Less	Equal	More
less than fewer than smaller than	the same as equal to equivalent to	more than greater than larger than times as many

Interpret the expressions below. Then compare their values without evaluating them.

Equivalent numerical expressions are numerical expressions with the same value.

a. $(30 + 100) \div 15$ and $(100 + 30) \div 15$

b. $4 + (2\frac{5}{6} - 1\frac{7}{6})$ and $5 + (2\frac{5}{6} - 1\frac{7}{6})$

Guided Instruction

Connect: What you know about writing and interpreting numerical expressions

Jamal and Katie bring water bottles to the soccer tournament for the team. Jamie brings three cases of twenty-four bottles, plus four extra bottles. Katie brings three cases of twenty-four bottles, but she and her brother drink two of the bottles on the way to the tournament.

Write numerical expressions to represent how many water bottles Jamal and Katie each bring to the soccer tournament. How does the number of water bottles that Jamal brings compare to the number that Katie brings?

Step 1

Write word phrases and numerical expressions to represent how many water bottles Jamal and Katie bring.

Jamal: three *groups of* twenty-four plus four *more*.
$3 \times 24 + 4$

Katie: three *groups of* twenty-four *less* two.
$3 \times 24 - 2$

Step 2

Interpret the expressions.

Both expressions contain 3×24, or 3 groups of 24.
Jamal's expression is 4 *more than* 3×24.
Katie's expression is 2 *less than* 3×24.

Step 3

Compare the values of the expressions.

The value of $3 \times 24 + 4$ is *greater than* the value of $3 \times 24 - 2$.

Both expressions contain 3×24, but the value of Jamal's expression is greater than the value of Katie's expression because it adds 4 to 3×24 instead of subtracting 2.

➡ Jamal brings 6 more water bottles to the soccer tournament.

Guided Practice

Write a numerical expression for each phrase. The first two are started for you.

1. eleven plus three and seven-eighths

   11 ____ $3\frac{7}{8}$

2. ten less than one hundred twenty

   120 ________

3. five more than eight groups of seven-tenths

   ____

4. eight more than the result of dividing three hundred fifty by two

   ____

Interpret and explain the two expressions without evaluating them. The first one is started for you.

5. $7 \times (4 + 8)$ and $4 + 8$

   $7 \times (4 + 8)$ is 7 times as much as $4 + 8$ because

6. $(19 - 2\frac{3}{4}) + 5$ and $(19 - 2\frac{3}{4}) - 5$

Think • Pair • Share

MP7 7. Two students compared the expressions below.

$12 + 3 - \frac{2}{3}$ and $(12 + 3 - \frac{2}{3}) \times 2$

Tricia says $(12 + 3 - \frac{2}{3})$ is half as much as $(12 + 3 - \frac{2}{3}) \times 2$.

Ava says $(12 + 3 - \frac{2}{3}) \times 2$ is twice as much as $(12 + 3 - \frac{2}{3})$.

Explain why both students are correct.

Independent Practice

Complete the numerical expression for each phrase.

1. thirteen multiplied by eight and one half

   13 ____ $8\frac{1}{2}$

2. twenty-one less than two hundred thirty

   230 ____ 21

3. seventeen added to two groups of five

   17 ____ 2 ____ 5

4. nine less than the result of dividing twelve by four

   12 ____ 4 ____ 9

Complete the phrase for each numerical expression.

5. $18 \times (9 - 1)$

   eighteen ____________ the number that is one ____________ nine

6. $7 + (10 - 4)$

   seven ____________ than ten ____________ four

7. $(6 + 4\frac{3}{4}) \div 2$

   the ____________ of six and four and three-fourths ____________ by two

8. $(4 \times \frac{3}{4}) - 5$

   five ____________ than the ____________ of four and three-fourths

Without evaluating, compare the two expressions. Tell whether the value of the first expression is *less than*, *greater than*, or *equal to* the value of the second expression.

9. $7 + \frac{11}{13}$ and $3 \times (7 + \frac{11}{13})$

   ____

10. $(8 - 2) \times (5 - 1)$ and $(5 - 1) \times (8 - 2)$

    ____

11. $15\frac{1}{4} \times 2$ and $(15\frac{1}{4} \times 2) \div 3$

    ____

12. $(15 - 6) - 7 \times 2$ and $(15 - 6) - 4 \times 2$

    ____

Independent Practice

Write a numerical expression for each phrase.

13. twenty minus four and two-thirds plus two

____

14. seven less than the product of five and sixty

____

15. eighteen and five-sixths divided by three

____

16. twice the sum of three and nineteen

____

Write a word phrase for each numerical expression.

17. $5 + 10 - 2$

18. $903 \times (1 + 7)$

19. $(13\frac{2}{3} + 3) \div 8$

20. $17 - (12 \div 6)$

Interpret and explain the two expressions without evaluating them.

21. $3 + (16 \div 2)$ and $16 \div 2$

22. $(10 - 4\frac{3}{4}) + 9$ and $9 + (10 - 4\frac{3}{4})$

Independent Practice

Solve the problems.

MP3 **23.** Luke said that "three divided by twenty-one" is the same as "twenty-one divided by three". Is Luke correct? Explain why or why not.

MP3 **24.** Is "seven and one seventh less than the product of two times five" the same as "two multiplied by five and then decreased by seven and one seventh"? Explain why or why not.

MP2 **25.** Tyrone has $(17 + 2) \times 100$ baseball cards. Evelyn has $17 + 2$ baseball cards. Without evaluating, explain how the number of Tyrone's baseball cards compares to the number of Evelyn's baseball cards.

MP7 **26.** Jaime has $14 \div 2 - 3\frac{1}{3}$ feet of string. Charlotte has $14 \div 2$ feet of string. Without evaluating, compare the expressions to tell who has more string. Explain.

Independent Practice

MP2 **27.** Petra and Billy have stamp collections. Petra has three groups of one hundred stamps, plus nine more. Billy has three groups of one hundred stamps.

Write numerical expressions to show how many stamps Petra and Billy have. How do the expressions compare? Who has more stamps?

Answer ______________________________

Justify your answer using words, drawings, or numbers.

MP2 **28.** Rajit and Samantha are playing a game. Rajit scored seven hundred plus the result of subtracting eleven from two hundred nineteen points. Samantha scored the result of subtracting eleven from two hundred nineteen, increased by seven hundred points.

Write numerical expressions to represent each player's score. How do the expressions compare? Who scored more points?

Answer ______________________________

Justify your answer using words, drawings, or numbers.

MP3 **29.** Janelle says that "two groups of nine, plus four and two-thirds" is the same as "nine plus four and two-thirds, multiplied by two." What is her error?

Lesson 3

Analyze Numerical Patterns

Essential Question:
How can you identify relationships between corresponding terms of two numerical patterns?

5.OA.3

Words to Know:
- numerical pattern
- corresponding terms
- coordinate plane
- *x*-axis
- *y*-axis
- origin
- ordered pair
- coordinates

Guided Instruction

In this lesson you will generate two numerical patterns using two rules. You will identify relationships between them and graph corresponding terms of the two patterns.

Understand: How to generate and analyze two numerical patterns

Carlos saves $1 each week. Ana saves $3 each week. After 4 weeks, how does the amount Ana saved compare to the amount Carlos saved?

To find how the amounts Carlos and Ana save increase each week, generate numerical patterns. A numerical pattern is a list of numbers that follows a constant rule. This rule is an expression that tells how to complete the numerical pattern.

Carlos saves $1 the first week and then adds $1 to his savings each week. So, to generate a pattern for Carlos's savings, start with 1 and use the rule: *add 1*.

+1 +1 +1 +1

Carlos: 1, 2, 3, 4, 5, . . .

Ana saves $3 the first week and then adds $3 to her savings each week. So, to generate a pattern for Ana's savings, start with 3 and use the rule: *add 3*.

+3 +3 +3 +3

Ana: 3, 6, 9, 12, 15, . . .

Corresponding terms are terms that are in the same position in the two patterns. Pairs of corresponding terms are circled below.

Carlos:	1,	2,	3,	4,	5
Ana:	3,	6,	9,	12,	15

Notice that all the terms in Ana's pattern are three times the corresponding terms in Carlos's pattern.

To compare the amounts saved after four weeks, look at the fourth pair of corresponding terms. Carlos saved $4 and Ana saved $12. You can find how much more Ana saved than Carlos by subtracting: $\$12 - \$4 = \$8$.

$3 \times \$4 = \$12$ shows that Ana saved three times as much as Carlos.

➡ Ana saved $8 more than Carlos, or three times as much as Carlos.

Guided Instruction

Understand: How to graph ordered pairs of corresponding terms from two patterns

Below are Carlos and Ana's patterns with corresponding terms circled.

Carlos: 1, 2, 3, 4, 5
Ana: 3, 6, 9, 12, 15

Write the corresponding terms as ordered pairs and graph them on a coordinate plane. Describe the pattern of points.

Ordered pairs are pairs of numbers in the form (x, y), in which the order of the numbers is important. Below are ordered pairs for Carlos and Ana's patterns. Notice that Carlos's value comes first in each pair.

(1, 3) (2, 6) (3, 9) (4, 12) (5, 15)

The numbers in an ordered pair are called coordinates. The first number is called the x-coordinate, and the second is called the y-coordinate. Carlos's values are the x-coordinates, and Ana's are the y-coordinates.

On a coordinate plane, ordered pairs are located using a horizontal number line, called the x-axis, and a vertical number line, called the y-axis. The x-axis and y-axis intersect to form perpendicular number lines. The two number lines meet at their 0 points. This intersection point is called the origin, or (0, 0).

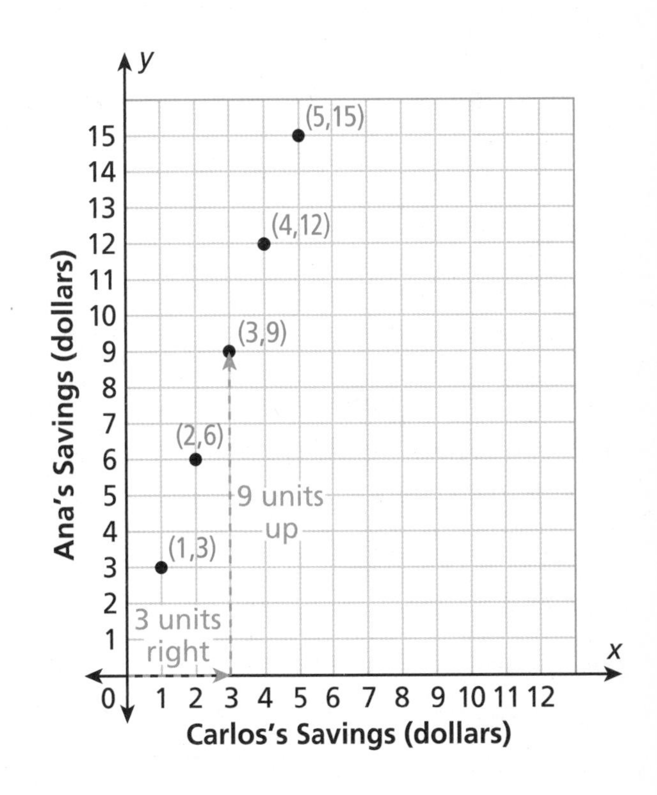

Here, the x-axis represents Carlos's savings and the y-axis represents Ana's savings.

To graph an ordered pair, start at the origin, or (0, 0), and move right the number of units indicated by the x-coordinate, and then move up the number of units indicated by the y-coordinate. For example, to graph (3, 9), move right 3 units and up 9 units.

➡ The ordered pairs for Carlos and Ana's patterns are shown on the coordinate plane. The points follow a straight-line pattern that moves upward from left to right.

Guided Instruction

Connect: What you know about generating and relating two numerical patterns

A baker uses 3 cups of flour and 2 cups of berries in each loaf of blueberry bread. Generate numerical patterns to show how the number of cups of flour and berries used changes as the number of loaves increases.

Describe how the corresponding terms of the two patterns are related, and graph the pairs on a coordinate plane.

You can show the patterns in a table, where corresponding pairs are in the same column. There are 3 cups of flour in the first loaf, and 3 more cups for each additional loaf. The rule is *add 3*. There are 2 cups of berries in the first loaf, and 2 more cups for each additional loaf. The rule is *add 2*.

Cups of Flour: *add 3*	3	6	9	12	15
Cups of Berries: *add 2*	2	4	6	8	10

Look for relationships in the corresponding terms.
Here are some relationships:

The difference in the first pair of terms, 3 and 2, is 1. The differences of the next four pairs are 2, 3, 4, 5. The difference increases by 1 each time.

The sums of the pairs are 5, 10, 15, 20, and 25. The sum increases by 5 each time.

➡ Graph the ordered pairs (3, 2), (6, 4), (9, 6), (12, 8), and (15, 10). Notice that the points form a straight-line pattern that moves upward from left to right.

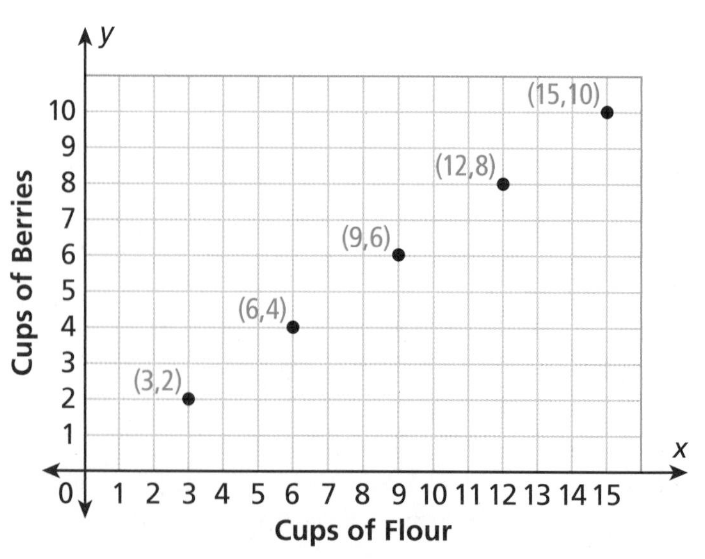

Guided Practice

1. Each fruit basket contains 3 apples and 1 orange. Use the rules to complete numerical patterns that show how the total number of apples and oranges increases with each basket.

Apples: *add 3*	Oranges: *add 1*
3	1
6	2

2. Describe two ways the corresponding terms in the patterns in exercise 1 are related:

   Each number of apples is ____ times the corresponding number of oranges.

   Each number of oranges is the corresponding number of apples divided by ____.

3. Write the corresponding terms in the pattern from exercise 1 as ordered pairs.

   (3, 1) (6, 2)

   (____, 3) (12, ____)

4. Graph the ordered pairs from exercise 3 on the coordinate plane.

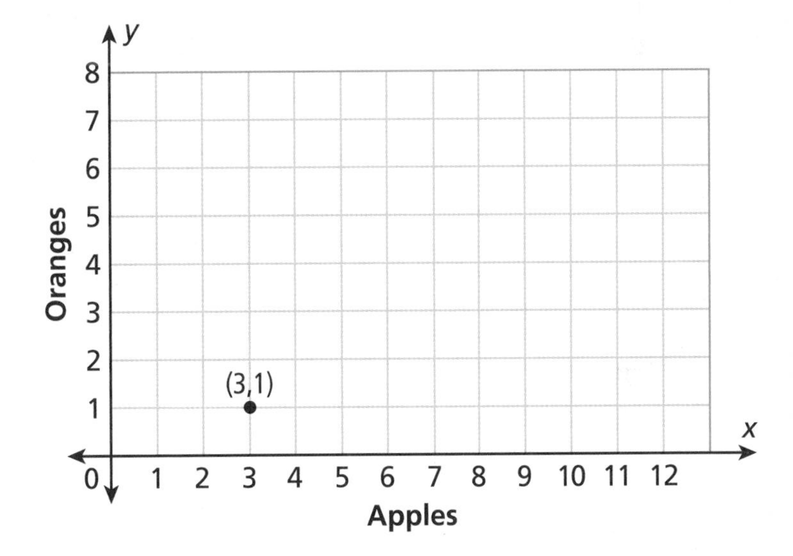

Think • Pair • Share

MP7 5. Two numerical patterns are shown below.

0, 8, 16, 24, 32, . . .
0, 4, 8, 12, 16, . . .

Analyze the patterns. Tell how they are the same and how they are different. Explain the relationship between the corresponding terms.

Independent Practice

Generate patterns using the two rules. Then, complete the statement about how the corresponding terms in each pair are related.

1. Rule 1: *add 4.* 0, 4, ____, ____, ____

   Rule 2: *add 12.* 0, 12, ____, ____, ____

   Relationship: Each term in the Rule 2 pattern is ____ times the corresponding term in the Rule 1 pattern.

2. Rule 1: *subtract 1.* 10, 9, ____, ____, ____

   Rule 2: *subtract 2.* 10, 8, ____, ____, ____

   Relationship: The difference between the Rule 1 term and the corresponding Rule 2 term increases by ____ with each term.

3. Rule 1: *add 10.* 0, 10, ____, ____, ____

   Rule 2: *add 100.* 0, 100, ____, ____, ____

   Relationship: ____________________

4. Rule 1: *add 5.* 20, 25, ____, ____, ____

   Rule 2: *add 10.* 20, 30, ____, ____, ____

   Relationship: ____________________

The numbers in the first two columns in each table are generated using a different rule. Identify the rule for the pattern in each column, and then complete the table. Form ordered pairs for the corresponding terms.

5. Pens: *add 10*. Pencils: __________.

Pens	Pencils	(Pens, Pencils)
10	8	(10, 8)
20	16	(20, 16)
30	24	

6. Points: __________. Penalties: __________.

Points	Penalties	(Points, Penalties)
12	10	(12, 10)
18	8	(18, 8)
24	6	

Independent Practice

The first two columns of each table show two patterns and their rules. In the third column, write the corresponding terms of the patterns as ordered pairs. Then graph the order pairs on the coordinate plane.

7.

Rule 1: *add 1*	Rule 2: *add 2*	Ordered Pairs (Rule 1, Rule 2)
1	2	(1, 2)
2	4	(2, 4)
3	6	
4	8	
5	10	

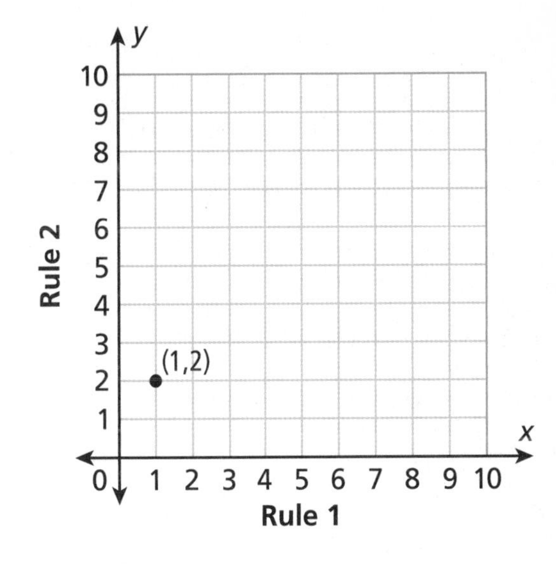

8.

Rule 1: *add 1*	Rule 2: *subtract 2*	(Rule 1, Rule 2)
1	10	(1, 10)
2	8	(2,)
3	6	
4	4	
5	2	

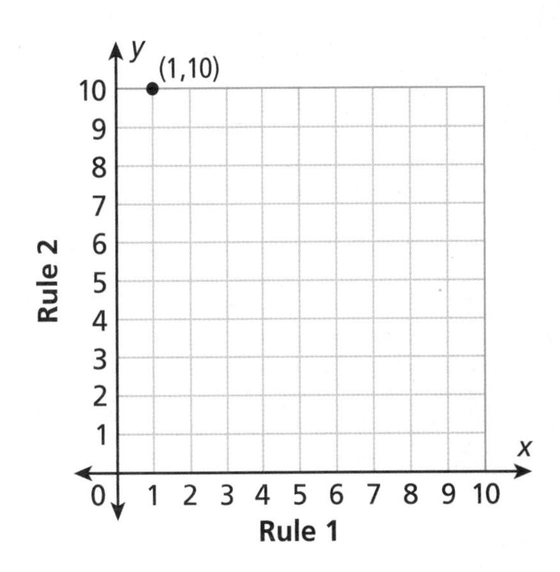

MP2 **9.** How are the patterns of points in exercises 7 and 8 the same? And, how are they different?

Independent Practice

MP8 **10.** Chandra and Joey are mountain biking. Chandra bikes 8 miles every hour. Joey bikes 9 miles every hour. After biking for 4 hours, how many miles have Chandra and Joey each traveled? Complete the table and find the answer.

Number of Hours	1	2	3	4	5
Chandra (Miles Biked)	8				
Joey (Miles Biked)	9				

Answer ______________________________

Justify your answer using words, drawings, or numbers.

MP8 **11.** Complete the order pairs for the points on the graph, and then complete the columns for Rule 1 and Rule 2. Give the rules for the patterns. Explain how you found the rules.

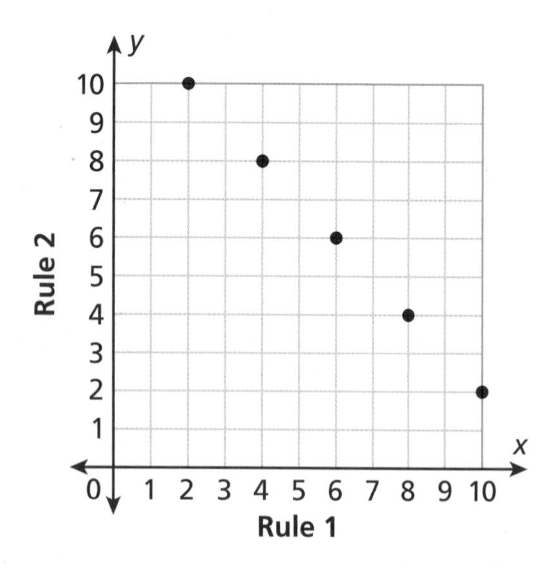

Ordered Pairs	Rule 1: ______	Rule 2: ______
(2, 10)	2	10
(4,)	4	
(, 6)		6
(8,)	8	
(, 2)		2

Independent Practice

MP4 **12.** Rita starts with $10 and saves $5 each month. Tara starts with $50 and spends $5 each month. Complete the tables. The ordered pairs for Rita's table are shown on the coordinate plane. Use a different color to add the points for Tara's table.

Are there any months when Rita and Tara have the same amount of money? Explain.

Month	Rita
0	10
1	15
2	
3	
4	
5	

Month	Tara
0	50
1	45
2	
3	
4	
5	

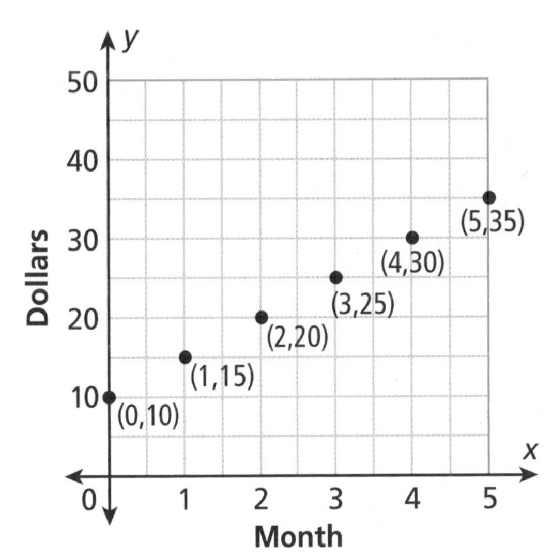

Solve the problem.

MP8 **13.** Kerry is making shapes out of toothpicks. She uses 3 toothpicks to make one shape, 6 toothpicks to make two shapes, 9 toothpicks to make three shapes, and so on. How many toothpicks does Kerry need to make five shapes?

Answer ____________________

Justify your answer using words, drawings, or numbers.

For exercises 1–2, evaluate the expression. Show your work.

1. $27 \div 3 + [38 - (6 \times 4)]$

Answer ________

2. $125 - (12 \times 5) + 75$

Answer ________

For exercises 3–4, list the operations in the order they should be performed. Do not evaluate.

3. $\{[(50 - 44) \div 2] + 10\} \times 5$

____
____
____
____

4. $75 - [60 \div (5 \times 2) + 32]$

____
____
____
____

5. Which numerical expression represents the phrase fourteen less than the product of five and thirty?

a. $5 + 30 - 14$

b. $5 \times 30 - 14$

c. $14 - 5 \times 30$

d. $14 - 5 \times 30$

6. Write a numerical expression for the phrase.
twelve times the result of dividing 20 by 2

7. Generate the two patterns using the given rules. Then compare corresponding terms and complete the sentence.

add 4	2	6			
add 8	2				

The difference between corresponding terms increases by ____ with each term.

8. Pam had $20 to spend at the museum. She bought an admission ticket for $8, a tote bag for $6, and spent the rest for lunch. Which expression shows how much she spent for lunch?

a. (8 + 6) − 20

b. 20 − 8 + 6

c. (20 − 8) + 6

d. 20 − (8 + 6)

MP2 9. Write and evaluate an expression to solve the problem.
A large packing box holds 20 toy cars. A small box holds 8 toy cars. How many toy cars can be shipped in 15 large boxes and 30 small boxes?

Expression: ______________________

Evaluate: ______________________

Answer ______________________

10. Which expression has the least value?

a. one more than five groups of two

b. two more than the result of dividing 15 by 3

c. two less than the result of dividing 15 by 3

d. three times the result of subtracting four from nine

11. Do these expressions have the same value? Explain your answer and show the expressions in numerical form.

"twenty less than the product of fifteen and six"

"six multiplied by fifteen and then decreased by twenty"

12. Generate the two patterns using the given rules. Then write the corresponding terms of the two patterns as ordered pairs.

multiply by 2	16	32			
divide by 2	16				

Ordered pairs: (16, 16), ________, ________, ________, ________

MP2 **13.** A gift basket of fruit contains 3 oranges, 2 peaches, and 3 bananas. How many pieces of fruit are there in 5 gift baskets? Write and evaluate an expression to solve.

Expression: ______________________

Answer ______________________

MP2 **14.** There are 16 boys and 18 girls in Ms. Watkins' fifth grade class. Ms. Watkins gave each person 3 pencils and 6 stickers. Write expressions for the number of pencils and stickers. Compare the expressions without evaluating them.

Pencils: ________________ **Stickers:** ________________

MP3 **15.** Explain how you can evaluate the expression mentally.
$(61 - 19) \times [16 \times (8 - 8)] \div (54 + 72)$

Complete the table. Then graph the ordered pairs on the coordinate plane.

MP4 **16.** Drama club starts with 2 members and adds 2 members each week. Debate club starts with 12 members and loses 3 members each week.

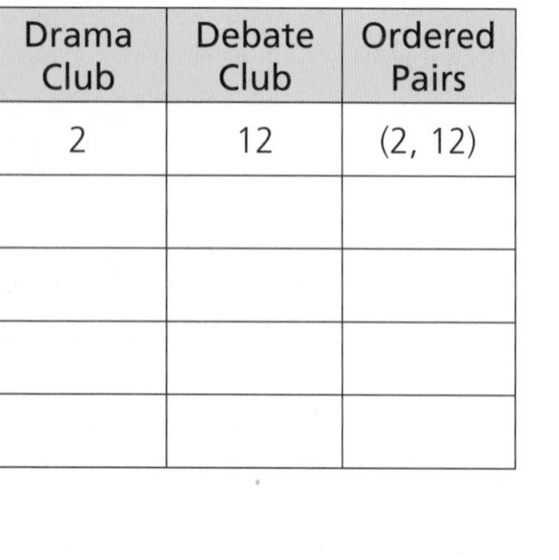

Drama Club	Debate Club	Ordered Pairs
2	12	(2, 12)

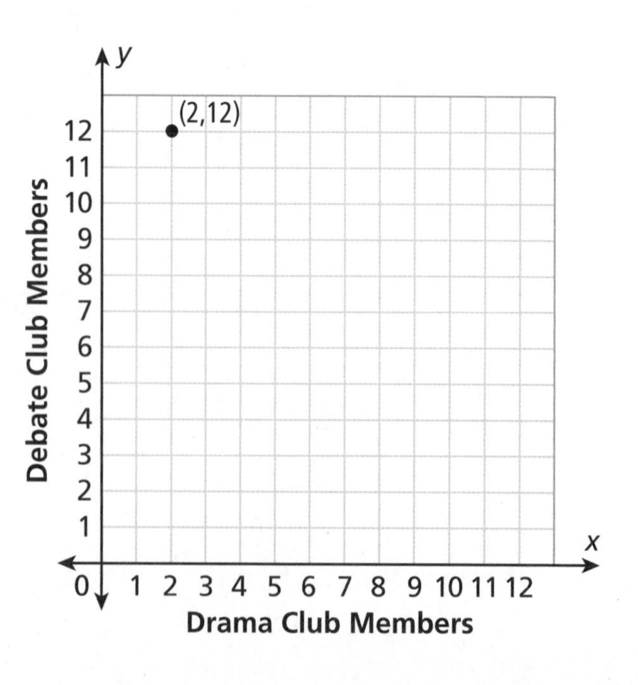

Progress Check

UNIT 2

Look at how the Common Core standards you have learned and will learn connect.

It is very important for you to understand the standards from the prior grade level so that you will be able to develop an understanding of number and operations in base ten in this unit and be prepared for next year. To practice your skills, go to sadlierconnect.com.

GRADE 4 I Can...	Before Unit 2	GRADE 5 Can I ?	After Unit 2	GRADE 6 I Will...
4.NBT.1 Understand place value in whole numbers	☐	**5.NBT.1** Understand place value in whole numbers and decimal numbers	☐	
4.NBT.1 Understand place value in whole numbers	☐	**5.NBT.2** Explain patterns when multiplying or dividing whole numbers and decimals by powers of 10	☐	**6.EE.1** Write repeated multiplication expressions as exponential expressions
	☐	Use whole number exponents to show powers of 10	☐	Evaluate numerical expressions involving exponents
4.NBT.2 Read, write, and compare whole numbers	☐	**5.NBT.3** Read, write, and compare decimals to thousandths	☐	
4.NBT.3 Round whole numbers to any place	☐	**5.NBT.4** Round decimals to any place	☐	
4.NBT.5 Multiply whole numbers	☐	**5.NBT.5** Fluently multiply whole numbers	☐	
4.NBT.6 Divide whole numbers by one-digit divisors	☐	**5.NBT.6** Divide whole numbers by two digit divisors	☐	**6.NS.2** Fluently divide multi-digit whole numbers
4.NF.5 Add two fractions with denominators of 10 and 100	☐	**5.NBT.7** Add, subtract, multiply, and divide decimals to hundredths	☐	**6.NS.3** Fluently add, subtract, multiply, and divide multi-digit decimals
4.NBT.4, 4.NBT.5, 4.NBT.6 Add, subtract, multiply, and divide whole numbers	☐		☐	

HOME ✦ CONNECT...

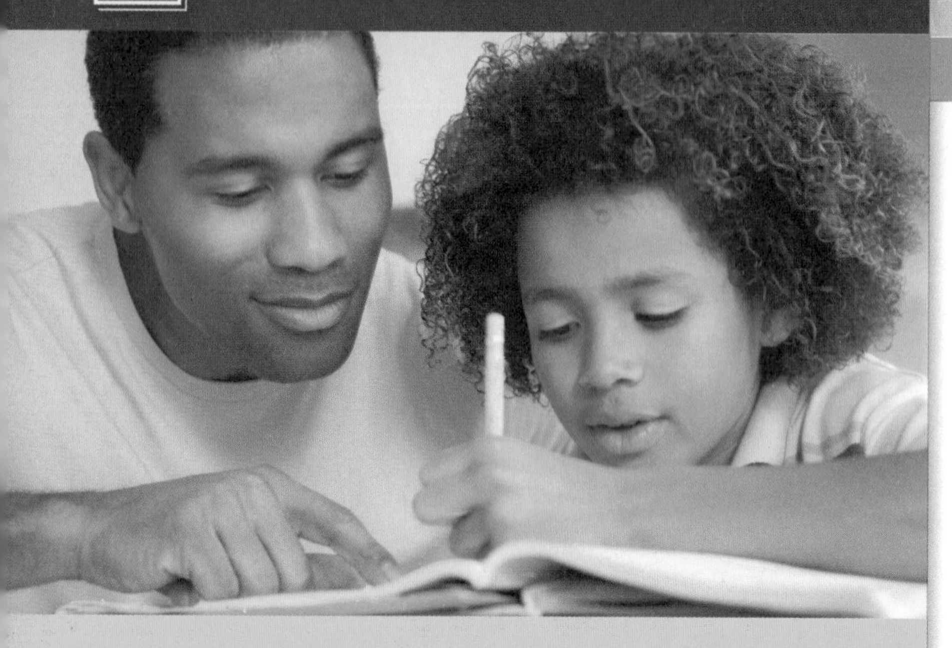

Place value and number sense have been a big part of your child's mathematics instruction. This understanding will now serve as the foundation for working with decimal numbers.

In our base-ten system, the value of a digit depends on its place in the number. Look at the place-value chart below. The number one hundred eleven and twenty-three thousandths is shown.

hundreds	tens	ones	.	tenths	hundredths	thousandths
1	1	1	.	0	2	3

The value of each place is *ten times* the value of the place to its right. The value of each place is also *one tenth* the value of the place to its left. Therefore, one hundred is *ten times* the value of ten, and ten is *one tenth* the value of one hundred.

Activity: You can think of hundredths as cents when you are talking about a sum of money. There are 100 cents in a dollar, so if you have $10.53, the 3 in the hundredths place represents 3 cents. Play a game with your child in which you round the prices of items from a circular to the nearest hundredth, tenth, or whole number.

In this unit your child will:

- Understand place value.
- Use patterns and whole-number exponents.
- Read, write, and compare decimals to thousandths.
- Round decimals using place value.
- Multiply fluently with multi-digit numbers.
- Divide whole numbers using place value and properties of operations.
- Add, subtract, multiply, and divide decimals to hundredths.

NOTE: All of these learning goals for your child are based on the Grade 5 Common Core State Standards for Mathematics.

Ways to Help Your Child

Remember not to give your child the answer to a problem. It is very important that your child learn to persevere in solving problems and think independently. Mistakes are an important part of the learning process. They can help your child and their teacher to determine where misunderstandings have occurred.

ONLINE

For more Home Connect activities, continue online at sadlierconnect.com

Focus on Number and Operations in Base Ten

UNIT 2

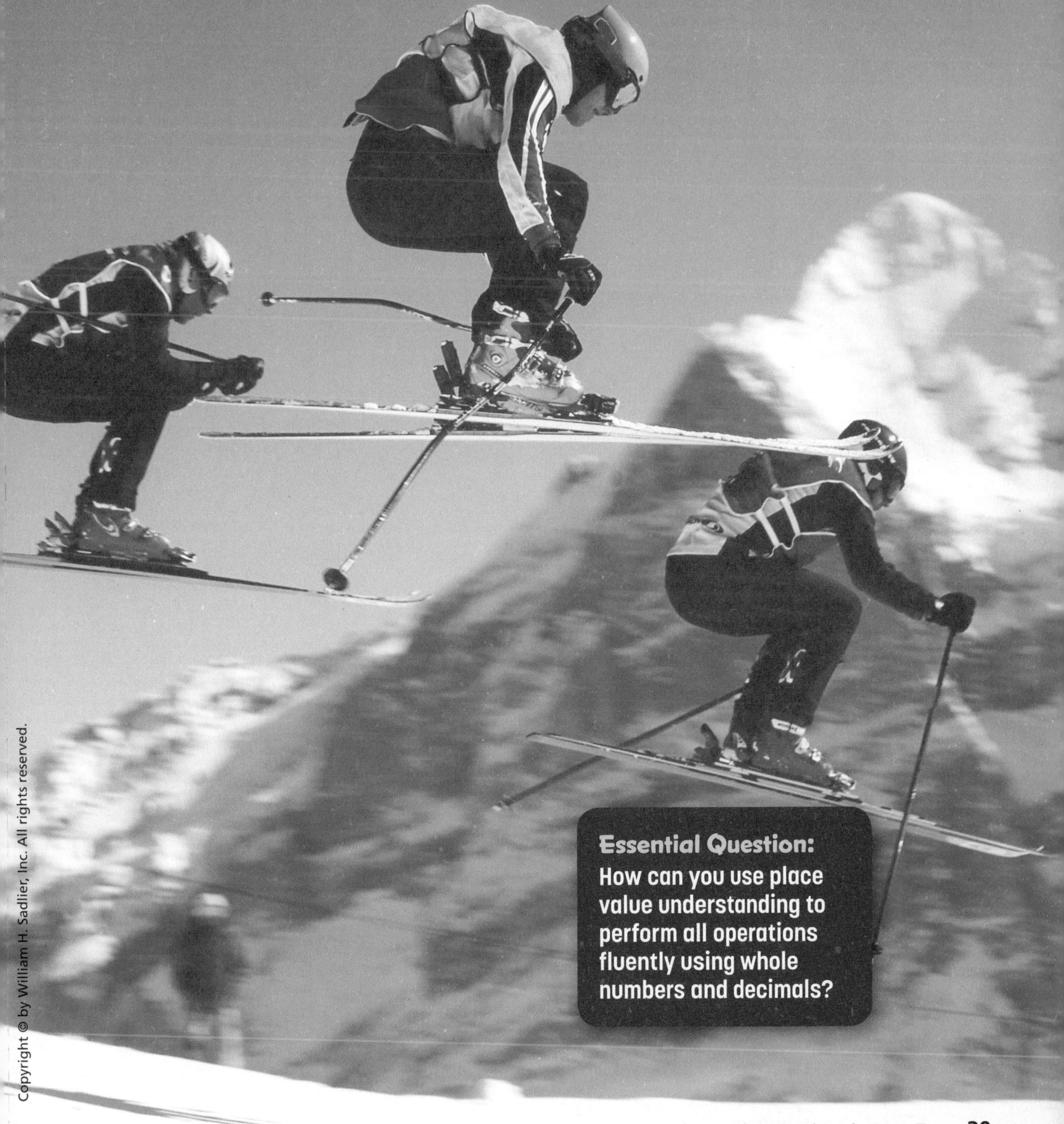

Essential Question:
How can you use place value understanding to perform all operations fluently using whole numbers and decimals?

Lesson

4 Understand Place Value

Essential Question:
What is the relationship between adjacent places in the base-ten system?

5.NBT.1

Guided Instruction

In this lesson you will learn about how the values of adjacent places in a number are related.

Understand: The relationships between 1, $\frac{1}{10}$, and $\frac{1}{100}$

Fill in the blanks to show how 1, $\frac{1}{10}$, and $\frac{1}{100}$ are related.

$\times$ ____ $\quad \times 10$

1 $\quad \frac{1}{10} \quad \frac{1}{100}$

$\div 10 \quad \div$ ____

Compare the area models for 1, $\frac{1}{10}$, and $\frac{1}{100}$.

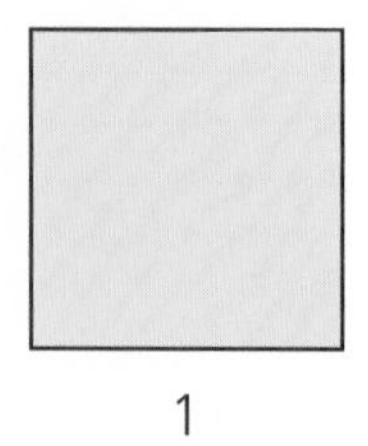

1

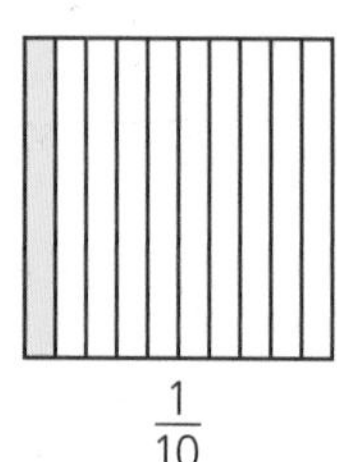

$\frac{1}{10}$

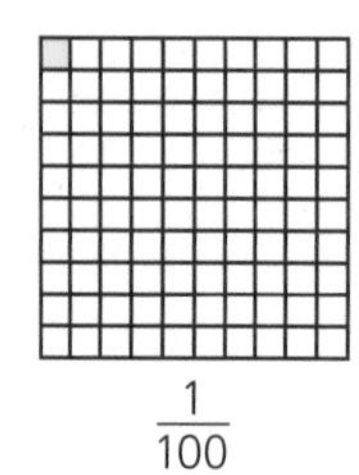

$\frac{1}{100}$

Compare 1 and $\frac{1}{10}$.

The $\frac{1}{10}$ model has one tenth the area of the 1 model. ⟶ $1 \div 10 = \frac{1}{10}$

The 1 model has ten times the area of the $\frac{1}{10}$ model. ⟶ $10 \times \frac{1}{10} = 1$

Compare $\frac{1}{10}$ and $\frac{1}{100}$.

The $\frac{1}{100}$ model has one tenth the area of the $\frac{1}{10}$ model. ⟶ $\frac{1}{10} \div 10 = \frac{1}{100}$

The $\frac{1}{10}$ model has ten times the area of the $\frac{1}{100}$ model. ⟶ $10 \times \frac{1}{100} = \frac{1}{10}$

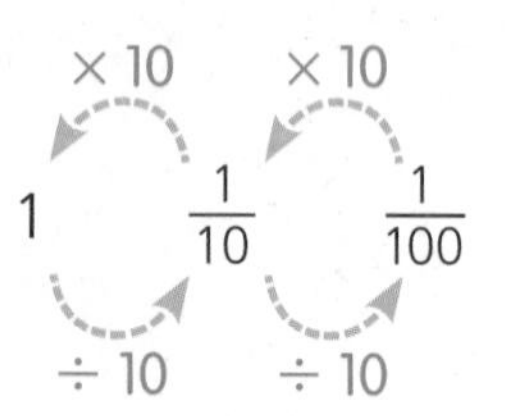

This diagram shows the same relationship but with decimals.

$\times 10 \quad \times 10$

1 $\quad$ 0.1 $\quad$ 0.01

$\div 10 \quad \div 10$

Understand: Decimal place values

Give the value of each digit in the number 76.54.

The chart below shows decimal place values through hundredths. Just as for whole numbers, the value of each place is ten times the value of the place to its right and one tenth the value of the place to its left.

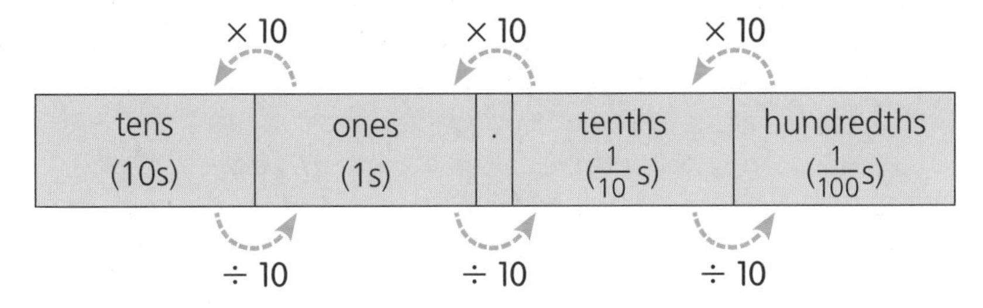

Write 76.54 in the place-value chart.

tens	ones	.	tenths	hundredths
7	**6**	**.**	**5**	**4**

The 7 is in the tens place, so it represents 7 tens.
Its value is $7 \times 10 = 70$.

The 6 is in the ones place, so it represents 6 ones.
Its value is $6 \times 1 = 6$.

The 5 is in the tenths place, so it represents 5 tenths.
Its value is $5 \times \frac{1}{10} = \frac{5}{10}$.

The 4 is in the hundredths place, so it represents 4 hundredths.
Its value is $4 \times \frac{1}{100} = \frac{4}{100}$.

➡ The value of each digit in the number 76.54 is 7 tens, 6 ones, 5 tenths, and 4 hundredths.

✏ Express the values of the digits 5 and 4 in the number 76.54 as decimals.

Guided Instruction

Connect: What you know about place value relationships

The digit 7 appears in a different place in each number below.

7 3.7 0.57

Each time 7 moves right one place, how does its place value change?
Each time 7 moves left one place, how does its place value change?

Use a place-value chart to identify the place value of the digit 7 in each number.

ones	.	tenths	hundredths	
7	.			← 7 ones = 7
3	.	7		← 7 tenths = $\frac{7}{10}$ = 0.7
0	.	5	7	← 7 hundredths = $\frac{7}{100}$ = 0.07

Look at how the value changes as 7 moves right:

A tenth is $\frac{1}{10}$ as much as a one, so 7 tenths is $\frac{1}{10}$ as much as 7 ones.

A hundredth is $\frac{1}{10}$ as much as a tenth, so 7 hundredths is $\frac{1}{10}$ as much as 7 tenths.

Remember!
Finding $\frac{1}{10}$ of a number is the same as dividing that number by 10.

Look at how the value changes as 7 moves left:

A tenth is 10 times as much as a hundredth, so 7 tenths is 10 times as much as 7 hundredths.

A one is 10 times as much as a tenth, so 7 ones is 10 times as much as 7 tenths.

➡ Each time 7 moves right one place, its value is divided by 10. Each time 7 moves left one place, its value is multiplied by 10.

Kami says that the value of the digit 5 in 0.15 is greater than the value of the digit 5 in 0.05 because the value of the 5 in 0.15 is ten times the value of the 5 in 0.05. Is she correct? Explain.

Guided Practice

For exercises 1–4, use the place-value chart to complete the sentences using *ten times* or *one tenth*.

ones	.	tenths	hundredths
1	**.**	**1**	**1**

1. One tenth is ____________ the value of one hundredth.

2. One hundredth is ____________ the value of one tenth.

3. One tenth is ____________ the value of one.

4. One is ____________ the value of one tenth.

For exercises 5–7, use the place-value chart to complete the statements about the number 26.13.

tens	ones	.	tenths	hundredths
2	**6**	**.**	**1**	**3**

5. The digit 3 is in the ____________ place, so its value is 3 × ____, or $\frac{3}{100}$.

6. The digit 2 is in the ____________ place, so its value is 2 × ____, or ____.

7. The digit 1 is in the ____________ place, so its value is 1 × ____, or ____.

Think • Pair • Share

MP3 8. Liam says the model at the right shows thirty hundredths. Anne says the model shows three tenths. Who is correct? Explain your reasoning.

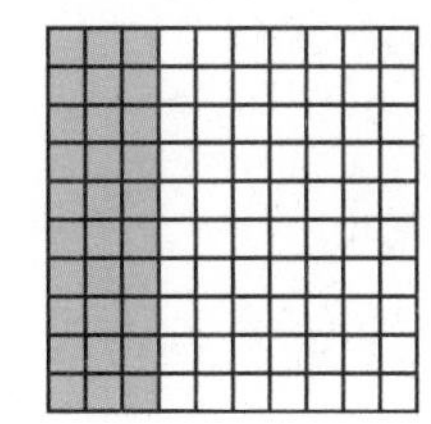

Independent Practice

1. Shade the models below to show 2, 0.2, and 0.02.

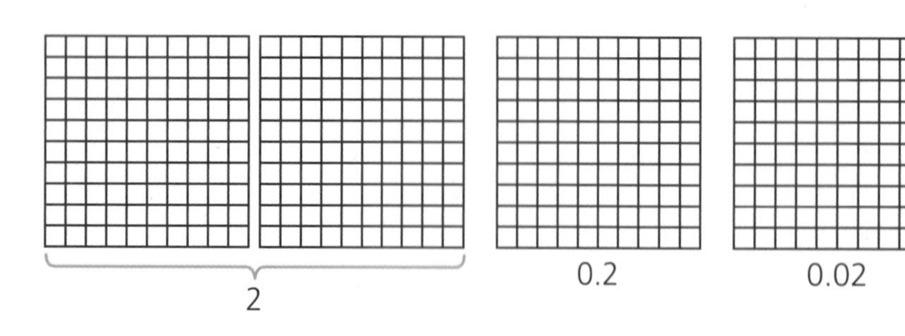

For exercises 2–5, use the models you shaded above to complete the sentences using *ten times* or *one tenth.*

2. 0.2 is ____________ as much as 0.02.

3. 0.2 is ____________ as much as 2.

4. 0.02 is ____________ as much as 0.2.

5. 2 is ____________ as much as 0.2.

6. Sam shaded a model to show one tenth of 0.7. Is he correct? Explain.

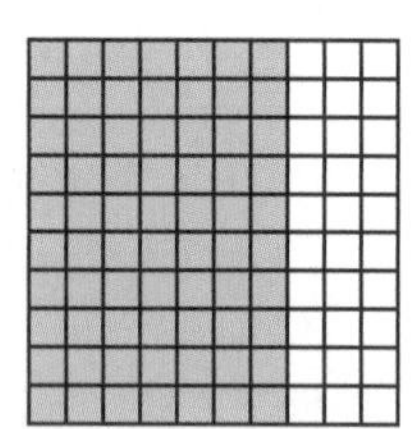

For exercises 7–8, use the number 6,125.89.

7. Which digit is in the hundredths place?

   a. 1 b. 2
   c. 8 d. 9

8. Which digit is in the tens place?

   a. 9 b. 8
   c. 5 d. 2

Independent Practice

For exercises 9–13, use the place-value chart to answer the questions.

tens	ones	.	tenths	hundredths
3	**0**			
	3			
	0	**.**	**3**	
	0	**.**	**0**	**3**

9. Which number is one tenth as much as 0.3? ______

10. Which number is ten times as much as 0.3? ______

11. Which number is ten times as much as 0.03? ______

12. Which number is one tenth as much as 3? ______

13. Which number is ten times as much as 3? ______

14. Which model shows one tenth the value of 5 tenths?

a. 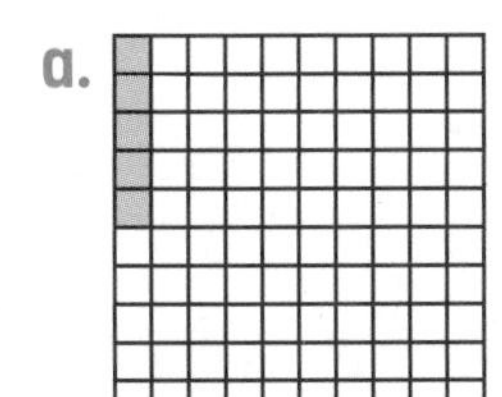

b. 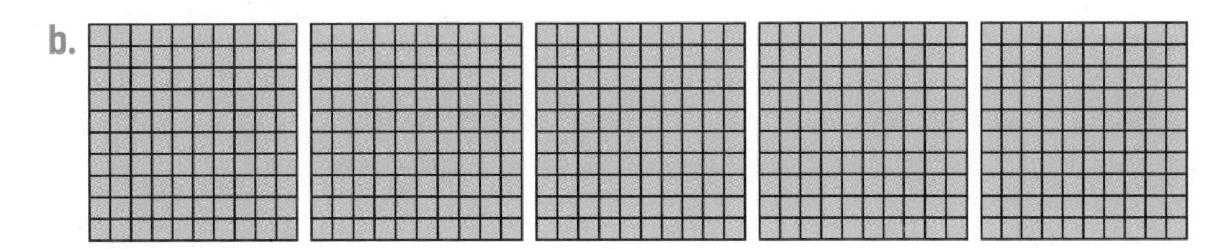

c. 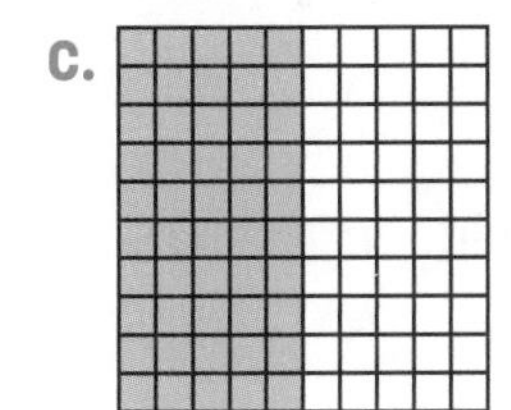

Independent Practice

Study the pattern. Complete the sentences to describe the pattern.

138.49 1,384.9 13,849 138,490

15. Reading the numbers from left to right, the digits shift __________ one place with each number.

16. In each number, the value of the digit 4 is __________ the value of the digit 4 in the number to its right.

17. In each number, the value of the digit 8 is __________ the value of the digit 8 in the number to its left.

Study the pattern. Complete the sentences to describe the pattern.

218,760 21,876 2,187.6 218.76

18. Reading the numbers from left to right, the digits shift __________ one place with each number.

19. In each number, the value of the digit 1 is __________ the value of the digit 1 in the number to its right.

20. In each number, the value of the digit 6 is __________ the value of the digit 6 in the number to its left.

For exercises 21–22, use the place-value chart below.

tens	ones	.	tenths	hundredths
6	**6**	**.**	**6**	**6**

21. Write two equations to show how the place values of the digits in the tens and ones place are related.

22. Write two equations to show how the place values of the digits in the tenths and hundredths places are related.

Independent Practice

MP6 **23.** Use the model below to show each number. Then explain the relationship between the values of the digit 3 in the numbers.

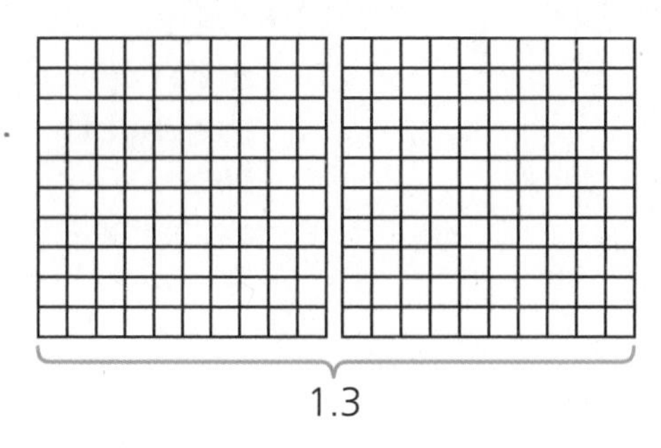

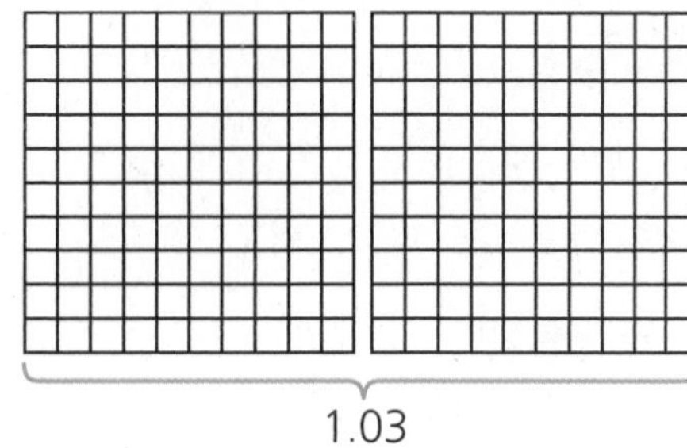

MP7 **For exercises 24–27, match each set of clues with the correct secret number. The key number is 13.57.**

24. The value of the digit 5 in the secret number has one tenth the value of the digit 5 in the key number.

25. The value of the digit 3 in the secret number has ten times the value of the digit 3 in the key number.

26. The value of the digit 1 in the secret number has one tenth the value of the digit 1 in the key number.

27. The value of the digit 7 in the secret number has ten times the value of the digit 7 in the key number.

a. 71.53

b. 53.71

c. 35.17

d. 17.35

MP7 **28.** Explain the relationship between the values of the digit 7 in these numbers: 270.5, 27.05, 2.70.

Lesson 5

Powers of 10: Use Patterns and Whole-Number Exponents

Essential Question: How can place value patterns help you multiply and divide by powers of 10?

5.NBT.2

Words to Know:
power of 10
base
exponent

Guided Instruction

In this lesson you will use your understanding of place value to help you multiply and divide by powers of ten.

Understand: Powers of 10

Lily reads in a science article that the average distance from Earth to the moon is about 4×10^5 kilometers. What does 10^5 represent? What is the average distance from Earth to the moon written as a whole number?

4×10^5 kilometers is a multiplication expression representing a number.

10^5 is a power of 10. A power of 10 is written with a base number of 10 and an exponent. The exponent tells how many times the base number is used as a factor. In 10^5, the exponent is 5.

10^5 is read as "ten to the fifth power."

10^5 ← exponent (5), base (10)

5 factors of 10.

$$10^5 = \underbrace{10 \times 10 \times 10 \times 10 \times 10}_{\text{5 factors of 10}} = 100{,}000$$

$$4 \times 10^5 = 4 \times 10 \times 10 \times 10 \times 10 \times 10 = 4 \times 100{,}000 = 400{,}000$$

➡ 10^5 is the product of five factors of 10. The average distance from Earth to the moon is about 400,000 kilometers.

For each power of 10 below, write the equivalent multiplication expression.

1. 10^3 ____________________

2. 10^7 ____________________

3. 10^4 ____________________

Guided Instruction

Understand: How to multiply whole numbers by powers of 10

In this chart, 24 is multiplied by increasing powers of 10. What pattern do you see? Why does this pattern occur?

Muliplication Expression	Factors	Product
24×10^1	24×10	240
24×10^2	$24 \times 10 \times 10$	2,400
24×10^3	$24 \times 10 \times 10 \times 10$	24,000
24×10^4	$24 \times 10 \times 10 \times 10 \times 10$	240,000

24×10^1 is 240, which has 1 zero.
24×10^2 is 2,400, which has 2 zeros.
24×10^3 is 24,000, which has 3 zeros.
24×10^4 is 240,000, which as 4 zeros.

Remember!
The value of each place is *10 times* the value of the place to the right.

➡ The number of zeros in the product is the same as the exponent, which is the number of factors of 10. This pattern occurs because each time you multiply by 10, the place values of 2 and 4 are multiplied by 10, so they each shift left to the next greater place.

Understand: How to divide whole numbers by powers of 10

In this chart, 37 is divided by increasing powers of 10. What pattern do you see? Why does this pattern occur?

Division Expression	Dividend ÷ Divisor	Quotient
$37 \div 10^1$	$37 \div 10$	3.7
$37 \div 10^2$	$37 \div (10 \times 10)$	0.37
$37 \div 10^3$	$37 \div (10 \times 10 \times 10)$	0.037

$37 \div 10^1 = 3.7$, so the digits shift right one place.
$37 \div 10^2 = 0.37$, so the digits shift right 2 places.
$37 \div 10^3 = 0.037$, so the digits shift right 3 places.

Remember!
The value of each place is *one tenth* the value of the place to the left.

➡ The exponent is the number of places 3 and 7 shift to the right. This pattern occurs because each time you divide by 10, the place values of 3 and 7 are divided by 10, so they shift right to the next smaller place.

Guided Instruction

Connect: What you know about multiplying and dividing by powers of 10 to decimals

Find the products and quotients.

$5.26 \times 10^1 =$ ______	$5.26 \div 10^1 =$ ______
$5.26 \times 10^2 =$ ______	$5.26 \div 10^2 =$ ______
$5.26 \times 10^3 =$ ______	$5.26 \div 10^3 =$ ______

The same patterns you found when multiplying and dividing whole numbers by powers of 10 apply to multiplying and dividing decimals by powers of 10.

Step 1

Multiply. Think about how many 10s you are multiplying by each time.

Each time you multiply a number by 10, the digits of that number shift left to the next greater place.

$5.26 \times 10^1 = 5.26 \times 10 = 52.6$ The digits shift left 1 place.
$5.26 \times 10^2 = 5.26 \times 10 \times 10 = 526$ The digits shift left 2 places.
$5.26 \times 10^3 = 5.26 \times 10 \times 10 \times 10 = 5,260$ The digits shift left 3 places.

Step 2

Divide. Think about how many 10s you are dividing by each time.

Each time you divide a number by 10, the digits of that number shift right to the next smaller place.

$5.26 \div 10^1 = 5.26 \div 10 = 0.526$ The digits shift right 1 place.
$5.26 \div 10^2 = 5.26 \div (10 \times 10) = 0.0526$ The digits shift right 2 places.
$5.26 \div 10^3 = 5.26 \div (10 \times 10 \times 10) = 0.00526$ The digits shift right 3 places.

$5.26 \times 10^1 = 52.6$	$5.26 \div 10^1 = 0.526$
$5.26 \times 10^2 = 526$	$5.26 \div 10^2 = 0.0526$
$5.26 \times 10^3 = 5,260$	$5.26 \div 10^3 = 0.00526$

Evaluate $4.5 \times 1,000$ and $4.5 \div 100$ using mental math. Explain your reasoning.

Guided Practice

Complete the expression for each power of 10, and find its value. Then complete how the power is read in words.

1. $10^1 =$ ______ "ten to the ____________ power"

2. $10^2 =$ ____ $\times$ ____ $=$ ______ "ten to the ____________ power"

3. $10^3 =$ ____ $\times$ ____ $\times$ ____ $=$ ______ "ten to the ____________ power"

Place the decimal point in each product. Add zeros if needed.

4. $2.5 \times 10^2 = 2\ 5$

5. $32.69 \times 10^3 = 3\ 2\ 6\ 9$

6. $1.94 \times 10 = 1\ 9\ 4$

7. $4 \times 10^3 = 4$

Place the decimal point in each quotient. Add zeros if needed.

8. $19 \div 10^2 = 1\ 9$

9. $52.6 \div 10 = 5\ 2\ 6$

10. $13{,}205 \div 10^3 = 1\ 3\ 2\ 0\ 5$

11. $5 \div 10^2 = 5$

MP3 12. Explain why you had to add zeros in the answers to exercises 7 and 11.

Independent Practice

Match each number to its equivalent power of ten.

1. 100,000 — a. ten to the sixth power

2. 1,000 — b. ten to the fifth power

3. 10,000 — c. ten to the third power

4. 1,000,000 — d. ten to the fourth power

For exercises 5–8, choose the correct factor or divisor.

5. $30 \times \blacksquare = 300$

   a. 10^7 b. 10^1 c. 10^2 d. 10^3

6. $4{,}000 \div \blacksquare = 40$

   a. 10^4 b. 10^1 c. 10^2 d. 10^3

7. $0.05 \times \blacksquare = 50$

   a. 10^4 b. 10^1 c. 10^2 d. 10^3

8. $80 \div \blacksquare = 0.08$

   a. 10^5 b. 10^1 c. 10^2 d. 10^3

Place the decimal point in each product or quotient. Add zeros if needed.

9. $15 \div 10^2 =$ 1 5

10. $32.63 \times 10 =$ 3 2 6 3

11. $723{,}356 \div 10^3 =$ 7 2 3 3 5 6

12. $35{,}526 \times 10^2 =$ 3 5 5 2 6

Independent Practice

For exercises 13–16, write each product or quotient in the place-value chart. Include zeros only where needed.

13. 5.1×10^3

ten thousands	thousands	hundreds	tens	ones	.	tenths	hundredths

14. $51 \div 10^2$

ten thousands	thousands	hundreds	tens	ones	.	tenths	hundredths

15. 0.51×10^2

ten thousands	thousands	hundreds	tens	ones	.	tenths	hundredths

16. $510{,}000 \div 10^3$

ten thousands	thousands	hundreds	tens	ones	.	tenths	hundredths

For exercises 17–22, find each product or quotient.

17. $83 \times 10^2 =$ ____________

18. $0.34 \times 10^3 =$ ____________

19. $37.5 \times 10^1 =$ ____________

20. $0.08 \times 10^2 =$ ____________

21. $978 \div 10 =$ ____________

22. $15{,}334 \div 10^3 =$ ____________

23. $88 \div 10^2 =$ ____________

24. $2{,}734 \div 10^1 =$ ____________

Independent Practice

25. What happens to the digits 2 and 4 when finding the product of 0.0024×10^4? What is the product?

26. Where do you put the decimal point in the quotient for $99{,}999.99 \div 10^5$? Explain.

For exercises 27–29, choose the correct factor or divisor.

27. $0.22 \times \blacksquare = 22$

a. 10^4 b. 10^3 c. 10^2 d. 10^1

28. $908.7 \div \blacksquare = 0.9087$

a. 10^1 b. 10^6 c. 10^5 d. 10^3

29. $30.05 \times \blacksquare = 30{,}050$

a. 10^3 b. 10^5 c. 10^2 d. 10^7

Solve the problems.

MP3 **30.** Last year, Josh earned $200 a month running errands for neighbors. He wants to earn $2,000 for a summer vacation. If he starts in January, will Josh earn enough by summer for his vacation? Explain your thinking.

MP1 **31.** Ms. Andrews earned $64,000 last year. She spent one tenth of her earnings on medical expenses. How much did Ms. Andrews spend on medical expenses? Explain how you determined the answer.

Independent Practice

MP3 **32.** Kent says that $360{,}534 \div 10^2 = 36{,}053.4$. Explain the error Kent made. Then give the correct answer.

Answer ______________________________

Justify your answer using words, drawings, or numbers.

MP6 **33.** What is the value of the expression below?

$(3 \times 1{,}000 + 4 \times 100 + 2 \times 10 + 5) \times 10^3$

Answer ______________________________

Justify your answer using words, drawings, or numbers.

MP7 **34.** Marisa divides a number by a power of ten and the quotient is 1.4. She says that if she multiplies the number by the same power of ten, the product is 14,000. What was the dividend in Marisa's original problem? Use patterns to explain your thinking.

Answer ______________________________

Justify your answer using words, drawings, or numbers.

Lesson 6

Read and Write Decimals to Thousandths

Essential Question:
How can you express a decimal to thousandths in different forms?
5.NBT.3a

Guided Instruction

In this lesson you will learn how to read and write decimals to thousandths in different forms.

Understand: How to express decimals to hundredths in more than one way

Andre jogs a distance of 1.45 miles. Express this distance in words, with a model, and in expanded form.

You can express Andre's jogging distance the following ways.

In words: Think of the decimal part as a fraction. The decimal 1.45 is the same as $1\frac{45}{100}$, and it is written and read as "one *and* forty-five hundredths."

With a model:

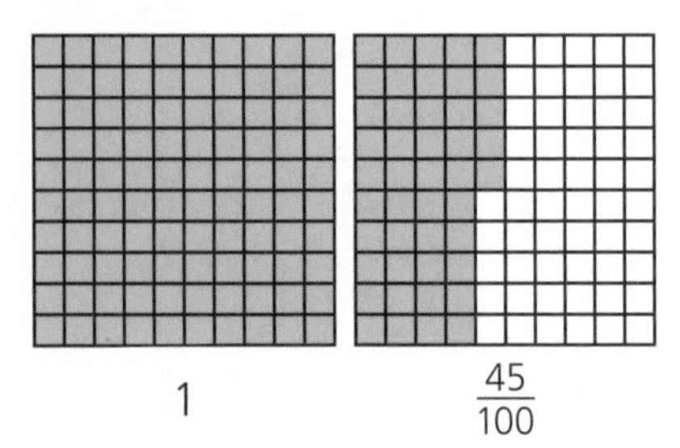

1 $\frac{45}{100}$

OR

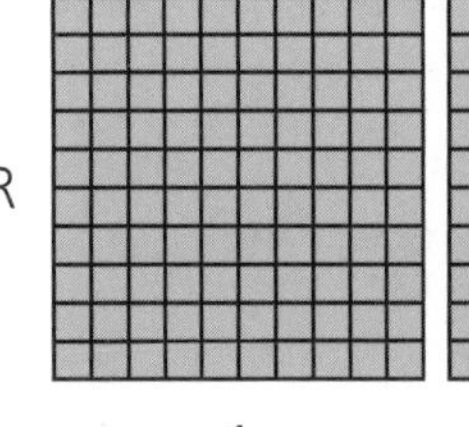

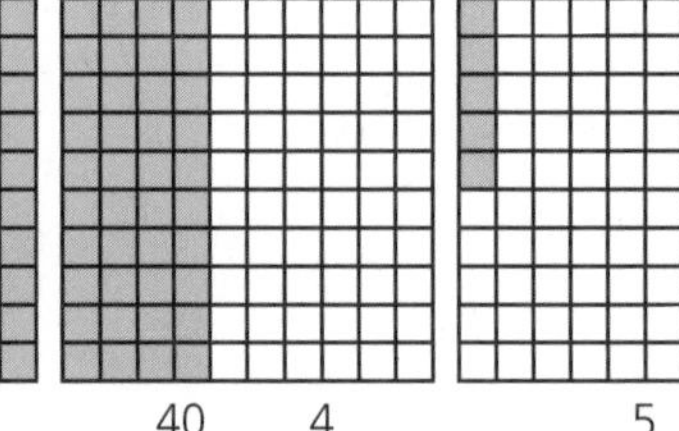

1 $\frac{40}{100} = \frac{4}{10}$ $\frac{5}{100}$

In expanded form: Use a place-value chart or a model to help you.

ones	.	tenths	hundredths
1	**.**	**4**	**5**

Below are four ways to write 1.45 in expanded form.

1.45 = 1 one + 4 tenths + 5 hundredths

$1.45 = 1 \times 1 + 4 \times \frac{1}{10} + 5 \times \frac{1}{100}$

$1.45 = 1 \times 1 + 4 \times 0.1 + 5 \times 0.01$

$1.45 = 1 + 0.4 + 0.05$

Express 0.03 in words and as a fraction.

Understand: How to express decimals to thousandths in more than one way

Express 0.417 in words, with a model, and in expanded form.

In words: The decimal 0.417 is equivalent to the fraction $\frac{417}{1,000}$. It is written and read as "four hundred seventeen thousandths."

With a model:

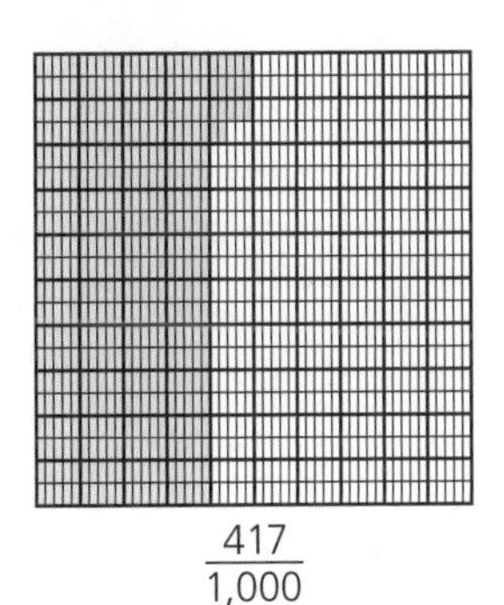

$\frac{417}{1,000}$

OR

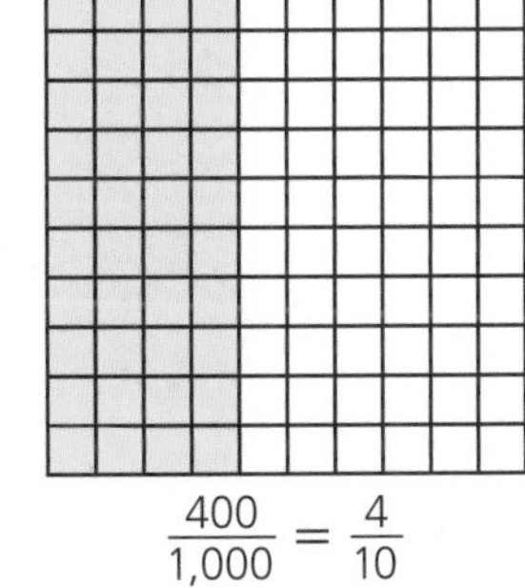

$\frac{400}{1,000} = \frac{4}{10}$

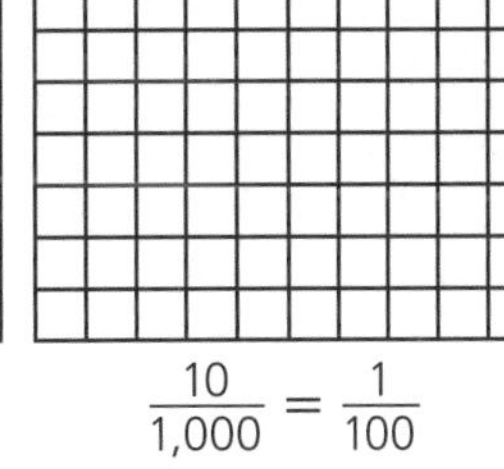

$\frac{10}{1,000} = \frac{1}{100}$

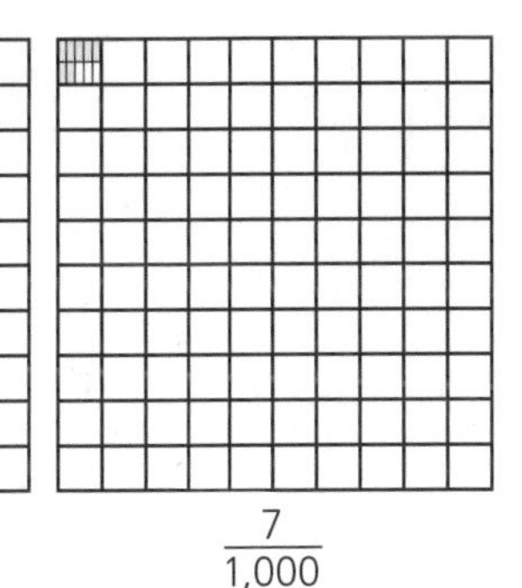

$\frac{7}{1,000}$

In expanded form: Use a place-value chart or a model to help you.

ones	.	tenths	hundredths	thousandths
0	**.**	**4**	**1**	**7**

Below are four ways to write 0.417 in expanded form.

0.417 = 4 tenths + 1 hundredth + 7 thousandths

$0.417 = 4 \times \frac{1}{10} + 1 \times \frac{1}{100} + 7 \times \frac{1}{1,000}$

$0.417 = 4 \times 0.1 + 1 \times 0.01 + 7 \times 0.001$

$0.417 = 0.4 + 0.01 + 0.007$

How would you write the decimal 63.076 in words?

Guided Instruction

Connect: What you know about reading and writing decimal numbers to thousandths

Alice planted a packet of 1,000 tomato seeds in her garden. After a week, 48 of them sprouted. In what ways can you express the fraction of the seeds that sprouted?

Step 1

Write a fraction.

48 out of 1,000 seeds sprouted, so the fraction of seeds that sprouted is $\frac{48}{1,000}$.

Step 2

Write a decimal.

$\frac{48}{1,000}$ written as a decimal is 0.048.

Show the decimal in a place-value chart.

ones	.	tenths	hundredths	thousandths
0	**.**	**0**	**4**	**8**

Step 3

Express the decimal number in expanded form.

Below are four ways to do this.

$0.048 = 0 \text{ tenths} + 4 \text{ hundredths} + 8 \text{ thousandths}$

$0.048 = 0 \times \frac{1}{10} + 4 \times \frac{1}{100} + 8 \times \frac{1}{1,000}$

$0.048 = 0 \times 0.1 + 4 \times 0.01 + 8 \times 0.001$

$0.048 = 0 + 0.04 + 0.008$

Step 4

Write the fraction or its decimal equivalent in words.

$\frac{48}{1,000}$, or 0.048, is written as "forty-eight thousandths."

➡ You can express the fraction of the plants that sprouted in more than one way: as a fraction, as a decimal, in expanded form, and in words.

Guided Practice

Write each fraction in decimal form.

1. $\frac{23}{100}$ ______

2. $35\frac{9}{100}$ ______

3. $200\frac{103}{1,000}$ ______

Write each decimal in fraction form.

4. 0.203 ______

5. 0.01 ______

6. 5.099 ______

Write the expanded form to show each decimal.

7. 0.35 ______

8. 0.326 ______

Write the decimal that represents the expanded form of the number.

9. $5 \times 10 + 0 \times 1 + 1 \times \frac{1}{10} + 4 \times \frac{1}{100} + 2 \times \frac{1}{1,000}$

Express each decimal in words.

10. 12.76 ______

11. 0.029 ______

12. 384.9 ______

13. 9.802 ______

Think • Pair • Share

MP3 14. Patrick says that 0.500 is greater than 0.50 and 0.5. Is he correct? Explain your reasoning.

Independent Practice

Which decimal does each model represent?

1.

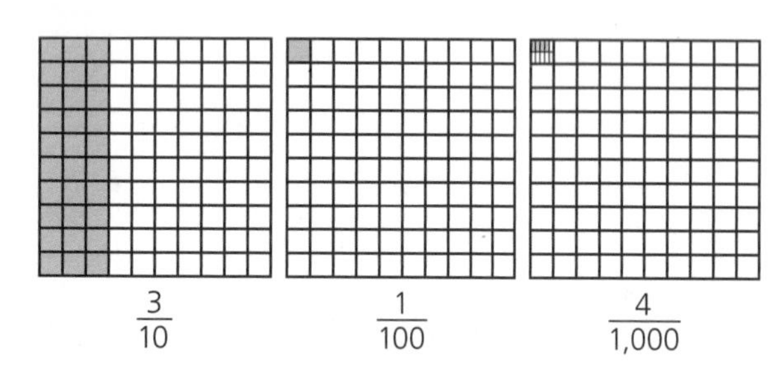

a. 0.413 b. 3.14

c. 0.314 d. 4,130

2.

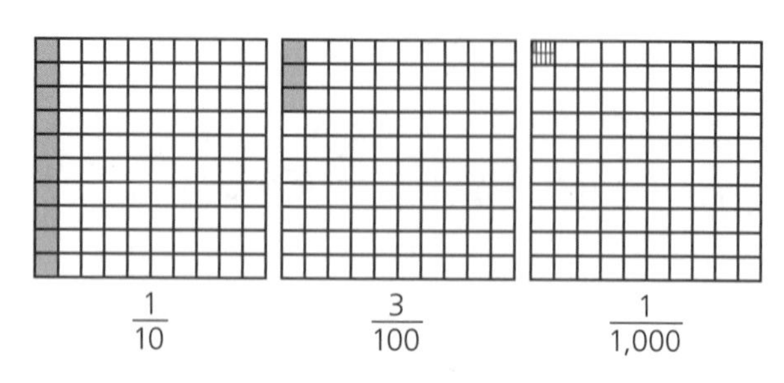

a. 0.131 b. 13.1

c. 1.31 d. 131

For exercises 3–6, write the decimals in expanded form.

3. 0.59

____

4. 9.099

____

5. 21.121

____

6. 100.930

____

Write the fractions as decimals.

7. $\frac{41}{100}$

____

8. $87\frac{33}{1,000}$

____

9. $1\frac{570}{1,000}$

____

10. $356\frac{242}{1,000}$

____

Independent Practice

Write each word phrase as a decimal.

11. forty-nine hundredths

_____

12. fourteen and ninety-nine thousandths

_____

13. two hundred thirty-one thousandths

_____

14. six hundred nine and two hundred and three thousandths

_____

15. eight hundredths

_____

16. one and four hundred seventy-three thousandths

_____

Write each decimal in words.

17. 0.01

_____

_____

18. 11.011

_____

_____

19. 0.719

_____

_____

20. 216.231

_____

_____

21. 0.910

_____

_____

22. 0.005

_____

_____

23. What is the decimal that represents ninety hundredths?

a. 0.09

b. 9.00

c. 0.90

d. 0.009

Independent Practice

MP2 **24.** Look at the decimals below. How are they alike? How are they different?

0.8 0.80 0.800

MP2 **25.** Explain how the value of the digit 4 in 0.47 relates to the value of the digit 4 in 0.704.

Solve the problems.

MP6 **26.** Farukh helps his father put a new part in the engine of his car. The part has a small gap between two pieces of metal. The gap must be no more than $\frac{16}{1,000}$ of an inch. What is this amount represented as a decimal?

MP6 **27.** Maria likes to watch Olympic swimmers on TV. In the closest race, her favorite swimmer lost by two thousandths of a second. What is this amount represented as a decimal?

MP4 **28.** Out of 100 students surveyed, 40 responded that they had an older brother or sister. What is this amount represented as a decimal?

29. What is the fraction represented by the decimal 0.001?

a. $\frac{1,000}{1}$ **b.** $\frac{1}{10}$

c. $\frac{1}{100}$ **d.** $\frac{1}{1,000}$

Independent Practice

MP3 **30.** Kai tells Juan that a housefly has a mass of twelve thousandths of a gram. Juan writes this as 0.12 grams. What is his error? Explain.

Answer ______________________________

Justify your answer using words, drawings, or numbers.

MP5 **31.** Represent the decimal 0.402 using a model, words, a fraction, and expanded form.

Model:

Words: ______________________________

Fraction: ______________________________

Expanded form: ______________________________

Lesson 7

Compare Decimals to Thousandths

Essential Question:
How can you compare decimal numbers?
5.NBT.3b

Guided Instruction

In this lesson you will learn how to compare decimal numbers to thousandths.

Understand: How to use a number line to compare decimal numbers

Sal and Pat store music on their mobile devices. They compare the unused storage each mobile device has left. Sal's mobile device has 9.869 gigabytes left, and Pat's mobile device has 9.863 gigabytes. Whose mobile device has more storage left?

To find whose mobile device has more storage left, plot the gigabyte values from 9.860 to 9.870 on a number line.

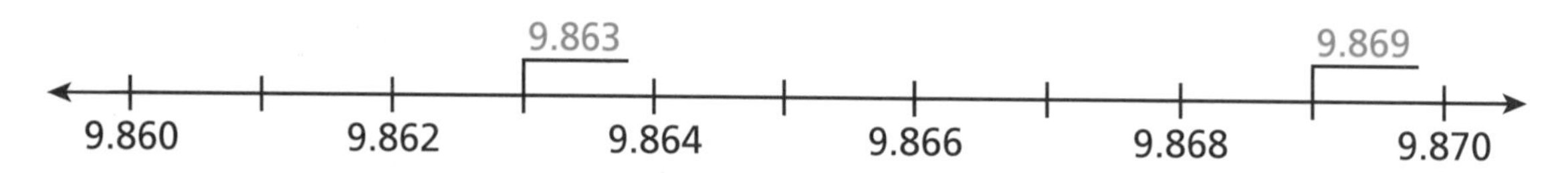

Because 9.869 is farther to the right on the number line, 9.869 > 9.863.

➡ Sal's mobile device has more storage left.

Understand: How to use fractions to compare decimal numbers

Tia's batting average is 0.358. Sam's batting average is 0.356. Who has the greater batting average?

To find who has the greater batting average, compare the batting averages using fractions.

Write 0.358 and 0.356 as fractions.

$0.358 = \frac{358}{1{,}000}$ $\quad\quad$ $0.356 = \frac{356}{1{,}000}$

The denominators are the same, so compare the numerators to find which fraction is greater.

$$358 > 356$$
$$\frac{358}{1{,}000} > \frac{356}{1{,}000}$$

➡ Tia has the greater batting average.

Guided Instruction

Understand: How to use place value to compare decimal numbers

Which is longer, 7.323 inches or 7.385 inches?

To compare 7.323 and 7.385, think about the place values of the digits.

ones	.	tenths	hundredths	thousandths
7	.	3	2	3
7	.	3	8	5

Compare the digits of the numbers place by place, starting with the greatest place, until you find digits that are different.

Compare ones: 7 ones = 7 ones
Compare tenths: 3 tenths = 3 tenths
Compare hundredths: 2 hundredths < 8 hundredths.

Because 7.385 has more hundredths, it is the greater number. You do not need to check thousandths.

➡ 7.385 inches is longer than 7.323 inches.

Understand: How to use expanded form to compare decimal numbers

A scientist records the lengths of two specimens. Specimen A is 3.452 centimeters long. Specimen B is 3.459 centimeters long. Which specimen is longer?

You can compare the measures using expanded notation.

Specimen A: $3.452 = 3 \times 1 + 4 \times \frac{1}{10} + 5 \times \frac{1}{100} + 2 \times \frac{1}{1{,}000}$

Specimen B: $3.459 = 3 \times 1 + 4 \times \frac{1}{10} + 5 \times \frac{1}{100} + 9 \times \frac{1}{1{,}000}$

Start with the greatest place value and compare. Both numbers have 3 ones, both numbers have 4 tenths, and both numbers have 5 hundredths. Now, compare the thousandths: 2 thousandths is less than 9 thousandths, so 3.452 < 3.459.

➡ Specimen B is longer than Specimen A.

Guided Instruction

Connect: What you know about place value and comparisons

Compare 0.23 and 0.234.

Step 1

Write the numbers in a column, lining up like place values. Add a zero to the thousandths column of 0.23 to help you align each digit with its correct corresponding place value.

0.230
0.234

Step 2

Compare the digits in the same place, starting from the left. The digits in the ones place are both 0.

0.230
0.234

Step 3

Compare the digits in the tenths place. The digits are both 2.

0.230
0.234

Step 4

Compare the digits in the hundredths place. The digits are both 3.

0.230
0.234

Step 5

Compare the digits in the thousandths place.
The digits are different:
0 thousandths < 4 thousandths

0.230
0.234

The number 0.230 is less than 0.234.

➡ 0.23 < 0.234

Willa says that 0.276 is greater than 0.88 because 276 is greater than 88. Explain why Willa's reasoning is incorrect.

Guided Practice

1. Compare 1.237 and 1.234.

   a. Write the decimals in a place-value chart.

ones	.	tenths	hundredths	thousandths
	.			
	.			

   Compare the digits starting from the left.

   Ones: 1 one = 1 one

   Tenths: ____ tenths = ____ tenths

   Hundredths: ______________________________

   Thousandths: ______________________________

   b. Write < or >. 1.237 ____ 1.234

For exercises 2–4, compare the numbers using place value.

2. 0.029 and 0.030

   Step 1: Which is the first place from the left that has different digits?

   ____

   Step 2: Which digit is greater? ____

   Step 3: So 0.029 ____ 0.030

3. 1.109 and 1.019

   1.109 ____ 1.019

4. 0.27 and 0.269

   0.27 ____ 0.269

MP2 5. Caleb wants to put three batting averages in order from least to greatest. They are 0.276, 0.283, and 0.279. Explain how can he do this.

Independent Practice

Compare using a place-value chart.

1. Compare 1.135 and 1.153.

   a. Write the decimals in a place-value chart.

ones	.	tenths	hundredths	thousandths
	.			
	.			

   b. Compare the digits in the same place value columns.

   Ones: 1 one = 1 one

   Tenths: ____________________

   Hundredths: ____________________

   c. Since the 3 in the hundredths place of 1.135 is less than the 5 in the hundredths place of 1.153, 1.135 ____ 1.153.

Compare using expanded form. Show your work.

2. 0.023 and 0.198

   Step 1:
   Write 0.023 in expanded notation.

   $0 \times 1 + 0 \times \frac{1}{10} + \_\_\_\_ \times \_\_\_\_ + 3 \times \frac{1}{1,000}$

   Step 2:
   Write 0.198 in expanded notation.

   $0 \times 1 + \_\_\_\_ \times \_\_\_\_ + 9 \times \frac{1}{100} + \_\_\_\_ \times \_\_\_\_$

   Step 3:
   Compare the tenths.

   $0 \times \frac{1}{10}$ ____ $1 \times \frac{1}{10}$

   0.023 ____ 0.198

Independent Practice

Compare. Use place value.

3. 1.121 and 1.211

   1.121 ____ 1.211

4. 0.37 and 0.370

   0.37 ____ 0.370

5. 0.298 and 0.289

   0.298 ____ 0.289

Compare. Use expanded form.

6. 3.544 and 3.455

   3.544 ____ 3.455

7. 0.109 and 0.190

   0.109 ____ 0.190

8. 0.12 and 0.119

   0.12 ____ 0.119

Choose the correct answer.

9. The lengths of two nails are 0.785 inch and 0.768 inch. At which place should you look to decide which nail is longer?

   a. ones
   b. hundredths
   c. tenths
   d. thousandths

10. For the number 3.124, which of the following correctly shows the place value of the digit 4 in expanded form?

   a. $4 \times \frac{1}{10}$
   b. $4 \times \frac{1}{100}$
   c. $4 \times \frac{1}{1,000}$
   d. 4×1000

11. Which of the following decimals is to the left of 0.354 on a number line?

   a. 0.355
   b. 0.35
   c. 0.364
   d. 1.333

Independent Practice

Compare the decimals using the number line.

12. 2.543 ____ 2.549

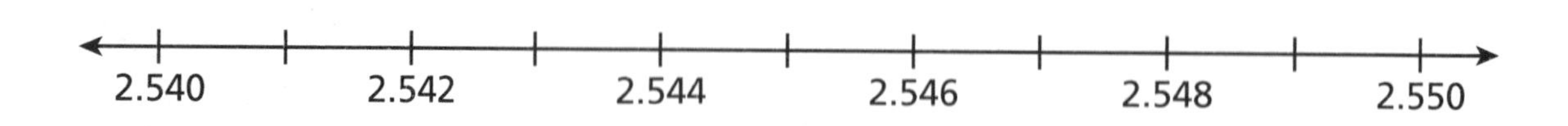

Solve the problems.

MP6 **13.** Explain some ways you can compare decimals.

MP3 **14.** To compare 5.147 and 5.139, Emily looked at the thousandths place. She said since 9 is greater than 7, 5.139 is greater than 5.147. What is her error? Explain how to correct it.

MP6 **15.** A quarter is 1.750 millimeters thick. A nickel is 1.950 millimeters thick. Write the sizes as mixed numbers. Which is thicker? Explain.

MP6 **16.** A dime has a mass of 2.268 grams. A penny has a mass of 2.500 grams. Write the masses as mixed numbers. Which coin has a greater mass? Explain.

Independent Practice

MP5 **17.** One gram of anchovies has 0.199 grams of B vitamins. One gram of sturgeon has 0.101 grams of B vitamins. Tuna has more B vitamins than sturgeon but less than anchovies. The number of B vitamins in tuna is a number listed as a, b, or c below. Which number is correct for tuna?

a. 0.099 grams per gram

b. 0.211 grams per gram

c. 0.188 grams per gram

Show your work. Use a place-value chart.

MP4 **18.** Karen wants to drill a hole for a screw. The hole must be a little smaller than the screw. She has three drill bits with diameters of 0.389 inch, 0.362 inch, and 0.352 inch. She has three screws with diameters of 0.385 inch, 0.362 inch, and 0.348 inch. Which are the best drill bit and screw combination that Karen should use? Explain your reasoning.

Show your work. Use the number line

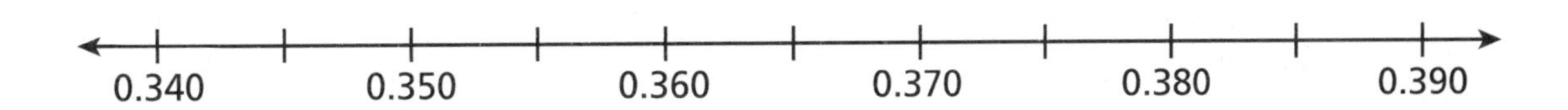

Lesson 8

Round Decimals: Use Place Value

Essential Question:
How do you use place value to round decimal numbers?
5.NBT.4

Guided Instruction

In this lesson you will learn how to round decimals using place value.

Understand: How to round decimal numbers to the nearest whole number

A jewelry designer records the mass of a necklace as 32.748 grams. What is the mass of the necklace to the nearest gram?

To find the mass of the necklace to the nearest gram, you can round 32.748 using the same steps you apply to round whole numbers.

Write 32.748 in a place-value chart. Identify the place you are being asked to round to. Rounding to the nearest gram means you are rounding to the nearest *whole number*. So, you are rounding to the ones place.

tens	ones	.	tenths	hundredths	thousandths
3	2	.	**7**	**4**	**8**

Use a number line to help you round 32.748 grams to the ones place.

- Draw a number line. Since 32.748 is between **32** and **33**, start and end with these whole numbers. Separate the line into tenths.

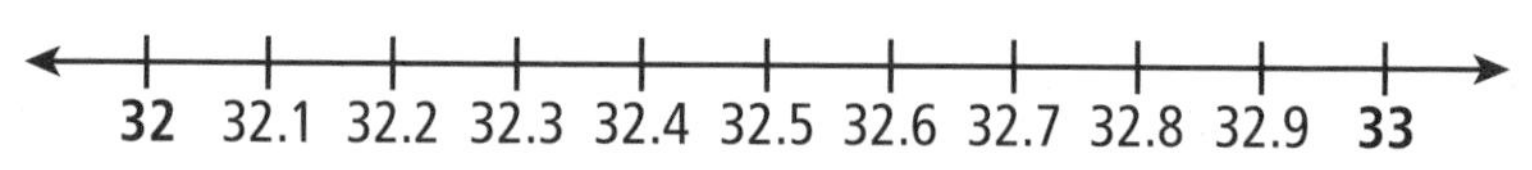

- Plot the approximate location of 32.748.

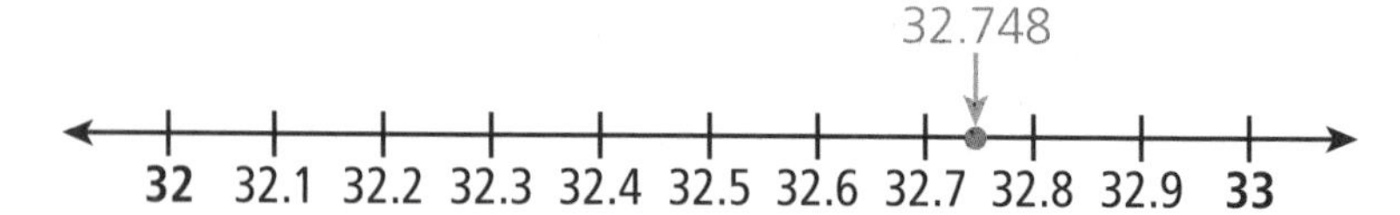

- Identify the whole number closest to 32.748 on the number line. 32.748 is closer to 33 than to 32.

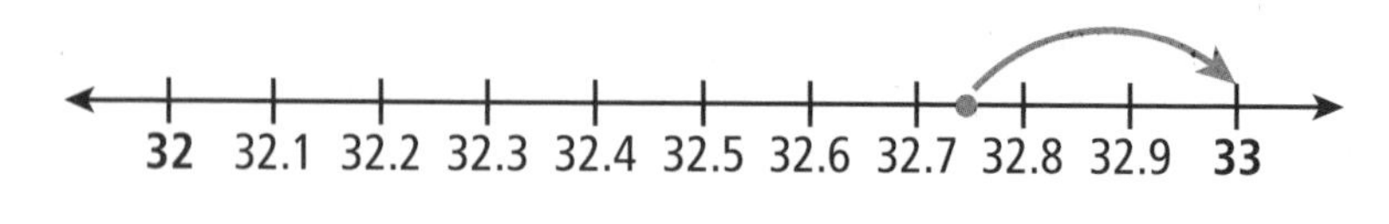

To the nearest gram, the mass of the necklace is 33 grams.

Guided Instruction

Understand: How to round decimal numbers to the nearest tenth

Now the jewelry designer wants to know what the mass of the necklace, 32.748 grams, is to the nearest tenth of a gram.

Use a number line to help you round 32.748 grams. The answer will be in tenths because you are asked to round to the nearest *tenth* of a gram.

- 32.748 is between the tenths values **32.7** and **32.8**. Divide the interval from 32.7 to 32.8 into ten parts to show hundredths.

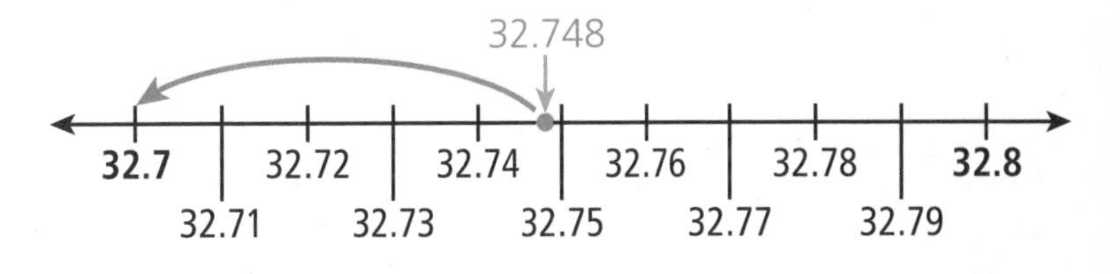

- The point for 32.748 is closer to 32.7 than 32.8.
- 32.748 rounded to the nearest *tenth* is 32.7.

➡ To the nearest tenth of a gram, the mass of the necklace is 32.7 grams.

Understand: How to round decimal numbers to the nearest hundredth

Round 32.748 grams to the nearest hundredth of a gram.

Use a number line to help you round 32.748 grams. The answer will be in hundredths because you are asked to round to the nearest *hundredth* of a gram.

- 32.748 is between the hundredths values **32.74** and **32.75**. Divide the interval between these numbers into ten parts to show thousandths.

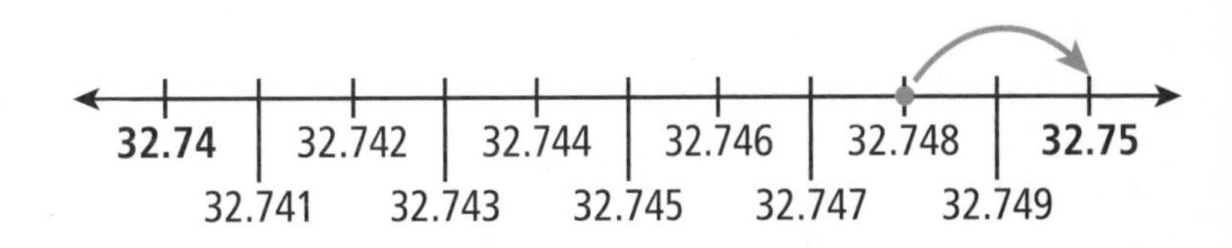

- The point for 32.748 is closer to 32.75 than 32.74.
- 32.748 rounded to the nearest *hundredth* is 32.75.

➡ To the nearest hundredth of a gram the mass is 32.75 grams.

Guided Instruction

Connect: What you know about place value and rounding decimal numbers

A biologist records the lengths of three lizards in centimeters.

What is the length of lizard A to the nearest centimeter?
What is the length of lizard B to the nearest tenth of a centimeter?
What is the length of lizard C to the nearest hundredth of a centimeter?

Lizard	Length (cm)
A	14.612
B	13.844
C	15.036

Step 1

To find the length of lizard A to the nearest centimeter, round 14.612 to the ones place. The rounding rules for decimals are the same as for whole numbers. Write 14.612 in a place-value chart.

tens	ones	.	tenths	hundredths	thousandths
1	4	.	6	1	2

To round to the ones place, look at the digit in the tenths place: $6 > 5$, so round 4 up to get 15.

Remember!
To round, look at the digit to the right of the rounding place.
- If it is 5 or more, round the digit in the rounding place up.
- If it is less than 5, leave the digit in the rounding place as it is.

Step 2

To find the length of lizard B to the nearest tenth of a centimeter, round 13.844 to the tenths place.

Look at the hundredths place: 13.844. Since $4 < 5$, leave the number in the tenths place, 8, as it is. 13.844 rounds to 13.8.

Step 3

To find the length of lizard C to the nearest hundredth of a centimeter, round 15.036 to the hundredths place.

Look at the digit in the thousandths place: 15.036. Since $6 > 5$, round 3 hundredths up to 4 hundredths. 15.036 rounds to 15.04.

➡ To the nearest centimeter, lizard A is 15 cm long. To the nearest tenth of a centimeter, lizard B is 13.8 cm long. To the nearest hundredth of a centimeter, lizard C is 15.04 cm long.

Guided Practice

For exercises 1–2, use the number line given to complete the sentences and round each number.

1. 8.215 to the nearest whole number

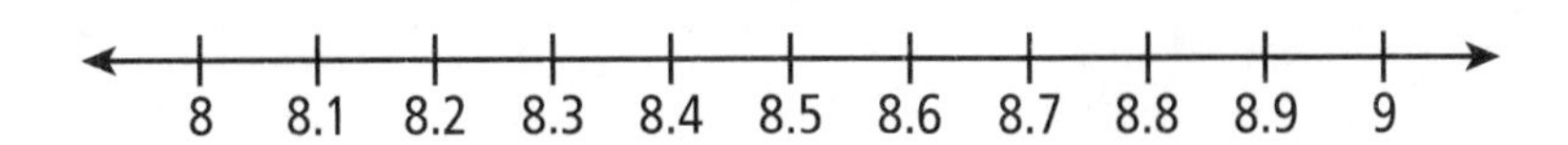

8.215 is closer to ____ than ____ on the number line.

8.215 rounded to the nearest whole number is ____.

2. 19.837 to the nearest hundredth

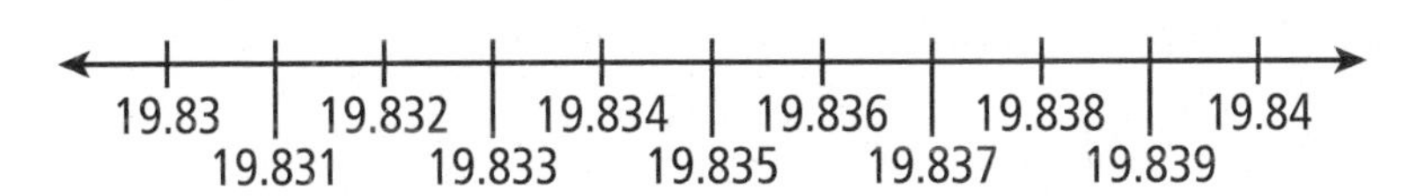

19.837 is closer to __________ than __________ on the number line.

19.837 rounded to the nearest hundredth is __________.

Use the place-value chart to round 0.376 to the nearest tenth and nearest hundredth.

3.

ones	.	tenths	hundredths	thousandths
0	**.**	**3**	**7**	**6**

Nearest tenth: ____

Nearest hundredth: ____

Think • Pair • Share

MP2 4. Explain why 1.999 rounded to the nearest hundredth is 2.

Independent Practice

Use the number line to help you round the number.

1. 0.762 to the nearest tenth

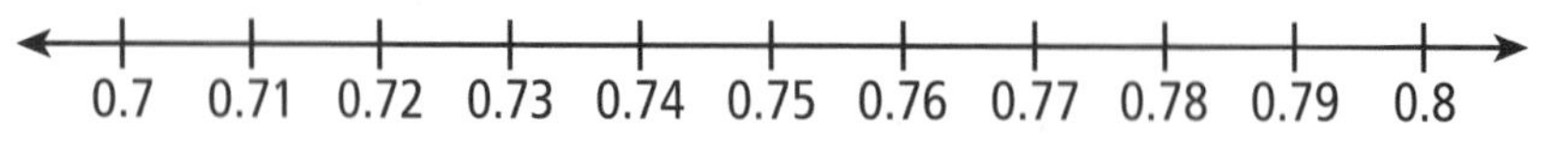

0.762 rounded to the nearest tenth is ____.

2. 6.308 to the nearest hundredth

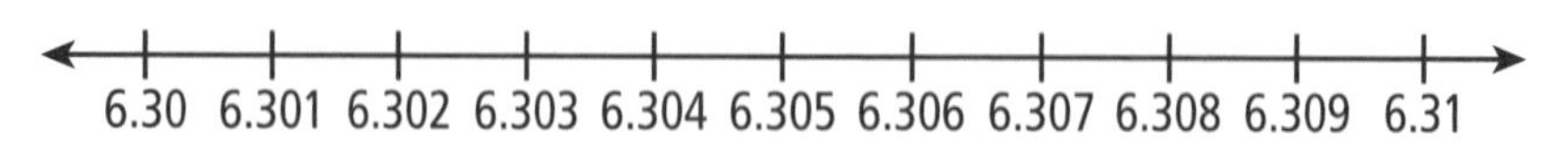

6.308 rounded to the nearest hundredth is ____.

Use the place-value charts to round each decimal to the nearest whole number, nearest tenth, and nearest hundredth.

3. 67.822

tens	ones	.	tenths	hundredths	thousandths

Nearest whole number: ______

Nearest tenth: ______

Nearest hundredth: ______

4. 2.467

ones	.	tenths	hundredths	thousandths

Nearest whole number: ______

Nearest tenth: ______

Nearest hundredth: ______

5. Which of the following decimals does NOT round to the nearest tenth as 45.3?

a. 45.28

b. 45.331

c. 45.373

d. 45.317

Independent Practice

6. Round a, b, c, and d on the number line to the nearest hundredth.

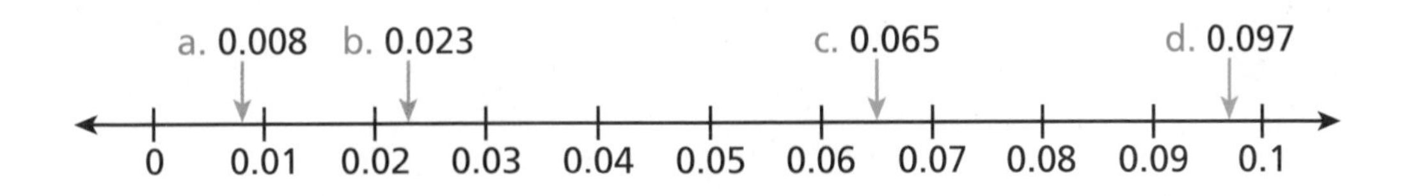

a. ____ b. ____ c. ____ d. ____

For exercises 7–10, write the place value that each number was rounded to.

7. 4.55 rounded to 4.6

____

8. 0.129 rounded to 0.13

____

9. 66.4 rounded to 66

____

10. 583.476 rounded to 583.48

____

For exercises 11–14, round the decimals to the nearest one, tenth, and hundredth.

	one	tenth	hundredth
11. 0.344	______	______	______
12. 1.545	______	______	______
13. 9.624	______	______	______
14. 89.799	______	______	______

15. Which number rounds up when rounded to the tenths place?

a. 65.938

b. 65.527

c. 65.409

d. 65.152

Independent Practice

16. The mass of a sample at the start of a science experiment is 10.951 grams. What is the sample's mass rounded to the nearest tenth of a gram?

a. 10.0 grams
b. 10.9 grams
c. 10.95 grams
d. 11.0 grams

Solve the problems.

MP2 **17.** Explain how 8.557 can be rounded correctly to 9, 8.6, or 8.56.

MP3 **18.** Mia has exactly $10.25. She wants to buy a box of pens for $6.49 and a notebook for $4.28. She rounds both prices to the nearest dollar to get $6 and $4. She thinks, "When I add the rounded prices I get $10. I have more than enough money." Is Mia correct? Explain.

MP7 **19.** A rectangular yard has a length of 7.3 meters and a width of 4.8 meters. Use rounding to estimate the perimeter and area of the yard.

Show your work.

Answer ______________________________

Independent Practice

MP1 **20.** Josie finished a sprinting race in 31.183 seconds. Wynne finished the race in 28.927 seconds. Estimate the difference in times by rounding the times to the nearest tenth of a second and subtracting by using a number line or another method. About how much sooner did Wynne finish?

Show your work.

Answer ______________________________

MP3 **21.** Pam bought a box of cereal for $4.39 and a gallon of milk for $3.42. Sam bought a carton of orange juice for $3.59 and a loaf of bread for $3.65. Estimate the amount each person paid by rounding the prices to the nearest dollar and adding. Then find the actual total each person paid. Whose estimated total is greater? Whose actual total is greater? Why do you think this happens?

Show your work.

Answer ______________________________

MP1 **22.** Use the hints below to identify the missing digit in the decimal number.

27.■62

- When rounded to the nearest whole number, the number is 27.
- When rounded to the nearest tenth, the number is 27.4.

Answer ______________________________

Lesson 9

Multiply Fluently with Multi-Digit Numbers

Essential Question:
How can you multiply multi-digit numbers by using the standard algorithm?

5.NBT.5

Words to Know:
partial product

Guided Instruction

In this lesson you will multiply multi-digit numbers by using the standard algorithm.

Understand: How to multiply a multi-digit number by a one-digit number

The path around the town park is 729 yards long. Cam ran around the park 6 times. How many yards did he run?

To find the distance Cam ran, multiply 729 by 6. You can use the standard multiplication algorithm.

$$\begin{array}{r} \scriptstyle 5 \\ 729 \\ \times \quad 6 \\ \hline 4 \end{array}$$

Multiply 9 ones by 6. You get 54 ones, or 5 tens and 4 ones.

Write 4 in the ones place of the answer and record the 5 tens over the tens place to be added in at the next step.

$$\begin{array}{r} \scriptstyle 1\,5 \\ 729 \\ \times \quad 6 \\ \hline 74 \end{array}$$

Multiply 2 tens by 6. You get 12 tens. Add the 5 tens from the previous step to get 17 tens, or 1 hundred and 7 tens.

Write 7 in the tens place of the answer and record the 1 hundred over the hundreds place to be added in the next step.

$$\begin{array}{r} \scriptstyle 1\,5 \\ 729 \\ \times \quad 6 \\ \hline 4{,}374 \end{array}$$

Multiply 7 hundreds by 6. You get 42 hundreds. Add the 1 hundred from the previous step to get 43 hundreds or 4 thousands and 3 hundreds.

Write 3 in the hundreds place of the answer and write 4 in the thousands place of the answer.

➡ Cam ran 4,374 yards in all.

Guided Instruction

Understand: How to multiply a two-digit number by a two-digit number

A health club orders 86 boxes of protein bars. Each case contains 24 bars. How many protein bars does the health club order in all?

To find the total number of protein bars, multiply 86 by 24.

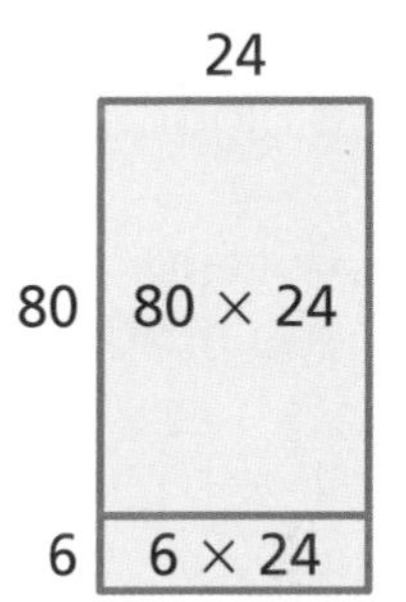

This area model shows that 86 × 24 can be calculated by adding the products of 6 × 24 and 80 × 24. Each of these products is called a partial product.

This idea can help you understand how to use the standard algorithm to multiply by a two-digit number.

$$\begin{array}{r} ^{2} \\ 24 \\ \times\ 86 \\ \hline 144 \end{array}$$

Multiply 24 by 6.
This will give you the first partial product. Follow the same steps used to multiply by a one-digit number on the previous page.

Multiply 24 by 80.
This will give you the second partial product.

$$\begin{array}{r} ^{3} \\ ^{2} \\ 24 \\ \times\ 86 \\ \hline 144 \\ 1{,}920 \end{array}$$

Remember that 80 × 24 is 10 times as much as 8 × 24. So, calculate the product just as you would calculate 8 × 24, but shift the digits in the partial product one place to the left. Put a 0 in the ones place.

8 × 24 = 192, so
80 × 24 = 1,920

$$\begin{array}{rl} ^{3} & \\ ^{2} & \\ 24 & \\ \times\ 86 & \\ \hline 144 & \leftarrow 6 \times 24 \\ +1{,}920 & \leftarrow 80 \times 24 \\ \hline 2{,}064 & \end{array}$$

Add the partial products to get the product of 24 × 86.

The health club orders 2,064 protein bars in all.

Guided Instruction

Connect: How to multiply numbers using the standard algorithm

A resort hotel has 36 floors. Each floor has 115 guest rooms. How many guest rooms are in the hotel?

To find how many guest rooms are in the hotel, multiply 115 guest rooms on each floor by 36 floors. Use the standard algorithm.

The model shows that the product of 36×115 is the sum of the products of 6×115 and 30×115.

	115
30	30×115
6	6×115

Step 1

$$\begin{array}{r} {\scriptstyle 3} \\ 115 \\ \times\ 36 \\ \hline 690 \end{array}$$

Multiply 115 by 6.
This will give you the first partial product.

Step 2

Multiply 115 by 30.
This will give you the second partial product.

$$\begin{array}{r} {\scriptstyle 1} \\ {\scriptstyle 3} \\ 115 \\ \times\ 36 \\ \hline 690 \\ 3{,}450 \end{array}$$

Remember that 30×115 is 10 times as much as 3×115. So, calculate the product just as you would calculate 3×115, but shift the digits in the partial product one place to the left. Put a 0 in the ones place.

Remember!
$3 \times 115 = 345$, so
$30 \times 115 = 3{,}450$

Step 3

$$\begin{array}{rl} {\scriptstyle 1} & \\ {\scriptstyle 3} & \\ 115 & \\ \times\ 36 & \\ \hline 690 & \leftarrow 6 \times 115 \\ +3{,}450 & \leftarrow 30 \times 115 \\ \hline 4{,}140 & \end{array}$$

Add the partial products to get the product of 36×115.

➡ The hotel has 4,140 guest rooms.

Guided Practice

Label the area model to show the partial products for the given multiplication problem.

1. 32 × 64

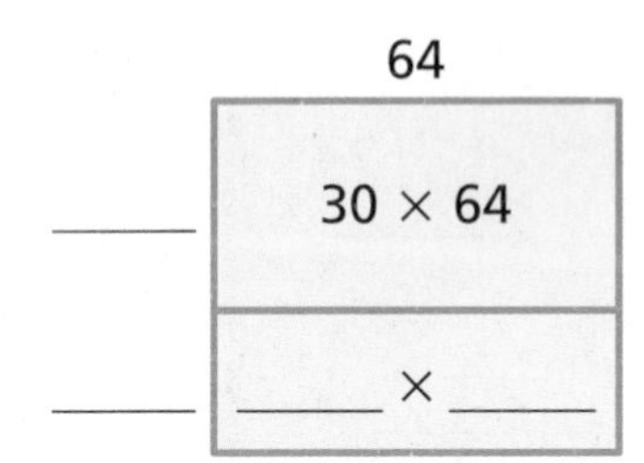

2. 84 × 152

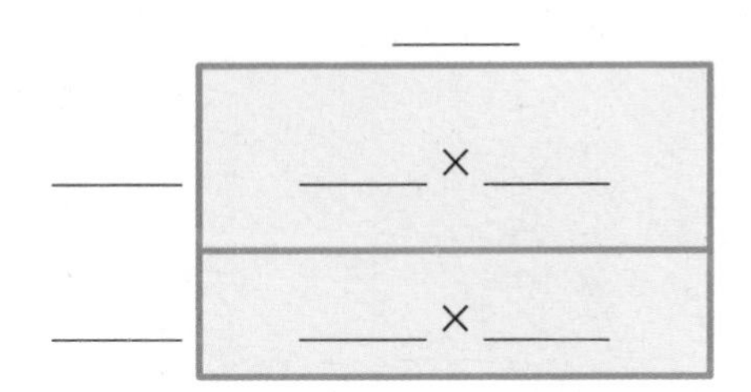

The products are calculated using the standard algorithm. Fill in the missing partial products and products.

3.

```
   607
×    5
------
[    ]
```

4.

```
      74
×     52
--------
     148  ← 2 × 74
+ [    ]  ← 50 × 74
--------
   3,848
```

5.

```
      29
×     68
--------
  [    ]  ← 8 × 29
+  1,740  ← 60 × 29
--------
  [    ]
```

6.

```
     435
×     16
--------
  [    ]  ← 6 × 435
+ [    ]  ← 10 × 435
--------
  [    ]
```

Think • Pair • Share

MP3 7. To multiply 225 times 40, Casey breaks apart 225 as 200 and 25. She knows that 25 times 4 is 100, so 25 times 40 is 1,000. Then she multiplies 200 times 40 to get 8,000. Finally, she adds 1,000 and 8,000 to get a final product of 9,000. Is Casey's answer correct? Explain your reasoning. Can you think of another way to break up the factors?

Independent Practice

Label the area model to show the partial products for the given multiplication problem.

1. 27 × 51

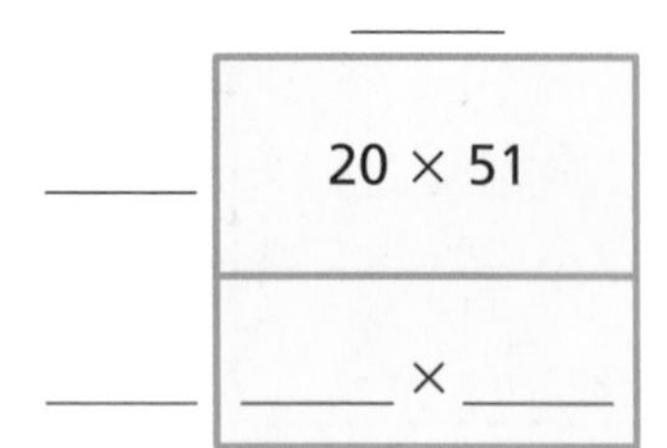

2. 93 × 294

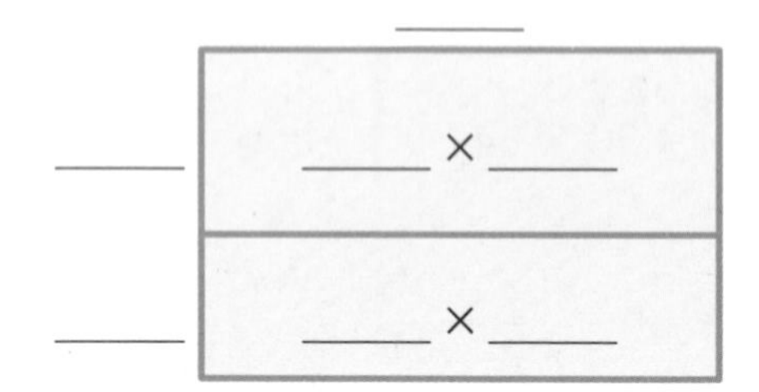

The products are calculated using the standard algorithm. Fill in the missing partial products and products.

3.
```
  838
×   4
-----
[   ]
```

4.
```
  620
×   9
-----
[   ]
```

5.
```
     51
×    27
-------
  [   ]  ← 7 × 51
+ 1,020  ← 20 × 51
-------
  [   ]
```

6.
```
   224
×   93
------
   672  ← 3 × 224
+[   ]  ← 90 × 224
------
 [   ]
```

7.

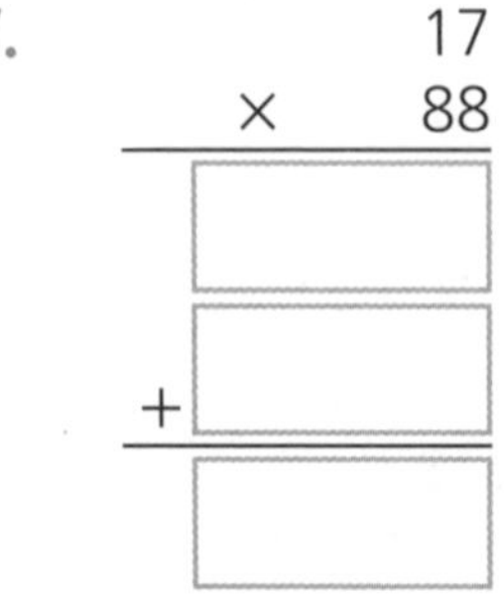

```
   17
×  88
-----
[   ]
+[   ]
-----
[   ]
```

8.
```
  108
×  49
-----
[   ]
+[   ]
-----
[   ]
```

Independent Practice

Multiply. Show your work.

9. $\begin{array}{r} 105 \\ \times\ 19 \\ \hline \end{array}$

10. $\begin{array}{r} 325 \\ \times\ 25 \\ \hline \end{array}$

11. $\begin{array}{r} 240 \\ \times\ 22 \\ \hline \end{array}$

12. $\begin{array}{r} 298 \\ \times\ 56 \\ \hline \end{array}$

13. $\begin{array}{r} 721 \\ \times\ 14 \\ \hline \end{array}$

14. $\begin{array}{r} 386 \\ \times\ 75 \\ \hline \end{array}$

For exercises 15–17, choose the correct answer.

15. A car company has a large automobile plant that produces 148 cars per hour. The automobile plant operates 24 hours a day. How many cars does the automobile plant produce in a day?

    a. 148
    b. 888
    c. 3,422
    d. 3,552

16. A school group is raising money for a trip. The trip will cost $135 per student. If there are 67 students in the group, how much must the group raise?

    a. $9,450
    b. $9,045
    c. $8,100
    d. $1,755

17. A catering hall can hold 165 tables. Each table can seat 12 people. How many people can be seated in the catering hall?

    a. 495
    b. 1,650
    c. 1,870
    d. 1,980

Independent Practice

MP4 **18.** To multiply 247 by 64, Jacob draws the area model below. What is his error? Explain how he can correct his model.

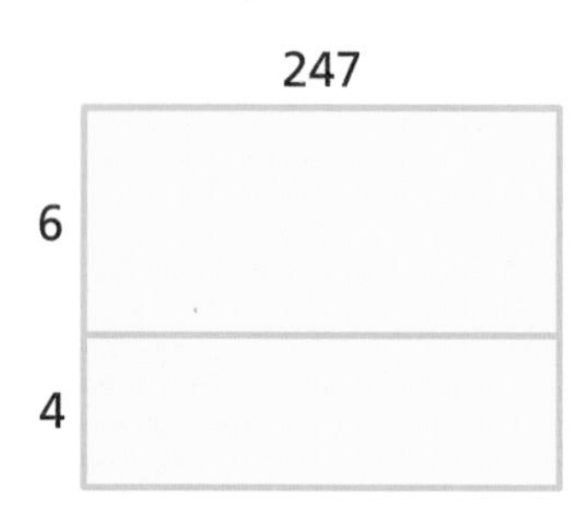

MP3 **19.** Explain two strategies you can use to find the product of 450×50.

Solve the problems.

MP1 **20.** Delilah is making necklaces. Each necklace will have 285 beads. She wants to make 37 necklaces. How many beads will Delilah need?

Show your work.

Answer ______________________________

MP1 **21.** Francis counts 863 books in a full bookcase at the library. The library has 95 full bookcases. If each bookcase has 863 books, how many books are in the library?

Show your work.

Answer ______________________________

Independent Practice

MP8 **22.** A fruit orchard has 65 lemon trees. On average, each lemon tree produces about 407 lemons in 5 years. About how many lemons will the orchard produce in 5 years?

Show your work.

Answer ______________________________

MP1 **23.** A diner is open for 24 hours a day, every day of the year except for 10 holidays. How many hours is the diner open in a year?

Answer ______________________________

Justify your answer using words, drawings, or numbers.

MP8 **24.** A honeybee flaps its wings about 237 times per second. Approximately, how many times does the bee flap its wings in 1 minute?

Answer ______________________________

Justify your answer using words, drawings, or numbers.

Lesson

10 Divide Whole Numbers: Use Place Value Strategies

Essential Question:
How can you use place value strategies to divide whole numbers?

5.NBT.6

Words to Know:
partial quotient

Guided Instruction

In this lesson you will learn methods for dividing a multi-digit number by a two-digit number.

Understand: How to divide using an area model

An aid organization has 3,842 bottles of water to divide equally among 15 shelters. How many bottles will each shelter get?

To find the solution divide: 3,842 bottles ÷ 15 shelters. Because 3,842 is between $15 \times 100 = 1{,}500$ and $15 \times 1{,}000 = 15{,}000$ the quotient is between 100 and 1,000. $15 \times n = 3{,}842$, so $n = 3{,}842 \div 15$.

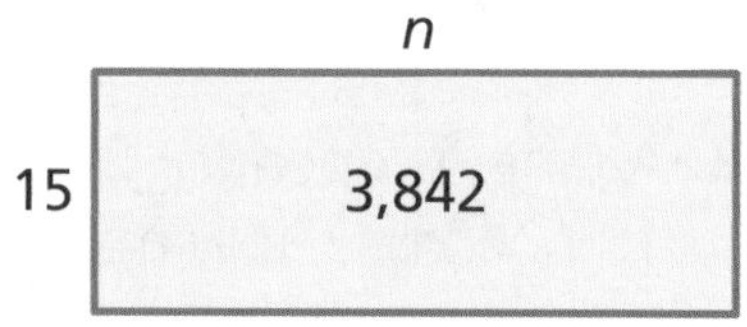

	n
15	3,842

Use an area model. The unknown side length, n, is the quotient of 3,842 ÷ 15. You will build the quotient place by place, redrawing the rectangle in sections as you go. The quotient for each section is called a partial quotient.

Think: 15 times what hundreds number gives a product closest to 3,842, without going over? $15 \times 200 = 3{,}000$ and $15 \times 300 = 4{,}500$, so use 200.

Draw the first section of the rectangle, and write 200 at the top. The area of this section is $15 \times 200 = 3{,}000$. Subtract 3,000 from 3,842 to find how much area is left, and insert or draw another section for this leftover area.

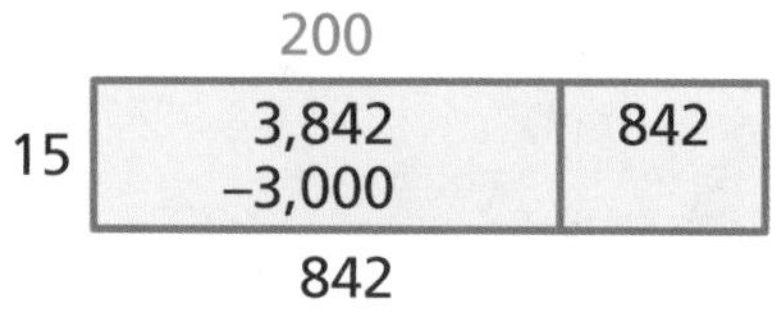

	200	
15	3,842 −3,000	842
	842	

Think: 15 times what tens number gives a product closest to 842, without going over? $15 \times 50 = 750$ and $15 \times 60 = 900$, so use 50. Write 50 at the top of the second section, subtract the area of that section from 842, and add a new section.

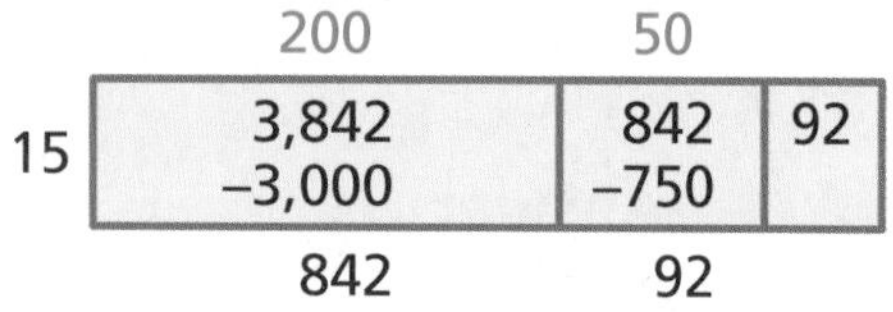

	200	50	
15	3,842 −3,000	842 −750	92
	842	92	

Think: 15 times what ones number gives a product closest to 92, without going over? $15 \times 6 = 90$ and $15 \times 7 = 105$, so use 6. Write 6 at the top of the third section, and subtract 90 from 92. The difference 2 is less than 15, so it is the remainder.

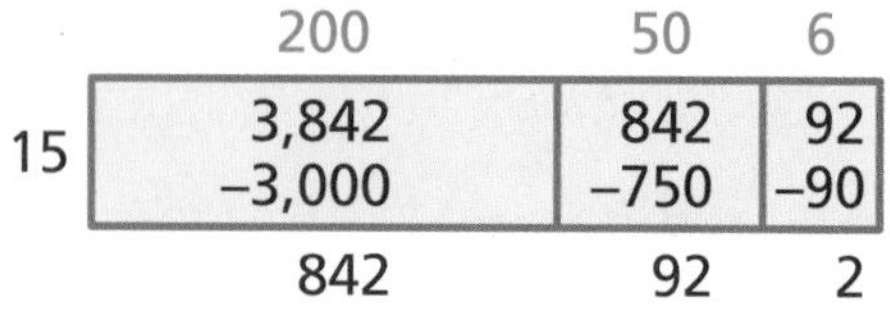

	200	50	6
15	3,842 −3,000	842 −750	92 −90
	842	92	2

Add the partial quotients, $200 + 50 + 6 = 256$, to get the quotient.

➡ Each shelter will get 256 bottles and there will be 2 bottles left.

Guided Instruction

Understand: How to divide using partial quotients

A publisher shipped 8,496 copies of a new book to stores. The books were shipped in boxes of 24. How many boxes were shipped?

Divide the total number of books by the number of books in each box: 8,496 ÷ 24.

Represent the problem as a long division.

divisor → 24)8,496 ← dividend; ■ ← quotient

Think: 24 times what hundreds number gives a product closest to 8,496 without going over?

24 × 300 = 7,200 and 24 × 400 = 9,600, so use 300.

Write 300 above the division symbol. It is the *first partial quotient*. Write 7,200, which is 24 × 300, under 8,946, and subtract to see how much is left to divide.

```
     300
24)8,496
  -7,200
   1,296
```

Think: 24 times what tens number gives a product closest to 1,296 without going over?

24 × 50 = 1,200 and 24 × 60 = 1,440, so use 50.

Write 50, the *second partial quotient*, above 300. Write 1,200 under 1,296, and subtract.

```
      50
     300
24)8,496
  -7,200
   1,296
  -1,200
      96
```

Think: 24 times what ones number gives a product close to 96 without going over?

24 × 4 = 96, so use 4.

Write 4, the *third partial quotient*, above 50. Write 96 under 96 and subtract to get 0. The division is complete. There is no remainder.

Add the partial quotients: 300 + 50 + 4 = 354.

```
       4
      50
     300
24)8,496
  -7,200
   1,296
  -1,200
      96
     -96
       0 ← no remainder
```

➡ 354 boxes of books were shipped.

Guided Instruction

Connect: Division methods to the standard division algorithm

A sports drink company paid participants $32 each to take part in a taste test. They paid $5,632 total. How many people participated in the taste test?

Divide the total amount the company paid by the amount it paid to each person: 5,632 ÷ 32. Use the standard division algorithm.

Think: You cannot divide 5 by 32. Try 56. What number times 32 will give a product close to 56 without going over? Answer: 1

Write 1 in the hundreds place of the quotient, above the 6. Multiply 1 × 32 and write the result, 32, below 56.

Subtract to see that 24 is left, and bring down the digit from the next place to make 243.

```
     1
32)5,632
  - 32
    243
```

Think: What number times 32 will give a product close to 243? Answer: 7

Write 7 in the tens place of the quotient, above the 3. Multiply 7 × 32 and write the result, 224, below 243.

Subtract to get 19, and bring down the digit from the next place to make 192.

```
     17
32)5,632
  - 32
    243
  - 224
     192
```

Think: What number times 32 will give a product close to 192? Answer: 6

Write 6 in the ones place of the quotient, above the 2. Multiply 6 × 32 and write the result, 192, below 192.

Subtract. There is nothing left. The quotient is complete.

```
     176
32)5,632
  - 32
    243
  - 224
     192
    -192
       0
```

➡ 176 people participated in the taste test.

Mel said, "At the start of the division, we are really finding how many times 32 divides into 5,600. That is why the 1 belongs in the hundreds place in the quotient." What do you think Mel means?

Guided Practice

1. Find 2,101 ÷ 15 by completing the area model.

	100	40
15	2,101 – ______	601 – ______
	601	1

Add the partial quotients:

100 + ______ = ______.

The remainder is ______.

2. Complete the steps to divide.

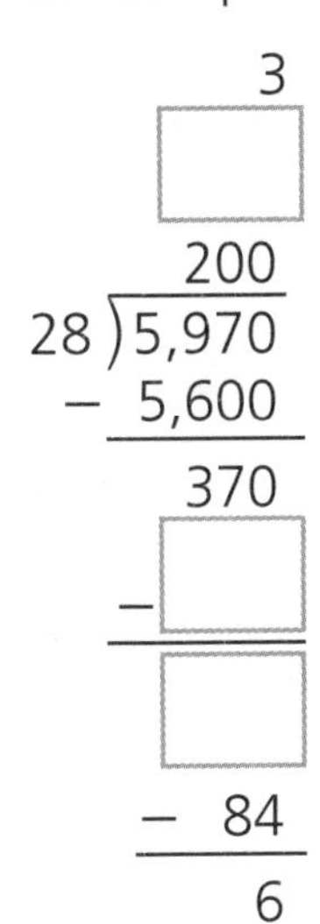

Add the partial quotients:

______ + 10 + ______ = ______.

The remainder is ______.

5,970 ÷ 28 = __________

3. Divide using the standard algorithm.

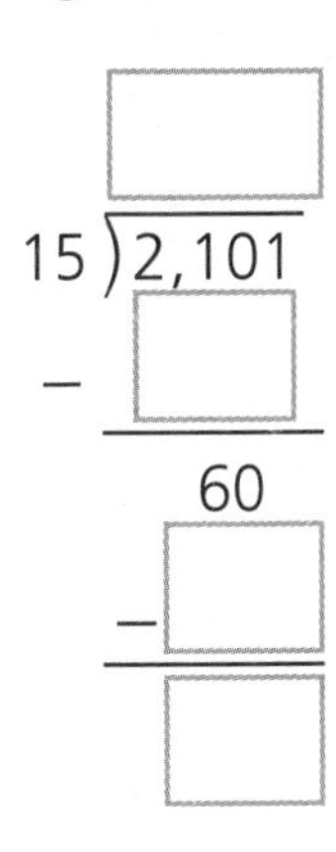

2,101 ÷ 15 = __________

Think • Pair • Share

MP3 4. Compare and contrast the area model method used in exercise 1 and the standard division algorithm method used in exercise 3.

Independent Practice

For exercises 1–2, evaluate the division expressions by using an area model.

1. $2{,}020 \div 15$

   Area Model

   Answer ______________________

2. $1{,}145 \div 35$

   Area Model

   Answer ______________________

3. Find $2{,}729 \div 22$ by using the partial-quotients method.

   Answer ______________________

4. Divide $5{,}648 \div 17$ using the standard division algorithm.

   Answer ______________________

Independent Practice

MP3 **5.** Adam is dividing 1,640 by 20. He says he can divide 1,640 by 10 and then multiply the answer by 2. Is Adam correct? How would you adjust his strategy? Explain.

MP3 **6.** To divide 1,110 by 10, Aliyah draws the area model below. What is her error? Explain how she can correct her model.

	100	1
10	1,110 −1,000	10 −10
	10	0

Choose the correct answer.

7. A roll of industrial wire is 7,776 inches long. It is cut into 36 pieces of the same size. What is the length of each piece of wire?

a. 22 inches
b. 216 inches
c. 36 inches
d. 1,296 inches

8. Kayla is packing 1,864 books. If 32 books can fit in one box, how many boxes does she need?

a. 55
b. 58
c. 56
d. 59

Independent Practice

Find each quotient. Show your work.

9. 4,750 ÷ 25

Answer ____________________

10. 5,026 ÷ 44

Answer ____________________

11. 2,889 ÷ 70

Answer ____________________

12. 3,080 ÷ 19

Answer ____________________

Solve the problems.

MP1 **13.** A school has 1,235 students that will be divided into 19 groups for sports day. How many students will be in each group? Are there any students who will not be in a group?

Show your work.

Answer ____________________

MP4 **14.** A factory has 1,368 vases to be boxed and shipped. Each box will contain 30 vases. How many boxes can be shipped with 30 vases? If there are vases left over, what is the number?

Show your work.

Answer ____________________

Independent Practice

MP1 **15.** A chapter in a book has 8,565 words. The chapter is 25 pages long. About how many words are on each page?

Show your work.

Answer ______________________________

MP5 **16.** A bus company has been booked to transport 1,957 passengers from Philadelphia to New York. A bus will seat 50 passengers. How many buses will it take to transport all the passengers?

Answer ______________________________

Justify your answer using words, drawings, or numbers.

MP8 **17.** A farmer's chickens lay 1,421 eggs a year. The farmer has 120 egg cartons, each of which holds a dozen eggs. Will the farmer need all the egg cartons to package the eggs for the year?

Answer ______________________________

Justify your answer using words, drawings, or numbers.

Lesson

11 Divide Whole Numbers: Use Properties of Operations

Essential Question:
How can you use properties of operations to divide whole numbers?

5.NBT.6

Guided Instruction

In this lesson you will divide whole numbers using properties of operations and the relationship between multiplication and division.

Understand: How to divide using the Distributive Property

A company has 5,535 boxes of soccer balls to deliver overseas. Before being loaded onto a cargo ship, the boxes are divided equally among 45 shipping containers. How many boxes are in each shipping container?

You have used the Distributive Property to multiply a sum $(a + b)$ by a number c. You can also use the Distributive Property to divide a sum $(a + b)$ by a number c.

Remember!
Distributive Property
$c \times (a + b) = c \times a + c \times b$
$(a + b) \div c = a \div c + b \div c$

Use the Distributive Property to divide 5,535 by 45. First break apart 5,535 into a sum of numbers that can be easily divided by 45.

Find multiples of 45, and use place values of 10, 100, and 1,000 to look for addends of 5,535 that are easy to divide by 45.

Since the greatest place value in 5,535 is thousands, first look for a 4-digit number. Try 45 × 100, or 4,500. 5,535 − 4,500 = 1,035.

sum = addends
5,535 = 4,500 + 1,035

Next, look for addends of 1,035. Find a number that is easy to divide by 45. Try 900, or 45 × 20. 1,035 − 900 = 135.

5,535 = 4,500 + 900 + 135

Then look for addends of 135. Try 90, or 45 × 2. 135 − 90 = 45. So, you have exactly 45 × 1, or 45, as the last addend.

5,535 = 4,500 + 900 + 90 + 45

Now, use the Distributive Property to find the quotient.

$$
\begin{aligned}
5{,}535 \div 45 &= (4{,}500 + 900 + 90 + 45) \div 45 \\
&= 4{,}500 \div 45 + 900 \div 45 + 90 \div 45 + 45 \div 45 \\
&= 100 \qquad\quad + 20 \qquad\quad + 2 \qquad\quad + 1 \\
&= 123
\end{aligned}
$$

➡ There are 123 boxes in each of the 45 shipping containers.

✏ Explain how you can use multiplication to check your answer.

Guided Instruction

Understand: How to divide by using the relationship between multiplication and division

The school band has 1,386 concert tickets to sell. Band members are organized into 11 teams. To sell out the concert, how many tickets must each team sell?

Let t be the number of tickets each team must sell. To find the value of t, divide the number of tickets by the number of teams. Write this as a division equation:

$t = 1{,}386 \div 11$

Use the relationship between multiplication and division to write a related multiplication equation:

$11 \times t = 1{,}386$

To find the value of t, first choose a number for t that you think may be reasonable.

Because $11 \times 100 = 1{,}100$ and $11 \times 200 = 2{,}200$ you know that t must be between 100 and 200, and it is closer to 100. Looking at $11 \times t = 1{,}386$ you know that the ones digit of t must be 6.

Try $t = 136$.

$11 \times 136 = 1{,}496$

Notice that the product is greater than 1,386. So, try another factor less than 136.

Try $t = 126$.

$11 \times 126 = 1{,}386$

$t = 126$ is the solution to the multiplication equation.

➡ Each team must sell 126 tickets.

James says that the solution to $y = 322 \div 23$ is $y = 15$. Without doing any calculations, how can you tell that James is incorrect?

Guided Instruction

Connect: What you know about the properties of operations to check a division answer

Lee needs 3,156 yards of red ribbon for her craft store. She buys the ribbon in rolls of 24 yards each. How many rolls does she need to buy?

Step 1

Write an expression.

To find the number of rolls she needs to buy, divide the total amount of yards Lee needs by the number of yards in each roll.

$3{,}156 \div 24$

Step 2

Use an area model to divide.

	100	30	1
24	3,156 −2,400	756 −720	36 −24
	756	36	12

$3{,}156 \div 24 = (100 + 30 + 1)\text{ R}12 = 131\text{ R}12$

Step 3

Use the Distributive Property to check.

When you multiply 131 by 24 and then add 12, the result should be the 3,156. You can use the Distributive Property to make the multiplication easier.

$$\begin{aligned} 24 \times 131 + 12 &= 24 \times (100 + 30 + 1) + 12 \\ &= 2{,}400 + 720 + 24 \quad + 12 \\ &= 3{,}156 \end{aligned}$$

Step 4

Interpret the answer.

If Lee buys 131 rolls, she will still need 12 more yards. So, she must buy 132 rolls to have enough.

➡ Lee needs to buy 132 rolls of red ribbon.

Guided Practice

1. Complete the steps to calculate $6{,}816 \div 32$.

   Write 6,816 as a sum of numbers that are easy to divide by 32:

   $6{,}816 = 6{,}400 + 320 +$ _____

   Use the Distributive Property.

   $6{,}816 \div 32 = (6{,}400 + 320 +$ _____ $) \div 32$

   $= 6{,}400 \div 32 + 320 \div$ _____ $+$ _____ $\div$ _____

   $= 200 +$ _____ $+$ _____

   $=$ _____

2. Complete the steps to solve $n = 3{,}094 \div 17$.

   Write an equivalent multiplication equation: $n \times$ _____ $=$ _____

   Because $17 \times 100 = 1{,}700$ and $17 \times 200 = 3{,}400$, the quotient must be between 100 and 200, and it must be closer to _____ since 3,400 is closer to 3,094 than 1,700 is.

   Looking at $n = 3{,}094 \div 17$ the ones digit of n must be _____.

   Try 172.

   $17 \times 172 = 2{,}924$. Since the product 2,924 is less than 3,094, try another number greater than 172.

   Try 182.

   $17 \times 182 =$ _____

   The solution is $n =$ _____.

Think • Pair • Share

Explain your reasoning.

MP7 3. Explain how knowing that $80 \times 24 = 1{,}920$ can help you find the quotient of $1{,}920 \div 40$.

Independent Practice

1. Complete the steps to calculate 6,594 ÷ 21.

   Write 6,594 as a sum of numbers that are easy to divide by 21:

   6,594 = 6,300 + 210 + ______

   Use the Distributive Property.

   6,594 ÷ 21 = (6,300 + 210 + ______) ÷ 21

   = 6,300 ÷ ______ + 210 ÷ ______ + ______ ÷ ______

   = ______ + ______ + ______

   = ______

Complete the area model to find the quotient of 2,510 ÷ 18.

2.

18	2,510 −	 −	 −
	710	170	8

   2,510 ÷ 18 = ____ with a remainder of ____

3. Show how you can check your answer to example 2 using the Distributive Property.

Independent Practice

Complete each division.

4.

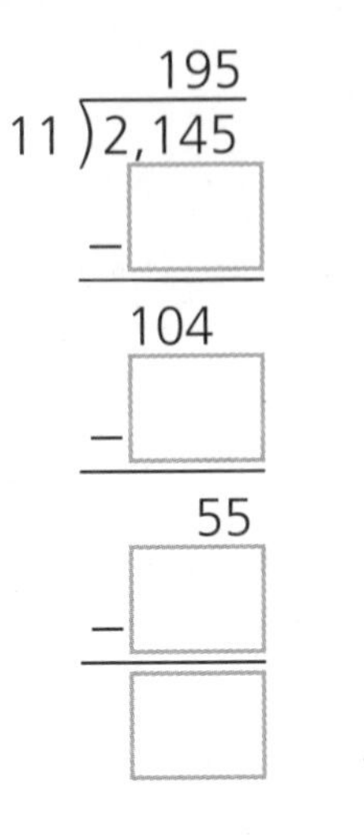

$2,145 \div 11 =$ ________

5.

19)1,056
− 95
− 95

$1,056 \div 19 =$ ________

For exercises 6–7, find each quotient. Show your work.

6. $3,310 \div 13$

Answer ________

7. $4,125 \div 20$

Answer ________

For exercises 8–9, choose the correct answer.

8. The area of a rectangular cornfield is 7,140 square feet. The width of the field is 68 feet. What is the length of the field?

a. 150 feet
b. 115 feet
c. 105 feet
d. 15 feet

9. Carla spent 2,430 hours doing homework last year. About how many hours did she spend doing homework each month?

a. 2,000 hours
b. 200 hours
c. 20 hours
d. 2 hours

Independent Practice

MP3 **10.** Justin's family is going on vacation. They will drive 3,290 miles in 11 days. Justin and his sister, Jackie, use two different ways to estimate how many miles they will drive each day. Whose approach is correct? Explain.

Justin: 3,290 rounds to 3,000 and 11 rounds to 10. Then, I can divide.
Jackie: 3,290 rounds to 3,300. I know that $11 \times 3 = 33$, $11 \times 30 = 330$, and $11 \times 300 = 3{,}300$.

MP3 **11.** Yani divides 1,542 by 19. She writes a multiplication equation for the problem and says the dividend becomes the product. Is Yani correct? Explain.

Solve the problems.

MP1 **12.** A pet store has 1,289 fish. A maximum of 12 fish can fit in a tank. What is the least number of tanks the pet store will need to contain all the fish?

Show your work.

Answer ____________________

MP2 **13.** A caterer is making 1,350 sandwiches for a party. If the catering staff can make 60 sandwiches in an hour, how many hours will it take to make all the sandwiches?

Show your work.

Answer ____________________

Independent Practice

MP6 **14.** Volunteers working in 16 teams are filling sandbags to prevent flooding in a beach town. Each sandbag weighs about 35 pounds. If there are 2,900 pounds of sand, how many sandbags can be filled?

Answer ____

Justify your answer using words, drawings, or numbers.

MP6 **15.** Serena has 1,532 photographs. She has 40 photo albums. Each album holds 36 photographs. Does Serena have enough albums to hold all the photographs?

Answer ____

Justify your answer using words, drawings, or numbers.

MP6 **16.** A group of 1,058 people are called in for jury duty. A jury is made up of 12 jurors and 2 alternates. How many complete juries can be formed from the jury pool?

Answer ____

Justify your answer using words, drawings, or numbers.

Lesson

12 Add and Subtract Decimals to Hundredths

Essential Question:
How do you add and subtract decimal numbers?

5.NBT.7

Guided Instruction

In this lesson you will learn how to add and subtract decimal numbers.

Understand: How to add decimals using a number line

Dan rode his bike 1.75 miles from school to the library. Later, he rode 0.75 miles home from the library. How many miles did Dan ride?

To find the total number of miles, add 1.75 + 0.75 using a number line.

- Move along the number line from 0 to 1.75. This represents the 1.75 miles Dan rode from school to the library.
- Add 0.75 to 1.75 by moving along the number line another 0.75. This shows the 0.75 miles Dan rode home.
- The sum is 2.5. This is the total number of miles Dan rode.

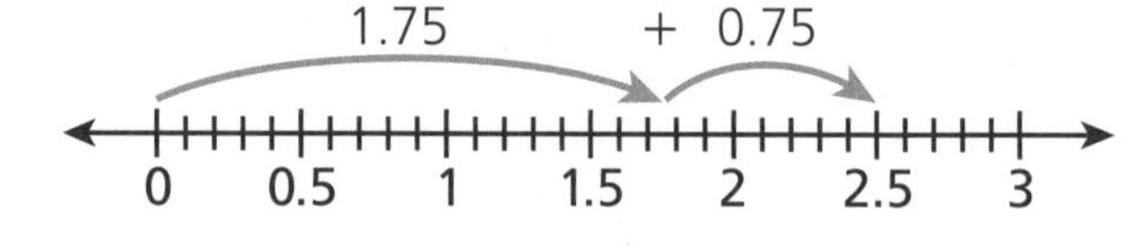

1.75 miles + 0.75 miles = 2.5 miles

➡ Dan rode 2.5 miles.

Understand: How to estimate the value of an expression

What is the approximate value of the expression 4.85 + 6 − 3.61?

To find the approximate value of the expression, estimate by rounding each term to the nearest whole number. Then evaluate.

➡ The approximate value of the expression is 7.

Guided Instruction

Understand: How to subtract decimals using hundreds grids

Lana had $1.30 to buy a snack. She spent $0.68 on a banana.
How much money does Lana have left?

Write a subtraction equation and use hundreds grids.

Subtraction equation: $1.30 − $0.68 = ■

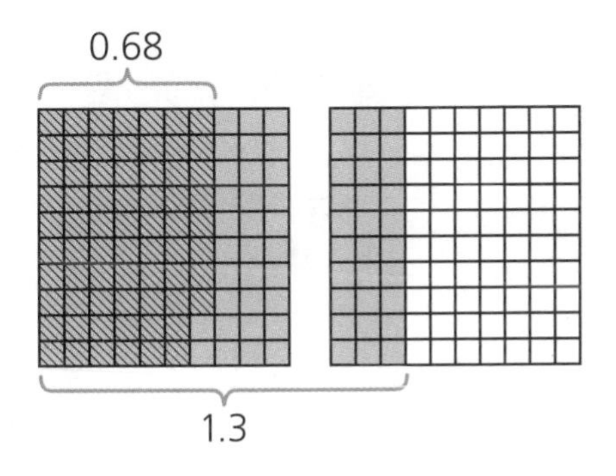

Remember!
- 1.30 or 1.3 is represented with 1 whole grid and 3 tenths of a grid.
- 0.68 is represented with 6 tenths of a grid and 8 hundredths of a grid.

Shade 1.30. Cross out 0.68 of the shaded part.
The shaded part that is *not crossed out* is the difference.
$1.30 - 0.68 = 0.62$

➡ Lana has $0.62 left.

Understand: How to add or subtract decimals using place value

Evaluate: 3.5 + 1.86

Line up like place values. Write 3.5 as 3.50 to help you align the digits correctly.

Add the columns from right to left, as if you were adding whole numbers. Regroup 13 tenths as 1 one and 3 tenths.

Write the decimal point in the answer.

	ones	.	tenths	hundredths
	1			
	3	.	5	0
+	1	.	8	6
	5		3	6

➡ The expression 3.5 + 1.86 has a value of 5.36.

✎ Evaluate: 3.5 − 1.86 using place value.

Guided Instruction

Connect: What you know about adding and subtracting decimal numbers

May and Will ran a relay race. May ran the first 100 yards in 18.49 seconds (s). Will ran the next 100 yards in 22.55 seconds (s). He lost 4.5 seconds because he tripped on a rock and fell. What would their total running time have been if Will had not fallen?

Step 1

Add the actual running times.

	tens	ones	.	tenths	hundredths
	1	1		1	
	1	8	.	4	9
+	2	2	.	5	5
	4	1	.	0	4

Remember!
Line up the numbers by place value, and then add the digits from right to left, regrouping when needed.

Step 2

Subtract the time Will lost from the actual combined running time.

	tens	ones	.	tenths	hundredths
	3	10		10	
	~~4~~	~~1~~	.	~~0~~	4
−		4	.	5	0
	3	6	.	5	4

Remember!
Write 4.5 as 4.50 to help you line up the digits correctly.

Step 3

Check the reasonableness of your answer.

Round each running time to the nearest second. ⟶ 18.49 rounds down to 18; 22.55 rounds up to 23

Round the time Will fell. ⟶ 4.5 rounds up to 5

Add and subtract the rounded times. ⟶ $18 + 23 - 5 = 36$

The running time of 36.54 s is close to the estimated time of 36 s.

➡ The total time would have been 36.54 s had Will not fallen.

Guided Practice

Estimate the value of each expression to the nearest whole number.

1. 6.87 + 3.1

   6.87 rounds up to 7

   3.1 rounds down to ____

   Estimate: ____

2. 5.84 – (1.23 + 2.09)

   5.84 rounds up to ____

   1.23 rounds down to ____

   2.09 rounds down to ____

   Estimate: ____

Use the hundreds grids to solve each equation.

3. 1.3 + 0.45 = ______

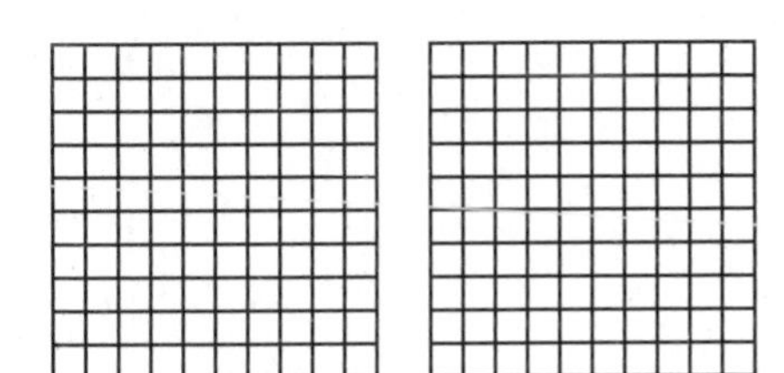

4. 1.85 – 1.22 = ______

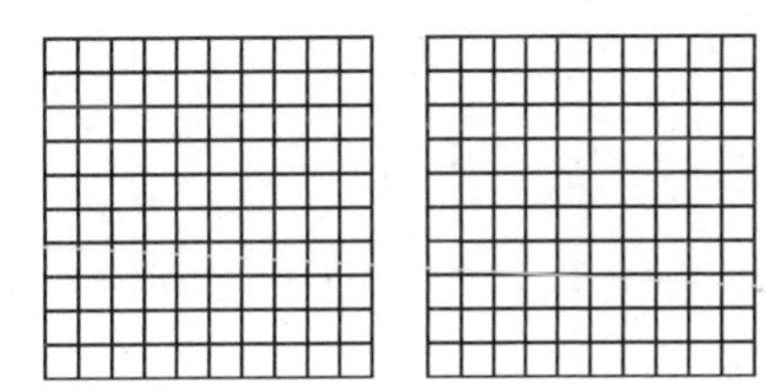

Use the place-value chart to solve each equation.

5. 7.81 + 1.75 = ______

	ones	.	tenths	hundredths
	7	.	8	1
+	1	.	7	5

6. 4.7 – 1.25 = ______

	ones	.	tenths	hundredths
–				

Think • Pair • Share

MP1 7. Chris is going shopping for school supplies. He wants to buy a binder for $3.15 and a pack of folders for $1.95. Tax is already included.

a. Estimate how much Chris will spend on the supplies. ____________

b. If Chris has $5, does he have enough to buy the supplies? Explain your reasoning.

Independent Practice

Complete the steps to estimate each answer to the nearest whole number.

1. 2.09 + 1.84

   ____ + 2

   ____

2. 48.85 − 3.22

   ____ − ____

   ____

3. 5.7 + 8.15 + 3.72

   ____ + ____ + ____

   ____ + ____

   ____

4. 32.2 + (12.91 − 4.75)

   ____ + (____ − ____)

   ____ + ____

   ____

Use the model to find the value of the expression.

5. 1.4 − 0.55

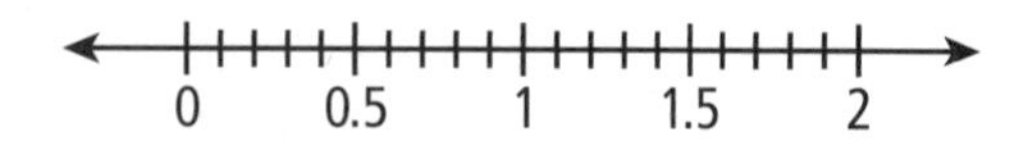

1.4 − 0.55 = ____________

6. 1.3 + 1.5 − 1.14

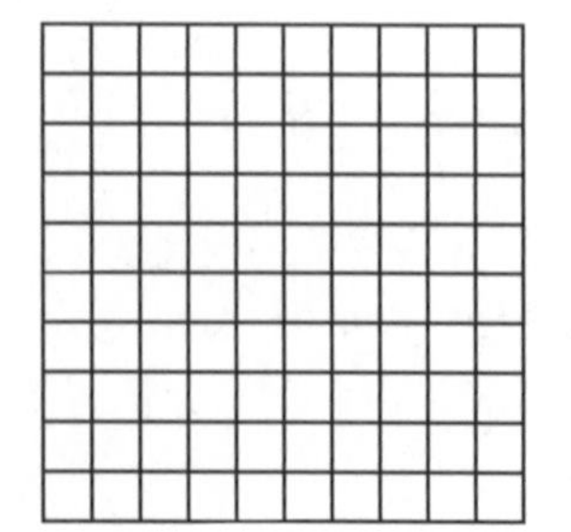
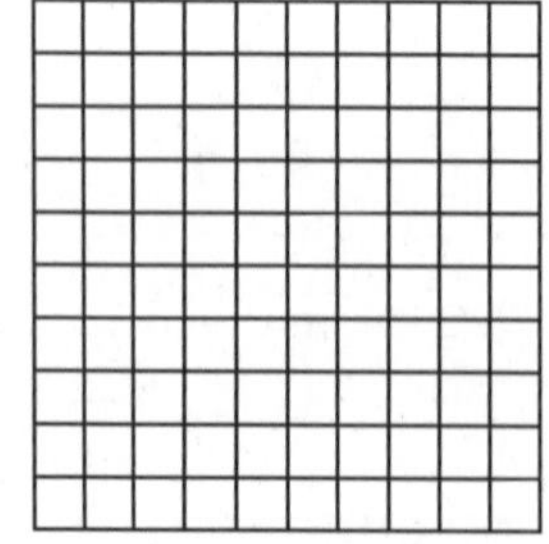
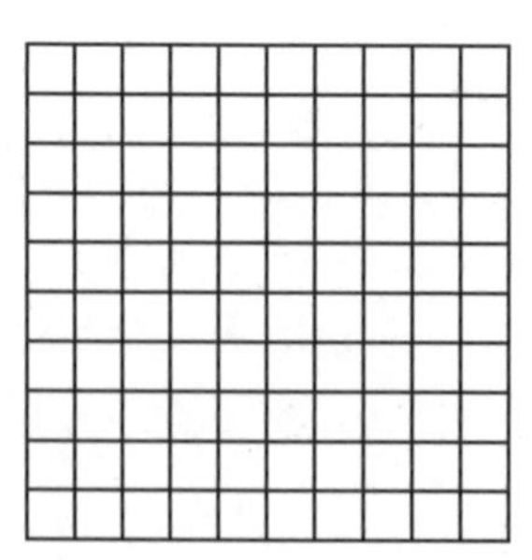

1.3 + 1.5 − 1.14 = ____________

Independent Practice

Use the place-value chart to solve each equation.

7. 3.89 − 2.43 = ______

	ones	.	tenths	hundredths
−				

8. 5.12 + 2.7 + 0.23 = ______

	ones	.	tenths	hundredths
+				

9. 200.9 + 37.48 + 89 = ____________

	hundreds	tens	ones	.	tenths	hundredths
+						

Evaluate. Show your work.

10. 11.5 + 7.78

____

11. 130.84 − 13.9

____

12. 42.2 + 20.85

____

13. 3.17 + 109 − 12.95

____

14. What is the value of 27.09 + 13.5 − 8.85?

a. 19.59

b. 21.74

c. 31.74

d. 32.55

Independent Practice

MP3 **15.** Renee says that the value of 21.9 − 1.16 is 1.03. Her work is shown below. What error did Renee make? What is the correct answer?

$$\begin{array}{r} 21.9 \\ -1.16 \\ \hline 1.03 \end{array}$$

Solve the problems.

MP1 **16.** Gary's backpack weighs 1.2 pounds. His math textbook weighs 3.75 pounds, and his science textbook weighs 2.85 pounds. How much will his backpack weigh with the math and science textbooks in it? Check the reasonableness of your answer.

Show your work.

Answer ______________________________

MP2 **17.** Steven made punch by mixing 2.8 liters of orange juice, 0.75 liters of pineapple juice, and 1.2 liters of sparkling water. How many liters of punch did Steven make? Check the reasonableness of your answer.

Show your work.

Answer ______________________________

Independent Practice

MP1 **18.** The table below shows the cost of fruits at a produce stand. Alberto bought two bananas, a kiwi, and a pound of apples. How much did he spend?

Fruit	Cost
Apples	$2.05 per pound
Bananas	$0.39 each
Kiwis	$0.50 each

Show your work.

Answer ____

MP2 **19.** Radha now pays $45.50 per month for unlimited calls and texts. She can switch to a new wireless company and pay $42.49 per month for unlimited calls plus $3.99 for unlimited texts. Should Radha switch? Explain.

Show your work.

Answer ____

MP3 **20.** Tammy's kitten weighed 1.87 pounds when he was a month old. Now he weighs 3.9 pounds. Tammy says her cat gained more than 2 pounds. Is she correct? Explain.

Show your work.

Answer ____

Lesson 13

Multiply Decimals to Hundredths

Essential Question:
How do you multiply decimal numbers?
5.NBT.7

Guided Instruction

In this lesson you will learn how to multiply decimal numbers.

Understand: How to use a model to multiply a decimal by a whole number

Sara has 2 bags of dried fruit. Each bag weighs 0.83 ounce. How many ounces of dried fruit does Sara have in all?

To find the total ounces Sarah has in 2 bags of dried fruit, multiply 0.83 ounce by 2. Use a model.

1. Model the problem.

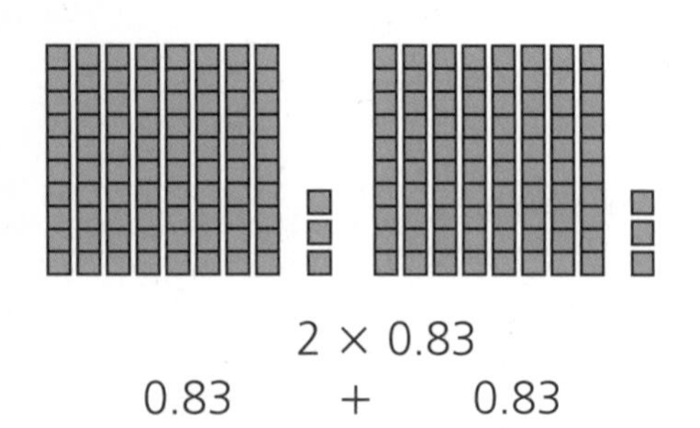

2 × 0.83
0.83 + 0.83

2. Add the tenths.

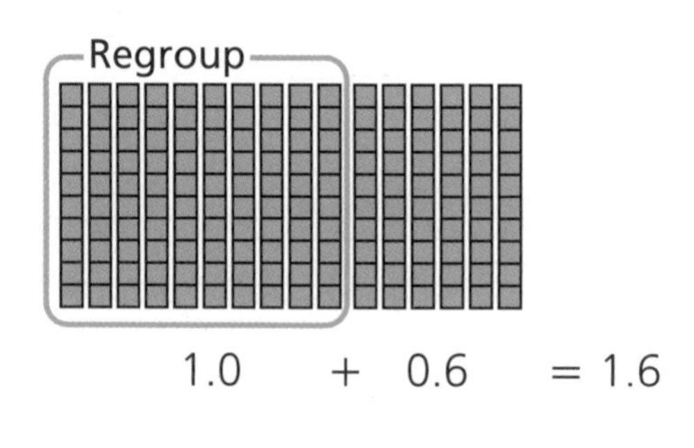

1.0 + 0.6 = 1.6

3. Add the hundredths.

0.03 + 0.03 = 0.06

4. Add the two sums.

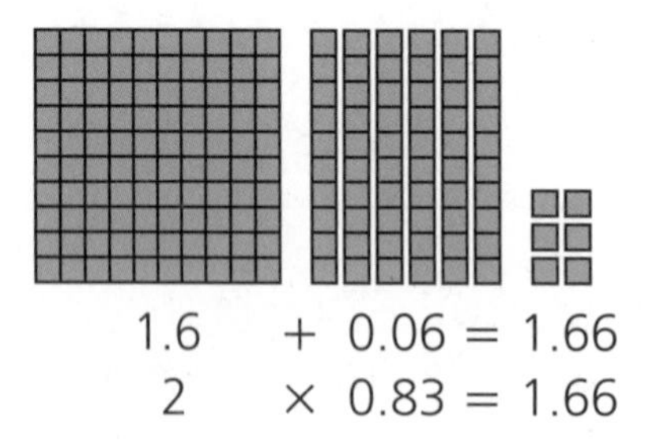

1.6 + 0.06 = 1.66
2 × 0.83 = 1.66

Sara has 1.66 ounces of dried fruit.

A grocery store sells mushrooms for $1.75 per pound. If Cecilia buys 4.2 pounds of mushrooms, about how much will she spend? Use estimation to find the answer. *Hint:* Round each factor to the nearest whole number.

Understand: Methods for Multiplying Two Decimals

Peaches cost $1.30 per pound. How much do 2.8 pounds of peaches cost?

To find the cost, multiply the cost per pound by the number of pounds: 2.8×1.3.

Remember!
$1.30 = 1.3$

Here are two possible methods for finding the product.

Method 1

To find 2.8×1.3, first calculate 28×13.

$$\begin{array}{r} \scriptstyle 2 \\ 13 \\ \times\ 28 \\ \hline 104 \\ +260 \\ \hline 364 \end{array}$$

28 is 10 times as much as 2.8. So, $28 = 10 \times 2.8$.
13 is 10 times as much as 1.3. So, $13 = 10 \times 1.3$.
28×13 is 10×10, or 100 times, as much as 2.8×1.3.
So, $28 \times 13 = 100 \times 2.8 \times 1.3$.

To find 2.8×1.3, divide 364 by 100:
$2.8 \times 1.3 = 364 \div 100 = 364 \times \frac{1}{100} = \frac{364}{100} = 3.64$.

Method 2

Ignore the decimal points and multiply as you would with whole numbers.

$$\begin{array}{r} \scriptstyle 2 \\ 1.3 \\ \times\ 2.8 \\ \hline 104 \\ +260 \\ \hline 364 \end{array}$$

Use estimation to place the decimal point: 2.8×1.3 is about 3×1, or 3. The decimal point should be between the 3 and the 6.

$$\begin{array}{r} \scriptstyle 2 \\ 1.3 \\ \times\ 2.8 \\ \hline 104 \\ +260 \\ \hline 3.64 \end{array}$$

➡ 2.8 pounds of peaches cost $3.64.

Guided Instruction

Connect: What you know about multiplying decimals

Nectarines cost $0.89 per pound. How much do 4.2 pounds of nectarines cost?

To find the cost, multiply the cost per pound by the number of pounds: 4.2×0.89.

You can use the standard multiplication algorithm.

Step 1

Ignore the decimal points and multiply as you would with whole numbers.

$$\begin{array}{r} {}^{3\,3} \\ {}^{1\,1} \\ 0.89 \\ \times \quad 4.2 \\ \hline 178 \\ +3560 \\ \hline 3738 \end{array}$$

Step 2

Find the total number of decimal places in the two factors.

0.89 has 2 decimal places.
4.2 has 1 decimal place.

There is a total of 3 decimal places.

Step 3

Place the decimal point in the product so the number of decimal places equals the total you found in Step 2.

$$\begin{array}{r} {}^{3\,3} \\ {}^{1\,1} \\ 0.89 \\ \times \quad 4.2 \\ \hline 178 \\ +3560 \\ \hline 3.738 \end{array}$$

The product has 3 decimal places.

Because the answer is a price, round to the nearest cent to get $3.74.

➡ 4.2 pounds of nectarines cost $3.74.

 Find 4.2×0.89 by first multiplying 42×89 and then adjusting the product as you did in Method 1 on page 113.

Guided Practice

1. Use the model to find 3×1.4.

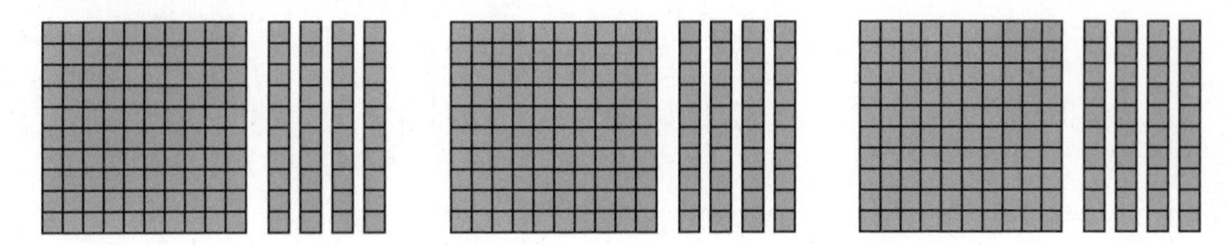

$3 \times 1.4 =$ ____

For exercises 2–5, use the given whole number product to find the decimal product.

2. $73 \times 14 = 1{,}022$, so

   $7.3 \times 1.4 =$ ________

3. $7 \times 32 = 224$, so

   $0.7 \times 32 =$ ________

4. $25 \times 16 = 400$, so

   $0.25 \times 1.6 =$ ________

5. $62 \times 44 = 2{,}728$, so

   $62 \times 0.44 =$ ________

Complete to find each product.

6. $\begin{array}{r} 1.6 \\ \times\ 0.8 \\ \hline \end{array}$

   ____ decimal place

   ____ decimal place

   ____ decimal places

7. $\begin{array}{r} 21.05 \\ \times\ \ \ 3.2 \\ \hline \\ + \qquad \\ \hline \end{array}$

   ____ decimal places

   ____ decimal place

   ____ decimal places

MP6 8. Explain how the model below shows that $0.4 \times 0.2 = 0.08$.

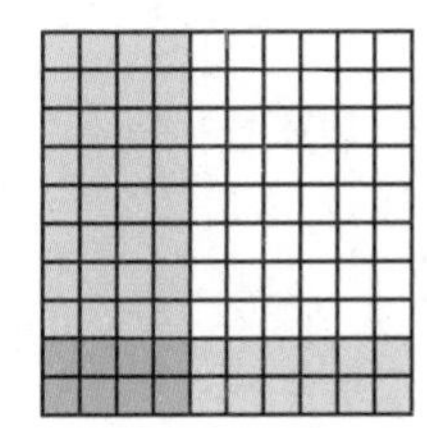

Independent Practice

1. Which expression does the model represent?

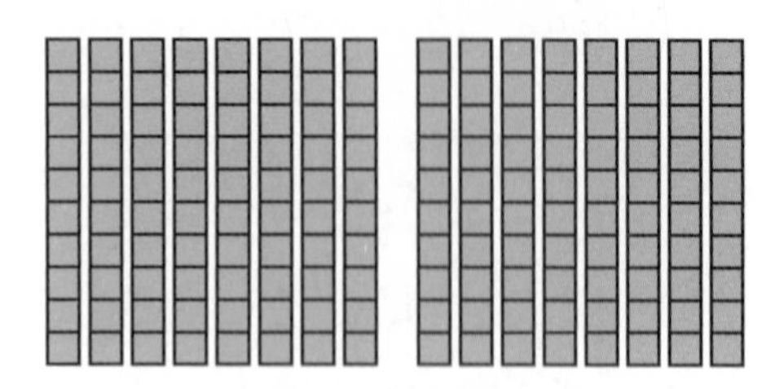

a. 2×8 b. 0.2×8

c. 2×0.8 d. 0.2×0.8

Make a model to find each answer.

2. $3 \times 0.75 =$ ____

3. $0.7 \times 2 =$ ____

For exercises 4–7, put the decimal point in the correct place in the product.

4.
```
     9.2
×    3.1
      92
+ 2760
  2852
```

5.
```
       2
       2
    0.55
×    5.5
     275
+   2750
    3025
```

6.
```
    4
   46
×  0.8
  368
```

7.
```
   25.8
×  0.11
    258
+  2580
   2838
```

MP2 8. Use estimation to determine which of the following expressions is greater. Explain how you got your answer.
$5 \times (1.9 + 3.15)$ and $6.9 \times (0.2 + 3.2)$

Independent Practice

Evaluate each expression. Show your work.

9. 0.8×0.9

10. 0.2×0.5

11. 6.7×2.2

12. 2.15×0.9

13. 15.8×10.25

14. $(9.5 + 12) \times 3.05$

15. $7 \times [(8 + 2.8) \times 1.5]$

16. $(3.5 + 17.92) \times (21 - 4.5)$

Write an equation for each situation. Let *n* represent the unknown amount. Then solve.

MP4 **17.** Dana is skipping down the sidewalk. She jumps over 2.5 sections of sidewalk with each skip. How many sections will she cover after 12 skips?

Answer: Dana will cover ____________ sections in 12 skips.

MP4 **18.** Jodie makes $11.70 an hour working at a clothing store. How much will Jodie earn for working a six and a half hour shift?

Answer: Jodie will earn ____________.

Independent Practice

19. Look back at question 18. Jodie estimated her pay by multiplying 12 by 6.5. Is her estimate more than or less than her actual pay?

MP3 20. Laura says the product of 5.05 × 20 is 101. Jeremy says Laura's answer is incorrect, because the product must have 2 decimal places. How would you convince Jeremy that Laura's answer is correct?

For exercises 21–22, use the information from the table below to answer questions.

Cost of manufacturing tablet readers	
Number of tablet readers	Cost per tablet reader
1 – 25	$57.55
26 – 50	$52.30
51 – 100	$48.18

MP5 21. How much will it cost to manufacture 15 tablet readers?

Show your work.

Answer ______________________________

MP5 22. Is it cheaper to manufacture 48 tablet readers or 52 tablet readers? Explain.

Independent Practice

MP6 **23.** Explain why estimating 17.09×4.1 and 17.1×4.09 by rounding the factors to the nearest whole number will not help you determine which product is greater. Then, find the actual products and compare.

Answer ______________________________

MP7 **24.** Explain how you can use the equation given below to find the product of 89.7×15.38.

$897 \times 1{,}538 = 1{,}379{,}586$

Answer ______________________________

MP3 **25.** Ian made the model shown below to represent 0.5×0.14 and found that $0.5 \times 0.14 = 0.07$. Do you agree with Ian's use of the model and his answer? Explain why or why not.

× 0.5 or one half → = 0.07

Answer ______________________________

Lesson 14

Divide Decimals to Hundredths

Essential Question:
How do you divide decimal numbers?
5.NBT.7

Guided Instruction

In this lesson you will learn methods for dividing with decimals.

Understand: How to divide a decimal by a whole number.

Evaluate 5.32 ÷ 4.

Use a model to help you visualize the division.

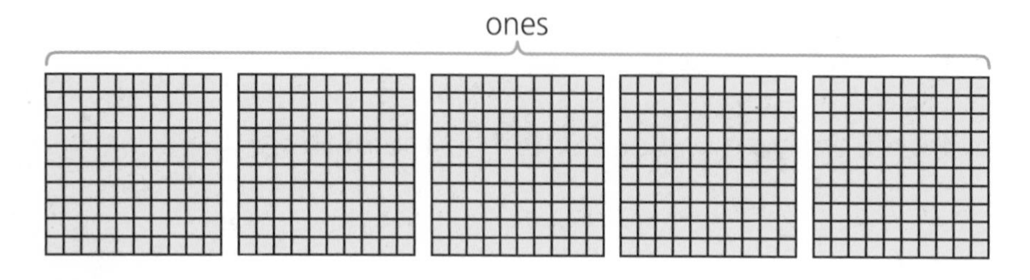

Step 1

Divide the 5 ones into 4 equal groups. There will be 1 one in each group with 1 one left over.

$$\begin{array}{r} 1 \\ 4\overline{)5.32} \\ -4 \\ \hline 1 \end{array}$$

Step 2

Ungroup the leftover one as 10 tenths, and combine them with the original 3 tenths making 13 tenths.

Divide the 13 tenths among the 4 groups. There will be 3 tenths in each group with 1 tenth left over.

$$\begin{array}{r} 1 \\ 4\overline{)5.32} \\ -4 \\ \hline 13 \end{array} \longrightarrow \begin{array}{r} 1.3 \\ 4\overline{)5.32} \\ -4 \\ \hline 13 \\ -12 \\ \hline 1 \end{array}$$

Step 3

Ungroup the leftover tenth as 10 hundredths and combine them with the original 2 hundredths making 12 hundredths.

Divide the 12 hundredths among the 4 groups. There will be 3 hundredths in each group.

When you divide 5.32 by 4 each group will have 1 ones, 3 tenths, and 3 hundredths.

$$\begin{array}{r} 1.3 \\ 4\overline{)5.32} \\ -4 \\ \hline 13 \\ -12 \\ \hline 12 \end{array} \longrightarrow \begin{array}{r} 1.33 \\ 4\overline{)5.32} \\ -4 \\ \hline 13 \\ -12 \\ \hline 12 \\ -\ 12 \\ \hline 0 \end{array}$$

➡ 5.32 ÷ 4 = 1.33.

Understand: How to divide by 0.1 and 0.01

Evaluate 4.8 ÷ 0.1 and 4.8 ÷ 0.01.

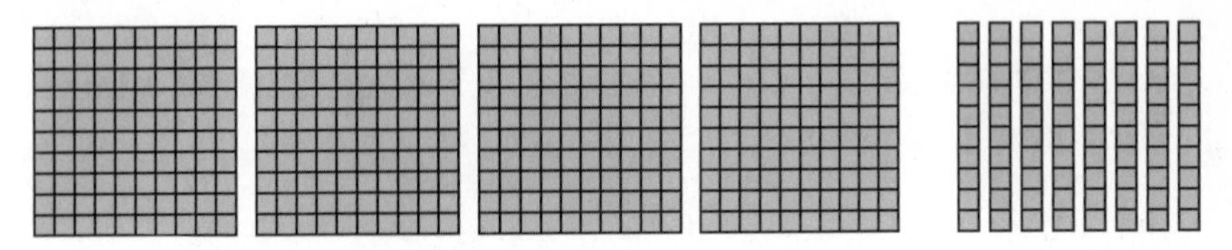

- To evaluate 4.8 ÷ 0.1, find the number of tenths in 4.8.
  There are 10 tenths in each of the ones, so there are 40 tenths in 4.
  There are 8 tenths in 0.8.
  Altogether, there are 48 tenths in 4.8. So, 4.8 ÷ 0.1 = 48.

- To evaluate 4.8 ÷ 0.01, find the number of hundredths in 4.8.
  There are 100 hundredths in each of the ones, so there are 400 hundredths in 4.
  Because 0.8 = 0.80, there are 80 hundredths in 0.8.
  Altogether, there are 480 hundredths in 4.8. So, 4.8 ÷ 0.01 = 480.

Notice that 4.8 ÷ 0.1 = 4.8 × 10 and 4.8 ÷ 0.01 = 4.8 × 100.

➡ 4.8 ÷ 0.1 = 48 and 4.8 ÷ 0.01 = 480.

Understand: How to relate dividing by a decimal to dividing by a whole number

Explain why 4.8 ÷ 0.6 is equivalent to 48 ÷ 6.
Explain why 4.8 ÷ 0.06 is equivalent to 480 ÷ 6.

➡ 4.8 = 48 tenths and 0.6 = 6 tenths. So, to evaluate 4.8 ÷ 0.6, find the number of groups of 6 tenths in 48 tenths. This is the same as calculating 48 ÷ 6. So, 4.8 ÷ 0.6 = 48 ÷ 6 = 8.

Notice that to get from 4.8 ÷ 0.6 to 48 ÷ 6, you multiply both numbers by 10. The quotient stays the same.

4.8 = 480 hundredths and 0.06 = 6 hundredths. So, to evaluate 4.8 ÷ 0.06, find the number of groups of 6 hundredths in 480 hundredths. This is the same as calculating 480 ÷ 6. So, 4.8 ÷ 0.06 = 480 ÷ 6 = 80.

Notice to get from 4.8 ÷ 0.06 to 480 ÷ 6, you multiply both numbers by 100. The quotient stays the same.

✏ Explain why 0.5 ÷ 0.25 is the same as 50 ÷ 25.

Guided Instruction

Connect: What you know about place value and dividing decimals

Kim earned $43.75 for working a 3.5-hour shift at a bakery. How much did she earn per hour?

Step 1

Write an expression for the situation.

Divide the amount Kim earned by the number of hours she worked: $43.75 \div 3.5$.

Step 2

Change the problem to an equivalent problem with a whole number divisor.

Multiply both 43.75 and 3.5 by 10 to get $437.5 \div 35$. This does not change the quotient.

In long division format, move the decimal points in the divisor and dividend the same number of places to get a whole-number divisor.

$3.5\overline{)43.75}$

Step 3

Evaluate $437.5 \div 35$.

a.) Divide 43 tens into 35 groups. There is 1 ten in each group, and there are 8 tens left.

b.) Ungroup 8 tens as 80 ones. Bring down the 7 ones making 87 ones.

c.) Divide 87 ones into 35 groups. There are 2 ones in each group with 17 ones left.

d.) Ungroup the 17 ones as 170 tenths and bring down the 5 original tenths to get 175 tenths.

e.) Divide 175 tenths into 35 groups. There are 5 in each group with none left.

Because the answer is a money amount, show the decimal to the hundredths place: $12.5 = 12.50$.

a.)
```
      1
35)437.5
  -35
    8
```

b.)
```
      1
35)437.5
  -35
    87
```

c.)
```
      12
35)437.5
  -35
    87
   -70
    17
```

d.)
```
      12
35)437.5
  -35
    87
   -70
    175
```

e.)
```
      12.5
35)437.5
  -35
    87
   -70
    175
   -175
      0
```

When the divisor is a whole number, the decimal point in the quotient is placed directly above the decimal point in the dividend.

➡ Kim earned $12.50 per hour.

Guided Practice

1. Write the division equation that is modeled below.

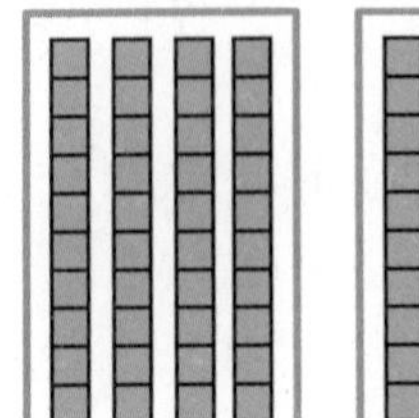
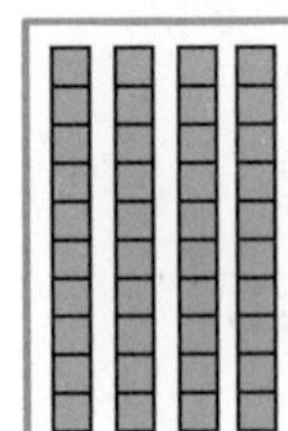
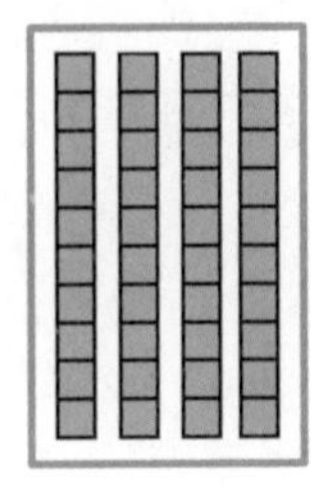
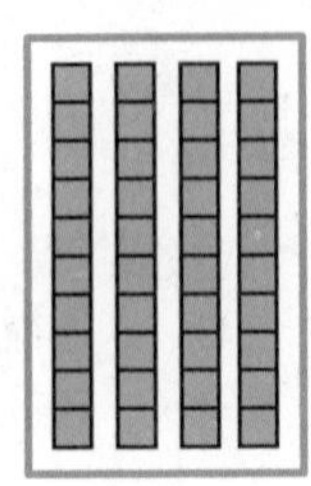
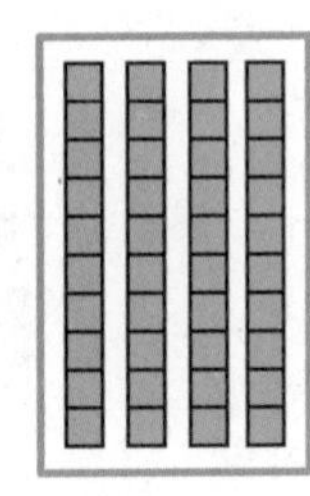

____

2. Complete the statements to find $8 \div 0.01$.

There are ____ hundredths in 1.

So, there are ____ hundredths in 8.

This means that $8 \div 0.01 =$ ____.

3. Complete the statements to find $2.9 \div 0.1$.

There are ____ tenths in 2.

There are ____ tenths in 0.9.

So, $2.9 \div 0.1 =$ ____.

Complete the statements.

4. $5.4 \div 0.6$ has the same quotient as $54 \div$ ____.

5. $36.5 \div 0.05$ has the same quotient as ________ $\div 5$.

Rewrite the expression as an equivalent expression with a whole-number divisor.

6. $9.48 \div 2.7$

____

7. $5.8 \div 0.65$

____

MP7 **8.** Find and compare the quotients of $0.4 \div 0.02$, $4 \div 0.2$, and $40 \div 2$. Explain the relationship among the three expressions.

Independent Practice

1. Use the model to complete the sentences below and answer the question.

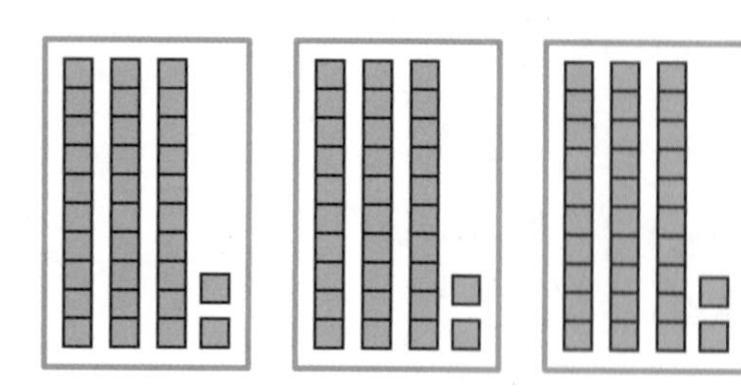

a. The model shows _____ ones, _____ tenths, and _____ hundredths in all.

b. There are _____ groups in all.

c. Each group has _____ tenths and _____ hundredths.

d. What division equation is modeled above? ____________________

2. Complete the statements to find $2.39 \div 0.01$.

There are _____ hundredths in 2.

There are _____ hundredths in 0.3.

There are _____ hundredths in 0.09.

So, $2.39 \div 0.01 =$ _____.

Complete the statements.

3. $30 \div 0.5$ has the same quotient as _____ $\div 5$.

4. $2.1 \div 0.42$ has the same quotient as $210 \div$ _____.

Rewrite the expression as an equivalent expression with a whole-number divisor.

5. $1.44 \div 1.2$

____

6. $0.49 \div 0.07$

____

Independent Practice

For exercises 7–12, find each quotient. Show your work.

7. $8\overline{)78.4}$

8. $5\overline{)50.5}$

9. $1.2\overline{)0.24}$

10. $0.9\overline{)7.47}$

11. $8.2\overline{)123}$

12. $0.03\overline{)0.75}$

MP1 **13.** Christopher needs to fill 45 cubic feet of his garden with soil. He already has 7.5 cubic feet of soil. If there are 2.5 cubic feet in each bag of soil, then how many bags should he purchase?

a. 2

b. 15

c. 18

d. 21

14. Insert one pair of parentheses in the expression below to make it true.

$2.5 \times 3 + 1.6 \div 1.25 - 0.85 - 2 = 9.5$

Independent Practice

MP2 **15.** Write and solve two division equations that include the numbers 2 and 0.8. Write one equation that has a quotient greater than the divisor and the dividend. Write another one that has a quotient less than the divisor and the dividend.

MP2 **16.** Explain why you can move the decimal point in the divisor to the right, as long as you move the decimal point in the dividend the same number of places to the right.

MP2 **17.** Explain how you can determine if $9 \div 0.36$ is greater than or less than $0.9 \div 0.36$ without finding each quotient.

18. Compare the values of each pair of expressions using >, <, or =.

$7 \div 3.5$ ◯ $7 \div 0.35$

$7 \div 0.35$ ◯ $7 \div 35$

$0.85 \div 0.5$ ◯ $8.5 \div 5$

$8.5 \div 5$ ◯ $85 \div 5$

MP4 **19.** Hal is installing a new floor in his office. He uses 352.5 square feet of tile to cover the rectangular floor. The room is 12.5 feet wide. How many feet long is the room?

a. 0.282 feet

b. 2.82 feet

c. 28.2 feet

d. 282 feet

Independent Practice

Solve each problem.

MP6 **20.** The gas tank in Don's car hold 12 gallons of gas. The car can drive for 415.2 miles on one full tank of gas. How many miles per gallon of gas does Don's car get?

Show your work. Check the reasonableness of your answer.

Answer ______________________

MP6 **21.** Casey gets paid \$2.55 per hour waiting tables. On Friday she earned \$72 in tips and made a total of \$82.20. How many hours did she work Friday?

Show your work.

Answer ______________________

MP3 **22.** Describe two different ways you could explain to a friend that $127.5 \div 1.7$ cannot have a quotient of 750.

Answer ______________________

Study the pattern. Complete the sentences to describe the pattern.

256,730   25,673   2,567.3   256.73

1. In each number, the value of 2 is ____________ the value of 2 in the number to its right.

2. In each number, the value of 7 is ____________ the value of 7 in the number to its left.

Write the expression in exponent form. Determine its value.

3. ten to the fourth power   exponent form: ____   value: ____________

For exercises 4–5, choose the correct answer.

4. $0.67 \times \blacksquare = 67$

   a. 10^1 b. 10^2

   c. 10^3 d. 10^4

5. $532.8 \div \blacksquare = 0.5328$

   a. 10^3 b. 10^4

   c. 10^5 d. 10^6

6. How many times as great is the value of the digit 8 in 18.43 than the value of the digit 8 in 14.83?

   a. 10 times   b. 100 times

   c. 1,000 times   d. 10,000 times

Write each word phrase as a decimal.

7. four hundred nine thousandths ____________

8. five hundred twenty-one and six hundred fourteen thousandths ____________

Write each decimal in words.

9. 0.751 ________________________________

10. 39.06 ________________________________

Compare. Use place value. Write <, >, or =.

11. 9.610 ◯ 9.609   12. 2.04 ◯ 2.040   13. 3.895 ◯ 3.985

Round each decimal to the ones, tenths, and hundredths places.

	ones	tenths	hundredths
14. 0.554	______	______	______
15. 8.497	______	______	______

Answer the questions.

16. What happens to the digits in 610.24 when you divide by 10^3? What is the quotient?

____

17. How do you write 23.504 in expanded form?

____

Find each product. Show your work.

18. $\begin{array}{r} 362 \\ \times\ 45 \\ \hline \end{array}$

19. $\begin{array}{r} 631 \\ \times\ 27 \\ \hline \end{array}$

20. $\begin{array}{r} 3.45 \\ \times\ 7.6 \\ \hline \end{array}$

Find each quotient. Show your work.

21. 3,647 ÷ 26

22. 6,095 ÷ 53

23. 17.28 ÷ 1.2

Evaluate each expression.

24. 67.4 + 25.82 ______

25. 260.31 − 43.6 ______

26. 6.15 + 128 + 34.59 ______

Solve the problems using any strategy.

MP3 **27.** Cole says there are 2,190 hours in a year. His work is below. What mistake did Cole make? How many hours are in a year?

$$\begin{array}{r} {\scriptstyle 1\,1} \\ {\scriptstyle 2\,2} \\ 365 \\ \times\ \ 24 \\ \hline 1{,}460 \\ 730 \\ \hline 2{,}190 \end{array}$$

MP4 **28.** The business manager for a swim club wants to order tote bags imprinted with the swim club's logo as end-of-the-season gifts for its 2,108 members. The tote bags are sold in bundles of 36. How many bundles must the business manager order?

Show your work.

Answer ______________________________

MP4 **29.** At the grocery store, Sunil buys 5 pounds of chicken breast for $1.59 per pound. He also buys a jar of tomato sauce that costs $3.98. Sunil has a coupon for half off the price of the sauce. He gives the cashier the coupon and a $20 bill. How much change should Sunil receive? Explain how to check the reasonableness of your answer.

Look at how the Common Core standards you have learned and will learn connect.

It is very important for you to understand the standards from the prior grade level so that you will be able to develop an understanding of fractions in this unit and be prepared for next year. To practice your skills, go to sadlierconnect.com.

GRADE 4 I Can...	Before Unit 3	GRADE 5 Can I ?	After Unit 3	GRADE 6 I Will...
4.NF.3 Add and subtract fractions with like denominators	☐	**5.NF.1** Add and subtract fractions with unlike denominators	☐	
4.NF.3 Add and subtract fractions with like denominators to solve word problems	☐	**5.NF.2** Add and subtract fractions to solve word problems	☐	
	☐	**5.NF.3** Interpret a fraction as division	☐	
	☐	Solve problems where fractions are answers to divisions	☐	
4.NF.4 Multiply a unit fraction and a fraction by a whole number	☐	**5.NF.4** Multiply a fraction or whole number by a fraction	☐	
4.OA.1 Interpret a multiplication equation as a comparison	☐	**5.NF.5** Interpret multiplication as scaling (resizing)	☐	
4.NF.4 Multiply fractions by whole numbers to solve problems	☐	**5.NF.6** Multiply fractions and mixed numbers to solve problems	☐	
4.NF.4 Multiply a unit fraction by a whole number	☐	**5.NF.7** Divide unit fractions by whole numbers and whole numbers by unit fractions	☐	**6.NS.1** Divide whole numbers by fractions Divide fractions by fractions
	☐	**5.NF.7** Solve problems involving division with unit fractions and whole numbers	☐	

HOME ✦ CONNECT...

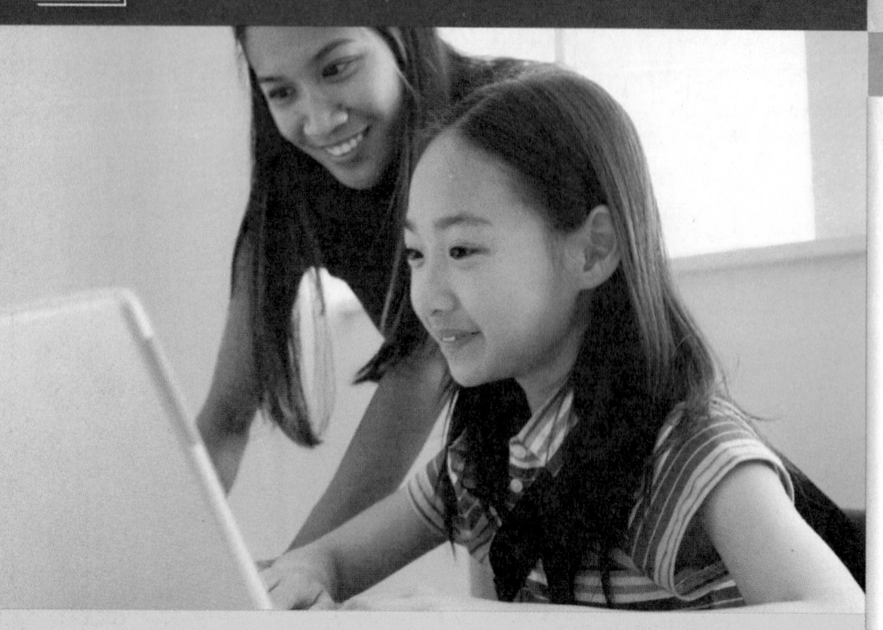

Your child will solve real-world problems using the addition, subtraction, multiplication and division of fractions with unlike denominators. Support your child by using the following problem-solving model.

- **Read** Read the problem. Focus on the facts and the questions. Ask: *What facts do you know? What do you need to find out?*
- **Plan** Outline a plan. Plan how to solve the problem. Ask: *What operation will you use? Do you need to use 1 step or 2 steps? Will you draw a picture? How have you solved similar problems?*
- **Solve** Follow your plan to solve the problem. Ask: *Did you answer the question? Did you label your answer?*
- **Check** Test that the solution is reasonable. Ask: *Does your answer make sense? If not, review and revise your plan? How can you solve the problem a different way? Is the answer the same? How can you estimate to check your answer?*

Conversation Starters: Using a model or drawing is a method your child will use. Talk about real-world problems that can be organized and solved by using visual supports. For example: determine the area or perimeter of a space in your home with mixed number measures. Ask questions such as: *How can a model of the space help in finding the area or perimeter? What model(s) can we draw?*

In this unit your child will:

- Add and subtract fractions with unlike denominators.
- Interpret fractions as division.
- Interpret products of fractions.
- Find areas of rectangles.
- Interpret multiplication of fractions as scaling.
- Multiply fractions and mixed numbers.
- Divide unit fractions by whole numbers and whole numbers by unit fractions.

NOTE: All of these learning goals for your child are based on the Grade 5 Common Core State Standards for Mathematics.

Ways to Help Your Child

As your child solves more and more complex real-world problems in math, continue to make everyday math part of your daily conversations at home. Talk about the ways you use math for your own work, or in making a recipe or keeping a budget. Involve your child in tasks that require math.

ONLINE

For more Home Connect activities, continue online at sadlierconnect.com

Focus on Number and Operations—Fractions

UNIT 3

Essential Question:
How can you use models and equivalent fractions to perform all operations with fractions or mixed numbers?

Lesson

15 Add and Subtract Fractions with Unlike Denominators

Essential Question:
How can you add and subtract fractions with unlike denominators?

5.NF.1

Words to Know:
unlike denominators
common denominator

Guided Instruction

In this lesson you will learn how to add and subtract fractions and mixed numbers with unlike denominators.

Understand: How to use a model to subtract fractions with unlike denominators

A one-gallon pitcher was $\frac{3}{4}$ full of juice. Then, Ada drank $\frac{1}{8}$ gallon of the juice in the pitcher. How full was the pitcher after that?

To find the amount of juice left in the pitcher, subtract $\frac{3}{4} - \frac{1}{8}$. You can use fraction strips.

Use three $\frac{1}{4}$ pieces to model $\frac{3}{4}$.

To see how you can take away $\frac{1}{8}$ from $\frac{3}{4}$, use $\frac{1}{8}$ pieces to build a fraction equivalent to $\frac{3}{4}$. Notice that $\frac{3}{4} = \frac{6}{8}$.

Now take away one $\frac{1}{8}$. There are five $\frac{1}{8}$ pieces left. So, $\frac{3}{4} - \frac{1}{8} = \frac{6}{8} - \frac{1}{8} = \frac{5}{8}$.

➡ After Ada drank, the pitcher was $\frac{5}{8}$ full.

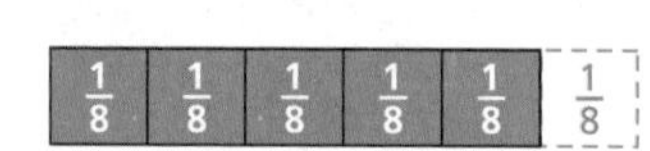

Understand: How to use a model to add fractions with unlike denominators

Use fraction strips to find $\frac{1}{2} + \frac{1}{3}$.

Combine fraction strips for $\frac{1}{2}$ and $\frac{1}{3}$.
You can see the sum, but you need to find a way to name it.

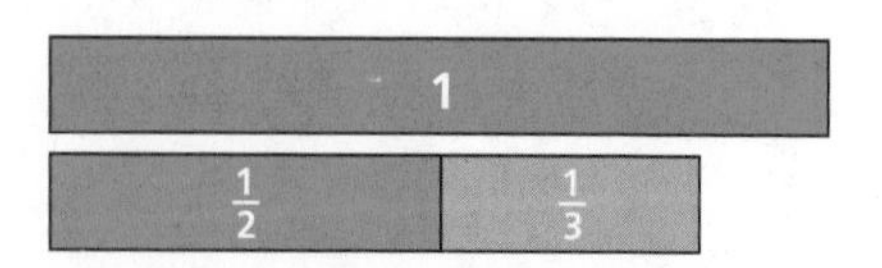

To name the sum, use same-size pieces to build a strip the same length as the sum. By using $\frac{1}{6}$ pieces, you can build $\frac{1}{2}$ and you can build $\frac{1}{3}$. Notice that $\frac{1}{2} = \frac{3}{6}$ and $\frac{1}{3} = \frac{2}{6}$.

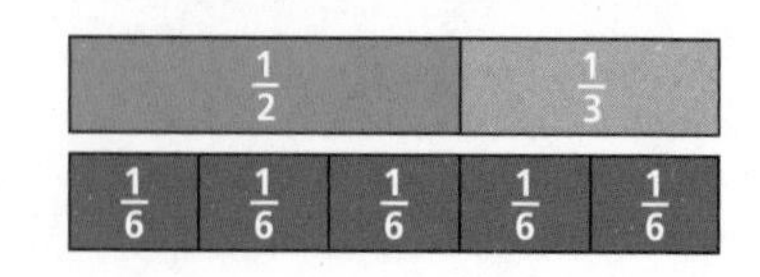

➡ $\frac{1}{2} + \frac{1}{3} = \frac{3}{6} + \frac{2}{6} = \frac{5}{6}$.

Guided Instruction

Understand: How to add fractions with unlike denominators by using equivalent fractions

Henry is designing a playground. He plans to cover $\frac{1}{4}$ of the playground with sand and $\frac{3}{10}$ with grass. What fraction of the playground will be covered with sand or grass?

To find the fraction of the playground that will be covered with sand or grass, add: $\frac{1}{4} + \frac{3}{10}$.

$\frac{1}{4}$ and $\frac{3}{10}$ have unlike denominators. This means they are made up of different unit fractions. Before adding, rewrite them as equivalent fractions that have a common denominator or common multiple.

Method 1

- List the first few multiples of 4 and of 10.
  Look for a multiple that is on *both* lists.

  Multiples of 4: 4, 8, 12, 16, 20, 24, 28
  Multiples of 10: 10, 20, 30, 40, 50, 60, 70

  20 is on both lists. You can use it as a common denominator of both $\frac{1}{4}$ and $\frac{3}{10}$.

- Rewrite $\frac{1}{4}$ and $\frac{3}{10}$ as equivalent fractions with the denominator 20.
  $\frac{1}{4} = \frac{1 \times 5}{4 \times 5} = \frac{5}{20}$ $\qquad$ $\frac{3}{10} = \frac{3 \times 2}{10 \times 2} = \frac{6}{20}$

- Add the fractions: $\frac{1}{4} + \frac{3}{10} = \frac{5}{20} + \frac{6}{20} = \frac{5 + 6}{20} = \frac{11}{20}$

To find a fraction equivalent to a given fraction, multiply or divide *both* the numerator *and* the denominator by *the same* number.

Method 2

- For $\frac{1}{4}$ and $\frac{3}{10}$ you can also use the product of the denominators, 4×10, or 40, as the common denominator.
  $\frac{1}{4} = \frac{1 \times 10}{4 \times 10} = \frac{10}{40}$ $\qquad$ $\frac{3}{10} = \frac{3 \times 4}{10 \times 4} = \frac{12}{40}$

- Add the fractions: $\frac{1}{4} + \frac{3}{10} = \frac{10}{40} + \frac{12}{40} = \frac{10 + 12}{40} = \frac{22}{40}$
  Simplify $\frac{22}{40}$ by finding an equivalent fraction. $\frac{22}{40} \div \frac{2}{2} = \frac{11}{20}$.

➡ The fraction of the playground that will be covered with sand or grass is $\frac{11}{20}$.

Guided Instruction

Connect: How to add and subtract mixed numbers with unlike denominators

Ted had $6\frac{1}{4}$ cups of flour. Then, he used $1\frac{3}{4}$ cups to make a piecrust and $2\frac{2}{3}$ cups to make a loaf of bread. How much flour does Ted have now?

Step 1

Add $1\frac{3}{4} + 2\frac{2}{3}$ to find how much flour Ted used.

To add $1\frac{3}{4} + 2\frac{2}{3}$, rewrite the fraction parts as equivalent fractions with a common denominator. You can use 12 as a common denominator.

$1\frac{3}{4} = 1\frac{3 \times 3}{4 \times 3} = 1\frac{9}{12}$ $\quad$ $2\frac{2}{3} = 2\frac{2 \times 4}{3 \times 4} = 2\frac{8}{12}$

Remember! You can use the product of the denominators to find the common denominator.

Add the mixed numbers. Add the whole number parts and fraction parts separately.

$$\begin{array}{r} 1\frac{9}{12} \\ +\ 2\frac{8}{12} \\ \hline 3\frac{17}{12} \end{array}$$

$\frac{17}{12}$ is more than 1 whole, so regroup:

$3\frac{17}{12} = 3 + \frac{12}{12} + \frac{5}{12} = 3 + 1 + \frac{5}{12} = 4\frac{5}{12}$.

Step 2

Subtract $4\frac{5}{12}$ from $6\frac{1}{4}$ to find how much flour Ted has left.

$$\begin{array}{r} 6\frac{1}{4} \\ -\ 4\frac{5}{12} \\ \hline \end{array} \xrightarrow{\text{Rewrite with a common denominator.}} \begin{array}{r} 6\frac{3}{12} \\ -\ 4\frac{5}{12} \\ \hline \end{array} \xrightarrow{\text{Since } \frac{5}{12} > \frac{3}{12}\text{, regroup } 6\frac{3}{12}.} \begin{array}{r} 5\frac{15}{12} \\ -\ 4\frac{5}{12} \\ \hline 1\frac{10}{12} \end{array}$$

$6 = 5 + \frac{12}{12}$. So, $6\frac{3}{12} = 5 + \frac{12}{12} + \frac{3}{12} = 5\frac{15}{12}$

You can simplify $1\frac{10}{12}$ to get $1\frac{5}{6}$.

➡ Ted has $1\frac{5}{6}$ cups of flour left.

Guided Practice

Use the model to help you find the sum or difference.

1. $\frac{7}{8} - \frac{3}{4}$

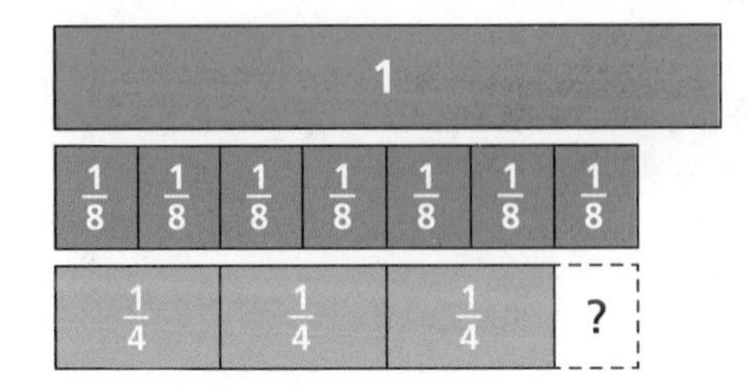

$\frac{7}{8} - \frac{3}{4} =$ ____

2. $\frac{1}{9} + \frac{2}{3}$

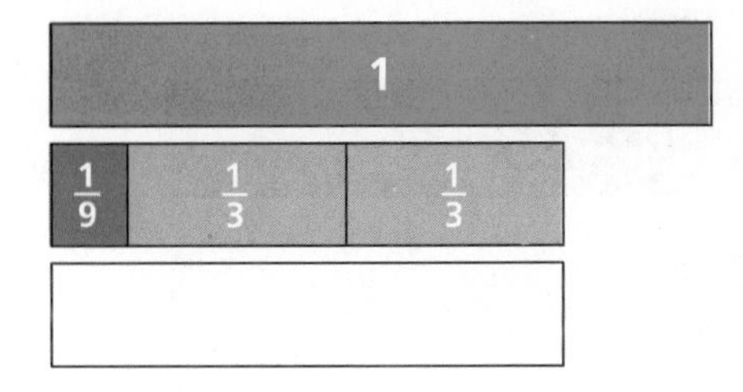

$\frac{1}{9} + \frac{2}{3} =$ ____

Complete the steps to find each sum or difference.

3. $\frac{2}{7} + \frac{1}{3}$

$\frac{2}{7} = \frac{}{21}$

$\frac{1}{3} = \frac{}{21}$

$\frac{}{21} + \frac{}{21} = \frac{ + }{21} = \frac{}{21}$

$\frac{2}{7} + \frac{1}{3} =$ ____

4. $1\frac{9}{11} - \frac{1}{3}$

$1\frac{9}{11} = 1\frac{}{33}$

$\frac{1}{3} = \frac{}{33}$

$1\frac{}{33}$

$- \frac{}{33}$

Think • Pair • Share

MP5 5. Which of the following expressions can the given model represent? Explain your answer.

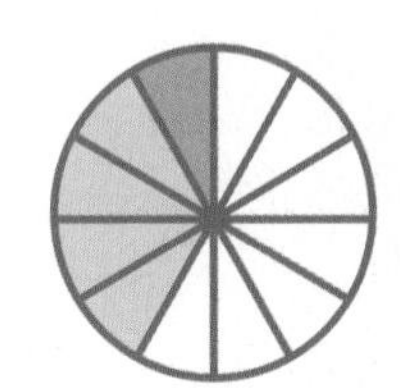

a. $\frac{1}{5} + \frac{4}{5}$ b. $\frac{1}{12} + \frac{2}{6}$ c. $\frac{2}{24} + \frac{1}{3}$ d. $\frac{1}{12} + \frac{4}{6}$

Independent Practice

Use the model to help you find the sum or difference.

1. $\frac{4}{5} - \frac{1}{10}$

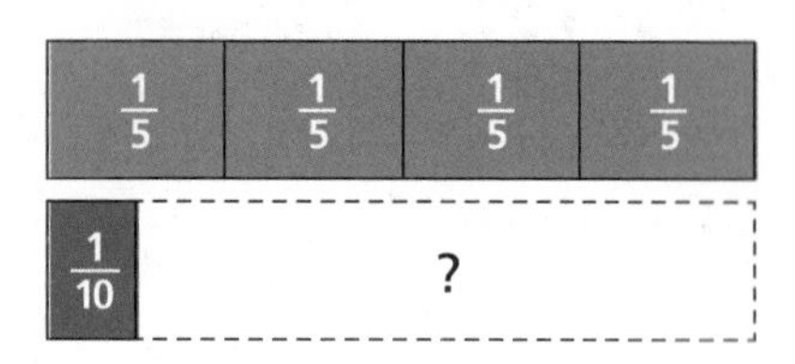

$\frac{4}{5} - \frac{1}{10} =$ ____

2. $\frac{2}{5} + \frac{1}{2}$

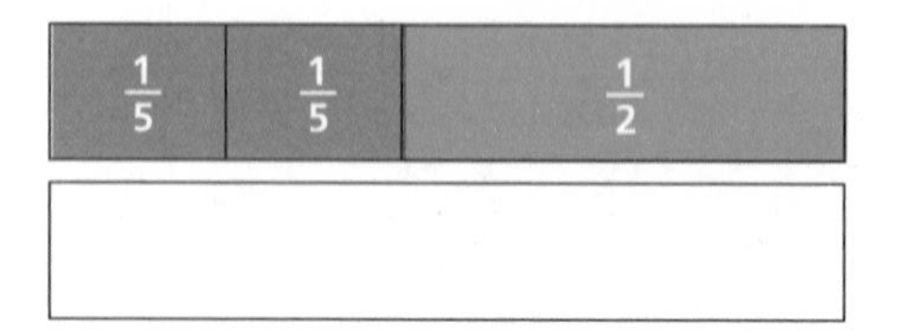

$\frac{2}{5} + \frac{1}{2} =$ ____

Complete the steps to find the sum or difference.

3. $2\frac{1}{6} + \frac{3}{4}$

$2\frac{1}{6} = 2\frac{\ }{12}$

$\frac{3}{4} = \frac{\ }{12}$

$2\frac{\ }{12} + \frac{\ }{12} =$ ____

$2\frac{1}{6} + \frac{3}{4} =$ ____

4. $1\frac{7}{8} - \frac{2}{3}$

$1\frac{7}{8} =$ ____

$\frac{2}{3} =$ ____

$\begin{array}{r} 1\ \frac{\ }{24} \\ -\ \ \frac{\ }{24} \\ \hline \end{array}$

$1\frac{7}{8} - \frac{2}{3} =$ ____

5. Which expressions are equivalent to $\frac{5}{18} - \frac{1}{4}$?

a. $\frac{5 - 1}{18 - 4}$

b. $\frac{5}{18} - \frac{1}{18}$

c. $\frac{10}{36} - \frac{9}{36}$

d. $\frac{20}{72} - \frac{18}{72}$

Independent Practice

6. Which expressions are equivalent to $4\frac{2}{7} + 1\frac{3}{4}$?

   a. $4\frac{16}{56} + 1\frac{42}{56}$
   b. $4\frac{10}{36} + 1\frac{27}{36}$
   c. $4\frac{2}{28} + 1\frac{3}{28}$
   d. $4\frac{8}{28} + 1\frac{21}{28}$

Evaluate each expression. Show your work.

7. $\frac{1}{3} + \frac{1}{8}$

8. $\frac{7}{13} - \frac{5}{39}$

9. $1\frac{5}{9} - \frac{1}{2}$

10. $4\frac{3}{8} + 2\frac{3}{4}$

11. $3 - 1\frac{7}{15}$

12. $1\frac{1}{2} - (\frac{1}{6} + \frac{2}{15})$

Solve each problem.

MP3 13. Samantha found the sum of $3\frac{1}{3} + \frac{3}{4}$. Her work is shown below. Is her answer correct? Explain.

$$3\frac{1}{3} + \frac{3}{4} = 3\frac{4}{12} + \frac{9}{12} = 3\frac{13}{12}$$

MP3 14. Manuel says that there is always more than one common denominator for a set of fractions. Do you agree? Explain why or why not.

Independent Practice

MP2 **15.** Desiree is driving from Raleigh, North Carolina to Key West, Florida. She drives $\frac{1}{5}$ of the way the first day. She drives $\frac{5}{8}$ of the way the second day. How much of the driving has Desiree completed?

Show your work.

Answer ______________________

MP1 **16.** Last summer, Ronald grew from $5\frac{7}{12}$ feet tall to $6\frac{1}{8}$ feet tall. How much did Ronald grow last summer?

Show your work.

Answer ______________________

MP1 **17.** Sammi makes $4\frac{1}{2}$ cups of granola. She gives $1\frac{1}{2}$ cups to her brother and $\frac{3}{4}$ of a cup to her friend. How much granola does Sammi have left?

Show your work.

Answer ______________________

MP6 **18.** The long-jump record at Tremell High School was $20\frac{3}{4}$ feet in 2000. In 2008, the record was broken by $\frac{1}{8}$ inch. In 2013, it was broken again by an additional $\frac{5}{12}$ inch. What is the new long-jump record?

Show your work.

Answer ______________________

Independent Practice

MP7 **19.** Complete the equations below.

$\frac{1}{2} - \frac{1}{4} =$ ____

$\frac{1}{5} - \frac{1}{10} =$ ____

$\frac{1}{8} - \frac{1}{16} =$ ____

Describe how the equations are similar. Can you apply the same pattern to find $\frac{1}{30} - \frac{1}{60}$ without determining a common denominator? Explain.

MP1 **20.** Which expression below has the greater value?

a. $2 - (\frac{4}{5} + \frac{2}{7})$

b. $\frac{2}{7} + \frac{1}{2}$

Show your work.

Answer ____

MP4 **21.** Evaluate $\frac{9}{12} - (\frac{1}{2} + \frac{1}{6})$. Draw a model to justify your answer.

Show your work.

Answer ____

Lesson

16 Problem Solving: Add and Subtract Fractions

Essential Question:
How can you use the addition and subtraction of fractions to solve real world problems?

5.NF.2

Guided Instruction

In this lesson you will solve problems using the addition and subtraction of fractions.

Understand: How to use the addition of fractions to solve problems

Ellen is collecting shells for an art project. Each day she collects them in the same size bucket. The first day Ellen collects $\frac{2}{3}$ of a bucket of shells. The second day she collects $\frac{3}{5}$ of a bucket of shells. How many buckets of shells does Ellen have? If she needs 1 full bucket for her project, does Ellen have enough?

To solve the problem, determine whether the total amount of shells Ellen collected over the two days is more or less than 1 full bucket.

Ellen collected $\frac{2}{3}$ bucket the first day and $\frac{3}{5}$ bucket the second day. To find the total for both days, add: $\frac{2}{3} + \frac{3}{5}$.

$\frac{2}{3}$ and $\frac{3}{5}$ have unlike denominators. Before you can add them, you need to rewrite them as equivalent fractions with a common denominator. You can use the product of the denominators 3 × 5, or 15, as the common denominator.

$\frac{2}{3} = \frac{2 \times 5}{3 \times 5} = \frac{10}{15}$ $\qquad$ $\frac{3}{5} = \frac{3 \times 3}{5 \times 3} = \frac{9}{15}$

Now, calculate the sum.

$\frac{2}{3} + \frac{3}{5} = \frac{10}{15} + \frac{9}{15} = \frac{19}{15}$

The numerator of $\frac{19}{15}$ is greater than the denominator, so it is greater than 1. It represents more than 1 full bucket. You can rewrite this fraction as a mixed number.

$\frac{19}{15} = \frac{15}{15} + \frac{4}{15} = 1\frac{4}{15}$

Ellen has 1 full bucket and $\frac{4}{15}$ of another bucket.

➡ Ellen has $1\frac{4}{15}$ buckets of shells. She has more than 1 bucket full of shells, so she has enough for her art project.

Guided Instruction

Understand: How to use the subtraction of fractions to solve problems

Javier rides his bike to visit his friend Abe. Abe's house is $5\frac{1}{2}$ miles away. The first $4\frac{2}{3}$ miles of the trip are on flat land, but the rest is uphill. How many miles of the trip are uphill?

You can make a drawing to help you make sense of the problem.

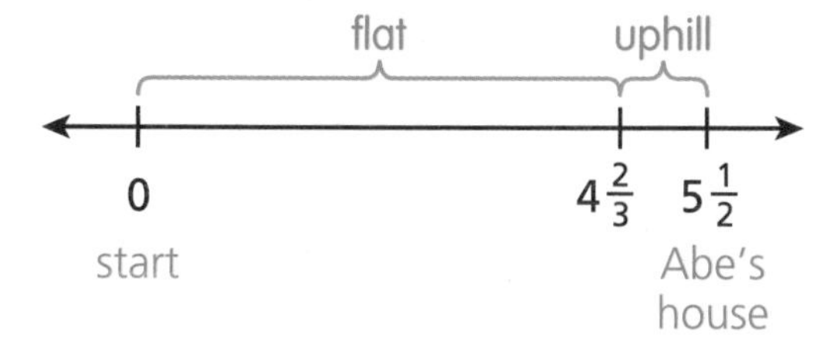

To find the distance that is uphill, you must subtract: $5\frac{1}{2} - 4\frac{2}{3}$.

Before subtracting, rename the fractions so that they have a common denominator. You can use the product of the denominators 2 × 3, or 6, as a common denominator.

$5\frac{1}{2} = 5\frac{1 \times 3}{2 \times 3} = 5\frac{3}{6}$ $4\frac{2}{3} = 4\frac{2 \times 2}{3 \times 2} = 4\frac{4}{6}$

Now, calculate the difference.

$$\begin{array}{r} 5\frac{3}{6} \\ -\ 4\frac{4}{6} \\ \hline \end{array}$$

Since $\frac{4}{6} > \frac{3}{6}$, regroup $5\frac{3}{6}$.

$$\begin{array}{r} 4\frac{9}{6} \\ -\ 4\frac{4}{6} \\ \hline \frac{5}{6} \end{array}$$

Remember!
$5\frac{3}{6} = 4 + \frac{6}{6} + \frac{3}{6} = 4\frac{9}{6}$

Use estimation to check that the answer is reasonable. Because $4\frac{2}{3}$ is a little more than $4\frac{1}{2}$, $5\frac{1}{2} - 4\frac{2}{3}$ should be a little less than $5\frac{1}{2} - 4\frac{1}{2}$, which is 1. So, $\frac{5}{6}$ is a reasonable answer.

➡ $\frac{5}{6}$ mile of Javier's trip is uphill.

Suppose Javier walks his bike during the last $\frac{1}{3}$ mile. How many miles does he ride uphill? Show your work.

Guided Instruction

Connect: What you know about the addition or subtraction of fractions to solve problems

Jill and her brother Ray grow tomatoes. Jill picks $3\frac{2}{3}$ pounds and Ray picks $2\frac{1}{2}$ pounds. They give 4 pounds to Uncle Joe and the rest to Uncle Pete. How many pounds of tomatoes do they give to Uncle Pete?

Step 1

Make sense of the problem. Write a word equation to represent the situation.

total pounds picked − pounds given to Uncle Joe = pounds given to Uncle Pete

Step 2

Rewrite the equation using the information from the problem. The sum in parentheses is the total number of pounds Jill and Ray picked. The number of pounds Uncle Pete gets is not known.

$(3\frac{2}{3} + 2\frac{1}{2}) - 4 = ■$

Step 3

Use the product of the denominators as the common denominator of the mixed numbers.

$3\frac{2}{3} = 3\frac{2 \times 2}{3 \times 2} = 3\frac{4}{6}$ $2\frac{1}{2} = 2\frac{1 \times 3}{2 \times 3} = 2\frac{3}{6}$

Step 4

Solve. $(3\frac{4}{6} + 2\frac{3}{6}) - 4 = 5\frac{7}{6} - 4 = 1\frac{7}{6} = 2\frac{1}{6}$

Remember!

You can use addition to undo subtraction and use subtraction to undo addition.

Step 5

Check your answer by working backward.

First find the sum of $2\frac{1}{6}$ and 4. → $2\frac{1}{6} + 4 = 6\frac{1}{6}$

Then subtract the amount Jill picked. → $6\frac{1}{6} - 3\frac{2}{3}$

The difference should be the amount Ray picked, $2\frac{1}{2}$. → $6\frac{1}{6} - 3\frac{4}{6} = 2\frac{3}{6} = 2\frac{1}{2}$

➡ Uncle Pete will get $2\frac{1}{6}$ pounds of tomatoes.

Guided Practice

Tell whether to add or subtract to solve the problem. Draw a diagram or model and solve.

1. Jack is making a family recipe. He uses $\frac{3}{8}$ teaspoon of curry and $\frac{1}{3}$ teaspoon of rosemary. How much spice does Jack use in all?

   Add or subtract? ______________

   Answer ______________

2. Stella had $\frac{7}{8}$ of a bag of popcorn. She gave $\frac{5}{6}$ of the bag to her friends. How much does Stella have left?

   Add or subtract? ______________

   Answer ______________

Solve the problem. Show your work.

3. Halley builds a model car for a competition. The maximum car length allowed is $8\frac{3}{4}$ inches. Halley's car measures $6\frac{9}{16}$ inches. How much shorter is her car than the maximum length allowed?

   Answer ______________

MP5 4. Show how you can estimate to check each answer in Exercises 1–3. Tell if your answers are reasonable. Hint: Use benchmark fractions.

Independent Practice

Solve the problems. Show your work.

MP1 **1.** Mr. Nguyen had $\frac{7}{8}$ pint of water in his water bottle. Then, he drank $\frac{2}{3}$ pint. How much water is left in the bottle?

____ pint of water is left in the water bottle.

MP1 **2.** Maria is writing a book report. The first week she wrote $\frac{5}{12}$ of the report. The next week she wrote $\frac{1}{4}$ of the report. What fraction of the whole report has Maria completed?

Maria has completed ____ of the report.

MP2 **3.** Bella fills her gas tank with $13\frac{1}{2}$ gallons of gas. After driving the car she has $11\frac{4}{5}$ gallons left. How much gas did Bella use?

Bella used ________________ of gas.

MP2 **4.** Teresa has $\frac{3}{4}$ hour to complete a 3-page test. She spends $\frac{1}{3}$ hour on the first page. Teresa spends $\frac{1}{4}$ hour on the second page. How much time is left for the last page?

____ hour is left for the last page.

MP2 **5.** There were $5\frac{1}{4}$ gallons of water in an aquarium. Then Bruce added $2\frac{2}{3}$ gallons of water. If the aquarium holds 15 gallons, how many more gallons does Bruce need to add to fill the aquarium?

Bruce needs to add ________________ to fill the aquarium.

Independent Practice

For exercises 6–7, choose the correct answer.

6. Penny buys $2\frac{1}{3}$ yards of cloth. She uses $\frac{3}{4}$ yard to make a skirt. Without solving the problem, what is the closest estimate of how much cloth Penny has left?

   a. less than $1\frac{1}{2}$ yards
   b. more than $1\frac{1}{2}$ yards
   c. more than 2 yards
   d. more than 3 yards

7. Franco walks $3\frac{1}{3}$ miles from his home to the store. Then he continues walking in the same direction another $1\frac{1}{4}$ miles to his friend's house. Later, Franco walks $2\frac{2}{3}$ miles back toward his home to another friend's house. Without solving the problem, what is the closest estimate of how far Franco is from home?

   a. more than 1 mile
   b. more than 2 miles
   c. more than 5 miles
   d. more than 7 miles

MP2 8. Lucia plans to bake a lemon dessert. She has $1\frac{1}{3}$ lemons in her refrigerator. The recipe lists $2\frac{3}{4}$ lemons for the filling and $1\frac{2}{3}$ lemons for the topping. Lucia estimates that if she buys 3 more lemons she will have enough for the recipe? Is Lucia correct? Explain.

MP2 9. Abraham and Kali solve the same problem in two different ways. Choose the approach that you prefer, and explain why you prefer it.

Abraham: $(2\frac{3}{8} + 1\frac{1}{2}) - \frac{3}{4}$

$(2\frac{3}{8} + 1\frac{4}{8}) - \frac{3}{4}$

$3\frac{7}{8} - \frac{6}{8}$

$3\frac{1}{8}$

Kali: $(2\frac{3}{8} + 1\frac{1}{2}) - \frac{3}{4}$

$(\frac{19}{8} + \frac{12}{8}) - \frac{3}{4}$

$\frac{31}{8} - \frac{6}{8}$

$\frac{25}{8} = 3\frac{1}{8}$

Independent Practice

MP4 **10.** Write a word problem that can be solved by evaluating $1\frac{3}{4} + 1\frac{2}{3} - 1\frac{1}{2}$.

MP4 **11.** Write a word problem that can be solved by evaluating $6 - 1\frac{5}{6} - 1\frac{4}{9}$.

Solve the problems.

MP4 **12.** Audrey has $3\frac{1}{3}$ boxes of comic books. Her cousin gives her $2\frac{1}{2}$ boxes. Audrey gives $1\frac{1}{6}$ boxes to her little sister. How many boxes of comic books does she have left? Write an equation and use the number line below.

Show your work.

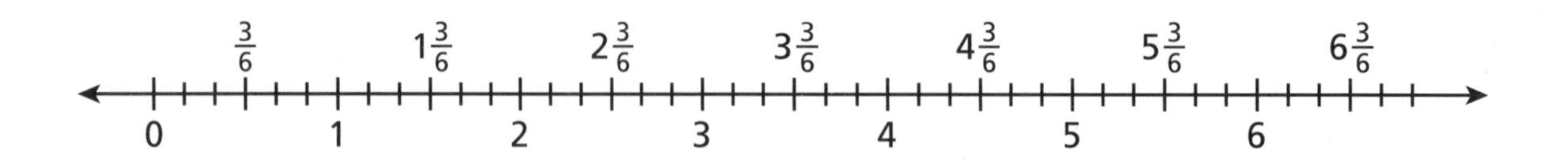

Answer ______________________________

Independent Practice

MP1 **13.** Rina has \$60 to spend at an amusement park. Her budget is listed below. What fraction of Rina's budget does she spend on food? About what fraction of Rina's budget does she spend on all tickets? What fraction of Rina's budget does she have left?

Ticket for entry: \$22.00
Tickets for special rides: 2 for \$8.00 each
Lunch: \$12.00
Popcorn: \$3.00
Ice cream: \$5.00

Show your work.

Answer ______________________________

MP4 **14.** Evaluate the expression below. Use the number line provided.

$(5\frac{3}{4} - 3\frac{1}{5}) + 2\frac{3}{10}$

Show your work.

Answer ______________________________

Lesson
17 Interpret Fractions as Division

Essential Question:
How are fractions related to division?
5.NF.3

Guided Instruction

In this lesson you will learn how to solve division problems that result in quotients that are a fraction or mixed number.

Understand: A fraction as the quotient of whole number division

> Amy is making raisin bread. She has 2 cups of raisins to divide equally among 3 batches of dough. How many cups should Amy put into each batch?

To find how many cups Amy should put into each batch of dough, divide 2 cups of raisins equally among 3 batches.

Draw a model. Divide each cup into thirds and then put $\frac{1}{3}$ from each cup in each batch of dough. Each batch gets two $\frac{1}{3}$ cups, which is $\frac{2}{3}$ cup.

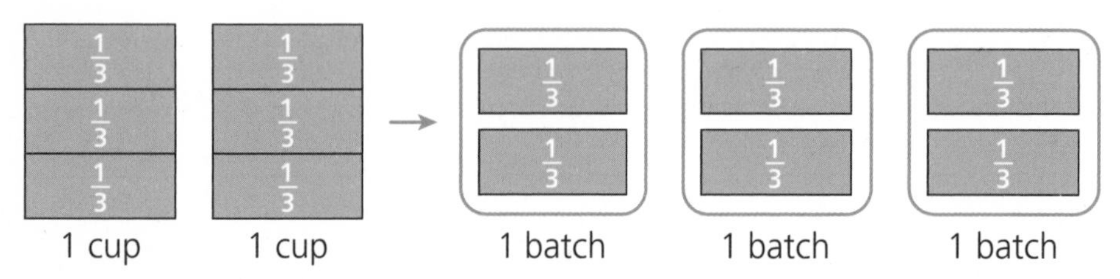

This shows that $2 \div 3 = \frac{2}{3}$.

Notice the relationship between the dividend and divisor of the division problem, and the numerator and denominator of the quotient.

$$\underset{\text{dividend}}{2} \div \underset{\text{divisor}}{3} = \frac{2}{3} \begin{array}{l}\text{numerator}\\ \text{denominator}\end{array}$$

In fact, you can think of any fraction as the result of dividing its numerator by its denominator.

In general for whole numbers a and b, with b not equal to zero,
$a \div b = \frac{a}{b}$. ← $\frac{a}{b}$ is the result of dividing a into b equal parts or groups.

➡ Amy should put $\frac{2}{3}$ cup of raisins into each batch of dough.

✏ Max has 3 ounces of a solution to pour equally into 4 beakers. How much should he pour into each beaker?

Guided Instruction

Understand: Division problems with mixed-number quotients

Vick brings 12 bags of granola on a hike to be shared equally among 5 people. How much granola will each person get?

To find how much granola each person will get, divide the 12 bags of granola by 5 people.

Method 1

Use what you learned in the previous problem:

$12 \div 5 = \frac{12}{5}$

Rewrite the fraction as a mixed number:

$\frac{12}{5} = \frac{10}{5} + \frac{2}{5} = 2\frac{2}{5}$

Remember!

In general for whole numbers a and b, with b not equal to zero, $a \div b = \frac{a}{b}$.

Method 2

Start by thinking about sharing just 1 bag.
If 5 people share 1 bag, then each person gets $\frac{1}{5}$ bag.
Vick has 12 bags, so each person gets 12 times this much:

$12 \times \frac{1}{5} = \frac{12}{5}$

This is the same as $2\frac{2}{5}$ bag.

Method 3

Use long division. Each person gets 2 whole bags, and there are 2 bags left. Each person gets $\frac{1}{5}$ of each of these leftover bags for a total of $\frac{2}{5}$ bag more.

$$\begin{array}{r} 2 \text{ R}2 \\ 5\overline{)12} \\ -10 \\ \hline 2 \end{array} \qquad 2\frac{2}{5}$$

➡ Each person will get $2\frac{2}{5}$ bags of granola.

Josh solved this problem: Eleven social studies books are being shipped to a school. One box fits 3 books. How many boxes will the publisher need? Josh said the answer is $\frac{11}{3}$ or $3\frac{2}{3}$. Explain why Josh's answer is not correct.

Guided Instruction

Connect: Solving division problems with quotients that are fractions or mixed numbers

These word problems are both solved using the same division expression, but the solutions are in different forms. Find the solutions and explain why they are in different forms.

Problem A
Four students sign up to work equal amounts of time at a class flower sale. If the sale is 7 hours long, how long must each student work?

Problem B
Four friends earned $7 at a carnival stand. If they divide the money equally, how much will each friend get?

Step 1

Write a division expression for each problem.

In **Problem A**, 7 hours is divided among 4 students.
In **Problem B**, $7 is divided among 4 friends.

Both problems can be represented by the expression $7 \div 4$.

Step 2

Divide.

$7 \div 4 = \frac{7}{4} = 1\frac{3}{4}$

Remember!
In general for whole numbers a and b, with b not equal to zero, $a \div b = \frac{a}{b}$.

Step 3

Interpret the quotient.

For **Problem A**, the answer means that each student must work $1\frac{3}{4}$ hours.

For **Problem B**, the answer means that each friend should receive $1 and $\frac{3}{4}$ of another dollar, which is 75¢.

➡ For **Problem A**, each student must work $1\frac{3}{4}$ hours. For **Problem B**, each friend will receive $1.75. It makes sense for the first answer to be a mixed number because it is common to talk about fractional parts of an hour. However, money amounts are usually given in dollars and cents, rather than as fractions of dollars.

Guided Practice

Draw a model to represent the division. Give the quotient as a fraction.

1. $3 \div 4 =$ ____

2. $5 \div 1 =$ ____

Solve each equation. Write the quotient as a fraction or mixed number.

3. $6 \div 11 =$ ____

4. $14 \div 4 =$ ____

5. $7 \div 10 =$ ____

6. $21 \div 5 =$ ____

7. $12 \div 7 =$ ____

8. $8 \div 15 =$ ____

9. $32 \div 4 =$ ____

10. $23 \div 11 =$ ____

Think•Pair•Share

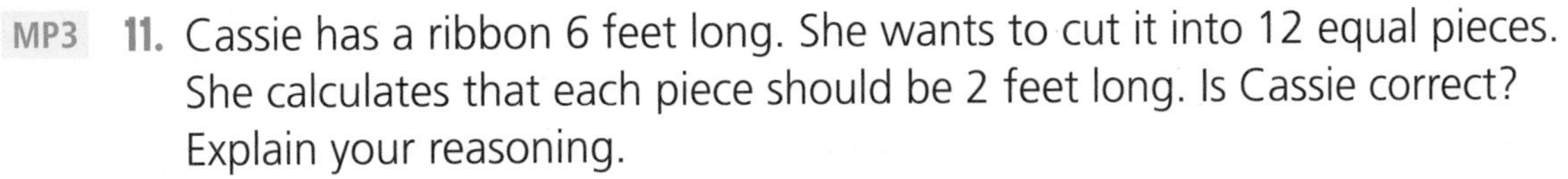

MP3 11. Cassie has a ribbon 6 feet long. She wants to cut it into 12 equal pieces. She calculates that each piece should be 2 feet long. Is Cassie correct? Explain your reasoning.

$12 \div 6 = \frac{12}{6} = \frac{2}{1} = 2$

Independent Practice

Draw a model to represent the division. Give the quotient as a fraction or mixed number.

1. $2 \div 7 =$ ____

2. $17 \div 3 =$ ____

3. $1 \div 4 =$ ____

4. $14 \div 6 =$ ____

Solve each equation. Write the quotient as a fraction or mixed number.

5. $19 \div 4 =$ ____

6. $5 \div 21 =$ ____

7. Choose a problem on this page and create a story problem that can be modeled by the problem. Then write the answer to your story problem.

Independent Practice

For exercises 8–11, give each quotient as a fraction or mixed number.

8. $11 \div 8 =$ ____

9. $7 \div 33 =$ ____

10. $9 \div 14 =$ ____

11. $45 \div 10 =$ ____

For exercises 12–13, choose the correct answer.

12. Which expression is represented by the model?

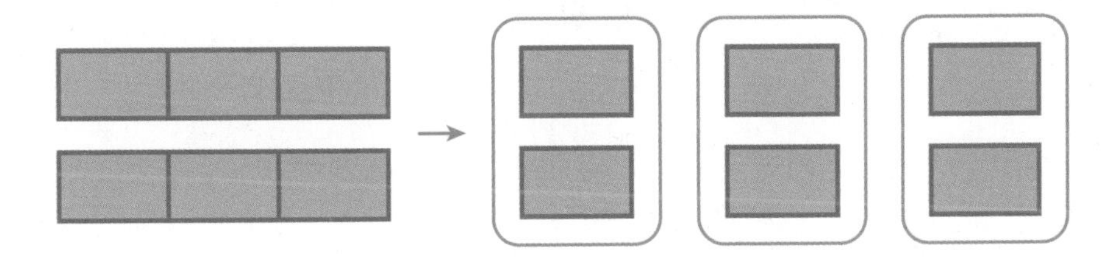

a. $2 \div 6$

b. $3 \div 6$

c. $2 \div 3$

d. $3 \div 2$

13. Tina has 4 apples to share among 5 people. Which fraction shows how much each person receives?

a. $\frac{5}{30}$

b. $\frac{4}{5}$

c. $\frac{5}{4}$

d. $\frac{30}{4}$

Solve the problems.

MP1 14. Fran and 5 friends must share 3 liters of water. How much water will each person get?

MP1 15. Dmitri has 16 inches of wire. He wants to bend the wire to make a triangle with 3 equal sides. How long will each side be?

Independent Practice

MP3 **16.** Annette buys swim goggles for her swim team at a wholesale store. There are 25 swimmers and the swim goggles are sold in a package of 6. Annette wants to give each swimmer 2 swim goggles, therefore, she buys 9 packages. Is Annette correct? Explain.

MP3 **17.** Jose has a 120-inch roll of wrapping paper. He needs an 18-inch piece to wrap each present. Does Jose have enough to wrap 7 presents? Explain.

MP1 **18.** Allen has 13 carrots. He wants to put an equal amount of carrots into 5 sandwich sized bags. How much should Allen put into each bag?

Show your work.

Answer ____________________

MP2 **19.** Deanna has 2 nutrition bars that she wants to share among herself and 2 other friends. How can Deanna divide the nutrition bars into equal portions?

Show your work.

Answer ____________________

Independent Practice

MP1 **20.** Greg completes his drills for football training camp in 75 minutes. He needs to record the time in hours. How many hours did Greg engage in drills. (Remember: There are 60 minutes in one hour.)

Show your work.

Answer ______________________

MP6 **21.** Darren and his 2 sisters want to equally share 17 tokens at an arcade. How many tokens will each of them get?

Show your work.

Answer ______________________

MP1 **22.** Mr. Fried plans to give fruit flies to 6 groups of lab students for an experiment. He wants to give the same number of flies to each group. He has different size bottles. How can Mr. Fried give each group the same number of fruit flies without opening the bottles?

2 large bottles: 12 fruit flies in each bottle
10 medium bottles: 8 fruit flies in each bottle
14 small bottles: 2 fruit flies in each bottle

Show your work.

Answer ______________________

Lesson

18 Interpret Products of Fractions

Essential Question:
How can you multiply a whole number or a fraction by a fraction?
5.NF.4a

Guided Instruction

In this lesson you will find the product of a fraction and a whole number and of two fractions.

Understand: How to multiply a whole number by a unit fraction when the whole number is divisible by the denominator

> Jorge has 20 autographed baseballs. One-quarter of them are autographed by pitchers. How many of Jorge's baseballs are autographed by pitchers?

To find how many of the baseballs are autographed by pitchers, find $\frac{1}{4}$ of 20, which is the same as $\frac{1}{4} \times 20$.

Draw a model. Use 20 circles to represent the baseballs. Divide the circles into four equal groups. Shade 1 of the 4 groups to show $\frac{1}{4}$ of 20.

$$\begin{aligned} \frac{1}{4} \times 20 &= \frac{1}{4} \text{ of } 20 \\ &= 20 \div 4 \\ &= 5 \end{aligned}$$

There are 5 circles shaded.

➡ 5 of Jorge's baseballs are autographed by pitchers.

Understand: How to multiply a whole number by a non-unit fraction when the whole number is divisible by the denominator

> Of Jorge's 20 baseballs, $\frac{3}{4}$ are autographed by American League players. How many of Jorge's baseballs are autographed by American League players?

Find $\frac{3}{4}$ of 20, which is the same as $\frac{3}{4} \times 20$.

Draw 20 circles and divide them into 4 equal groups. Shade 3 of the groups to represent $\frac{3}{4}$ of 20.

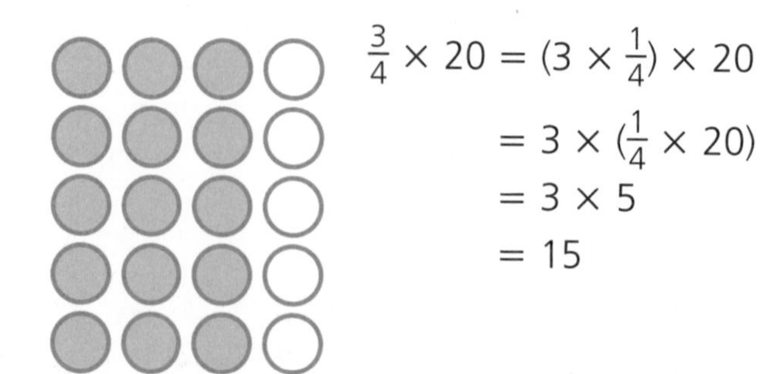

$$\begin{aligned} \frac{3}{4} \times 20 &= (3 \times \tfrac{1}{4}) \times 20 \\ &= 3 \times (\tfrac{1}{4} \times 20) \\ &= 3 \times 5 \\ &= 15 \end{aligned}$$

There are 15 circles shaded.

➡ 15 of Jorge's baseballs are autographed by American League players.

Guided Instruction

Understand: How to multiply a whole number by any unit fraction

Zoe bought 2 pounds of seaweed salad. She and her sister ate $\frac{1}{5}$ of it with their lunch. How much seaweed salad did Zoe and her sister eat with lunch?

To determine how much they ate, find $\frac{1}{5}$ of 2, which is the same as $\frac{1}{5} \times 2$.

Draw a model.

Each bar represents 1 whole pound. To find $\frac{1}{5} \times 2$ pounds, find $\frac{1}{5}$ of each pound and add.

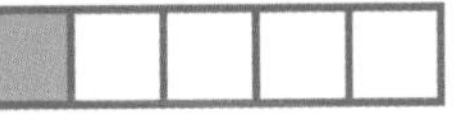

$$\frac{1}{5} \times 2 = \frac{1}{5} \text{ of } 2 = \frac{1}{5} + \frac{1}{5} = \frac{2}{5}$$

➡ Zoe and her sister ate $\frac{2}{5}$ pound of seaweed salad.

Understand: How to multiply a whole number by any non-unit fraction

Zoe also bought 3 pounds of bean salad. Her family ate $\frac{4}{5}$ of it with their dinner. How much bean salad did Zoe's family eat?

Find $\frac{4}{5}$ of 3, which is the same as $\frac{4}{5} \times 3$.

Draw a model.

Each bar represents 1 whole pound. To find $\frac{4}{5} \times 3$ pounds, find $\frac{4}{5}$ of each pound and add.

$$\frac{4}{5} \times 3 = \frac{4}{5} \text{ of } 3 = \frac{4}{5} + \frac{4}{5} + \frac{4}{5} = \frac{12}{5}$$

➡ Zoe's family ate $\frac{12}{5}$ pounds, or $2\frac{2}{5}$ pounds of bean salad.

If $\frac{a}{b}$ is a fraction and q is a whole number greater than 1, then $\frac{a}{b} \times q = \frac{a \times q}{b}$. Show that this general principle works for the four problems you have seen so far in this lesson.

Guided Instruction

Connect: What you know about multiplying by a fraction to multiply two fractions

Evaluate $\frac{1}{3} \times \frac{1}{4}$ and $\frac{2}{3} \times \frac{3}{4}$.

Step 1

Use a number line to find $\frac{1}{3} \times \frac{1}{4}$.

Divide the interval from 0 to 1 into fourths, and highlight $\frac{1}{4}$.

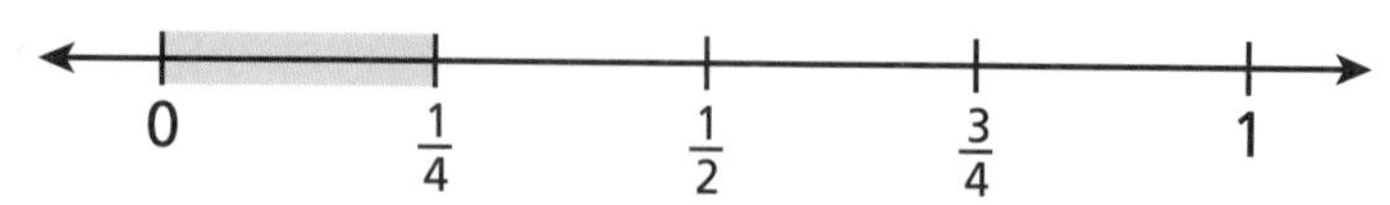

To find $\frac{1}{3} \times \frac{1}{4}$, or $\frac{1}{3}$ *of* $\frac{1}{4}$, divide each fourth into three equal intervals. This makes twelfths. Circle $\frac{1}{3}$ of the highlighted $\frac{1}{4}$. This interval represents $\frac{1}{12}$.

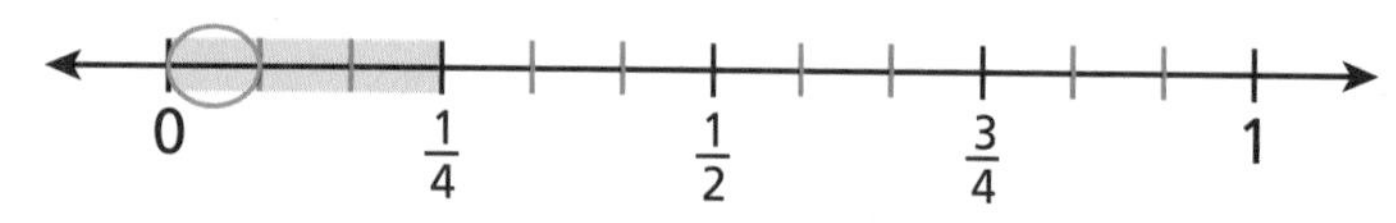

Step 2

Use a number line to find $\frac{2}{3} \times \frac{3}{4}$.

Divide the interval from 0 to 1 into fourths, and highlight $\frac{3}{4}$.

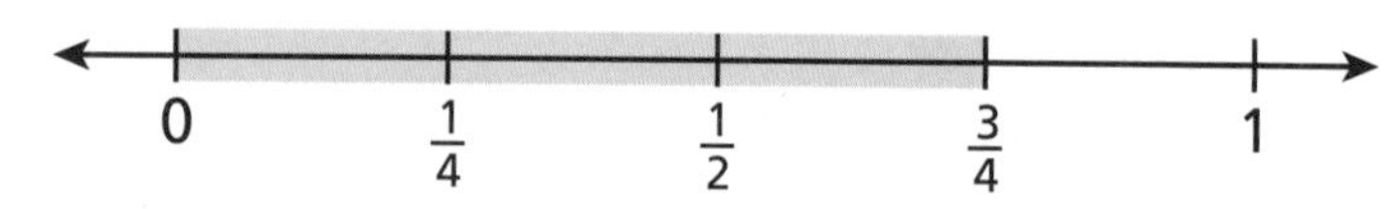

To find $\frac{2}{3} \times \frac{3}{4}$, or $\frac{2}{3}$ *of* $\frac{3}{4}$, divide each fourth into three equal parts.

This makes twelfths. Then circle $\frac{2}{3}$ of each of the 3 highlighted fourths.

The total amount circled is $\frac{2}{12} + \frac{2}{12} + \frac{2}{12} = \frac{6}{12}$.

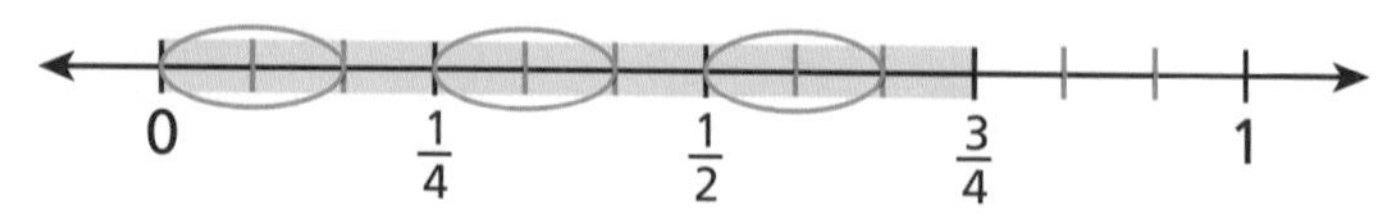

➡ $\frac{1}{3} \times \frac{1}{4} = \frac{1}{12}$ and $\frac{2}{3} \times \frac{3}{4} = \frac{6}{12}$

If $\frac{a}{b}$ and $\frac{c}{d}$ are any two fractions, with b, d not zero, then $\frac{a}{b} \times \frac{c}{d} = \frac{a \times c}{b \times d}$. Show that this general principle works for the two expressions on this page.

Guided Practice

Use the model to find each product.

1. $\frac{1}{6} \times 24$

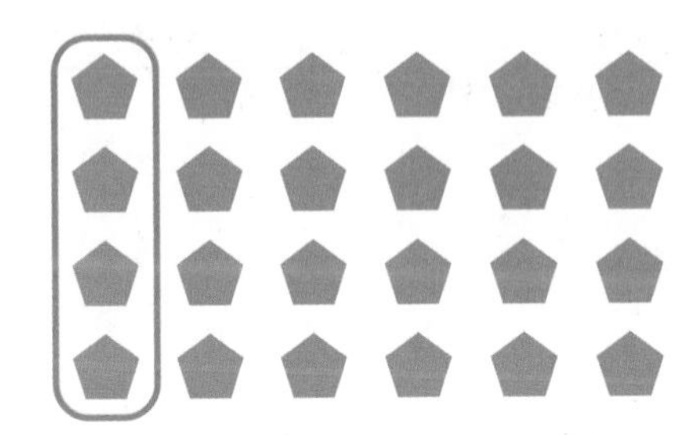

24 is divided into 6 groups of ____.

$\frac{1}{6} \times 24 =$ ____

2. $\frac{1}{4} \times \frac{1}{2}$

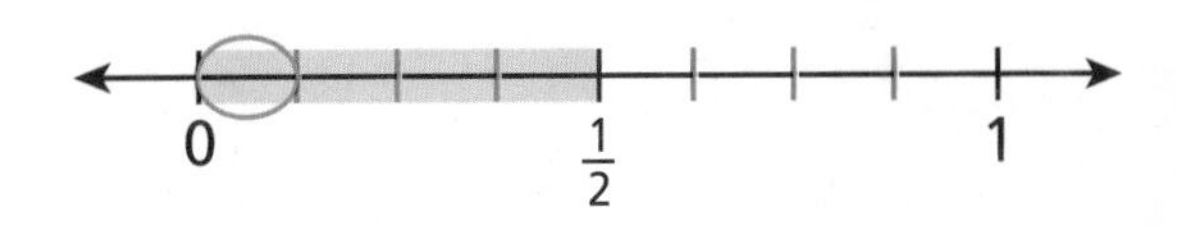

____ is highlighted.

Each half is divided into ____ intervals.

The circled interval represents ____.

$\frac{1}{4} \times \frac{1}{2} =$ ____

Find each product.

3. $\frac{4}{5} \times \frac{3}{8}$

$\frac{\quad\times\quad}{\quad\times\quad}$

$=$ —

4. $\frac{2}{5} \times 12$

$\frac{\quad\times\quad}{}$

$=$ —

$= 4$ —

Think • Pair • Share

MP3 5. Write a story problem for the equation $\frac{5}{6} \times \frac{2}{5} = \blacksquare$. What is the answer to your problem? Then ask a classmate to solve the equation two ways and interpret the product.

Independent Practice

Use the model to find each product.

1. $\frac{3}{5} \times 10$

$\frac{3}{5} \times 10 =$ ____

2. $\frac{5}{6} \times \frac{2}{3}$

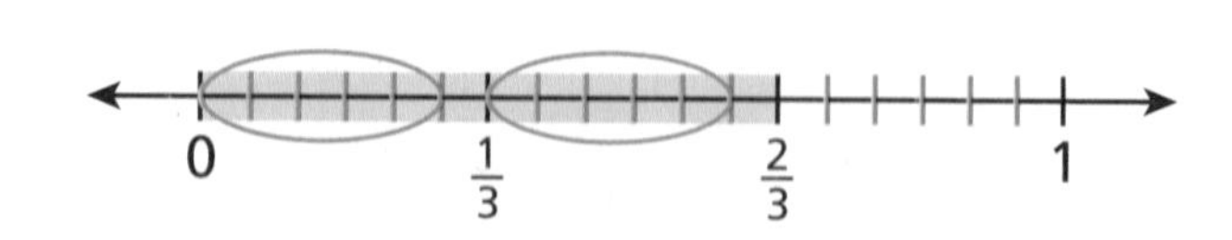

$\frac{5}{6} \times \frac{2}{3} =$ ____

Draw a model to find each product.

3. $\frac{2}{3} \times 9$

$\frac{2}{3} \times 9 =$ ____

4. $\frac{3}{5} \times \frac{6}{7}$

$\frac{3}{5} \times \frac{6}{7} =$ ____

Solve each equation. Show your work.

5. $\frac{1}{4} \times 44 =$ ____

6. $\frac{1}{5} \times \frac{2}{3} =$ ____

Independent Practice

7. $\frac{1}{6} \times \frac{4}{5} =$ ____

8. $\frac{2}{3} \times 20 =$ ____

9. $\frac{1}{4} \times 9 =$ ____

10. $\frac{5}{6} \times \frac{3}{4} =$ ____

11. $\frac{1}{5} \times \frac{2}{3} =$ ____

12. $\frac{5}{9} \times \frac{2}{5} =$ ____

Choose the correct answer.

13. Mel has a $\frac{1}{2}$ gallon of milk in the refrigerator. He drinks $\frac{1}{4}$ of the milk. How much milk does Mel drink?

a. $\frac{1}{8}$ gallon

b. $\frac{1}{6}$ gallon

c. $\frac{1}{4}$ gallon

d. $\frac{3}{4}$ gallon

Independent Practice

MP3 **14.** Amy multiplies $\frac{4}{5}$ and $\frac{2}{3}$ and says that the product is $\frac{6}{15}$. Identify the error Amy made and then find the correct answer.

MP4 **15.** Create a story problem for the expression below. Then find the answer to your problem.

$\frac{3}{4} \times 18$

Solve the problems.

MP1 **16.** A recipe calls for 6 cups of flour. Gunnar is only making $\frac{1}{4}$ of the recipe. How much flour does he need?

Show your work.

Answer ______________________________

MP1 **17.** Sarah is $\frac{3}{4}$ as old as Richardo. Richardo is 16 years old. How old is Sarah?

Show your work.

Answer ______________________________

Independent Practice

MP1 **18.** Jacob lives $\frac{3}{10}$ mile from school. Mia lives $\frac{2}{3}$ as far from school as Jacob. How far does Mia live from school?

Show your work.

Answer ______________________________

MP7 **19.** An apple weighs $\frac{9}{16}$ pound. A smaller apple is only $\frac{4}{5}$ as heavy. What is the weight of the smaller apple?

Show your work.

Answer ______________________________

MP4 **20.** Wylie is tiling a closet. Each tile is $\frac{3}{4}$ foot by $\frac{2}{3}$ foot. The closet floor is 6 square feet. How many tiles does Wylie need to cover the closet floor?

Show your work.

Answer ______________________________

Lesson 19

Find Areas of Rectangles: Tile and Multiply

Essential Question:
How do you find the area of rectangles with fractional side lengths?
5.NF.4b

Guided Instruction

In this lesson you will learn how to use tiling and multiplication to find the area of rectangles with fractional side lengths.

Understand: How to find the area of a rectangle with unit-fraction side lengths

Find the area of a rectangle with side lengths of $\frac{1}{3}$ unit and $\frac{1}{4}$ unit.

The model at the right shows that 3 × 4, or 12, $\frac{1}{3}$-unit by $\frac{1}{4}$-unit rectangles fit inside a unit square.

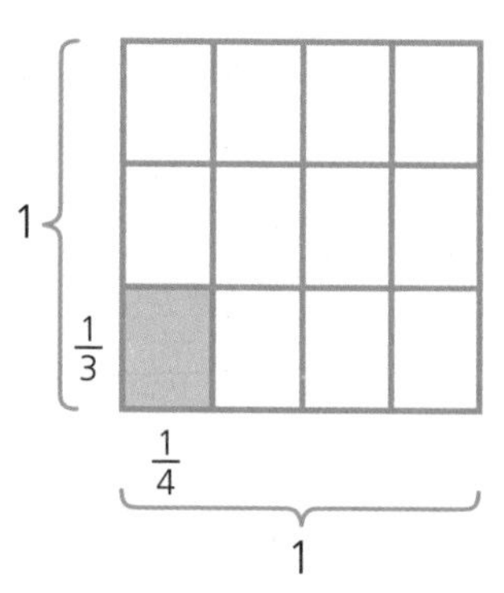

The area of the unit square is 1 square unit. So, the $\frac{1}{3}$-unit by $\frac{1}{4}$-unit rectangle has an area of $\frac{1}{12}$ square unit, or (unit)^2.

➡ The area of a rectangle with side lengths of $\frac{1}{3}$ unit and $\frac{1}{4}$ unit is $\frac{1}{12}$ square unit, or (unit)^2.

Understand: How to find the area of a rectangle with fractional side lengths

A rectangular field has side lengths of $\frac{2}{3}$ mile and $\frac{3}{4}$ mile. What is the area of the field.

The model at the right shows that a $\frac{2}{3}$-mi by $\frac{3}{4}$-mi rectangle can be tiled with $\frac{1}{3}$-mi by $\frac{1}{4}$-mi rectangles. From the previous problem, you know that each small rectangle has an area of $\frac{1}{12}$ mi^2. There are 2 × 3, or 6 of these *unit-fraction rectangles* inside the larger rectangle.

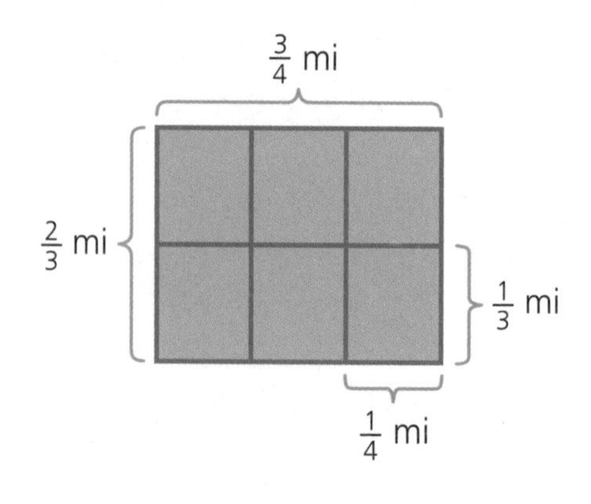

So, the area of the field is $6 \times \frac{1}{12} = \frac{6}{1} \times \frac{1}{12}$, or $\frac{6}{12}$ mi^2, which is the same as $\frac{1}{2}$ mi^2.

Notice that you get the same result if you multiply the side lengths.

$$\frac{2}{3} \times \frac{3}{4} = \frac{2 \times 3}{3 \times 4} = \frac{6}{12} = \frac{1}{2}$$

➡ The area of the field is $\frac{6}{12}$ mi^2, or $\frac{1}{2}$ mi^2.

Understand: How to find the area of a rectangle with mixed-number side lengths

Madeline made a banner to advertise the school carnival. The banner is $2\frac{1}{3}$ yards wide and $1\frac{1}{2}$ yards tall. What is the area of the banner?

Make a model or drawing of the banner. Divide it into rectangles with unit-fraction side lengths. Each unit-fraction rectangle has an area of $\frac{1}{2} \times \frac{1}{3}$ or $\frac{1}{6}$ yd^2.

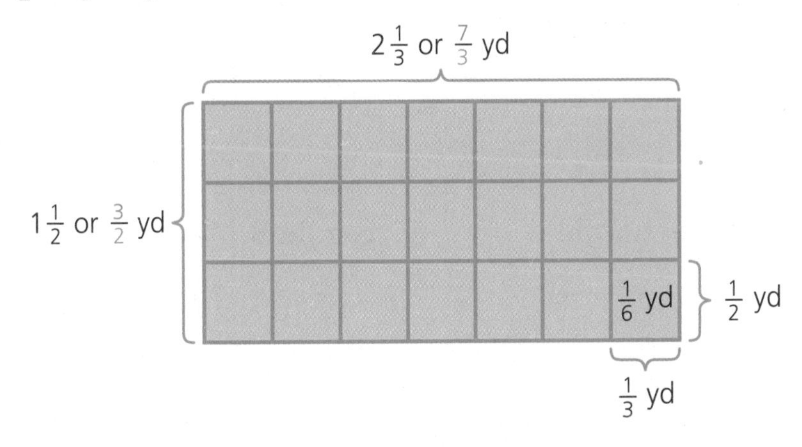

You can tile the banner with 3 × 7, or 21 unit-fraction rectangles. So the area of the banner in square yards is

$$21 \times \frac{1}{6} = \frac{21}{1} \times \frac{1}{6} = \frac{21}{6} = \frac{7}{2} = 3\frac{1}{2}.$$

Notice that you get the same result if you multiply the side lengths.

$$2\frac{1}{3} \times 1\frac{1}{2} = \frac{7}{3} \times \frac{3}{2}$$ → Rewrite the mixed numbers as fractions.

$$= \frac{7 \times 3}{3 \times 2}$$ → Multiply the fractions.

$$= \frac{21}{6} = \frac{7}{2} = 3\frac{1}{2}$$

In general, you can find the area of a rectangle with fractional or mixed number side lengths by multiplying the side lengths, just as you do for rectangles with whole number side lengths.

➡ The area of the banner is $3\frac{1}{2}$ yd^2.

Guided Instruction

Connect: How to find the area of rectangles with fractional side lengths

Rectangle A has side lengths of $\frac{3}{4}$ yard and $\frac{3}{5}$ yard. **Rectangle B** has side lengths of $\frac{2}{5}$ yard and $\frac{1}{2}$ yard. Which rectangle has the greater area?

Step 1

Write multiplication expressions to represent the areas.

Area of **Rectangle A**: $\frac{3}{4} \times \frac{3}{5}$

Area of **Rectangle B**: $\frac{2}{5} \times \frac{1}{2}$

Remember!
The area of a rectangle is *length* × *width*.

Step 2

Multiply the fractions to determine the areas.

Rectangle A	**Rectangle B**
$\frac{3}{4} \times \frac{3}{5} = \frac{9}{20}$	$\frac{2}{5} \times \frac{1}{2} = \frac{2}{10}$

Step 3

Compare the areas of **Rectangle A** and **Rectangle B**.

Rectangle A $= \frac{9}{20}$ yd^2.

Rectangle B $= \frac{2}{10}$, or $\frac{4}{20}$ yd^2.

Write an equivalent fraction for $\frac{2}{10}$ with a denominator of 20. $\frac{2}{10} = \frac{2 \times 2}{10 \times 2} = \frac{4}{20}$

$\frac{9}{20} > \frac{4}{20}$

Then compare the numerators.

Rectangle A > Rectangle B

➡ **Rectangle A** has the greater area.

Draw a model to represent a $\frac{3}{4}$ by $\frac{3}{5}$ rectangle. Then explain how your model shows that $\frac{3}{4} \times \frac{3}{5} = \frac{9}{20}$.

Guided Practice

Complete the statements.

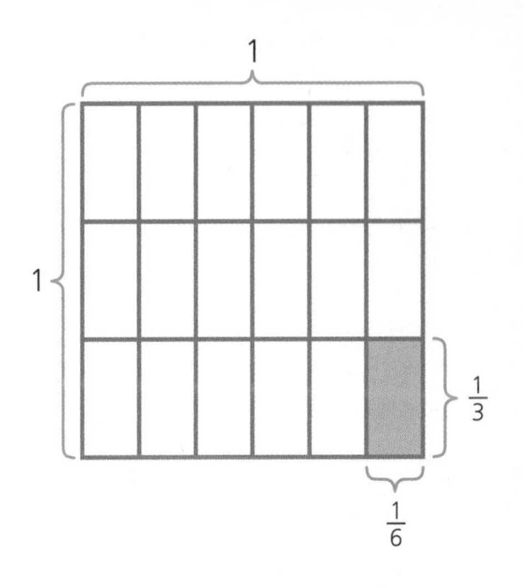

1. The unit square at the right is tiled with unit-fraction rectangles.

   The side lengths of each unit-fraction rectangle are $\frac{1}{3}$ unit and ____ unit.

   There are ____ unit-fraction rectangles in the unit square.

   Each unit-fraction rectangle has an area of ____ square unit.

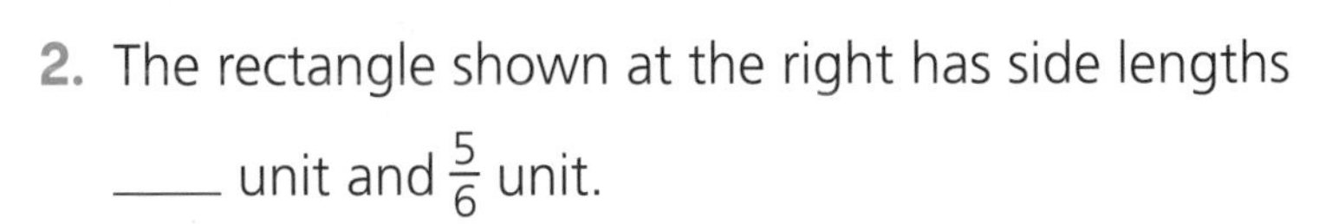

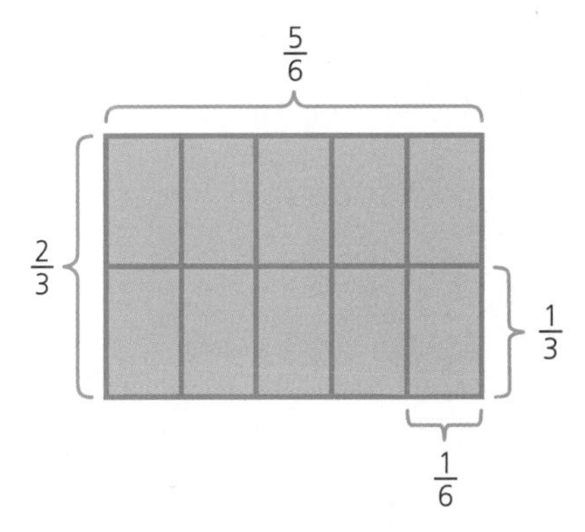

2. The rectangle shown at the right has side lengths ____ unit and $\frac{5}{6}$ unit.

   This rectangle is tiled with 2 × ____ or ____ unit-fraction rectangles.

   From exercise 1, you know that each unit-fraction rectangle, $\frac{1}{3} \times \frac{1}{6}$, has an area of ____ square unit.

   So, the area of this rectangle in square units is:

   $\_\_\_\_ \times \frac{1}{18} = \_\_\_\_.$

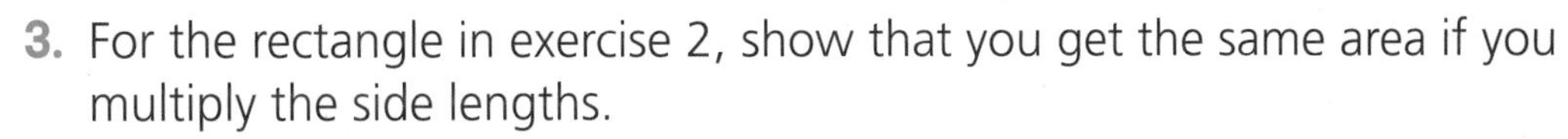

3. For the rectangle in exercise 2, show that you get the same area if you multiply the side lengths.

   $\frac{}{} \times \frac{5}{6} = \frac{\quad \times 5}{\quad \times 6} = \frac{}{}$

Think • Pair • Share

MP7 4. Explain two different ways you can find the area of a rectangle with a width of $\frac{2}{7}$ unit and a length of $\frac{3}{4}$ unit.

Independent Practice

Complete the statements.

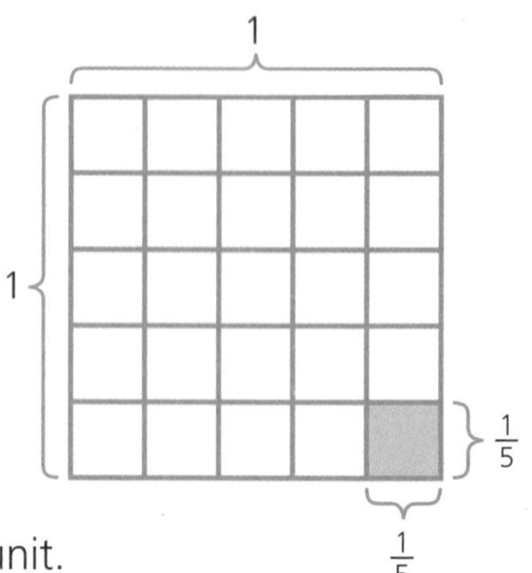

1. The unit square at the right is tiled with unit-fraction rectangles.

   The side lengths of each unit-fraction rectangle are $\frac{1}{5}$ and ____.

   There are ____ unit-fraction rectangles in the unit square.

   Each unit-fraction rectangle has an area of ____ square unit.

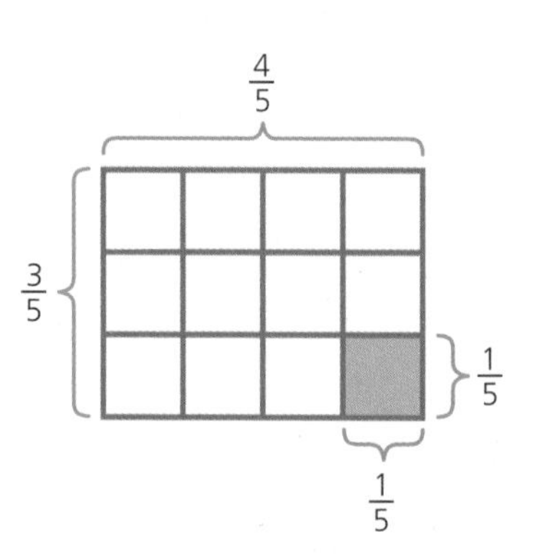

2. The rectangle shown here has side lengths ____ unit by ____ unit.

   This rectangle is tiled with ____ × ____ or ____, unit-fraction rectangles.

   From exercise 1, you know that each unit-fraction rectangle, $\frac{1}{5}$ × ____, has an area of ____ square unit.

   So, the area of this rectangle in square units is:

   ____ $\times \frac{1}{}$ = ____.

3. For the rectangle in exercise 2, show that you get the same area if you multiply the side lengths.

   $\frac{}{5} \times \frac{}{5} = \frac{ \times }{ \times } = \frac{}{}$

MP2 4. A rectangle has an area of $\frac{5}{18}$ square meter and a length of $\frac{5}{6}$ meter. What is its width? Explain your answer.

Independent Practice

Find the area of each figure. Show your work.

5. 

$\frac{5}{12}$ km

$\frac{5}{12}$ km

Area: ____________________

6.

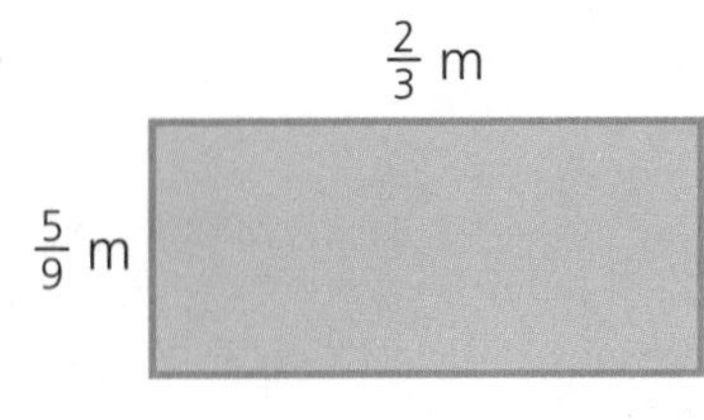

Area: ____________________

7. A square with side lengths of $\frac{7}{9}$ inches.

Area: ____________________

8. A rectangle with a width of $\frac{1}{2}$ cm and length of 10 cm.

Area: ____________________

9. A rectangle with a length of $\frac{1}{5}$ yd and width of $\frac{2}{3}$ yd.

Area: ____________________

10. A rectangle with a length of $\frac{2}{3}$ ft and width of $\frac{1}{2}$ ft.

Area: ____________________

For exercises 11–12, choose the correct answer.

11. A private beach is $\frac{6}{7}$ mile in length and $\frac{1}{4}$ mile in width. What is the area of the beach?

a. $\frac{3}{14}$ mi^2

b. $\frac{7}{11}$ mi^2

c. $\frac{1}{28}$ mi^2

d. $\frac{28}{6}$ mi^2

Independent Practice

12. What is the area of a rectangle with a width of $\frac{1}{3}$ yd and a length of $\frac{9}{10}$ yd?

   a. $\frac{9}{30}$ yd^2 b. $\frac{30}{9}$ yd^2

   c. $\frac{10}{13}$ yd^2 d. $\frac{27}{10}$ yd^2

MP3 13. If both sides of a rectangle are less than 1 unit long, will the area of that rectangle be less than or greater than 1 square unit? Explain your reasoning.

MP7 14. Without calculating the answer, explain how to find the area of the figure below.

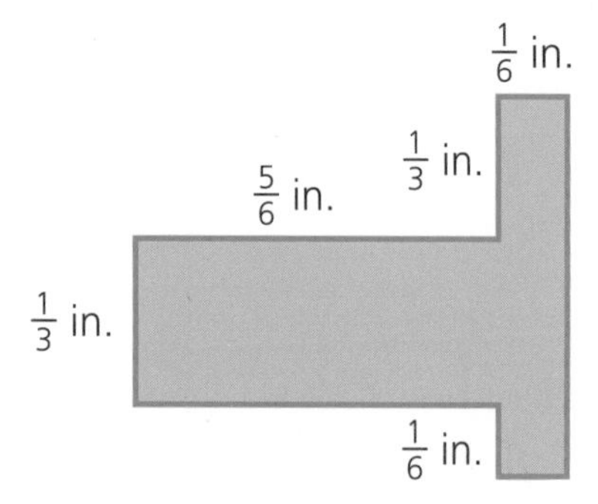

Solve the problems.

MP1 15. Ben has an herb garden in his backyard. The garden is a square. Each side measures $\frac{5}{6}$ foot. What is the area of Ben's herb garden?

Show your work.

Answer ______________________________

Independent Practice

MP1 **16.** The ancient Egyptians used the expression $\frac{1}{4} \times (a + c) \times (b + d)$ to find the area of four-sided figures. With a rectangle, a and c are the width and b and d are the length. Find the area of the rectangle shown below using the expression $\frac{1}{4} \times (a + c) \times (b + d)$. Also, find the area of the rectangle by multiplying the length by the width. Compare your answers.

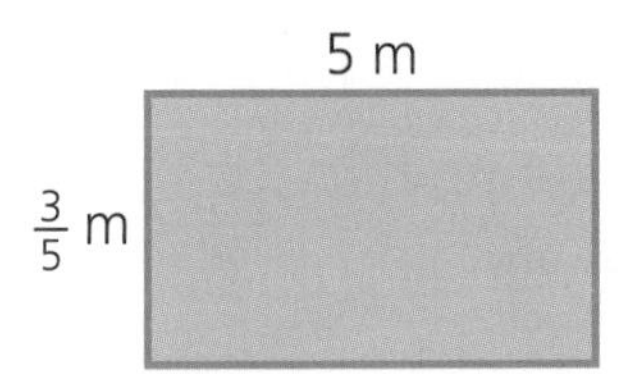

Show your work.

Answer ______________________________

MP1 **17.** Find the area of the shaded region below.

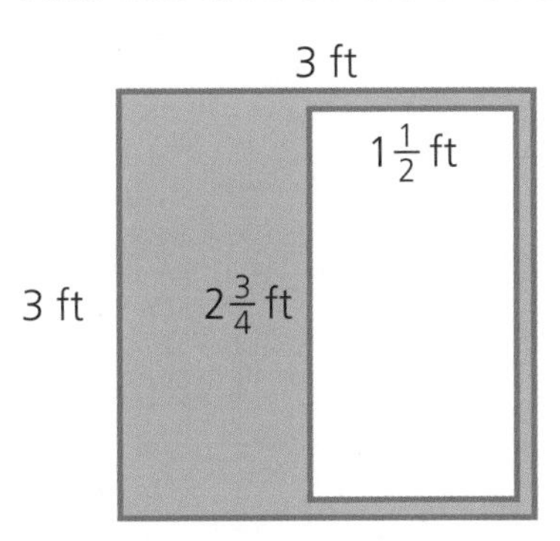

Show your work.

Answer ______________________________

Lesson
20 Interpret Multiplication of Fractions as Scaling

Essential Question:
When you multiply a number by a fraction, how does the product compare to the number?

5.NF.5a, 5.NF.5b

Words to Know:
scaling

Guided Instruction

In this lesson you will understand how multiplying by fractions less than or greater than 1 affects the size of products.

Understand: Comparing factors and products

Eli has 12 baseball cards. Marcos has $\frac{5}{4}$ as many cards as Eli. Lynne has $\frac{3}{4}$ as many cards as Eli. Without any computation, determine who has fewer cards than Eli and who has more cards than Eli.

To find who has fewer and more cards than Eli, you can use a model to visualize the numbers of baseball cards and make comparisons.

Eli has 12 baseball cards. Marcos has $\frac{5}{4}$ as many cards as Eli. Write an expression to show how many cards Marcos has. Notice the factor $\frac{5}{4}$ is $1\frac{1}{4}$, which is *greater than* 1 whole.

Expression: $\frac{5}{4} \times 12$

Eli has 12 baseball cards. Lynne has $\frac{3}{4}$ as many cards as Eli. Write an expression to show how many cards Lynne has. Notice the factor $\frac{3}{4}$ is *less than* 1 whole.

Expression: $\frac{3}{4} \times 12$

Draw a 3 by 4 model to represent Eli's 12 baseball cards.

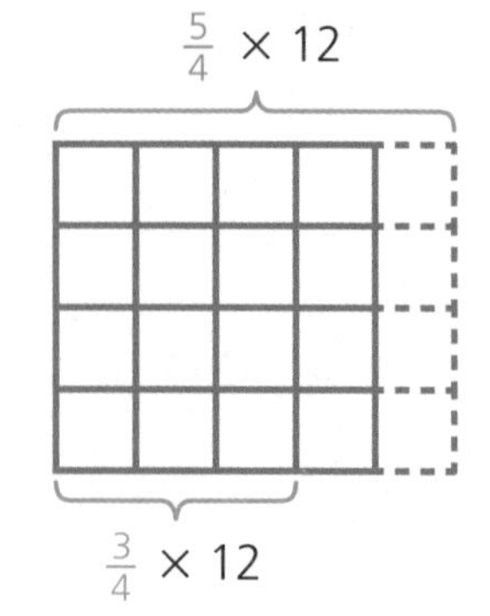

Marcos has $\frac{5}{4} \times 12$ cards. You can see from the model that the product of $\frac{5}{4} \times 12$ is *greater than* 12.

Lynne has $\frac{3}{4} \times 12$ cards. You can see from the model that product of $\frac{3}{4} \times 12$ is *less than* 12.

➡ Lynne has fewer cards than Eli. Marcos has more cards than Eli.

Guided Instruction

Connect: Multiplying fractions as scaling

When you multiply a number by a fraction, you are scaling, or resizing, that number. The size of the fraction determines whether the product will be less than, greater than, or equal to the original number.

- When you multiply a number by a fraction *less than* 1, the product is *less than* that number.
- When you multiply a number by a fraction *greater than* 1, the product is *greater than* that number.
- When you multiply a number by a fraction *equivalent* to 1, the product is *equal* to that number.

Remember!
The Identity Property of Multiplication: for any number a, $1 \times a = a \times 1 = a$.

Omar walks $\frac{3}{5}$ mile. Nate walks $\frac{4}{5}$ as far as Omar. Chris walks $\frac{4}{3}$ as far as Omar. Jen walks $\frac{4}{4}$ as far as Omar. Who walks a greater number of miles than Omar? Who walks fewer miles than Omar? Who walks the same number of miles as Omar? Find these answers without computing.

Write an expression to show how far Nate walks.
You are multiplying $\frac{3}{5}$ by a fraction that is *less than* 1.
The product will be *less than* $\frac{3}{5}$.

$\frac{4}{5} \times \frac{3}{5}$ | $\frac{4}{5} < 1$

$\frac{4}{5} \times \frac{3}{5} < \frac{3}{5}$

Write an expression to show how far Chris walks.
You are multiplying $\frac{3}{5}$ by a fraction that is *greater than* 1.
The product will be *greater than* $\frac{3}{5}$.

$\frac{4}{3} \times \frac{3}{5}$ | $\frac{4}{3} > 1$

$\frac{4}{3} \times \frac{3}{5} > \frac{3}{5}$

Write an expression to show how far Jen walks.
You are multiplying $\frac{3}{5}$ by 1.
The product will be *equal to* $\frac{3}{5}$.

$\frac{4}{4} \times \frac{3}{5}$ | $\frac{4}{4} = 1$

$\frac{4}{4} \times \frac{3}{5} = \frac{3}{5}$

➡ Chris walks a greater number of miles than Omar. Nate walks fewer miles than Omar. And Jen walks the same number of miles as Omar.

Without any computation, explain why 2×3 is greater than 3, and $\frac{1}{2} \times 3$ is less than 3.

Guided Practice

For exercises 1–4, use the models to determine whether the product is *less than*, *greater than*, or *equal to* the second factor.

1. $\frac{3}{5} \times 10$

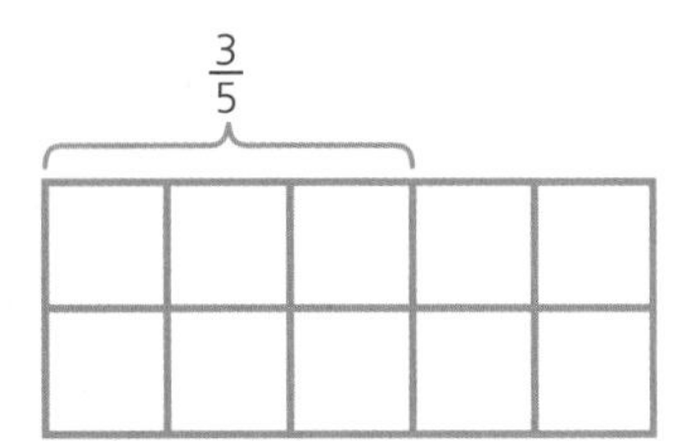

The product is ________ 10.

2. $\frac{7}{4} \times 16$

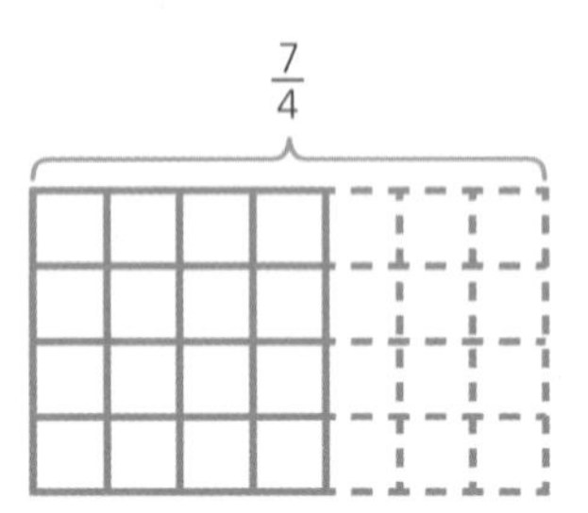

The product is ________ 16.

3. $\frac{6}{6} \times \frac{2}{3}$

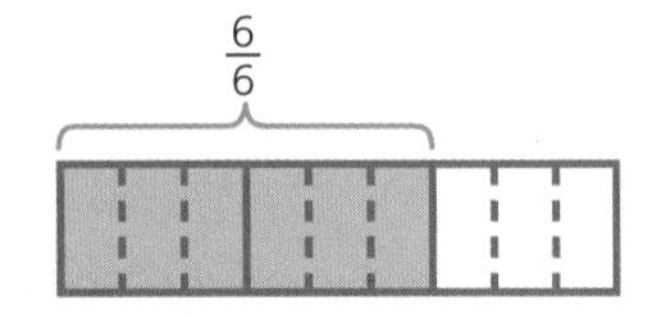

The product is ________ $\frac{2}{3}$.

4. $\frac{3}{2} \times \frac{3}{4}$

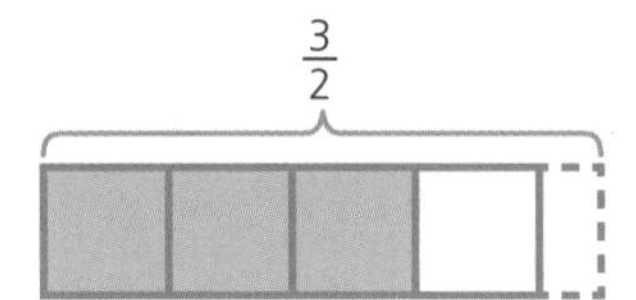

The product is ________ $\frac{3}{4}$.

For exercises 5–8, complete the statements to determine whether each product is *less than*, *greater than*, or *equal to* the second factor.

5. $\frac{6}{7} \times 64$

$\frac{6}{7}$ is ________ 1.

So, the product is

________ 64.

6. $\frac{7}{5} \times \frac{4}{13}$

$\frac{7}{5}$ is ________ 1.

So, the product is ________ $\frac{4}{13}$.

7. $\frac{12}{12} \times \frac{8}{11}$

$\frac{12}{12}$ is ________ 1.

So, the product is

________ $\frac{8}{11}$.

8. $\frac{9}{15} \times 112$

$\frac{9}{15}$ is ________ 1.

So, the product is ________ 112.

Guided Practice

Tell whether the product of each expression is *less than*, *greater than*, or *equal to* the second factor.

9. $\frac{1}{4} \times 109$ __________

10. $\frac{5}{3} \times \frac{2}{7}$ __________

11. $\frac{9}{9} \times 312$ __________

12. $\frac{3}{4} \times \frac{5}{9}$ __________

Complete each comparison with >, <, or =.

13. $\frac{1}{2} \times 87$ ____ 87

14. $\frac{5}{5} \times \frac{4}{20}$ ____ $\frac{4}{20}$

15. $\frac{11}{12} \times \frac{8}{11}$ ____ $\frac{8}{11}$

16. $\frac{8}{7} \times \frac{10}{13}$ ____ $\frac{10}{13}$

17. $\frac{2}{2} \times 55$ ____ 55

18. $\frac{9}{13} \times \frac{13}{9}$ ____ $\frac{13}{9}$

MP6 **19.** Complete the table below. Then ask a classmate to draw a model for each of your examples and verify your responses.

If a number is multiplied by . . .	then the product is . . .	Example:
a fraction less than 1,		
a fraction greater than 1,		
a fraction equal to 1,		

Independent Practice

For exercises 1–2, use the models to determine whether each product is *less than, greater than,* or *equal to* the second factor.

1. $\frac{7}{6} \times \frac{2}{3}$

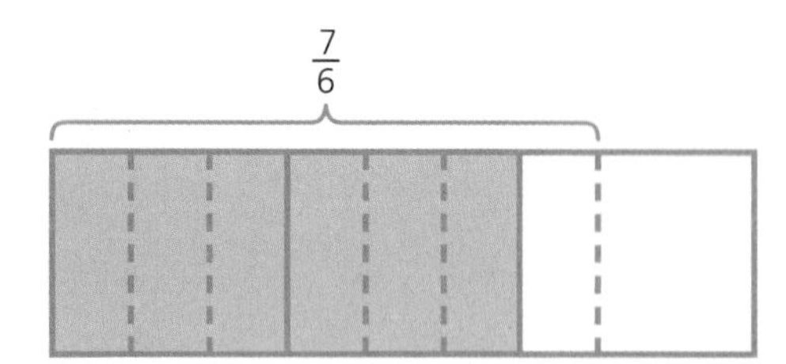

The product is ________ $\frac{2}{3}$.

2. $\frac{1}{2} \times 8$

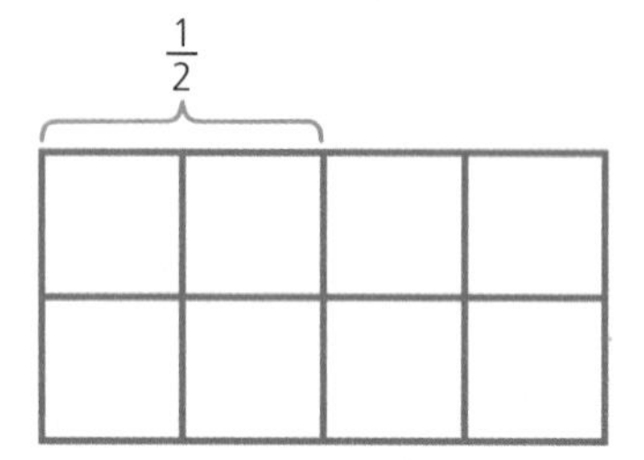

The product is ________ 8.

For exercises 3–6, write *less than, greater than,* or *equal to*.

3. $\frac{9}{5} \times 41$

$\frac{9}{5}$ is ________ 1.

So, the product is ________ 41.

4. $\frac{5}{7} \times \frac{3}{8}$

$\frac{5}{7}$ is ________ 1.

So, the product is ________ $\frac{3}{8}$.

5. $\frac{7}{17} \times \frac{6}{7}$

$\frac{7}{17}$ is ________ 1.

So, the product is ________ $\frac{6}{7}$.

6. $\frac{7}{7} \times \frac{4}{5}$

$\frac{7}{7}$ is ________ 1.

So, the product is ________ $\frac{4}{5}$.

For exercises 7–8, choose the correct answer.

7. Which of the following is true?

a. $\frac{1}{7} \times 24 > 24$

b. $\frac{5}{4} \times \frac{4}{5} > \frac{4}{5}$

c. $\frac{4}{4} \times \frac{3}{8} < \frac{3}{8}$

d. $\frac{3}{4} \times \frac{1}{2} > \frac{1}{2}$

Independent Practice

8. Franklin reads 6 pages in his textbook. Ann reads $\frac{1}{2}$ as many pages as Franklin. Billy reads $\frac{5}{3}$ as many pages as Franklin. Danny reads $\frac{4}{4}$ as many pages as Franklin. Which statement is correct?

   a. Ann reads fewer pages than Franklin.

   b. Danny reads more pages than Franklin.

   c. Billy reads the same number of pages as Franklin.

   d. Franklin reads the greatest number of pages.

Tell whether each product is *less than*, *greater than*, or *equal to* the second factor.

9. $\frac{8}{9} \times 212$ ____________

10. $\frac{5}{5} \times \frac{7}{5}$ ____________

Complete each comparison with >, <, or =.

11. $\frac{4}{7} \times \frac{19}{4}$ ____ $\frac{19}{4}$

12. $\frac{3}{11} \times 33$ ____ 33

13. $\frac{9}{9} \times \frac{5}{12}$ ____ $\frac{5}{12}$

14. $\frac{7}{8} \times \frac{2}{3}$ ____ $\frac{2}{3}$

15. $\frac{4}{3} \times 450$ ____ 450

16. $\frac{8}{8} \times \frac{13}{9}$ ____ $\frac{13}{9}$

Write a fraction that makes each comparison true.

17. ____ $\times 506 < 506$

18. ____ $\times \frac{5}{19} = \frac{5}{19}$

19. ____ $\times \frac{12}{13} > \frac{12}{13}$

20. ____ $\times \frac{6}{5} < \frac{6}{5}$

Independent Practice

Answer each question without multiplying.

MP3 **21.** Ari says that the product of $\frac{1}{18} \times 18$ is equal to 18. Is he correct? Explain your answer.

MP3 **22.** Marcy did this problem for her homework.

$\frac{1}{2} \times 6 = 3$

Her brother says that she is wrong because when you multiply, the product is always greater than either factor. In your own words, explain to Marcy's brother why her answer is correct.

MP2 **23.** A chef is making dinner for 12 people. She plans to use $\frac{1}{4}$ pound of turkey for each person. Will she need more than or less than 12 pounds of turkey? Explain your reasoning.

MP2 **24.** Mr. Amon's classroom has 30 desks. Ms. Wu's classroom has $\frac{4}{3}$ as many desks as Mr. Amon's classroom. Are there more than 30 desks, fewer than 30 desks, or exactly 30 desks in Ms. Wu's classroom? Explain your reasoning.

MP2 **25.** Grace is making soup for friends. The recipe calls for 5 cups of broth for 6 servings. Grace wants to make $\frac{1}{4}$ the number of servings. Does she need to use the amount of broth the recipe calls for, use less broth, or use more broth? Explain your reasoning.

Independent Practice

Solve the problems.

MP7 **26.** Kayla ran $\frac{9}{10}$ mile yesterday. Today, she ran $\frac{8}{9}$ the distance she ran yesterday. On which day did Kayla run more miles? Explain your reasoning.

MP4 **27.** Marta has $\frac{2}{3}$ yard of ribbon. Julian has a ribbon that is $\frac{1}{2}$ as long as Marta's ribbon. Is Julian's ribbon longer or shorter than $\frac{2}{3}$ yard?

Answer ______________________________

Justify your answer with a model, drawings, or numbers.

MP1 **28.** Matt is 60 inches tall. Jeff is $\frac{13}{12}$ as tall as Matt. Which statement is true?

a. Matt and Jeff are the same height.

b. Matt is taller than Jeff.

c. Jeff is taller than Matt.

Answer ______________________________

Justify your answer with a model, drawings, or numbers.

Lesson 21

Problem Solving: Multiply Fractions and Mixed Numbers

Essential Question:
How can you use the multiplication of fractions, mixed numbers, and whole numbers to solve real world problems?

5.NF.6

Guided Instruction

In this lesson you will solve word problems using the multiplication of fractions, mixed numbers, and whole numbers.

Understand: How to use a drawing to multiply a whole number by a fraction

On a typical day, Stan's Restaurant sells 9 homemade pies. If $\frac{1}{3}$ of the homemade pies sold are apple, how many apple pies are sold each day? How many are not apple?

To find how many homemade pies are apple, find $\frac{1}{3}$ of 9, or $\frac{1}{3} \times 9$. Use a drawing to represent the situation.

Draw 9 pies. Separate the 9 pies into thirds. $\frac{1}{3}$ are apple pies. The rest are *not* apple pies.

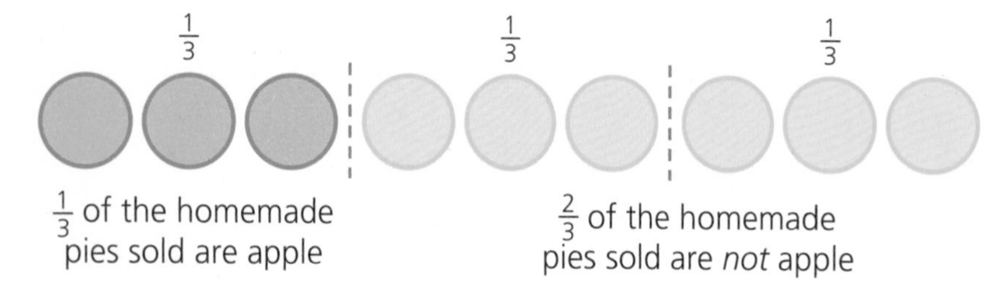

The drawing shows that 3 pies are apple and 6 pies are *not* apple.

You can also find the answers by multiplying.

$\frac{1}{3} \times 9 = \frac{9}{3} = 3$. Three homemade pies are apple.

To find how many homemade pies are *not* apple, multiply 9 by $\frac{2}{3}$.

$\frac{2}{3} \times 9 = \frac{18}{3} = 6$. Six homemade pies are *not* apple.

▶ On a typical day, Stan's Restaurant sells 3 apple pies and 6 pies that are not apple.

Use a drawing to represent and evaluate $\frac{3}{4} \times 8$.

Guided Instruction

Understand: How to find the area of a rectangle with mixed-number side lengths.

Ted is making a wall tapestry that is $3\frac{1}{2}$ feet by $4\frac{2}{5}$ feet. What is the area of the tapestry?

Method 1

Make a drawing and use logical reasoning.

The width is $3\frac{1}{2}$ feet, and the length is $4\frac{2}{5}$ feet.

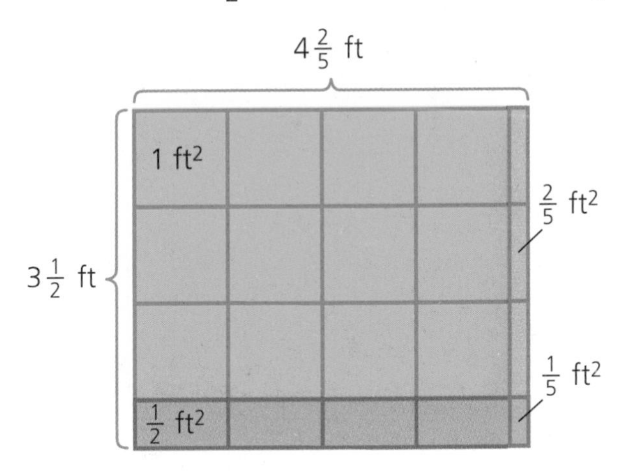

There are 12 squares that each represent 1 square foot.

There are 3 rectangles that each represent $\frac{2}{5}$ square foot.

There are 4 rectangles that each represent $1 \times \frac{1}{2}$, or $\frac{1}{2}$ square foot.

There is one rectangle that represents $\frac{2}{5} \times \frac{1}{2}$, or $\frac{1}{5}$ square foot.

$12 \text{ ft}^2 + \frac{6}{5} \text{ ft}^2 + \frac{4}{2} \text{ ft}^2 + \frac{1}{5} \text{ ft}^2 = 15\frac{2}{5} \text{ ft.}^2$

Method 2

Use the area formula for a rectangle to write an equation. Then, solve the equation.

$A = \ell \times w$	The area formula.
$A = 4\frac{2}{5} \times 3\frac{1}{2}$	Substitute the length and width values.
$A = \frac{22}{5} \times \frac{7}{2}$	Rewrite the mixed numbers as fractions.
$A = \frac{154}{10}$	Multiply.
$A = 15\frac{4}{10} = 15\frac{2}{5}$	Write the answer as a mixed number.

The area of the wall tapestry is $15\frac{2}{5}$ square feet.

Guided Instruction

Connect: What you know about multiplication with fractions, mixed numbers, and whole numbers to solve problems

In Doug's backyard, an oak tree is $\frac{3}{4}$ as tall as a maple tree. A pine tree is $1\frac{4}{5}$ times as tall as the oak tree. The maple tree is 30 feet tall. What is the height of the pine tree?

Step 1

Identify the key information: The maple tree is 30 feet tall.
The oak tree is $\frac{3}{4}$ as tall as the maple tree.
The pine tree is $1\frac{4}{5}$ times as tall as the oak tree.

Step 2

Write an equation for the situation. Use p to represent the height of the pine tree.

height of maple tree

$$p = 1\frac{4}{5} \times \underbrace{\frac{3}{4} \times 30}_{\text{height of oak tree}}$$

Step 3

Solve the equation.

$p = 1\frac{4}{5} \times \frac{3}{4} \times 30$

$p = \frac{9}{5} \times \frac{3}{4} \times \frac{30}{1}$ Write the mixed and whole numbers as fractions.

$p = \frac{9 \times 3 \times 30}{5 \times 4 \times 1}$ Multiply numerators and multiply denominators

$p = \frac{810}{20} = 40\frac{10}{20} = 40\frac{1}{2}$ Simplify.

Step 4

Estimate to check the reasonableness of your answer.

$\frac{3}{4}$ of 30 is a little more than $\frac{3}{4}$ of 28 which is 21.

$1\frac{4}{5}$ is close to 2, and $2 \times 21 = 42$

42 is close to $40\frac{1}{2}$, so $40\frac{1}{2}$ is a reasonable answer.

➡ The height of the pine tree is $40\frac{1}{2}$ feet.

Guided Practice

Use the given drawing or model to solve each problem.

1. Christine is paid \$12 an hour to stock shelves at a grocery store. Jon gets paid $\frac{5}{6}$ as much as Christine to bag groceries. How much does Jon get paid per hour?

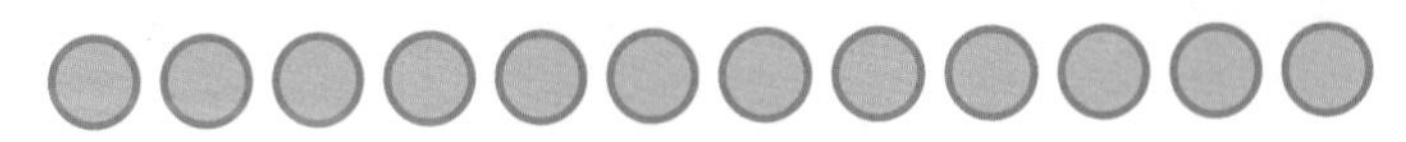

2. Ross's gray pet mouse is $5\frac{5}{8}$ inches long. His white mouse is $1\frac{1}{2}$ times as long as his gray mouse. How long is the white mouse?

$5\frac{5}{8}$ in.

$1\frac{1}{2}$ in.

Solve. Show your work.

3. $8 \times \frac{5}{6} \times 1\frac{3}{5} =$ ______________

4. A produce company is filling an order of vegetables for a local restaurant. The restaurant ordered $3\frac{3}{4}$ small crates of onions. Each crate of onions weighs $4\frac{1}{2}$ pounds.

   a. Write an expression to represent the total weight of the restaurant's order.

   b. How many pounds of onions did the restaurant order?

   c. If each pound of vegetables costs \$2, how much did the restaurant spend? Write your answer as a mixed number and a decimal.

Think•Pair•Share

MP1 5. Write a story problem that represents the expression $\frac{5}{6} \times 7$.

Independent Practice

Use the given model to solve each problem.

1. The original price of a comic book is $10, but it is on sale for $\frac{2}{5}$ off the original price. What is the sale price of the comic book?

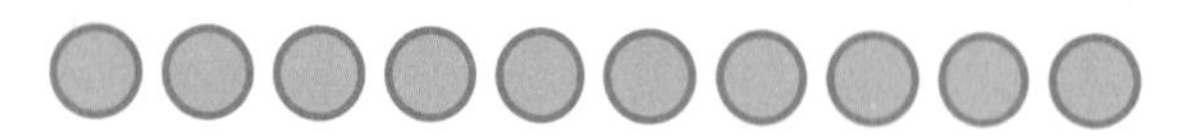

2. A photograph is $3\frac{1}{2}$ inches by $4\frac{1}{2}$ inches. Find the area of the photograph.

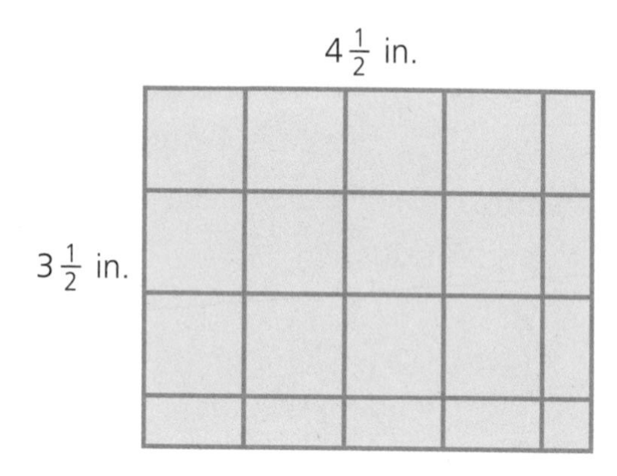

Make a model to represent each problem and solve.

3. A basket contains 16 pieces of fruit. $\frac{1}{4}$ are bananas, $\frac{1}{2}$ are apples, and the rest are oranges. How many oranges are there?

4. Cheng made a batch of her famous seafood gumbo. She made $5\frac{1}{2}$ servings of $1\frac{2}{3}$ cups. How many cups of gumbo did Cheng make?

Independent Practice

Evaluate each expression. Show your work.

5. $8\frac{1}{2} \times 1\frac{1}{2}$

______

6. $\frac{2}{9} \times 2 \times 3\frac{7}{12}$

______

7. $\frac{8}{11} \times \frac{9}{12} \times 6$

______

8. $2\frac{2}{3}\left(\frac{9}{10} + \frac{4}{5}\right)$

______

Solve the problems.

MP1 **9.** Louis has 20 rocks in his rock collection. $\frac{3}{10}$ of the rocks are sedimentary, and $\frac{2}{5}$ of the rocks are metamorphic. The rest of the rocks are igneous. How many igneous rocks does Louis have in his collection?

Show your work.

Answer ______

MP1 **10.** Every weekday, Nelly runs $3\frac{1}{2}$ laps around her school track, which is $\frac{3}{5}$ of a mile long. How far does she run in a week?

Show your work.

Answer ______

Independent Practice

MP3 **11.** Walter says that $2\frac{2}{3} \times 5\frac{1}{7}$ is equivalent to $2 \times 5 + \frac{2}{3} \times \frac{1}{7}$. Explain why Walter is not correct.

MP2 **12.** A 1 dollar bill is about $6\frac{1}{10}$ inches in length and $2\frac{3}{5}$ inches in width. If you place two 1 dollar bills side by side, what is the area of the rectangle formed by the bills?

Show your work.

Answer ______________________________

MP2 **13.** Jerry is shipping his bike, which weighs $34\frac{4}{5}$ pounds.

a. To calculate the shipping charge in dollars, Shipping Company A will multiply the weight of his bike times $2\frac{1}{5}$. How much will Shipping Company A charge Jerry? Show your work.

b. Shipping Company B will multiply the weight of the bike by 3 and then subtract $15. How much will Shipping Company B charge Jerry? Show your work.

c. Which company will charge Jerry less?

Independent Practice

MP3 **14.** Samuel says that $7 \times (\frac{1}{2} \times 2\frac{3}{4})$ is equivalent to $(7 \times \frac{1}{2}) \times 2\frac{3}{4}$. Do you agree with Samuel?

Show your work.

Answer ______________________________

MP2 **15.** The area model below represents 1×1. Use the model to explain why the product of two mixed numbers will always be greater than one.

Answer ______________________________

MP3 **16.** Lucia and Julia evaluated the expression $2\frac{2}{3} \times 1\frac{4}{5}$ two different ways. Lucia wanted to multiply using decimals, so she evaluated 2.67×1.8. Julia wanted to multiply using equivalent fractions, so she evaluated $\frac{8}{3} \times \frac{9}{5}$. If both girls multiplied correctly, whose answer is accurate? Explain your answer.

Show your work.

Answer ______________________________

Lesson

22 Divide Unit Fractions by Whole Numbers

Essential Question:
How can you divide a unit fraction by a whole number?

5.NF.7a

Guided Instruction

In this lesson you will divide unit fractions by whole numbers.

Understand: How to use a model to divide a unit fraction by a whole number

Jake is planting a vegetable garden. He plans to divide the garden into four equal sections and use $\frac{1}{4}$ for peppers. He will use the other three sections for zucchini, lettuce, and kale. Jake divides the area for peppers into 3 equal parts to plant bell peppers, jalapeño peppers, and pimento peppers. What fraction of the entire garden will be used to plant bell peppers?

To find what fraction of the entire garden will be used to plant bell peppers, divide $\frac{1}{4}$, the fraction of the garden used to plant peppers, by the 3 types of peppers: $\frac{1}{4} \div 3$.

Remember!
A unit fraction has 1 in the numerator. Some examples are $\frac{1}{4}$, $\frac{1}{10}$, and $\frac{1}{16}$.

Use a model or drawing to represent the problem. First, draw the four equal sections of the garden.

peppers	zucchini	lettuce	kale
$\frac{1}{4}$	$\frac{1}{4}$	$\frac{1}{4}$	$\frac{1}{4}$

Divide each of the 4 sections into 3 equal parts. Shade the part of the garden used to plant bell peppers.

peppers	zucchini	lettuce	kale
$\frac{1}{12}$ bell			
jalapeño			
pimento			

One part is shaded, and there are 12 parts in all. So, $\frac{1}{4} \div 3 = \frac{1}{12}$.

➡ $\frac{1}{12}$ of the garden will be used to plant bell peppers.

Guided Instruction

Understand: How to use a number line or fraction strips to divide a unit fraction by a whole number

Max had a strip of wood that was $\frac{1}{2}$ yard long. He cut the strip into 4 pieces of equal length to use as the sides of a picture frame. How long was each of the four pieces?

To find the length of each piece, divide $\frac{1}{2}$ yard into 4 equal parts: $\frac{1}{2} \div 4$.
You can solve this using a number line or fraction strips.

Method 1 Use a number line.

Draw a number line divided into intervals of $\frac{1}{2}$ yard.
Divide each $\frac{1}{2}$-yard interval into four equal intervals.
Each smaller interval is $\frac{1}{8}$ yard.

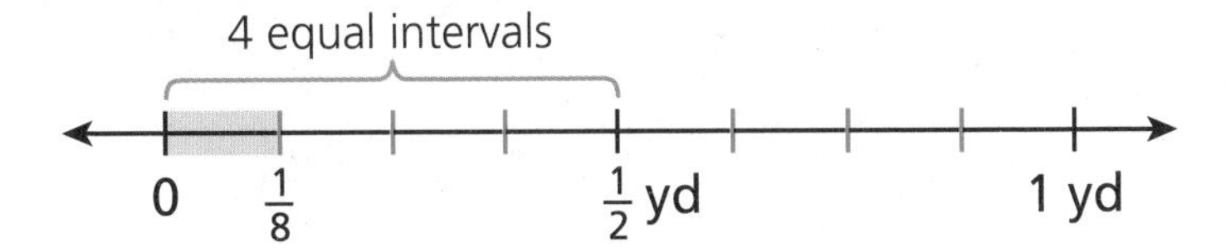

Method 2 Use fraction strips.

Use two $\frac{1}{2}$ strips to represent 1 yard.
Find the fraction strips that can be used to evenly divide $\frac{1}{2}$ into 4 equal parts.
Four $\frac{1}{8}$ strips will divide $\frac{1}{2}$ into 4 equal parts.

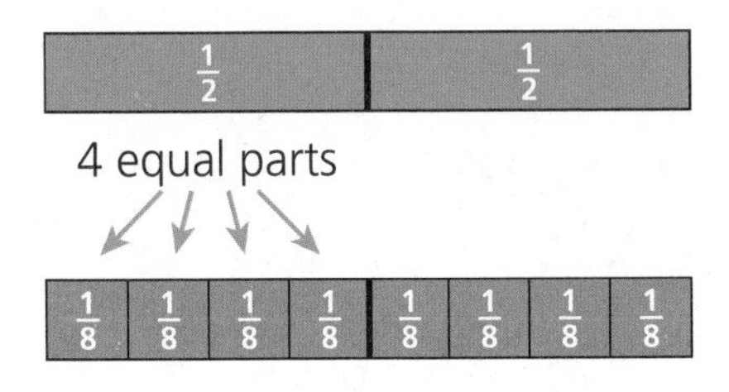

Each piece will be $\frac{1}{8}$ yard long.

Ryan said, "To divide a unit fraction by a whole number, you just multiply the denominator by the whole number." Show that Ryan's conclusion works for the two problems you have seen in this lesson.

Guided Instruction

Connect: Dividing a unit fraction by a whole number by relating division to multiplication

The May family plans to use $\frac{1}{5}$ of their monthly budget for recreation. Mrs. May further divides the recreation funds into 3 parts that are equal in dollars. One part is going to be used for family day trips. What fraction of the family's budget is going toward day trips?

To find what fraction of the family's budget is going toward day trips, divide the $\frac{1}{5}$ family recreation budget by 3. To solve, use what you know about the relationship between multiplication and division.

Step 1

Write a division expression to represent the problem. Mrs. May divides $\frac{1}{5}$ of the family's monthly recreation funds by 3.

$\frac{1}{5} \div 3$

Remember! Dividing a number by 3 means finding $\frac{1}{3}$ of the number. So, it is the same as multiplying the number by $\frac{1}{3}$.

Step 2

Rewrite the division expression as a multiplication expression.

$\frac{1}{5} \div 3 = \frac{1}{3} \times \frac{1}{5}$

Step 3

Multiply the fractions.

$\frac{1}{3} \times \frac{1}{5} = \frac{1}{15}$

➡ The May family will spend $\frac{1}{15}$ of their entire recreation budget on day trips.

How can you check the answer to this problem?

Guided Practice

1. Use the model and steps a–c below to find the quotient of $\frac{1}{5} \div 3$.

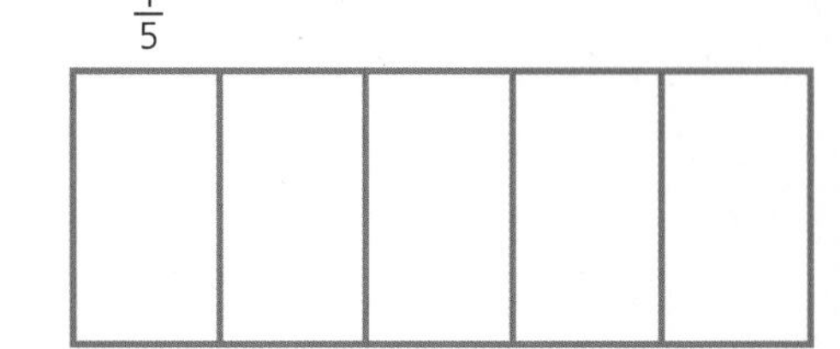

   a. The rectangle is divided in ____ equal parts.

      Each part is ____ of the whole.

   b. Draw ________ horizontal lines to divide the rectangle in 3 equal parts. Shade $\frac{1}{15}$.

   c. What is $\frac{1}{5}$ divided by 3? ____

2. Use the number line and steps a–c below to find the quotient of $\frac{1}{4} \div 2$.

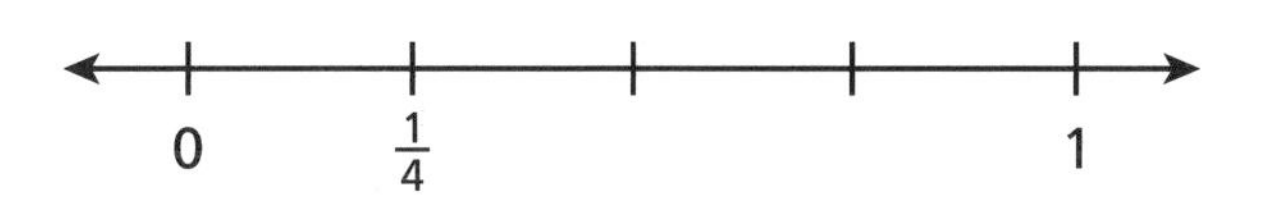

   a. To start, the number line is divided into intervals of ____.

   b. Divide each $\frac{1}{4}$ into ____ equal intervals.

      Each smaller interval represents ____.

   c. What is $\frac{1}{4}$ divided by 2? ____

For exercises 3–4, use the fraction strips.

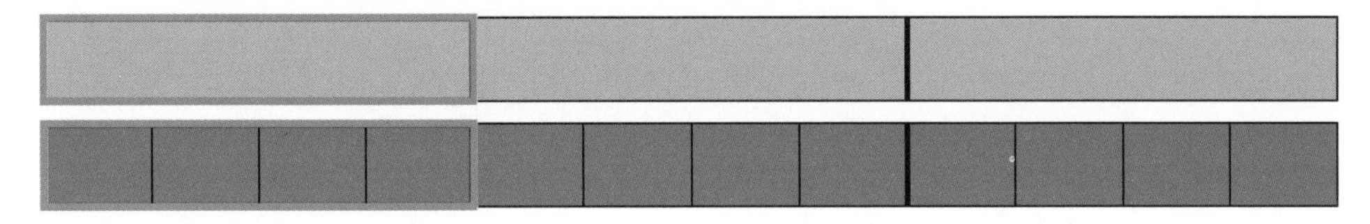

3. Look at the top fraction strip. What fraction of the whole strip does the green rectangle show? ____

4. Look at the bottom fraction strip. Into how many equal parts is the green rectangle partitioned? ____ What fraction of the whole fraction strip does one of these parts show? ____

Think•Pair•Share

MP4 5. What division equation does the model used for exercises 3 and 4 represent? Explain how the model shows the quotient.

Independent Practice

For exercises 1–2, use the models to answer the questions below.

1. $\frac{1}{4}$

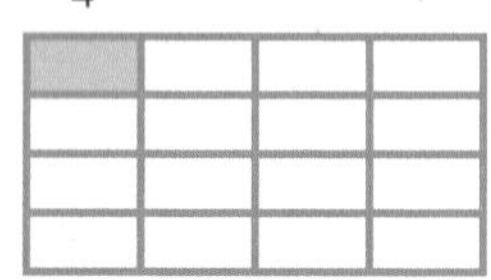

a. The vertical lines divide the rectangle into ________. Each column is what fraction of the whole rectangle? ____

b. The horizontal lines divide the rectangle into how many equal parts? ____

c. $\frac{1}{4} \div 4 =$ ____

2. $\frac{1}{6}$

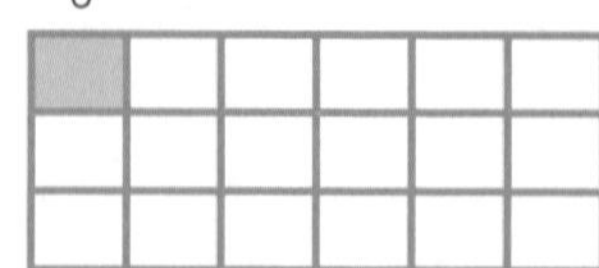

a. The vertical lines divide the rectangle into ________. Each column is what fraction of the whole rectangle? ____

b. The horizontal lines divide the rectangle into how many equal parts? ____

c. $\frac{1}{6} \div 3 =$ ____

For exercises 3–5, use the number lines below.

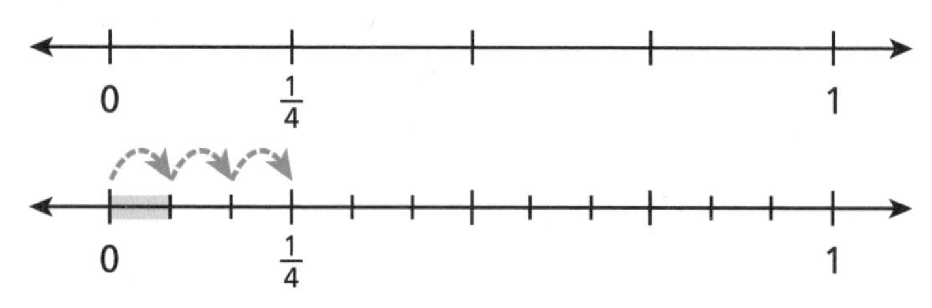

3. The top number line is divided into ____ equal parts. What fraction of the number line is one of these parts? ____

4. The bottom number line shows $\frac{1}{4}$ divided into ____ equal parts. What fraction of the number line is one of these parts? ____

5. Write the division equation represented by the bottom number line. ______________

6. Draw a number line model to show $\frac{1}{8}$ divided by 2.

Independent Practice

To complete exercises 7–9, use the fraction strips below.

$\frac{1}{5}$	$\frac{1}{5}$	$\frac{1}{5}$	$\frac{1}{5}$	$\frac{1}{5}$

2 equal parts

$\frac{1}{10}$									

7. The top strip is divided into ____ equal parts. What fraction of the strip is one of these parts? ____

8. The bottom strip shows $\frac{1}{5}$ being divided into ____ equal parts. What fraction of the strip is one of these parts? ____

9. Write the division equation shown by the model. ____________

10. Divide $\frac{1}{3}$ by 3. Use the fraction strips below to show the division.

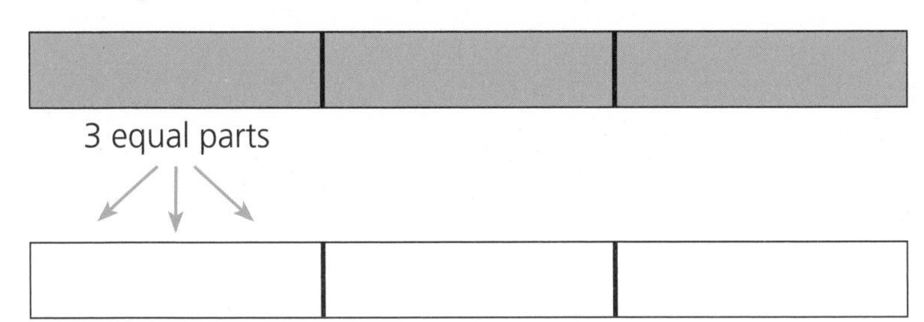

For exercises 11–14, use what you know about the relationship between multiplication and division to complete these problems.

11. $\frac{1}{12} \times 6 = \frac{1}{2}$

    So, this division equation is true:

    $\frac{1}{2} \div 6 =$ ____.

12. $\frac{1}{10} \times 2 = \frac{1}{5}$

    So, this division equation is true:

    $\frac{1}{5} \div 2 =$ ____.

13. Dividing by 4 is the same as multiplying by $\frac{1}{4}$. So, these equations show the same situation:

    $\frac{1}{5} \div 4 =$ ____ and $\frac{1}{4} \times \frac{1}{5} =$ ____.

14. Dividing by 8 is the same as multiplying by $\frac{1}{8}$. So, these equations show the same situation:

    $\frac{1}{3} \div 8 =$ ____ and $\frac{1}{8} \times \frac{1}{3} =$ ____.

Independent Practice

Choose the correct answer.

15. Sam has $\frac{1}{7}$ meter of rope. He divides it in 2 equal parts. What fraction of a meter is each part of the rope?

a. $\frac{1}{14}$ meter **b.** $\frac{1}{7}$ meter

c. $\frac{14}{7}$ meter **d.** $\frac{2}{7}$ meter

Solve the problems.

MP4 **16.** The figure is part of a number line model. Explain how the model represents a division equation.

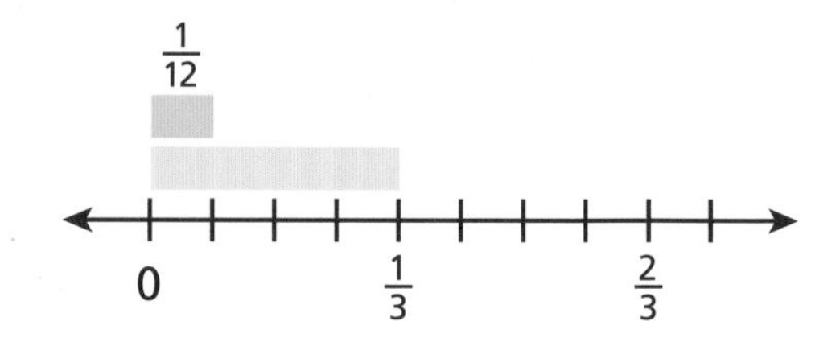

MP3 **17.** Tricia used a meter stick to help her divide $\frac{1}{4}$ by 5. Explain how she could have done this and give the answer as a fraction of a meter.

MP4 **18.** Three people have $\frac{1}{2}$ of a pizza to share equally. What fraction of a whole pizza will each person get?

Show your work. Include a model in your answer and explain the steps you use.

Answer ______________________________

Independent Practice

MP2 **19.** Vincent has $\frac{1}{3}$ pound of cherries. Create two story situations about Vincent's cherries, one that represents $\frac{1}{3} \div 4$ and another that represent $4 \times \frac{1}{3}$. Include the answers to the problems in your stories.

MP2 **20.** Use your stories from exercise 19 to compare dividing a fraction by 4 with multiplying that fraction by 4. How do the answers compare to the original fractions?

Justify your answer using words, drawings, or numbers.

MP2 **21.** Show that $\frac{1}{2} \div 5$ and $\frac{1}{5} \div 2$ result in the same quotient by renaming the fractions in both expressions as decimals.

Justify your answer using words, drawings, or numbers.

Lesson 23

Divide Whole Numbers by Unit Fractions

Essential Question:
How can you divide a whole number by a unit fraction?

5.NF.7b

Guided Instruction

In this lesson you will divide whole numbers by unit fractions.

Understand: How to use a model to show division of whole numbers by unit fractions

Katie ordered 5 pizzas. Each pizza is cut into eighths. How many pieces of pizza does Katie have?

To find how many pieces of pizza Katie has, use a model and division.

Draw 5 circles to represent the pizzas. Then divide each circle into eighths.

5 pizzas divided into eighths make 40 pieces of pizza. That is, $5 \div \frac{1}{8} = 40$.

➡ Katie has 40 pieces of pizza.

Understand: How to use a number line to divide whole numbers by unit fractions

Jessica uses $\frac{1}{4}$ yard of ribbon to trim a baby bib. How many bibs can she trim with 3 yards of ribbon?

To find how many bibs Jessica can trim, divide 3 yards by $\frac{1}{4}$ yard. That is, find $3 \div \frac{1}{4}$.

Draw a number line from 0–3 to show 3 yards of ribbon.
Divide each yard into fourths.

There are 4 fourths in each yard, so there are 12 fourths in 3 yards. That is, $3 \div \frac{1}{4} = 12$.

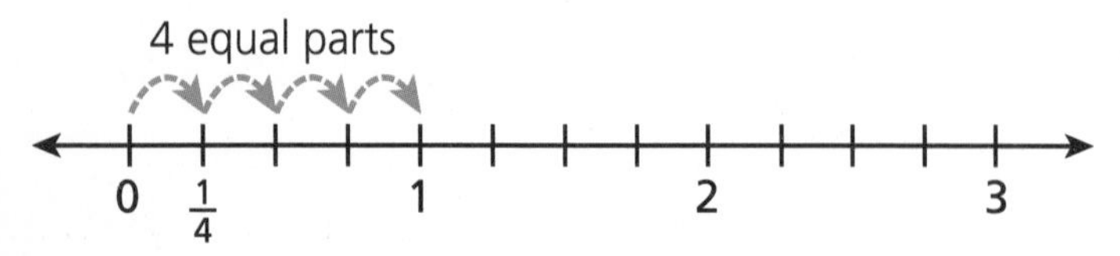

➡ Jessica can trim 12 baby bibs with 3 yards of ribbon.

Guided Instruction

Understand: How to divide whole numbers by unit fractions using the relationship between division and multiplication

One quart of milk is equivalent to $\frac{1}{4}$ gallon. How many quarts are there in 7 gallons?

Finding the number of quarts in 7 gallons is the same as finding the number of $\frac{1}{4}$ gallon in 7 gallons. So, divide 7 by $\frac{1}{4}$.

The two solution methods below both use multiplication to solve $7 \div \frac{1}{4}$.

Method 1 Think about the number of fourths in each whole.

There are 4 fourths in 1 whole.
So, to find the number of fourths in 7 wholes, multiply 4 by 7.

$7 \div \frac{1}{4} = 7 \times 4 = 28$

Method 2 Write a division equation as an equivalent multiplication equation.

If q equals the number of quarts in 7 gallons, then

$q = 7 \div \frac{1}{4}$.

Rewrite this as an equivalent multiplication equation with an unknown factor.

$q \times \frac{1}{4} = 7$

Because $28 \times \frac{1}{4} = \frac{28}{4} = 7$, $q = 28$.

There are 28 quarts of milk in 7 gallons.

Explain why $6 \div \frac{1}{5} = 6 \times 5$. Draw a model to justify your answer.

Guided Instruction

Connect: What you know about dividing whole numbers by unit fractions to write and solve story problems

Write a story problem that can be modeled by the expression $16 \div \frac{1}{2}$. Give the solution to your problem.

Step 1

Think of a situation in which you have to divide a whole-number amount by a unit fraction.

For example, you might have 16 cups of cereal in a storage container and want to know how many $\frac{1}{2}$-cup servings this is.

Step 2

Find the quotient.

Dividing by $\frac{1}{2}$ is the same as multiplying by 2.	$16 \div \frac{1}{2}$
So, rewrite the division expression as a multiplication expression.	16×2
Find the product.	32

There are 2 halves in 1. So, there are 16×2 halves in 16.

Step 3

Write a story problem.

Use the cereal example.

➡ Jaycee has 16 cups of cereal. She wants to pack $\frac{1}{2}$-cup servings into snack bags to share with her classmates. How many snack bags can she make? Jaycee can make 32 snack bags of cereal.

✏ Alex uses $\frac{1}{5}$ meter of wired ribbon to make a little picture frame. Use this idea to write a division story. Draw a number line or a model and include the solution in your story.

Guided Practice

Complete the problems below each model.

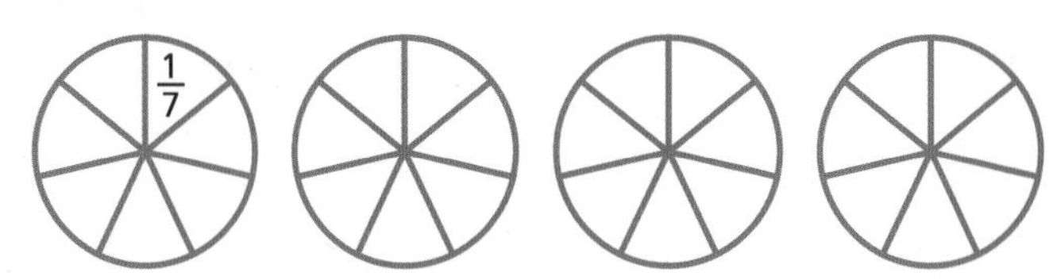

1. How many $\frac{1}{7}$s are there in 4? ____

2. What is value of the expression $4 \div \frac{1}{7}$? ____

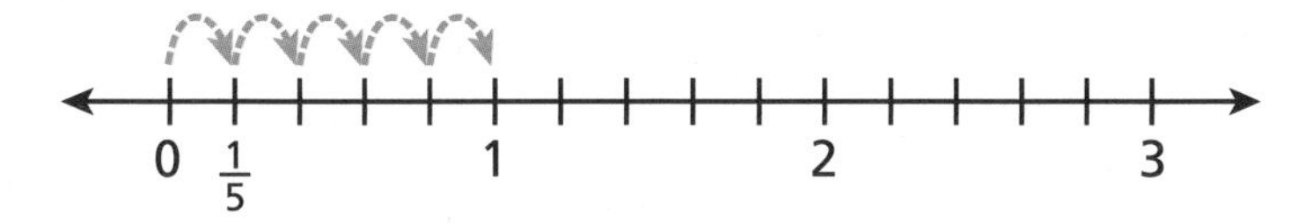

3. How many $\frac{1}{5}$s are there in 3? ____

4. What is the value of the expression $3 \div \frac{1}{5}$? ____

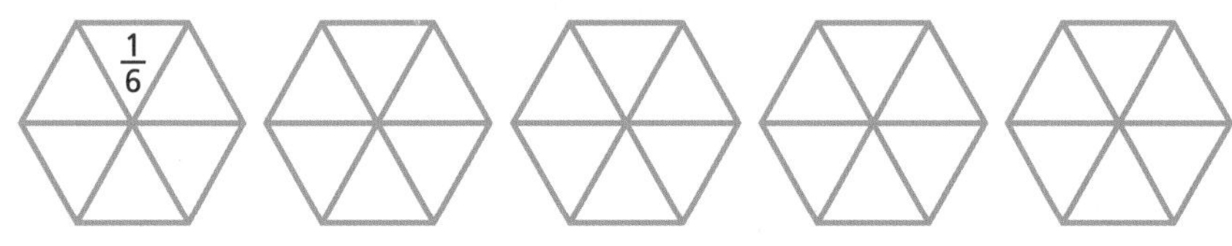

5. How many $\frac{1}{6}$s are there in 5? ____

6. What is the value of the expression $5 \div \frac{1}{6}$? ____

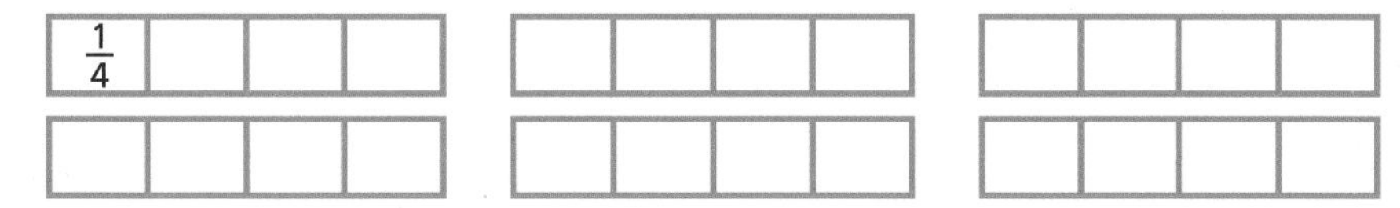

7. How many $\frac{1}{4}$s are there in 6? ____

8. What is the value of the expression $6 \div \frac{1}{4}$? ____

Think-Pair-Share

MP4 9. Write a division story problem about one of the models on this page. Then ask a classmate to solve your problem.

Independent Practice

Solve each problem.

MP4 **1.** A tortoise is moving at a speed of $\frac{1}{3}$ mile an hour. At this speed, how long will it take the tortoise to go 5 miles?

a. Complete this number line model for the story situation.

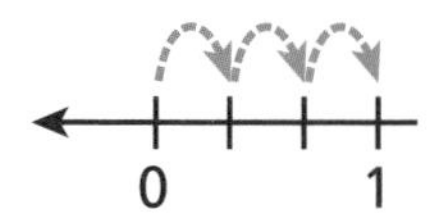

b. How many $\frac{1}{3}$s are there in 5? ____

c. What is the value of the expression $5 \div \frac{1}{3}$? ____

Answer ______________________________

MP4 **2.** Hal works in a bakery. He used $\frac{1}{6}$ of a large box of flour for a batch of muffins. How many batches can he make with 4 boxes of flour?

a. Complete this model for the story situation.

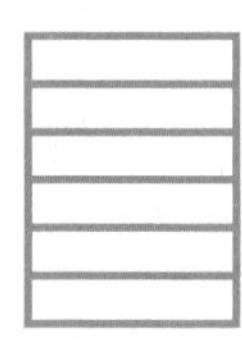

b. How many $\frac{1}{6}$s are there in 4? ____

c. What is the value of the expression $4 \div \frac{1}{6}$? ____

Answer ______________________________

MP4 **3.** Agnes is cutting squares into triangles for a quilt project. Each triangle is $\frac{1}{4}$ of a square. How many triangles can she cut from 5 squares?

a. Complete this model for the story situation.

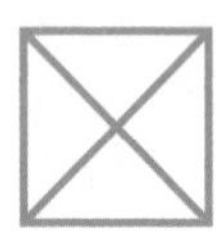

b. How many $\frac{1}{4}$s are there in 5? ____

c. What is the value of the expression $5 \div \frac{1}{4}$? ____

Answer ______________________________

Independent Practice

Fill in the blanks to write a division problem. Then write and solve a division equation for the problem.

4. ____________ [name] cuts a ____________ [thing] into ____________ [whole number] equal pieces.

   Each piece is ____________ [unit fraction] of a whole. How many pieces can be cut

   from ____________ [whole number] whole ____________ [thing]?

   Division Equation ____________

   Answer ______________________________

5. ____________ [name] uses ____________ [unit fraction] of a bag of ____________ [ingredient] to make a

   ____________ [thing]. How many ____________ [thing] can be made from

   ____________ [whole number] bags?

   Division Equation ____________

   Answer ______________________________

For exercises 6–7, choose the best answer.

6. It took Marsha 15 minutes to cut 20 pizzas into ninths. How many slices of pizza does she have? Choose the division expression that gives the answer.

   a. $\frac{1}{9} \div 20$
   b. $9 \div 20$
   c. $20 \div \frac{1}{9}$
   d. $(20 - 15) \div 9$

7. Ed plants trees in city parks. He used $\frac{1}{10}$ of a bag of fertilizer around the base of a newly planted tree. How many trees can Ed fertilize with 40 bags of fertilizer?

   a. 4
   b. 10
   c. 40
   d. 400

Independent Practice

For exercises 8–10, use the model below.

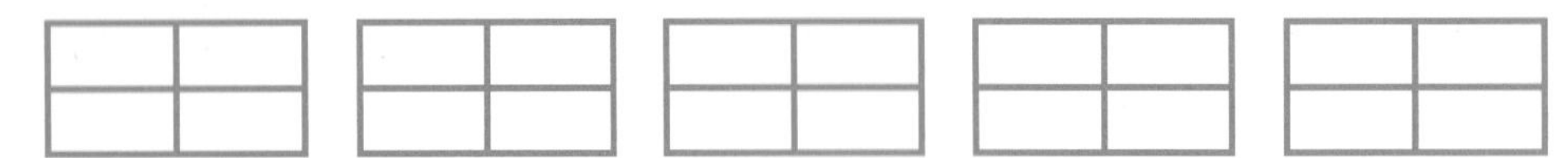

8. Explain how the model shows both $5 \div \frac{1}{4}$ and 5×4.

9. Complete this story situation for the model.

   Each student in an art class gets $\frac{1}{4}$ of a display board to present his or her project. How many students can display projects if . . .

10. Complete a different story situation for the model.

   Fred has 5 containers of fruit salad for the family reunion. Each person will get . . .

Complete the division equation to solve each problem.

11. Each rhombus is $\frac{1}{6}$ of this star.

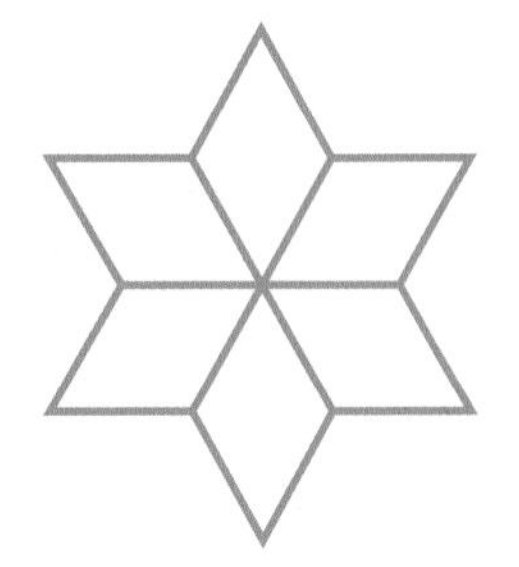

How many rhombuses are there in 50 of these stars?

____ ÷ ____ = ____

12. Each circle is $\frac{1}{21}$ of this pyramid.

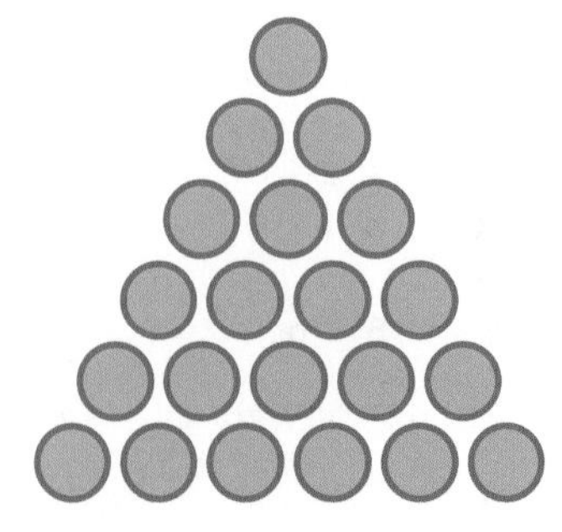

How many balls are there in 12 of these pyramids?

____ ÷ ____ = ____

Independent Practice

Solve the problems.

MP4 **13.** Use the large circle to model $\frac{1}{2} \div 4$. Use the four small circles to model $4 \div \frac{1}{2}$. Explain why the two expressions have different meanings.

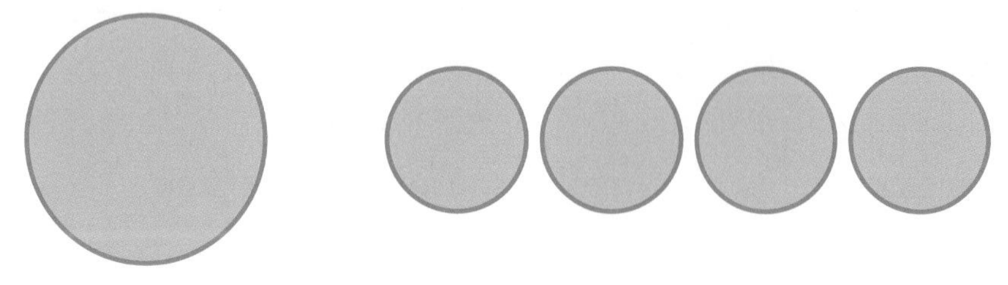

MP2 **14.** It takes Camilla $\frac{1}{4}$ hour to make a customized basket. How many baskets can she make in 6 hours?

Show your work.

Answer ______________________

MP2 **15.** The distance traveled by a moving object equals the rate of speed multiplied by the time. This can be represented by the formula $d = r \times t$. Find the speed of a moving car that goes 11 miles in $\frac{1}{5}$ of an hour.

Show your work.

Answer ______________________

Lesson

24 Problem Solving: Divide Unit Fractions and Whole Numbers

Essential Question:
How can you use division with unit fractions and whole numbers to solve real world problems?

5.NF.7c

Guided Instruction

In this lesson you will solve problems using division with unit fractions and whole numbers.

Understand: How to solve problems that involve more than one step

Bert and Betty made snack boxes to sell at a school picnic. Each snack box had an apple and crackers and sold for \$2.50. They put $\frac{1}{10}$ of a bag of crackers in each box. They used 5 bags of crackers and sold all the boxes they made. How much money did they earn?

First, divide to find the number of snack boxes Bert and Betty made with 5 bags. $5 \div \frac{1}{10} = 5 \times 10 = 50$

Then, multiply the 50 snack boxes you determined above by \$2.50 per box. \$2.50 × 50 snack boxes = \$125

➡ Bert and Betty earned \$125.

Understand: How to solve problems using a picture

The city has 10 trees to plant along a stretch of road that is $\frac{1}{4}$ mile long. The trees will be equally spaced. How far apart should the trees be?

To solve, first make a sketch showing the 10 trees.

Remember!
Drawing pictures can help you better understand a problem situation and avoid incorrect calculations.

Notice there are only 9 spaces between the 10 trees. Divide the $\frac{1}{4}$ mile road into 9 equal parts, *not* 10.

Write a division equation and solve. $\frac{1}{4} \div 9 = \frac{1}{9} \times \frac{1}{4} = \frac{1}{36}$

➡ The trees should be $\frac{1}{36}$ mile apart.

Understand: How to use division to solve a comparison problem

Kai has 4 cousins. This is $\frac{1}{6}$ as many cousins as Lucca has. How many cousins does Lucca have?

To find how many cousins Lucca has, start by writing a comparison statement in words.

The number of cousins Kai has is $\frac{1}{6}$ *times* as many cousins as Lucca has.

Use the statement to write a multiplication equation.

Let c represent the number of cousins Lucia has.

Multiplication equation: $4 = \frac{1}{6} \times c$

Use the fact that multiplication and division are inverse operations to write an equivalent division equation.

Division equation: $c = 4 \div \frac{1}{6}$

Now, solve.

$c = 4 \div \frac{1}{6}$
$c = 4 \times 6$ ← There are 6 sixths in 1, so there are 4×6 sixths in 4.
$c = 24$

➡ Lucca has 24 cousins.

It took Kara $\frac{1}{3}$ hour to finish a crossword puzzle. This is 4 times as long as it took Andre to complete the crossword puzzle. How long did it take Andre to complete the crossword puzzle?

Guided Instruction

Connect: What you know about division with unit fractions and whole numbers to solve problems

For the last 2 days, Juan and Kim have been selling lemonade for 50¢ a glass. They have a $\frac{1}{2}$ gallon left and pour an equal amount of the remaining lemonade in 8 glasses. What fraction of a gallon is in each glass?

Step 1

Identify the key information.

Juan and Kim are dividing $\frac{1}{2}$ gallon into 8 equal parts.

Step 2

Choose the operation you will use to solve. Write an equation.
Let x = the fraction of a gallon in each of the 8 glasses.

$\frac{1}{2} \div 8 = x$

Step 3

Use a model to visualize the division.

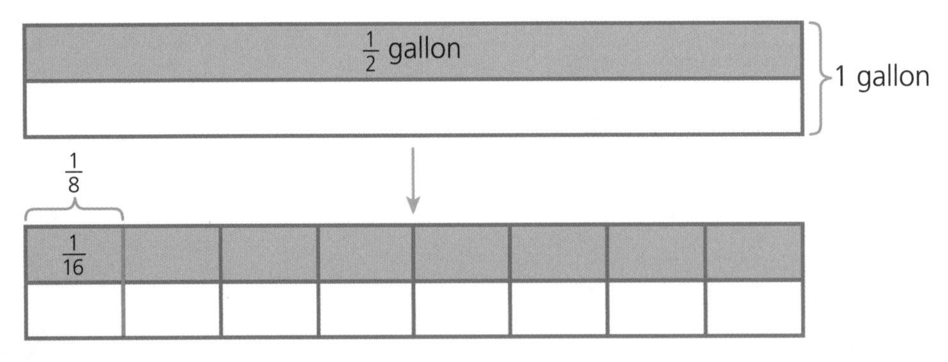

Step 4

Solve the equation. Verify your answer using the model.

$\frac{1}{2} \div 8 = x$

$\frac{1}{8} \times \frac{1}{2} = x$

$\frac{1}{16} = x$

➡ Each glass contains $\frac{1}{16}$ of a gallon.

Guided Practice

Use the problem below to answer exercises 1 and 2.

Vern and Tina are each planting $\frac{1}{2}$ of a rectangular garden. Tina plants vegetables in her half. Vern divides his half into 6 equal parts and plants marigolds in one of these sections. How much of the entire rectangular garden will be marigolds?

1. Will the answer to the problem be a fraction less than 1 or a whole number? Explain how you know.

2. Write an equation to represent the problem. Then solve.

Use the problem below to answer exercises 3–5.

Ruth is making pillows. She uses $\frac{1}{2}$ yard of fabric for each pillow. Her grandmother gives her a box of 15 spools of thread, 6 yards of fabric, and 40 zippers. How many pillows can Ruth make from the fabric?

3. What information is *not* needed to solve the problem?

4. Explain how division can be used to solve the problem.

5. Explain how multiplication can be used to solve the problem.

Think•Pair•Share

MP7 6. Compare the equations used to solve the garden and pillow problems. How are they the same? How are they different?

Independent Practice

Use the problem below to answer exercises 1– 4.

Paul uses $\frac{1}{5}$ liter of chicken broth and $\frac{1}{2}$ packet of noodles for a bowl of soup. How many bowls of soup can he make from 4 liters of chicken broth?

1. What numerical information is needed to solve the problem?

2. Which numbers should you divide to solve the problem? Explain why.

3. Write and solve an equation to answer the question in the problem.

4. Explain how to use multiplication to check your answer.

Use the problem below to answer exercises 5 and 6.

A quilt is made from squares, rectangles, and right triangles. One-third of the pieces are each shape. Sur divides the square pieces into 4 equal groups and makes one group from red fabric. What fraction of the quilt pieces will be red squares?

5. Complete this visual model to illustrate the problem.

squares	
rectangles	
right triangles	

6. Explain how to use equivalent fractions and logical reasoning to solve the problem.

Independent Practice

Problem Solving Strategies	
Draw a Picture or Diagram	Find a Pattern
Guess, Check, and Revise	Use Objects
Make an Organized List	Make a Table
Use a Number Sentence or Equation	Work Backwards
Use Logical Reasoning	Solve a Simpler Problem

Choose a problem solving strategy and explain how you use it.

7. An art teacher plans to give each student $\frac{1}{3}$ of a jar of paint. How many students can sign up for the art classes if the teacher has 20 paint jars?

Strategy: ______________________

Show your work.

Answer ______________________

a. Explain a way to check your answer.

8. Charlie has $\frac{1}{3}$ yard of gold braid to trim a jacket. He divides the braid into 2 equal pieces and uses 1 piece for the each sleeve. How long is the trim on each sleeve?

Strategy: ______________________

Show your work.

Answer ______________________

Independent Practice

9. A centimeter is equal to $\frac{1}{10}$ decimeter. How many centimeters are in 2 decimeters?

Strategy: ______________________

Show your work.

Answer ______________________

a. Explain a way to check your answer.

10. Gayle has enough gravel to cover 40 square yards. She is putting the gravel on a walkway that is $\frac{1}{2}$ yard wide. How much of the path can she cover with the gravel?

Strategy: ______________________

Show your work.

Answer ______________________

Choose the best answer.

11. What information is *not* needed to solve this problem?

Larry buys large bags of birdseed for $9.87 per bag. He uses $\frac{1}{6}$ bag of birdseed each week. He has 4 full bags of birdseed now. How long will it last?

a. The birdseed costs $9.87 per bag.

b. He uses $\frac{1}{6}$ bag per week.

c. He has 4 bags right now.

d. All this information is needed.

Independent Practice

Solve the problems.

MP4 **12.** John divides his food budget into 2 equal parts and spends one part on fruits and vegetables. He divides his book budget into 3 equal parts and uses one part for science books.

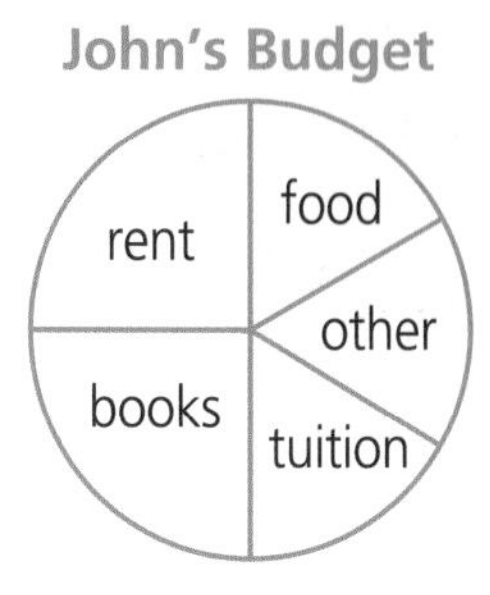

What fractional part of John's budget did he spend on fruits and vegetables and science books? Compare the fractional parts. Use both computation and a visual model in your answer.

Show your work.

Answer ______________________________

MP2 **13.** Explain how dividing something in thirds is different from dividing it by $\frac{1}{3}$. Create two story situations to illustrate your answer.

Story: Dividing in thirds ______________________________

____

Story: Dividing by $\frac{1}{3}$ ______________________________

____

MP5 **14.** Solve the problem below two ways, once using the fraction $\frac{1}{50}$ and once using its decimal equivalent.

A metal machine cuts very small parts that are $\frac{1}{50}$ of an inch long. How many of these parts can be cut from a 3-inch strip of metal?

Method 1: Use $\frac{1}{50}$: ______________________________

Method 2: Use a decimal: ______________________________

For exercises 1–4, evaluate. Show your work.

1. $3\frac{1}{2} \times 1\frac{3}{4}$ ____

2. $\frac{3}{4} \times 3 \times 5\frac{1}{3}$ ____

3. $\frac{1}{8} \div 2$ ____

4. $24 \div \frac{1}{3}$ ____

5. Write $23 \div 3$ as both a fraction and a mixed number.

   Fraction: ____ Mixed number: ____

6. Two-thirds of a science class is going on a field trip. One-fifth of this group is bringing cameras. What fraction of the class will be bringing cameras on the trip?

7. What is the area of a park that is $\frac{1}{2}$ mile wide and $\frac{7}{8}$ mile long?

For exercises 8–9, choose the correct answer.

8. In a number-guessing game, Paula chooses a fraction between 0 and 1. She multiplies 50 by her fraction. What must be true of the product?

   a. It is less than 50.

   b. It is greater than $\frac{1}{2}$ of 50.

   c. It is greater than 50.

   d. There is not enough information to decide.

9. Which expression is equivalent to $\frac{7}{9} - \frac{1}{6}$?

   a. $\frac{7}{9} - \frac{7}{18}$

   b. $\frac{7}{9} - \frac{1}{18}$

   c. $\frac{14}{18} - \frac{3}{18}$

   d. $\frac{7}{12} - \frac{2}{12}$

10. Describe a method for estimating this difference.

$5\frac{1}{3} - 2\frac{7}{8}$

11. Barb gets 6 pizzas to divide equally among 4 people. How much of a pizza can each person have?

12. Write an example problem for this rule. Then, explain why the product is greater than the original number.

When you multiply a number by a fraction *greater than* 1, the product is *greater than* that number.

13. A work crew is planting flowers along a stretch of road that is $\frac{3}{4}$ mile long. They plant $\frac{1}{3}$ mile the first day and $\frac{1}{4}$ mile the second day. How much of the job is left to complete on the final day? Show the equation you use.

Show your work.

Answer ______

14. Ms. Tompkins flies to San Francisco for a business trip. She decides to drive home. She drives $\frac{1}{3}$ of the way the first day, and then $\frac{3}{8}$ of the way the second day. How much of the trip has Ms. Tompkins completed so far?

Show your work.

Answer ______

15. There are 24 students in Rob's class. One-third of the students walk or ride a bike to school. How many students do not walk or ride a bike?

Show your work.

Answer ______

MP4 **16.** Explain how this model shows $\frac{1}{3} \div 3$. Include the quotient in your answer.

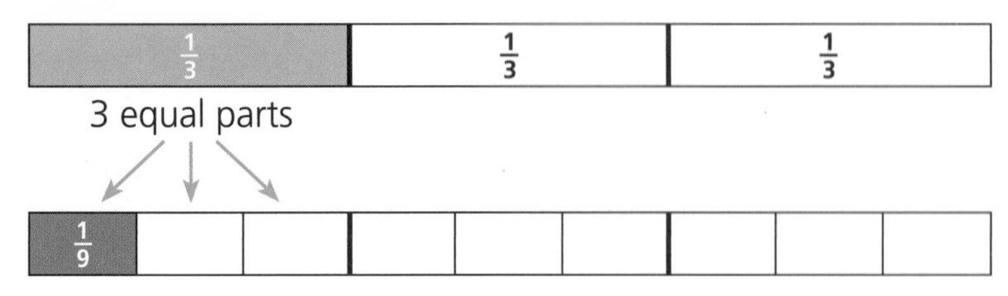

MP4 **17.** Explain how this model shows $\frac{2}{5} \times 15$. Include the product in your response.

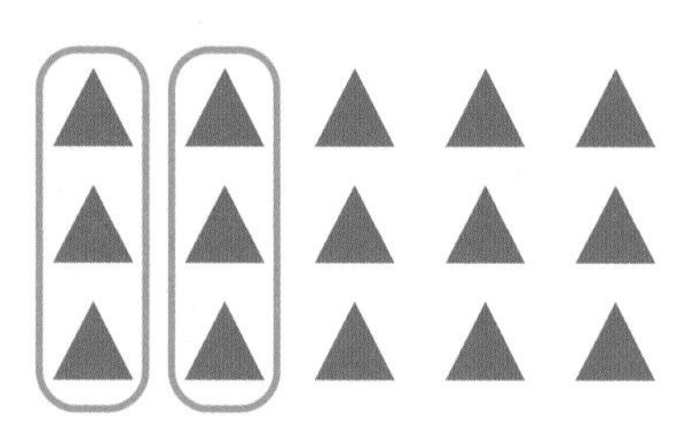

MP6 **18.** Greg has 60-inches of braided leather. He plans to cut 8-inch pieces to make leather key chains. Does Greg have enough to make 8 key chains? Explain.

MP1 **19.** Gina a square garden that is 20 yards on each side. She uses a rectangular area $\frac{1}{2}$ yard wide and 6 yards long for tulips. How much of the garden can be used for other plants?

Show your work.

Answer ______________________________

MP1 **20.** Janine is using an old silk dress for part of a quilt. She will make $\frac{1}{4}$ of the quilt from the dress. Janine divides this area into 2 equal parts and adds fancy stitching to one part. What fraction of the quilt will have dress fabric with fancy stitching?

Show your work.

Answer ______________________________

5.OA.1, 5.NBT.5, 5.NBT.6, 5.NF.1, 5.NF.2, 5.NF.4d, 5.NF.4b, 5.NF.5a, 5.NF.5b, 5.NF.6, 5.NF.7a, 5.NF.7b, 5.NF.7c

Performance Tasks

Performance Tasks show your understanding of the Math that you have learned. You will be doing various Performance Tasks as you complete your work in this text, ***Common Core Progress Mathematics***.

Beginning This Task

The next five pages provide you with the beginning of a Performance Task. You will be given 5 items to complete, and each item will have two or more parts. As you complete these items you will:

I Demonstrate that you have mastered mathematical skills and concepts

II Reason through a problem to a solution, and explain your reasoning

III Use models and apply them to real-world situations.

Extending This Task

Your teacher may extend this Performance Task with additional items provided in our online resources at sadlierconnect.com.

Scoring This Task

Your response to each item will be assessed against a rubric, or scoring guide. Some items will be worth 1 or 2 points, and others will be worth more. In each item you will show your work or explain your reasoning.

Performance Task 1

Yummy Strawberries at the Farmer's Market

1. Olga goes to the farmer's market to buy strawberries for a class party. There are 27 children in her class, but 9 of them do not like strawberries. Olga wants to buy 3 strawberries for each classmate who likes strawberries.

   a. Olga writes the expression $(3 \times 27) - 9$ to find the number of strawberries she should buy. What error did Olga make when she wrote the expression?

   b. Evaluate the expression that Olga wrote in item 1.a. above: $(3 \times 27) - 9$.

   c. Write a correct expression Olga can use to find the number of strawberries she should buy.

   d. Evaluate the expression you wrote in item 1.c. above. How many strawberries should Olga buy?

Boxes of Granola Bars

2. Ms. Sandino, the owner of a health food super store, receives 14 boxes of granola bars. Each box contains 248 bars.

   a. Find the total number of granola bars Ms. Sandino receives.

   b. Ms. Sandino wants to put an equal number of granola bars on each of 8 display racks. Find the number of granola bars she should put on each display rack. Use your answer from part a above.

   c. Show how you can use the relationship between multiplication and division to check your answer to item 2.b. above.

Bean Stew

3. Andrew purchases two kinds of beans to make stew. He buys $2\frac{1}{2}$ pounds of pinto beans and $1\frac{5}{8}$ pounds of kidney beans.

   a. Andrew estimates that he purchases about 3 pounds of beans altogether. Do you agree or disagree with his estimate? Explain.

   b. Find the exact weight of the beans Andrew purchases.

   c. Explain how knowing about equivalent fractions helped you find the exact weight of the beans in item 3.b. above.

   d. Andrew uses $\frac{3}{4}$ pound of the beans he buys to make a stew. How many pounds of beans does Andrew have left?

Advertising a Sale on Organic Avocados

4. Ms. Sandino makes a sign to advertise an unexpected bulk shipment of organic avocados. The sign is $\frac{3}{10}$ meter wide and $\frac{4}{5}$ meter long.

   a. What is the area of the sign?

   b. The store manager looks at the sign and says "I think you should make a new sign. The area of the new sign should be $\frac{5}{4}$ the area of this sign." Does the store manager want the new sign to be larger or smaller than the sign Ms. Sandino made? Explain how you know.

   c. Find the area for the sign that the store manager would like to have.

   d. Find the length and width of a sign that would have an area $\frac{5}{4}$ the area of Ms. Sandino's sign.

Performance Task 1

The Deli Counter

5. Terrence works the late afternoon shift at the deli counter. He uses 3 pounds of turkey breast to make sandwiches. He puts $\frac{1}{4}$ pound of turkey breast in each sandwich.

a. Draw a model that Terrence could use to find how many sandwiches he can make. Explain how your model shows the number of sandwiches Terrence can make.

b. Write a division equation that your model in item 5.a. above shows.

c. Use the relationship between multiplication and division to show that your division equation is correct.

d. After Terrance finishes making the sandwiches, he begins to slice some cheddar cheese. He writes the expression $\frac{1}{2} \div 10$. Write and solve a story problem that matches Terrence's expression.

Progress Check

Look at how the Common Core standards you have learned and will learn connect.

It is very important for you to understand the standards from the prior grade level so that you will be able to develop an understanding of measurement and data in this unit and be prepared for next year. To practice your skills, go to sadlierconnect.com.

GRADE 4 I Can...	Before Unit 4	GRADE 5 Can I ?	After Unit 4	GRADE 6 I Will...
4.MD.1 Express measurements in a larger unit in terms of a smaller unit within the same system	☐	**5.MD.1** Convert among different-sized measurement units within the same measurement system	☐	**6.RP.3** Use ratio reasoning to convert measurement units
	☐	Convert among measurement units while solving real-world problems	☐	
4.MD.4 Display a set of measurements in half units, quarter units, and eighth units on a line plot	☐	**5.MD.2** Display a set of measurements in half units, quarter units, and eighth units on a line plot	☐	**6.SP.4** Display numerical data in plots on a number line, including dot plots, histograms, and box plots
Add and subtract fractions to solve problems using information in line plots	☐	Perform operations on fractions to solve problems using information in line plots	☐	
	☐	**5.MD.3** Understand volume and volume measurement	☐	
	☐	**5.MD.4** Measure volume by counting unit cubes	☐	
4.MD.3 Apply the area and perimeter formulas for rectangles in real-world and mathematical problems	☐	**5.MD.5** Find the volume of a rectangular prism by multiplying the edge lengths	☐	**6.G.2** Find the volume of rectangular prisms using formulas
	☐	Apply the volume formulas for rectangular prisms in real-world and mathematical problems	☐	

HOME ✦ CONNECT...

If you have ever rented a truck during a move, you know how important it is to accurately estimate volume. Will all of your boxes and personal items fit into the moving truck? Not enough space presents a big problem, but so can too much extra space.

Volume is an attribute of three-dimensional space. It describes the amount of space that a solid figure like a cube occupies. There are two formulas for measuring the volume of a right rectangular prism:

Volume = length × width × height
Volume = area of the base × height

In the lessons that follow, your child will understand why these volume formulas work by obtaining a deeper conceptual understanding of volume.

Activity: Gather several boxes of different sizes and shapes. Ask your child to estimate the volume of each one. Then, find the volumes. Discuss together.

In this unit your child will:

- Convert customary and metric measurement units.
- Use line plots.
- Understand concepts of volume measurement.
- Measure volume using a variety of strategies and formulas.

NOTE: All of these learning goals for your child are based on the Grade 5 Common Core State Standards for Mathematics.

Ways to Help Your Child

Ask your child, "What did you learn today?" That question might sometimes be met with apathy, but be persistent. You will show that you are interested in their daily lives and care about your child's education. Additionally, it will keep you informed about what's happening in the classroom so you can help make connections at home.

ONLINE

For more Home Connect activities, continue online at sadlierconnect.com

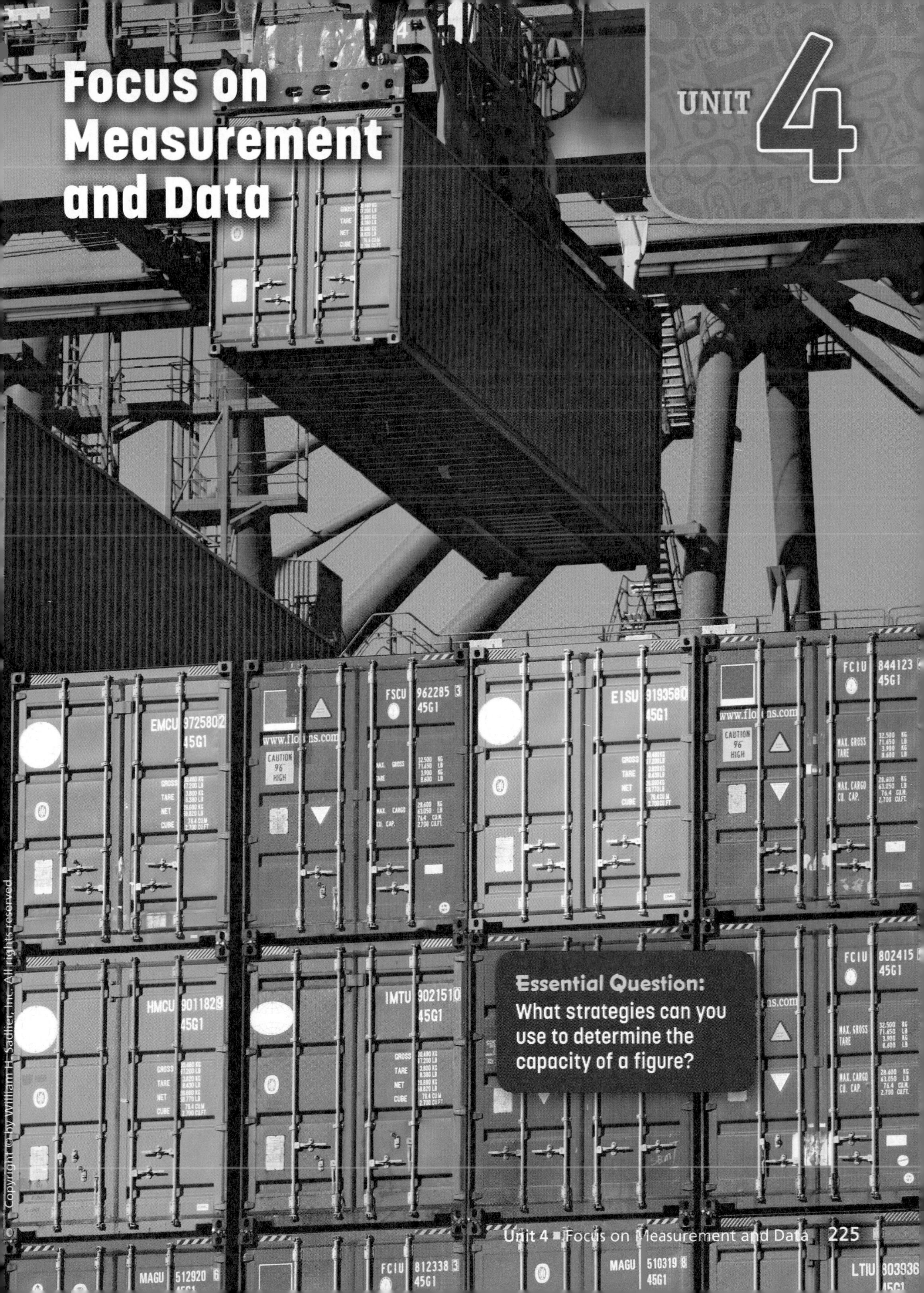

Focus on Measurement and Data

UNIT 4

Essential Question:
What strategies can you use to determine the capacity of a figure?

Lesson

25 Convert Customary Measurement Units

Guided Instruction

Essential Question:
How can you convert a measurement from one customary unit to another?

5.MD.1

Words to Know:
- customary units of liquid volume
- customary units of weight
- customary units of length

In this lesson you will learn how to convert customary units of measurement to solve real-world problems.

Understand: Converting larger customary units to smaller units

Jared buys 3 gallons of orange juice for a football team breakfast. The juice will be served in pitchers that hold 1 quart each. How many pitchers can Jared fill with juice?

To find the number of pitchers Jared can fill, you need to convert 3 gallons to the equivalent measurement in quarts. Look at the conversion chart for customary units of liquid volume. The chart shows that 1 gallon = 4 quarts.

Customary Units of Liquid Volume

1 pint (pt) = 2 cups (c)
1 quart (qt) = 2 pints
1 gallon (gal) = 4 quarts

Method 1 Make a bar model.

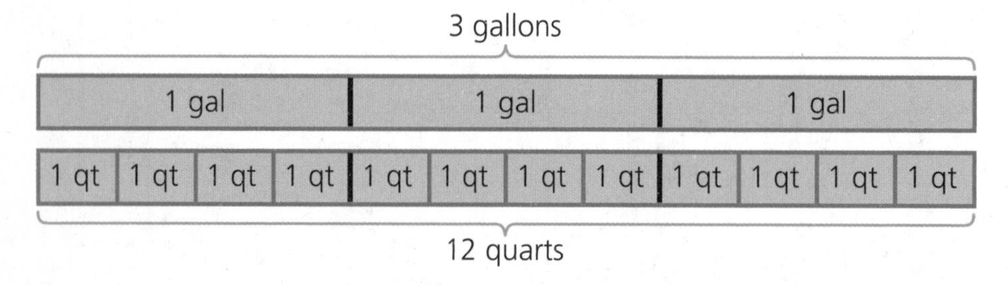

The model shows that there are 12 quarts in 3 gallons.

Method 2 Write and solve an equation.

A gallon is larger than a quart. To convert from a larger unit to a smaller unit, multiply. *Multiply* the number of gallons of juice by the number of quarts in 1 gallon. Use n for the unknown number of quarts.

number of gallons × number of quarts in 1 gallon = number of quarts

$$3 \times 4 = n$$

Since $12 = n$, 3 gallons = 12 quarts.

➡ Jared can fill 12 one-quart pitchers with juice.

Guided Instruction

Understand: Converting smaller customary units to larger units

A truck loaded with building supplies weighs about 72,000 pounds. The driver wants to use a bridge whose weight limit is 35 tons per vehicle. Can the truck use this bridge?

To determine if the truck can use the bridge, you need to convert 72,000 pounds to the equivalent weight in tons. Look at the conversion chart for customary units of weight.

Customary Units of Weight
1 pound (lb) = 16 ounces (oz)
1 ton (t) = 2,000 pounds

A ton is larger than a pound. To convert from a smaller unit to a larger unit, divide. *Divide* the number of pounds the truck weighs by the number of pounds in 1 ton.

number of pounds ÷ number of pounds in 1 ton = number of tons
$72{,}000 \div 2{,}000 = n$

Since $36 = n$, 72,000 pounds is equivalent to 36 tons.

The loaded truck weighs about 36 tons. This is greater than the bridge weight limit of 35 tons per vehicle.

The truck cannot use this bridge.

For each problem on pages 226 and 227, compare the number in the original measurement to the number in the converted measurement. Tell what you notice about those conversions.

Guided Instruction

Connect: What you know about customary units of measurement to solve real-world problems

Gia needs 130 feet of string. A spool of string contains 20 yards and costs $1.50. What is the total cost of the string that Gia must buy?

Step 1

Plan the solution.

To solve the problem, first convert 130 feet to yards. Next, determine how many spools of string Gia needs. Then multiply the number of spools by $1.50 to find the total cost of the string.

Step 2

Convert 130 feet of string to yards. Use the chart of customary units of length.

Customary Units of Length

1 foot (ft) = 12 inches (in.)
1 yard (yd) = 3 feet
1 mile (m) = 5,280 feet
1 mile (m) = 1,760 yards

You are converting from a smaller unit, feet, to a larger unit, yards, so divide.

Remember!
To convert from *larger units to smaller units*, multiply.
To convert from *smaller units to larger units*, divide.

number of feet ÷ number of feet in 1 yard = number of yards

$130 \div 3 = n$

Since $\frac{130}{3} = n$, 130 feet = $\frac{130}{3}$ yards, which equals $43\frac{1}{3}$ yards.

Step 3

Determine how many spools of string Gia needs. Two spools is 2×20, or 40 yards. This is not quite enough, therefore Gia must buy three spools.

Step 4

Multiply the number of spools Gia needs by the cost of one spool.

3 spools of string × $1.50 for each spool = $4.50

➡ Gia must buy $4.50 worth of string.

Guided Practice

Convert the measurements.

1. 5 feet = ■ inches

   1 foot = 12 inches

   An inch is smaller than a foot, so multiply.

   5 × 12 = ____

   5 feet = ____ inches

2. 14 cups = ■ pints

   1 pint = 2 cups

   A pint is ____________ than a cup,

   so ____________.

   14 ____ ____ = ____

   14 cups = ____ pints

3. 1,080 seconds = ■ minutes

   1 minute = 60 seconds

   A minute is ____________ than

   a second, so ____________.

   1,080 ____ 60 = ____

   1,080 seconds = ____ minutes

4. 176 ounces = ■ pounds

   1 pound = 16 ounces

   A pound is ____________ than

   an ounce, so ____________.

   176 ____ ____ = ____

   176 ounces = ____ pounds

Solve the problem.

5. Mariah has a new puppy that weighs 6 pounds 4 ounces. What is the weight of the puppy in ounces? Show your work.

Think • Pair • Share

MP6 6. Seth and Brian ran the 200-yard dash at the track meet. Brian reached the finish line in 30 seconds. Seth ran 25 feet per second. Who finished the race first? Explain your reasoning.

Independent Practice

Complete the tables to convert from one customary unit to another.

1.

miles	× or ÷	feet
1	× 5,280	5,280
2		
3		

2.

minutes	× or ÷	hours
60	÷ 60	1
300		
720		

3.

cups	× or ÷	pints
1	× 2	2
4		
8		

4.

pounds	× or ÷	tons
2,000	÷ 2,000	1
6,000		
12,000		

Convert the measurements.

5. 45 yards = ■ feet

1 yard = 3 feet

A foot is smaller than a yard, so multiply.

45 × 3 = ______

45 yards = ______ feet

6. 9 gallons = ■ quarts

1 gallon = 4 quarts

A quart is ______________ than a gallon, so ______________.

9 ____ ______ = ______

9 gallons = ______ quarts

7. 3,000 pounds = ■ tons

1 ton = 2,000 pounds

A ton is ______________ than a pound, so ______________.

3,000 ____ ______ = ______

3,000 pounds = ______ tons

8. 780 inches = ■ feet

1 foot = 12 inches

A foot is ______________ than an inch, so ______________.

780 ____ ______ = ______

780 inches = ______ feet

Independent Practice

Circle every correct answer.

9. Which of the following are equal to 440 yards?

   a. 15,840 inches
   b. $146\frac{2}{3}$ feet
   c. 1,320 feet
   d. $\frac{1}{4}$ mile

Order the measurements from *largest* to *smallest*. Show your work.

10. 15 gallons, 260 cups, 80 quarts

    Answer ____________________

11. 0.5 tons, 1,800 pounds, 27,200 ounces

    Answer ____________________

Complete parts a–d to solve the problem.

12. Josiah is building a fence around the perimeter of his garden, which is shaped like a rectangle. His garden is 39 feet long and 45 feet wide. One yard of fencing costs \$15. How much will Josiah spend on fencing?

    a. Find the perimeter of Josiah's garden in feet. ______ feet

    b. Convert the perimeter in feet to yards.

       A yard is __________ than a foot, so __________.

       ______ ____ 3 = ______. So, ______ feet = ______ yards

    c. Multiply the number of yards by the cost of one yard of fencing.

       ______ yards × \$______ = ______

    d. Answer the question.

       Josiah will spend ______ on fencing.

Independent Practice

MP2 **13.** Suppose the width of Josiah's garden from exercise 12 is 40 feet instead of 39 feet. This would change the perimeter of the garden from 56 yards to 170 feet, or 56 yards and 2 feet. How would this change affect the answer to the problem?

MP3 **14.** The capacity of an insulated cooler is 344 cups. Michele says the cooler will hold 22.25 gallons. Sharon says the cooler will only hold 21.5 gallons. Who is correct? Explain.

Solve the problems.

MP1 **15.** Nine of the houses on Marina's street are getting their driveways paved. It takes about $2\frac{3}{4}$ tons of blacktop to pave each driveway. How many pounds of blacktop will be used in all?

Show your work.

Answer ______________________________

Independent Practice

MP2 **16.** A serving of cheese weighs 3.5 ounces. How many whole servings of cheese are there in a 40-pound wheel of cheese? How much is left over?

Show your work.

Answer ______________________________

MP3 **17.** Arun needs 3 rods of wood with lengths of 26 inches, 17 inches, and 37 inches. At the local lumberyard, wood rods are sold in 6-foot, 8-foot, and 10-foot lengths. Which length should Arun buy so that the least amount of scrap wood is left over?

Answer ______________________________

Justify your answer using words, drawings, or numbers.

MP3 **18.** Michaela is mailing a 12.25-pound package to her grandmother. The shipping service charges $0.26 for every ounce mailed. Or, Michaela can use a flat-rate box that costs $25. Which is the less expensive option?

Answer ______________________________

Justify your answer using words, drawings, or numbers.

Lesson

26 Convert Metric Measurement Units

Essential Question:
How can you convert a measurement from one metric unit to another?

5.MD.1

Words to Know:
metric units of length
base unit
metric units of liquid volume
metric units of mass

Guided Instruction

In this lesson you will learn how to convert metric measurements to solve real-world problems.

Understand: Converting metric units of length

Anari hikes 3250 meters. How many kilometers does he hike?

To solve this problem, you need to convert 3250 meters to kilometers.

The chart below shows metric units of length from largest to smallest. The meter is the base unit of length. The bottom row of the chart shows how the other units compare to 1 meter. The most commonly used units are shown in red.

kilometer	hectometer	dekameter	meter	decimeter	centimeter	millimeter
km	hm	dam	m	dm	cm	mm
1000×1 m	100×1 m	10×1 m	1 m	$\frac{1}{10} \times 1$ m	$\frac{1}{100} \times 1$ m	$\frac{1}{1000} \times 1$ m

Each metric unit is 10 times the next smaller unit and $\frac{1}{10}$ the next larger unit.

To convert from a larger unit to a smaller unit, *multiply by 10* for each unit you move in the chart.

To convert from a smaller unit to a larger unit, *divide by 10* for each unit you move in the chart.

Remember!
Multiplying a number by 10 shifts the digits 1 place to the left.
Dividing a number by 10 shifts the digits 1 place to the right.

To convert from meters to kilometers, you move three units on the chart, so divide 3250 by $10 \times 10 \times 10$, or 1000.

3250 meters $\div$ 1000 = 3.250 kilometers

Anari hikes 3.25 kilometers.

Rename each unit of measure.

a. 3.78 centimeters = ______ millimeter(s)

b. 2 dekameters = ______ kilometer(s)

Guided Instruction

Understand: **Converting metric units of liquid volume**

A chemist needs to convert 2.5 liters of a solution to milliliters to present an experiment. How many milliliters is 2.5 liters?

To solve this problem, you need to convert 2.5 liters to milliliters.

This chart shows the metric units of liquid volume from largest to smallest. The most commonly used units are shown in red. The liter is the base unit of liquid volume. Notice that the relationship among the units is the same as it is for the units of length.

kiloliter	hectoliter	dekaliter	liter	deciliter	centiliter	milliliter
kL	hL	daL	L	dL	cL	mL
1000×1 L	100×1 L	10×1 L	1 L	$\frac{1}{10} \times 1$ L	$\frac{1}{100} \times 1$ L	$\frac{1}{1000} \times 1$ L

Method 1 Use the chart.

To convert from a larger unit to a smaller unit, *multiply by 10* for each unit you move in the chart.

To convert from a smaller unit to a larger unit, *divide by 10* for each unit you move in the chart.

Milliliters are smaller than liters, and to get from liters to milliliters, you move three units on the chart. So, to convert 2.5 liters to milliliters, multiply 2.5 by $10 \times 10 \times 10$, or 1000.

Remember!
Multiplying a number by 10 shifts the digits 1 place to the left.

Dividing a number by 10 shifts the digits 1 place to the left.

2.5 liters $\times$ 1000 = 2500 milliliters

Method 2 Use basic equivalences.

At the right are the basic equivalences for the most commonly used metric units of liquid volume.

Metric Units of Liquid Volume
1 kiloliter (kL) = 1000 liters
1 liter (L) = 1000 milliliters (mL)

Milliliters are smaller than liters, so multiply.

Number of liters $\times$ number of milliliters in 1 liter = number of milliliters

$2.5 \times 1000 = n$

Since $2500 = n$, 2.5 liters = 2500 milliliters.

➡ 2.5 liters is equal to 2500 milliliters.

Guided Instruction

Connect: What you know about metric units to solve real-world problems

Fae has a 5-kilogram bag of corn meal. A recipe calls for 250 grams of corn meal to make one loaf of bread. How many loaves of bread can Fae make from the bag of corn meal?

Step 1

Plan the solution.

To solve the problem, first find the number of grams of corn meal in the 5-kilogram bag. Then, divide the answer by 250 grams to determine how many loaves of bread Fae can make.

Step 2

Convert 5 kilograms to grams.

The chart below shows the metric units of mass from largest to smallest. The most commonly used units are shown in red. The gram is the base unit of mass. The relationship among the units is the same as it is for units of length and liquid volume.

kilogram	hectogram	dekagram	gram	decigram	centigram	milligram
kg	hg	dag	g	dg	cg	mg
1000×1 g	100×1 g	10×1 g	1 g	$\frac{1}{10} \times 1$ g	$\frac{1}{100} \times 1$ g	$\frac{1}{1000} \times 1$ g

To convert 5 kilograms to grams, you can use the chart or the basic equivalences shown at the right.

Metric Units of Mass

1 kilogram (kg) = 1000 grams

1 gram (g) = 1000 milligrams (mg)

Grams are smaller than kilograms, so multiply.

5 kilograms $\times$ 1000 = 5000 grams

Step 3

Divide the total number of grams of corn meal by the number of grams of corn meal needed for one loaf of bread.

$5000 \div 250 = 20$

➡ Fae can make 20 loaves of bread from the one bag of corn meal.

Guided Practice

Convert the measurements.

1. 20 meters = ■ centimeters

   1 meter = 100 centimeters

   A centimeter is ______________

   than a meter, so ______________.

   20 ____ 100 = ______

   20 meters = ______ centimeters

2. 1700 meters = ■ kilometers

   1 kilometer = 1000 meters

   A kilometer is ______________

   than a meter, so ______________.

   1700 ____ ______ = ______

   1700 meters = ______ kilometers

3. 4569 grams = ■ kilograms

   1 kilogram = 1000 grams

   A kilogram is larger than a gram,

   so ______________.

   4569 ____ ______ = ______

   4569 grams = ______ kilograms

4. 1.5 kiloliters = ■ liters

   1 kiloliter = 1000 liters

   A liter is smaller than a kiloliter,

   so ______________.

   1.5 ____ ______ = ______

   1.5 kiloliter = ______ liters

Solve the problem.

5. Andrea bicycles 8.04 kilometers each day, going to and from school. How many meters does she bicycle each day?

   ____

Think • Pair • Share

MP7 6. Jacob has a 15-kilogram bag of rice. A serving of rice has a mass of 200 grams. Jacob wants to find the number of servings of rice the bag contains. Should Jacob convert kilograms to grams or grams to kilograms to get the answer? Explain your reasoning.

Independent Practice

Complete the table to convert from one metric unit to another.

1.

centiliters	× or ÷	milliliters
1	× 10	10
2		
3		

2.

meters	× or ÷	kilometers
2500	÷ 1000	2.5
3500		
4500		

3.

kilograms	× or ÷	grams
2	x 1000	2000
4		
6		

4.

grams	× or ÷	kilograms
3000	÷ 1000	3
6000		
12,000		

Convert the measurements.

5. 9845 milliliters = ■ liters

1 liter = 1000 milliliters

A liter is larger than a milliliter,

so ______________.

9845 ____ ________ = ________

9845 milliliters = ________ liters

6. 5.2 kilograms = ■ grams

1 kilogram = 1000 grams

A gram is smaller than a kilogram,

so ______________.

5.2 ____ ________ = ________

5.2 kilograms = ________ grams

7. 12 kilometers = ■ meters

1 kilometer = 1000 meters

A meter is ______________

than a kilometer, so ______________.

12 ____ 1000 = ________

12 kilometers = ________ meters

8. 6800 grams = ■ kilograms

1 kilogram = 1000 grams

A kilogram is ______________

than a gram, so ______________.

6800 ____ ________ = ________

6800 grams = ________ kilograms

Independent Practice

Circle every correct answer.

9. Which of the following are equal to 72 liters?

   a. 72,000 milliliters
   b. 720 centiliters
   c. 0.072 kilometers
   d. 0.072 kiloliters

Order the measurements from *largest* to *smallest*. Show your work.

10. 175 grams, 18,000 milligrams, 1.6 kilograms

    Answer ______________________________

11. 50 centimeters, 570 millimeters, 0.53 meters

    Answer ______________________________

Complete parts a–c to solve the problem.

12. Ann is making smoothies. She uses 1.2 kilograms of apples and 600 grams of kiwi. How many kilograms of fruit does Ann use in all?

    a. Convert the 600 grams of kiwi to kilograms.

       1 kilogram = 1000 grams. A kilogram is __________ than a gram,

       so you need to __________.

       ______ ______ 1000 = ______

       600 grams = ______ kilograms

    b. Add the number of kilograms of apples to the number of kilograms of kiwi.

       1.2 kilograms + ______ kilograms = ______ kilograms

    c. Answer the question.

       Ann uses ______ kilograms of fruit in all.

Independent Practice

MP2 **13.** Suppose you want to find the amount of fruit in exercise 12 in grams instead of kilograms. Without calculating, explain how you would find the answer.

MP3 **14.** Compare converting units in the metric system with converting units in the customary system. How are they the same? How are they different?

Solve the problems.

MP1 **15.** Jasper has a lemonade stand. One glass of lemonade has 4950 milligrams of sugar. One weekend, he sells 87 glasses of lemonade. How many grams of sugar does Jasper use that weekend?

Show your work.

Answer ______________________________

MP1 **16.** Quinn is a runner. As part of her training, she keeps detailed records about the distances she runs. Last year Quinn ran 1820 kilometers. On average, about how many meters did Quinn run each week last year?

Show your work.

Answer ______________________________

Independent Practice

MP2 **17.** Ryan has a rope that is 1.25 meters long. He cuts off a piece that is 33 centimeters. Then Ryan cuts off a piece that is 150 millimeters. How many centimeters of rope is left?

Show your work.

Answer ______________________________

MP3 **18.** Gemma is making three candles of different sizes. She will need 125 grams, 0.65 kilograms, and 130,000 milligrams of wax to make the candles. Gemma can buy a 1000-gram block of wax or a 0.8-kilogram block of wax. Which one should Gemma buy to make her candles?

Answer ______________________________

Justify your answer using words, drawings, or numbers.

MP2 **19.** Felix says 1000 kiloliters is a million milliliters. Is Felix correct? Explain.

Answer ______________________________

Justify your answer using words, drawings, or numbers.

Lesson

27 Problem Solving: Use Line Plots

Essential Question:
How can you solve real-world problems using line plots?

5.MD.2

Words to Know:
line plot

Guided Instruction

In this lesson you will learn how to solve real-world problems by representing and interpreting data on a line plot.

Understand: How to represent data using a line plot

As part of Mr. Hughes' health class, ten students tracked the distance they walked to school one morning. They record the distances to the nearest $\frac{1}{8}$ mile. The results are shown at the right.

Make a line plot of the data. How many students walked at least $\frac{1}{2}$ mile to school?

Student's Distances to School (miles)

$\frac{1}{2}$	$\frac{1}{2}$	$\frac{3}{4}$	1	$\frac{1}{8}$
$1\frac{1}{4}$	$\frac{5}{8}$	$\frac{1}{4}$	$\frac{1}{4}$	$\frac{3}{8}$

A line plot uses a number line to organize and display data.

To start, draw a part of a number line that includes all the values of the student's distances. Use intervals of $\frac{1}{8}$ because the distances are recorded to the nearest $\frac{1}{8}$ mile. Add a label or title below the line to show what the values on the plot will represent.

0 $\frac{1}{8}$ $\frac{1}{4}$ $\frac{3}{8}$ $\frac{1}{2}$ $\frac{5}{8}$ $\frac{3}{4}$ $\frac{7}{8}$ 1 $1\frac{1}{8}$ $1\frac{1}{4}$

Student's Distances to School

For each value in the data set, make an X above that value on the number line. For example there is a $\frac{1}{8}$ in the data set. Therefore, there is one X above $\frac{1}{8}$.

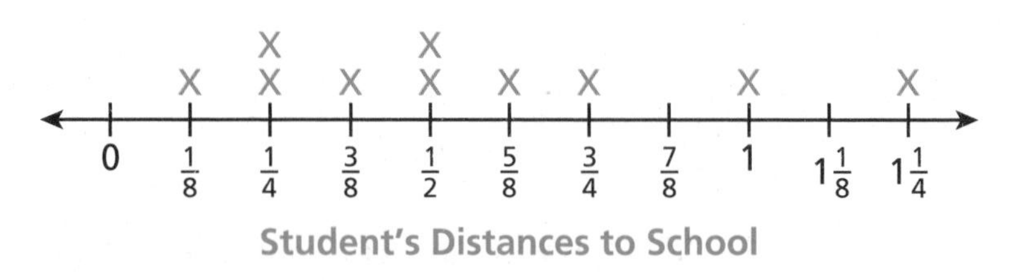

To answer the question, locate $\frac{1}{2}$ on the number line. Count the number of Xs above $\frac{1}{2}$ and above values greater than $\frac{1}{2}$. There are 6 Xs that represent values greater than or equal to $\frac{1}{2}$.

Six students walked at least $\frac{1}{2}$ mile to school.

How could you find the number of students who walked less than a $\frac{1}{2}$ mile to school?

Connect: What you know about line plots to solve problems

This line plot shows the amounts of punch in 10 pitchers.

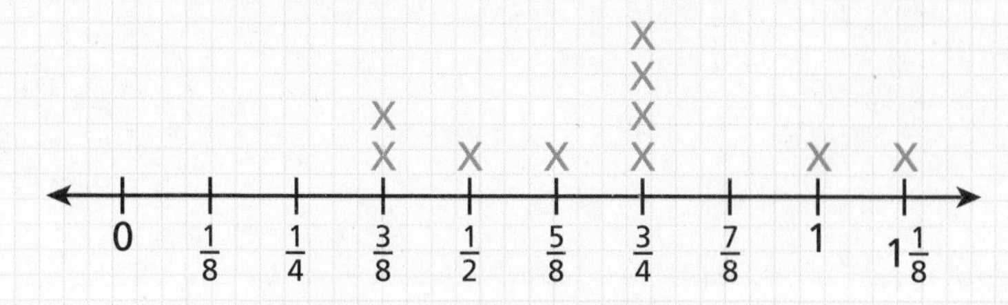

Javier wants to redistribute the punch so there is the same amount in each pitcher. How much punch will be in each pitcher after Javier has redistributed it?

To find how much punch will be in each pitcher after Javier has redistributed it, first find the total gallons of punch in all 10 pitchers. Do this by writing an expression that represents the total gallons of punch. Read the data values from the line plot.

$\underbrace{2 \times \frac{3}{8}}_{\text{2 pitchers have } \frac{3}{8} \text{ gal.}} + \frac{1}{2} + \frac{5}{8} + \underbrace{4 \times \frac{3}{4}}_{\text{4 pitchers have } \frac{3}{4} \text{ gal.}} + 1 + 1\frac{1}{8}$

Evaluate the expression.

$2 \times \frac{3}{8} + \frac{1}{2} + \frac{5}{8} + 4 \times \frac{3}{4} + 1 + 1\frac{1}{8}$ ← The original expression.

$\frac{6}{8} + \frac{1}{2} + \frac{5}{8} + \frac{12}{4} + 1 + 1\frac{1}{8}$ ← Multiply.

$\frac{6}{8} + \frac{4}{8} + \frac{5}{8} + 3 + 1 + 1\frac{1}{8}$ ← Rewrite $\frac{12}{4}$ as 3. Rewrite the other fractions so all have the denominator 8.

$5\frac{16}{8}$ ← Add.

7 ← Simplify.

Divide the total number of gallons by the 10 pitchers.

$7 \div 10 = \frac{7}{10}$

▶ Each pitcher will contain $\frac{7}{10}$ gallon of punch after Javier redistributes it.

Guided Practice

Use the data set below to make a line plot.

1.

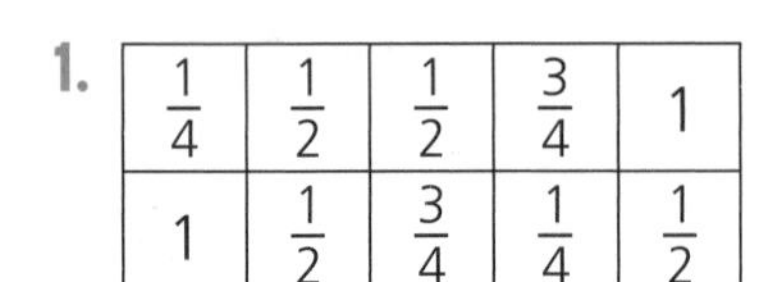

$\frac{1}{4}$	$\frac{1}{2}$	$\frac{1}{2}$	$\frac{3}{4}$	1
1	$\frac{1}{2}$	$\frac{3}{4}$	$\frac{1}{4}$	$\frac{1}{2}$

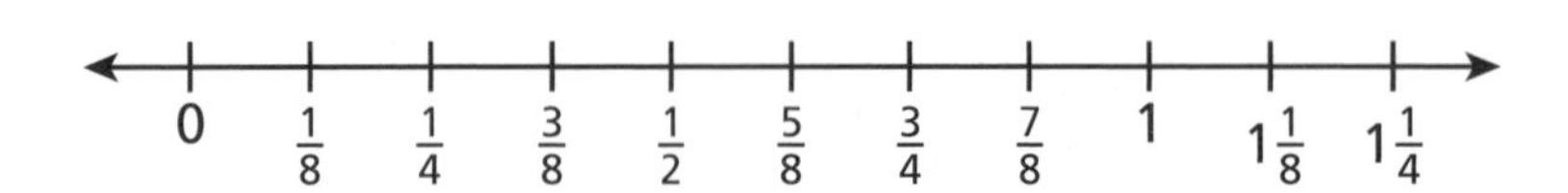

Solve.

2. The data set below lists the amounts of water in cups in 14 vases.

$\frac{7}{8}$	$\frac{1}{4}$	1	$\frac{3}{4}$	$\frac{3}{4}$	$\frac{1}{8}$	$\frac{5}{8}$
1	$\frac{1}{2}$	1	$\frac{1}{2}$	$\frac{3}{4}$	$1\frac{1}{8}$	$1\frac{1}{4}$

a. Make a line plot to organize and examine the data.

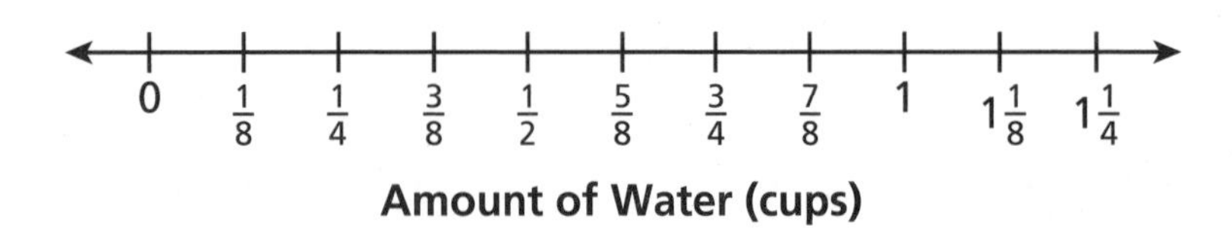

b. How many vases have less than $\frac{3}{4}$ cup of water?

____

c. How many vases have at least $\frac{1}{2}$ cup of water.

____

Guided Practice

3. Mr. Park has 10 bags of almonds. The line plot shows the weight of each bag.

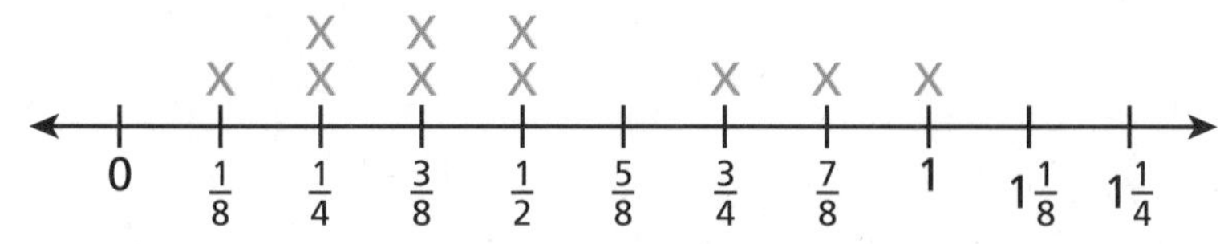

Weight of Almonds (pounds)

Mr. Park wants to redistribute the almonds so that each bag weighs the same. What will be the weight of each bag?

a. Complete this expression for the total weight of the almonds.

$\frac{1}{8} + 2 \times$ ____ $+ 2 \times$ ____ $+ 2 \times$ ____ $+ \frac{3}{4} + \frac{7}{8} + 1$

b. Evaluate the expression. Show your work.

c. Divide the total weight by the 10 bags. Give the answer as a fraction.

________________ = ________________

When the almonds are redistributed equally among 10 bags, the weight of each bag will be ____ pound(s).

Think • Pair • Share

MP3 **4.** Cassandra wrote this expression to represent the sum of the data shown on the line plot below. Is her expression correct? Why or why not? Explain your reasoning.

$\frac{1}{4} + \frac{1}{4} + (3 \times \frac{1}{2}) + (2 \times \frac{3}{4}) + 1$

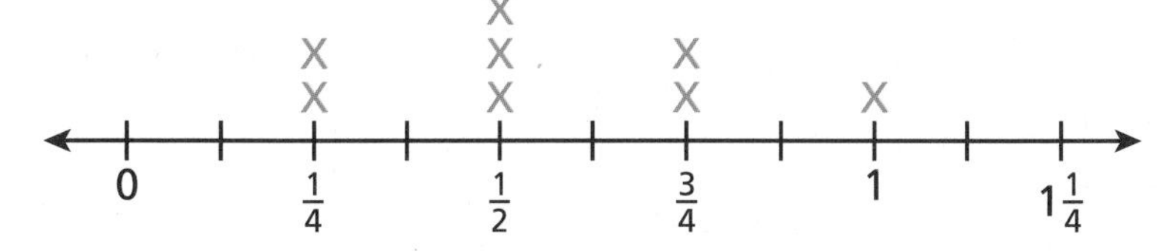

Independent Practice

Use the data set below to make a line plot.

1.

$\frac{2}{4}$	$\frac{1}{4}$	1	$\frac{3}{4}$	$\frac{1}{4}$	$\frac{1}{2}$
$\frac{3}{4}$	$\frac{1}{4}$	$\frac{1}{2}$	$\frac{3}{4}$	1	$\frac{5}{8}$

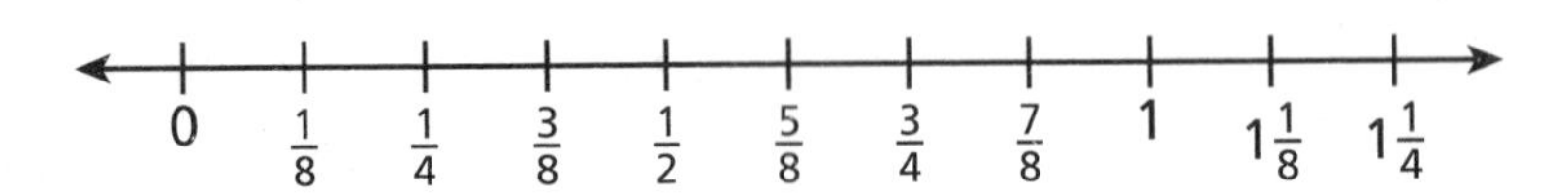

a. How many numbers on the line plot are greater than $\frac{5}{8}$? ____

Solve.

2. Mrs. Kelly has 10 square mosaic tiles. The data set below lists the side length of each tile in inches.

Lengths of Tile (inches)

$\frac{1}{2}$	1	$\frac{3}{4}$	$\frac{1}{2}$	$\frac{1}{2}$
$\frac{3}{4}$	$\frac{3}{8}$	$\frac{1}{4}$	$\frac{7}{8}$	1

a. Make a line plot to organize and examine the data set.

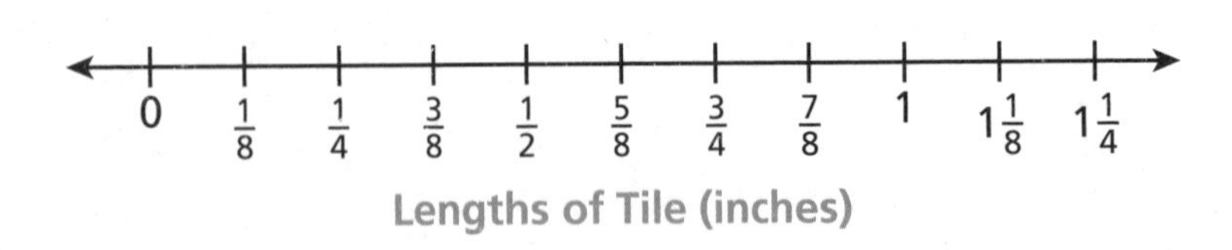

b. What is the sum of the lengths of the 10 tiles? Show your work.

Independent Practice

For exercises 3–4, circle the correct answer. Use the line plot below.

This line plot shows the weights of the deli meat Mr. Arlen sold to customers this morning.

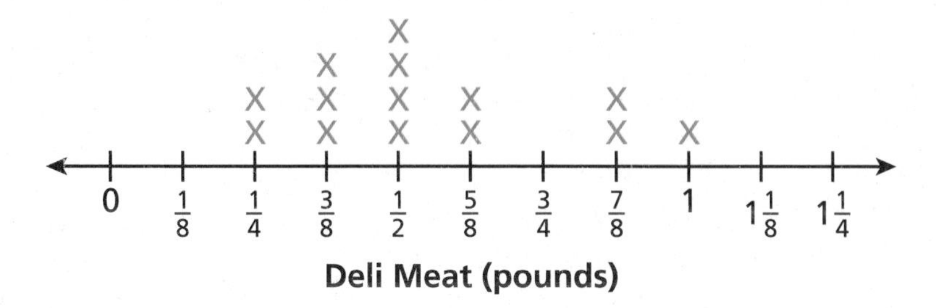

3. How many of the weights are less than $\frac{1}{2}$ pound?

   a. 6   b. 7

   c. 5   d. 9

4. How many of the weights are $\frac{3}{4}$ pound or more?

   a. 0   b. 2

   c. 5   d. 3

Solve.

5. Fourteen students in gym class ran the distances shown in the line plot below.

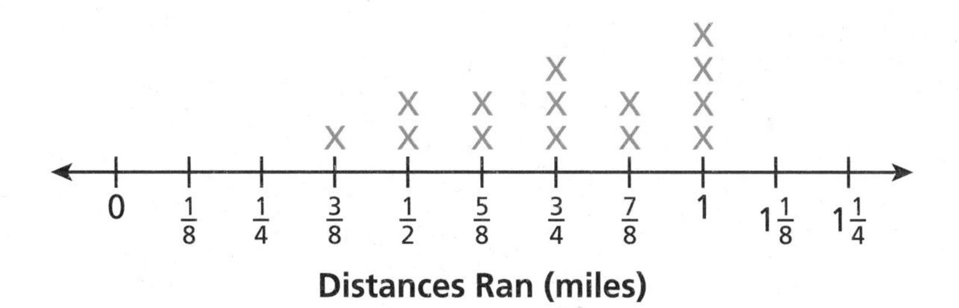

   a. What is the distance most of the students ran?

   ____

   b. What is the total distance that the 14 students ran?

   ____

Independent Practice

6. Ms. Quentin wants to find out how many students in her class correctly answered at least half of the problems on a 10-question quiz. Explain how she can use a line plot to find the answer. What fractions could Ms. Quentin use for her number line?

MP5 7. A tailor measures patches of fabric. The line plot shows his measurements. He wants to make a patchwork jacket, which requires $3\frac{7}{8}$ yards of fabric. Does the tailor have enough fabric to make the jacket? If so, how much fabric is left over? If not, how much additional fabric does he need?

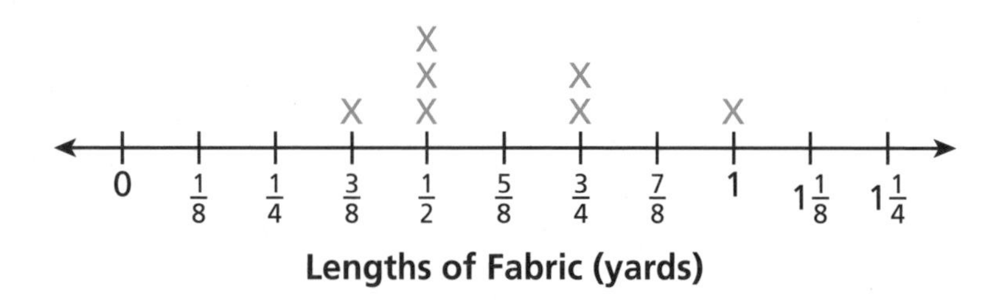

Show your work.

Answer ______________________________

Independent Practice

MP6 **8.** A painter measures the amount of paint in gallons left in 5 cans: $\frac{1}{2}$, $\frac{3}{4}$, 1, $\frac{1}{4}$, $\frac{1}{2}$. She wants to combine all the paint and pour it into the fewest number of cans possible. Each can holds a maximum of one gallon of paint. Make a line plot to show the data. How many cans of paint will she need?

Show your work.

Answer ______________________________

MP1 **9.** A baker needs $7\frac{1}{8}$ pounds of strawberries for the week. One shipment includes 8 baskets weighing the recorded pounds listed at the right. Make a line plot to show the data.

He gives away the baskets of strawberries that weigh less than $\frac{3}{4}$ pound. With the remaining baskets, will he have enough for the week? If so, how many pounds will he have left over? If not, how many additional pounds will he need?

Weights of Baskets (pounds)

$\frac{7}{8}$	1	$\frac{5}{8}$	$\frac{3}{4}$
1	$\frac{3}{4}$	$\frac{3}{4}$	$\frac{7}{8}$

Answer ______________________________

Justify your answer using words, drawings, or numbers.

MP5 **10.** Collect 10 classroom items that are 1 foot or less in length. Measure your items to the nearest inch. Record your measurements as fractions of a foot on a line plot. Make up a problem about your line plot. Give the solution to your problem.

Answer ______________________________

Justify your answer using words, drawings, or numbers.

Lesson 28

Understand Concepts of Volume Measurement

Essential Question:
What is volume and how do you measure it?

5.MD.3a; 5.MD.3b

Words to Know:
- unit cube
- volume
- cubic unit

Guided Instruction

In this lesson you will learn about using cubic units to measure volume.

Understand: Volume and cubic units

How many cubes like the one on the left below, will fit inside the box on the right?

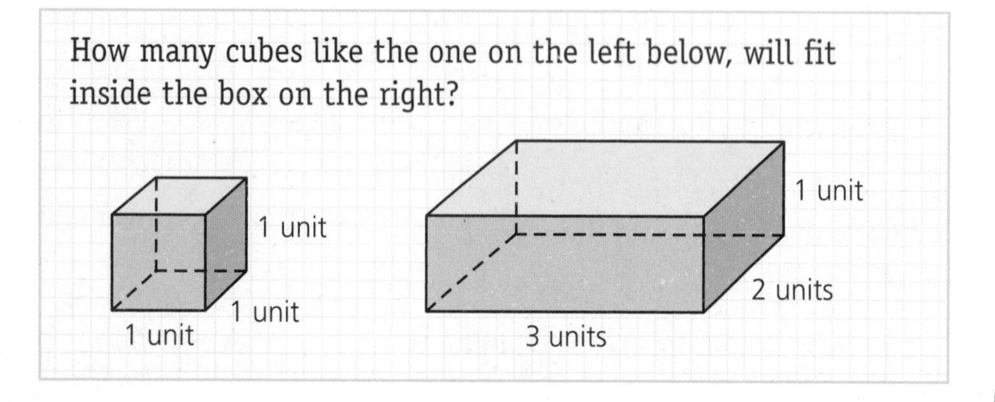

Remember!
A face is a flat surface of a solid figure surrounded by line segments. An edge is a line segment where two faces of a solid figure meet.

The cube above is called a unit cube because it has edge lengths of 1 unit.

The drawing below shows that 6 unit cubes fit inside the box.

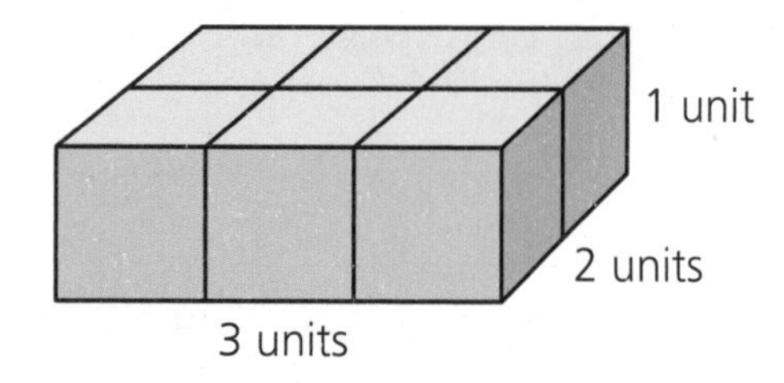

➡ 6 unit cubes will fit inside the box.

The volume of a three-dimensional figure is a measure of the amount of space the figure occupies or contains. A unit cube has a volume of 1 cubic unit. Because the box in the problem can be packed with 6 unit cubes *with no gaps or overlaps*, it has a volume of 6 cubic units.

What is the difference between area and volume?

Understand: Comparing volumes

The right rectangular prisms below are made with inch cubes. How do these volumes of the prisms compare?

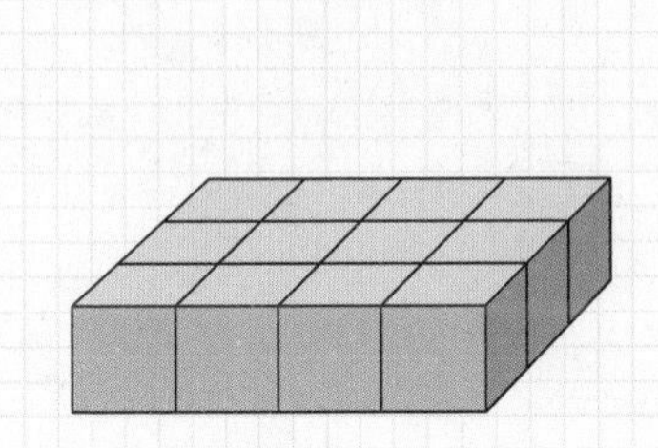

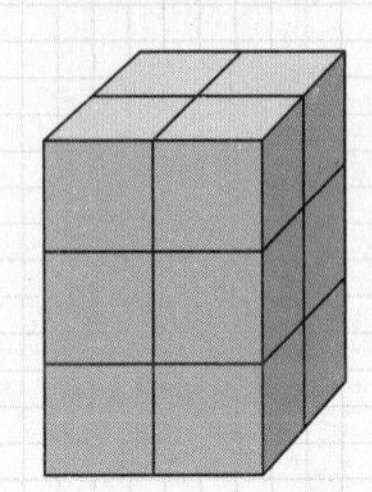

An inch cube has edge lengths of 1 inch. The volume of an inch cube is 1 cubic inch, which can also be written as 1 in.^{3}

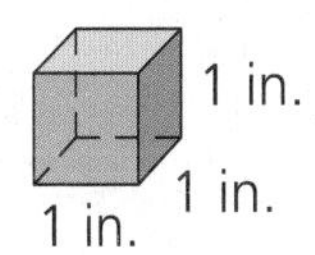

To find the volume of each prism, count the number of inch cubes that *pack* each prism.

The prism on the left is made up of 3 rows with 4-inch cubes in each row. So, it contains 4 + 4 + 4, or 12, inch cubes in all. Its volume is 12 cubic inches, or 12 in.^{3}

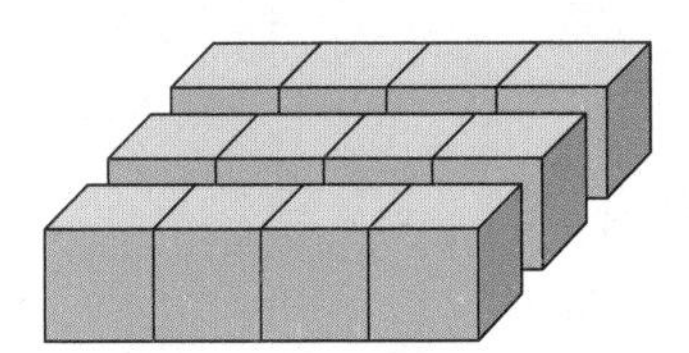

The prism on the right has 3 layers with 4 cubes in each layer. So, it contains 4 + 4 + 4, or 12 inch cubes. Its volume is 12 cubic inches, or 12 in.^{3}

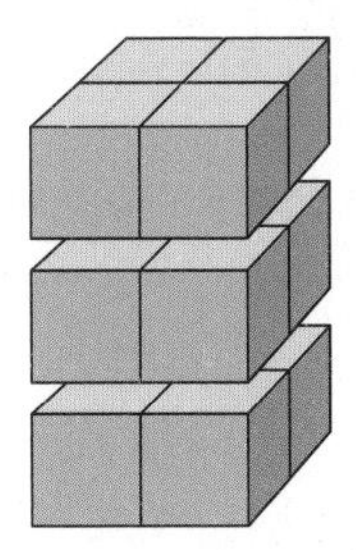

➡ The volumes of the right rectangular prisms are the same. Both have a volume of 12 cubic inches, or 12 in.^{3}

Guided Instruction

Connect: What you know about volume and liquid volume

A box the size of a centimeter cube will hold 1 milliliter of water.

Marley has a plastic box filled with centimeter cubes. The box is shown at the right. She wants to remove the cubes and fill the plastic box with 36 milliliters of water. Will all the water fit?

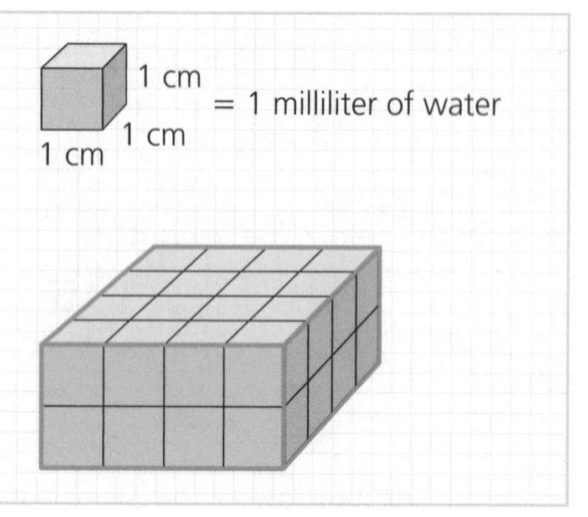

Step 1

Find the volume of the plastic box in cubic centimeters.

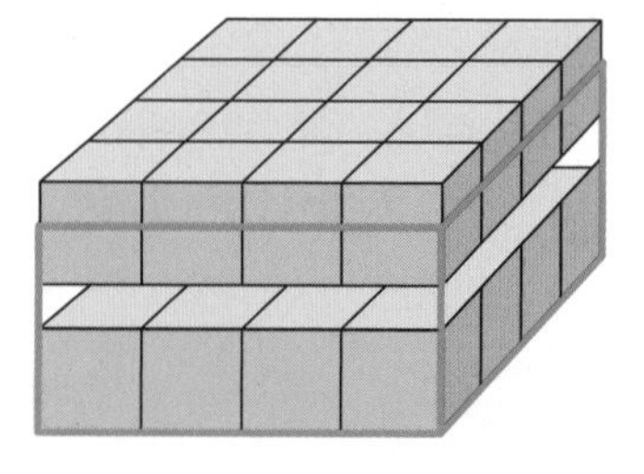

The plastic box contains 2 layers of centimeter cubes. Each layer has 16 cubes. The total number of centimeter cubes is 16 + 16. The volume of the plastic box is 32 cm^3.

Step 2

Find the liquid volume of the plastic box in milliliters.

The plastic box holds 32-centimeter cubes. If each of these cubes were an empty box, it could hold 1 milliliter of water. So, the liquid volume of the plastic box is 32 milliliters.

Step 3

Determine whether the water will fit in the plastic box.

Marley has 36 milliliters of water, but the plastic box holds only 32 milliliters.

➡ The water will not fit in the plastic box.

Guided Practice

Complete the statements.

1. Some unit cubes have already been placed in this box.

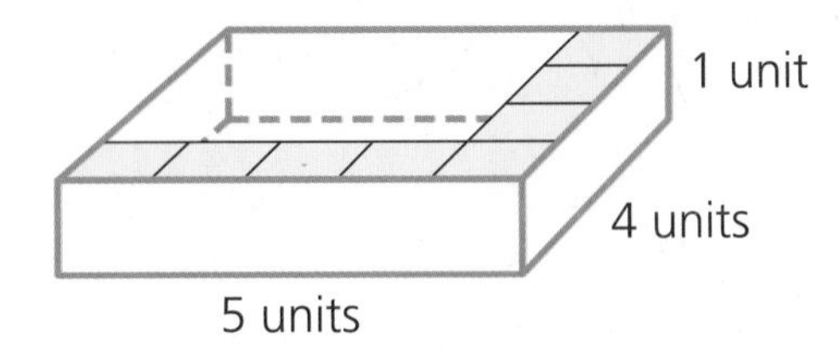

a. A total of ____ unit cubes can be packed into the box.

b. The volume of the box is ____ cubic units.

2. This right rectangular prism is made of centimeter cubes.

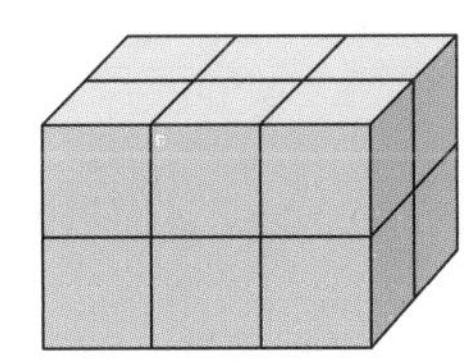

a. The prism has ____ layers of centimeter cubes.

There are ____ cubes in each layer.

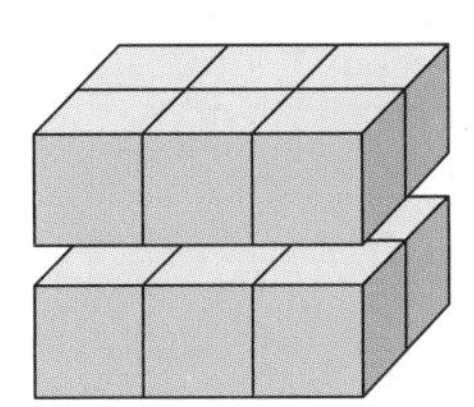

b. The volume of the prism is ____ cm^3.

Think • Pair • Share

MP3 3. Paulina and Jackson are measuring the volume of the same box using unit cubes. Paulina can fit 9 unit cubes inside the box without any gaps or overlaps. Jackson can fit 16 unit cubes inside the box without any gaps or overlaps. Is it possible that they are using unit cubes of the same size? Explain your reasoning.

Independent Practice

Complete the statements.

1. Some unit cubes have already been placed in this box.

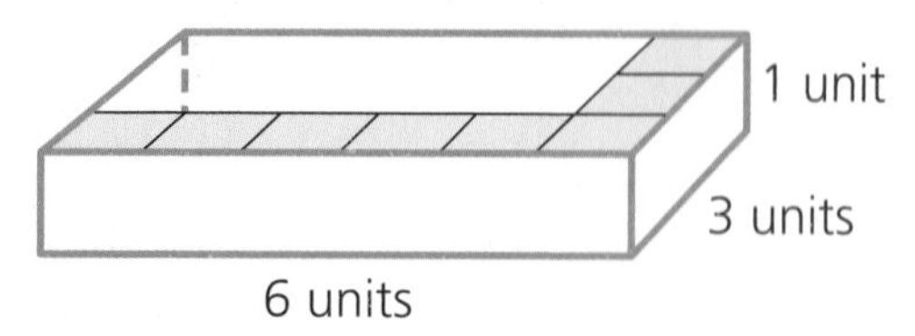

a. A total of ____ unit cubes can be packed into the box.

b. The volume of the box is ____ cubic units.

2. This right rectangular prism is made of inch cubes.

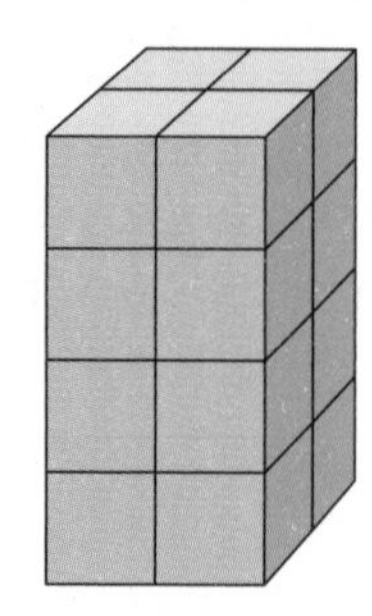

a. The prism has ____ layers of inch cubes.

There are ____ cubes in each layer.

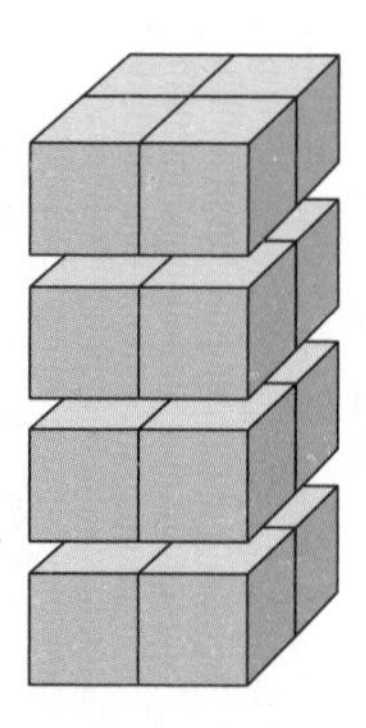

b. The volume of the prism is ____ $in.^3$

Fill in the blanks.

3. ________________ is the amount of space that a two-dimensional figure occupies.

4. ________________ is the amount of space that a three-dimensional solid occupies.

Independent Practice

Circle the most appropriate unit to measure the volume of each item.

5. a glass of orange juice

   a. square meters
   b. cubic yards
   c. cubic inches
   d. cups

6. a brick

   a. cubic centimeters
   b. liters
   c. ounces
   d. miles

7. a storage unit

   a. quarts
   b. cubic meters
   c. cubic mililiters
   d. square centimeters

Solve.

8. A crate can be filled with 4 layers of unit cubes. Each layer contains 6 unit cubes.

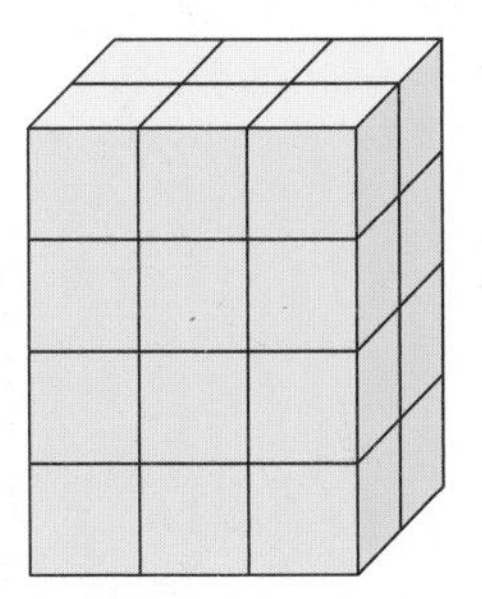

   a. What is the total number of unit cubes that can fill the crate?

   ____

   b. What is the volume of the crate? Express your answer in cubic units.

   ____

Independent Practice

MP3 **9.** Ambika found the volume of the solid below by counting the unit cubes. Then she wrote an expression for the volume.

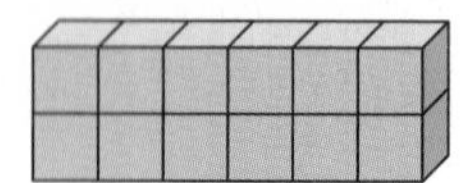

number of unit cubes in solid = 14
volume of solid = 14 square units

Is Ambika correct? If not, explain how she can correct her work.

MP3 **10.** Kevin filled a container with unit cubes. He was able to fit 16 unit cubes into the container, as shown below. He says the volume is 16 cubic units. Is his measurement accurate? Why or why not?

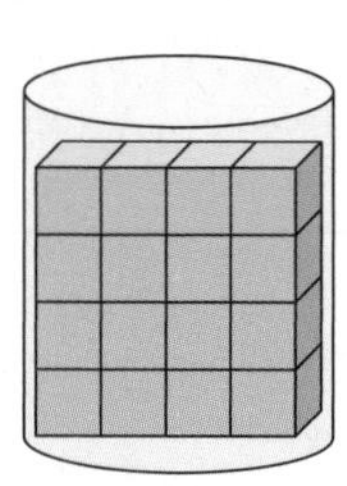

Solve the problems.

11. A solid figure is packed with 52 cubes. If the edge lengths of the cubes are 1 meter, what is the volume of the solid?

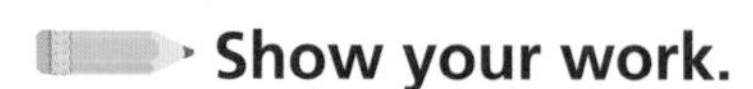 **Show your work.**

Answer ______________________________

12. Joey is packing books into a box. Each book has a volume of 125 cubic inches. Joey can fit 11 books into the box without any space in between or above them. What is the volume of the box?

Show your work.

Answer ______________________________

Independent Practice

MP1 **13.** A dresser has a volume of 120 cubic feet. A nightstand takes up exactly half the amount of space. What is the volume of the nightstand?

Show your work.

Answer ________________________

MP7 **14.** The volume of a stick of butter is 180 cubic centimeters. The volume of a jar of grape jam is 240 milliliters. What is the total volume of both items? Express your answer in cubic centimeters.

Answer ________________________

Justify your answer using words, drawings, or numbers.

MP7 **15.** A skyscraper has 27 floors. Each floor has 15 offices. The volume of 1 office is 1000 cubic meters. Hallways and other areas besides offices take up 100,000 cubic meters of space on each floor. What is the total volume of the skyscraper?

Answer ________________________

Justify your answer using words, drawings, or numbers.

Lesson

29 Measure Volume

Essential Question:
How do you measure the volume of a right rectangular prism?
5.MD.4

Guided Instruction

In this lesson you will learn how to measure volume by counting unit cubes.

Understand: Counting unit cubes

Marnie packs a rectangular box with inch cubes as shown below. What is the volume of the rectangular box?

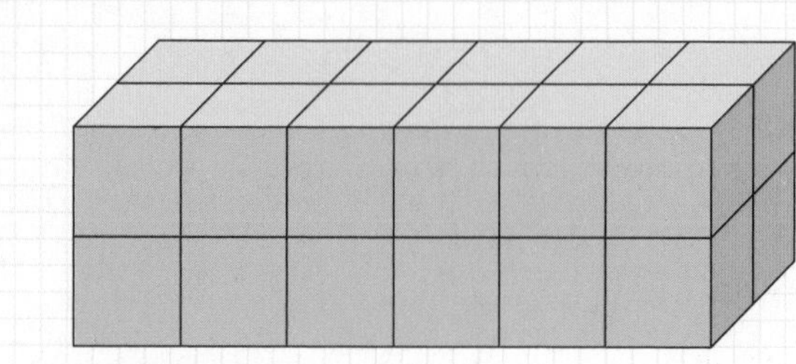

To find the volume of the rectangular box, count the number of inch cubes Marnie uses to pack the box.

There are two layers of inch cubes, like the one shown below. Each layer has 12 cubes.

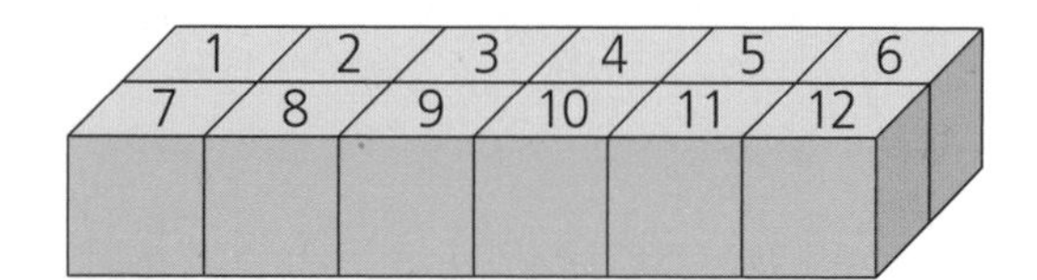

Remember!
An inch cube has edge lengths of 1 inch and a volume of 1 cubic inch. This volume can be written as 1 in.^{3}

There are 12 + 12, or 24, inch cubes in all.

➡ The volume of the rectangular box is 24 in^3.

Suppose Marnie's box rested on one of its square faces, rather than on a rectangular face. How would the volume change?

Connect: **What you know about measuring volume of right rectangular prisms with unit cubes**

A sporting goods store receives a shipment of basketballs. Each basketball is packed into a box that is a foot cube. These cubic boxes are packed into a larger box as shown. What is the volume of the larger box?

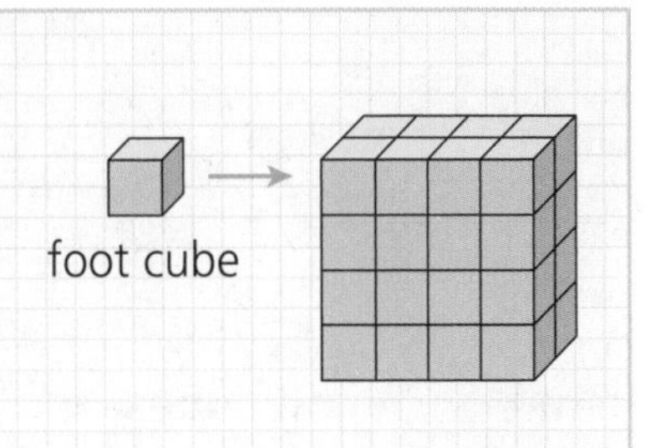

To find the volume of the larger box, you can count the cubes layer by layer.

Count the number of foot cubes in the first layer of the box.

There are 2 rows of 4 foot cubes, or 8 foot cubes in the first layer.

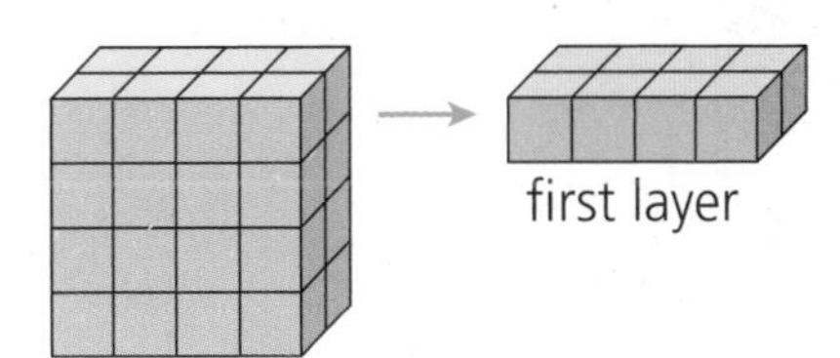

Count the number of layers of foot cubes that fill the box.

There are 4 layers.

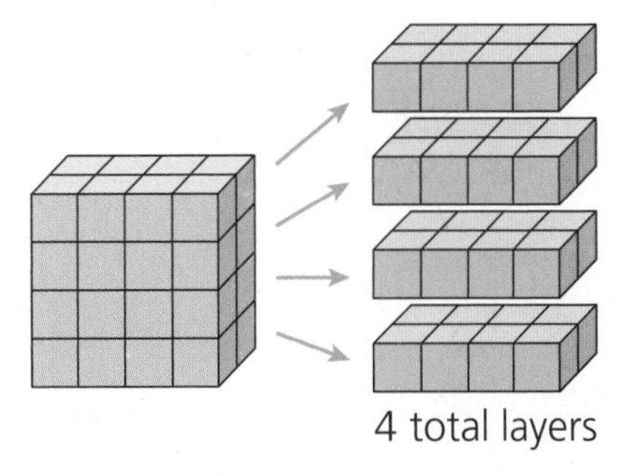

Add to find the total number of foot cubes in the four layers:
$8 + 8 + 8 + 8 = 32$

The volume of the larger box is 32 cubic feet, or 32 ft^3.

Livia packs a cubic box with 27 inch cubes. What is the length of each side of the box? Make a drawing to help you answer the question.

Guided Practice

For exercises 1–4, count the unit cubes to find the volume of each figure.

1.

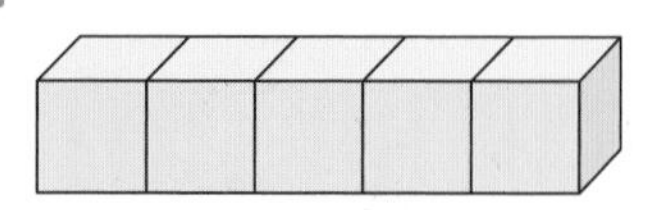

There are ____ unit cubes.

The volume is ____ cubic units.

2.

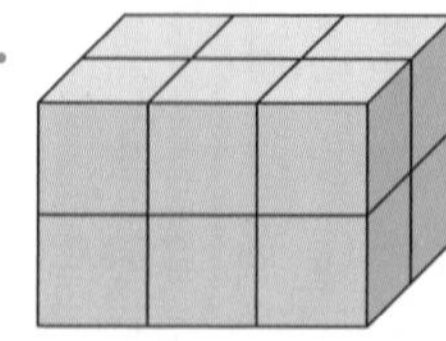

There are ____ unit cubes.

The volume is ____ cubic units.

3.

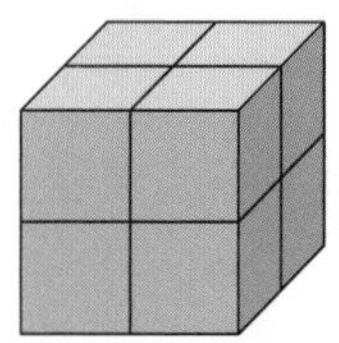

There are ____ unit cubes.

The volume is ____ cubic units.

4.

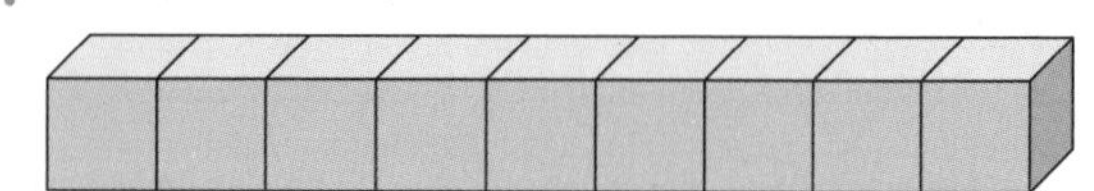

There are ____ unit cubes.

The volume is ____ cubic units.

5. This figure is made from inch cubes. Find the volume of the figure by following the instructions given in a–d.

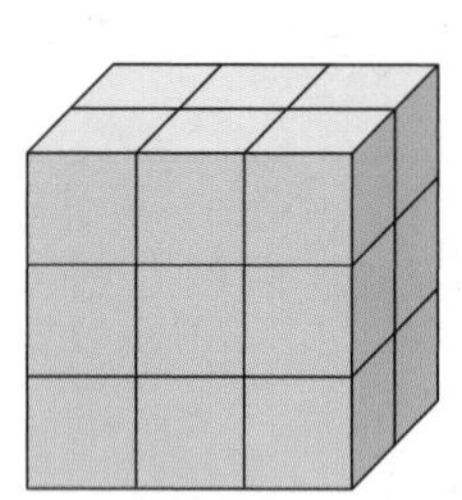

a. Count the number of inch cubes in the first layer of the figure.

There are ____ inch cubes in the first layer.

b. Count the number of layers. There are ____ layers.

c. Add the cubes in each layer to find the total number of cubes.

____ + ____ + ____ = ____

d. The volume of the figure is ____ cubic inches.

Guided Practice

Find the volume of each figure by counting the unit cubes.

6.

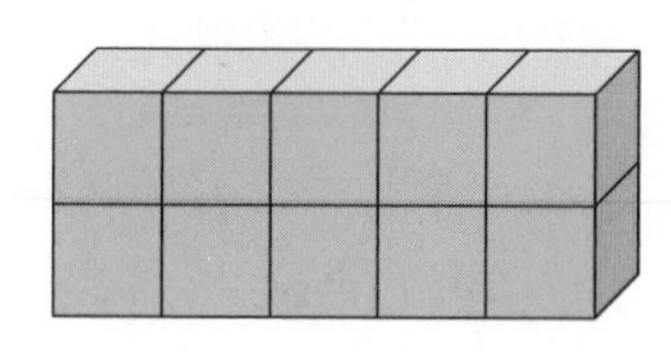

____ cubic units

7.

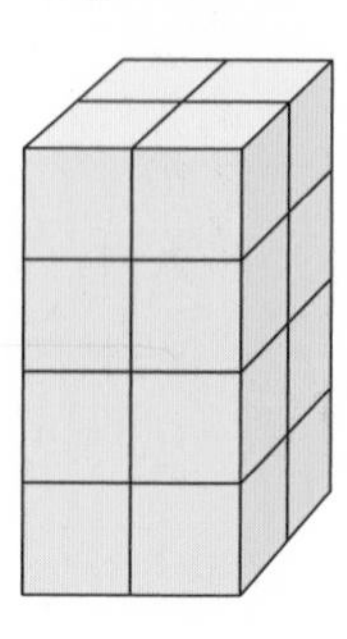

____ cubic units

8.

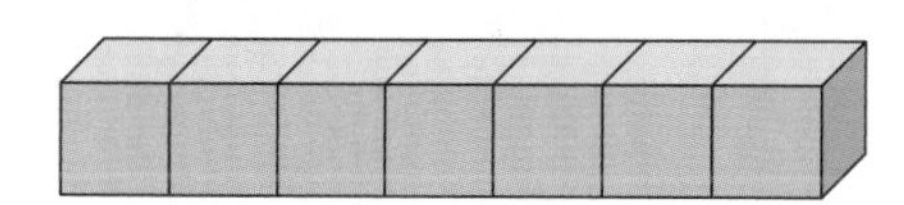

____ cubic units

9.

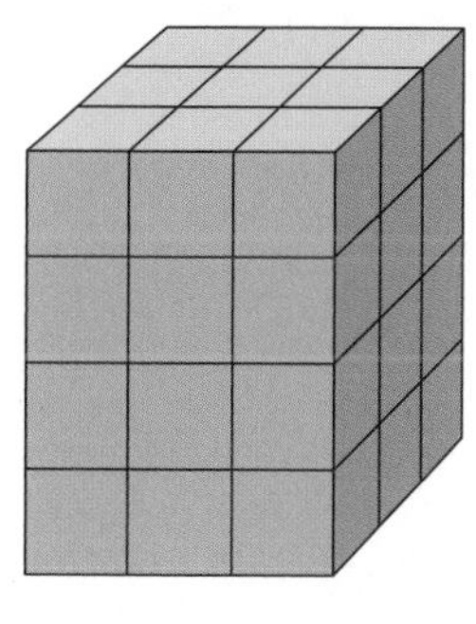

____ cubic units

Think • Pair • Share

MP3 **10.** Robert wants to measure the volume of the figure below. He says there are 4 cubic units in the bottom layer of the figure. Since there are 2 layers in the figure, he thinks he can add 4 + 4 to find the total volume of the figure. Is Robert's reasoning correct? If not, explain how you can find the volume.

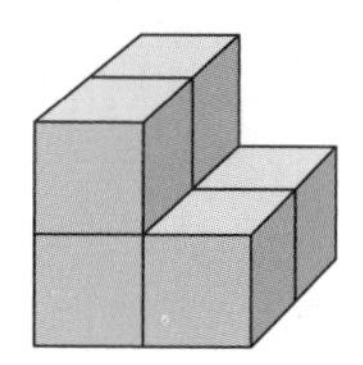

Independent Practice

For exercises 1–4, count the unit cubes to find the volume.

1.

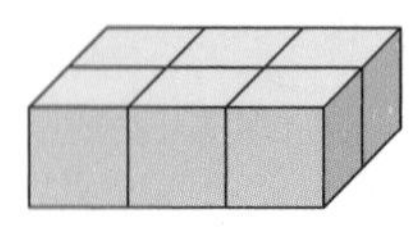

There are ____ unit cubes.

The volume is ____ cubic units.

2.

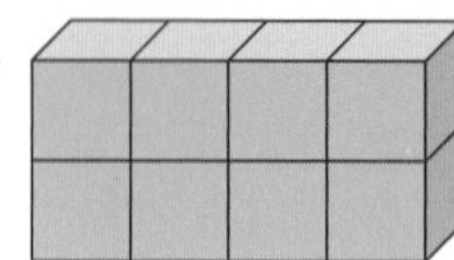

There are ____ unit cubes.

The volume is ____ cubic units.

3.

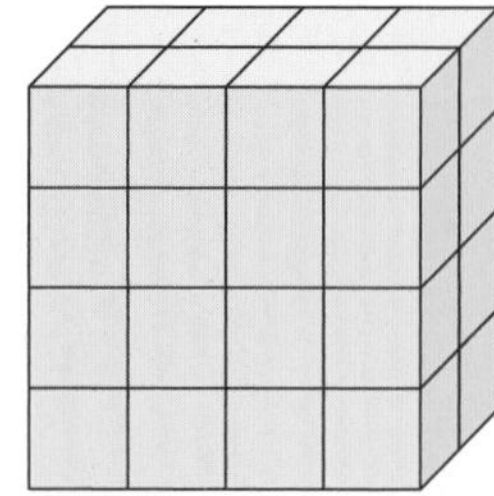

There are ____ unit cubes.

The volume is ____ cubic units.

4.

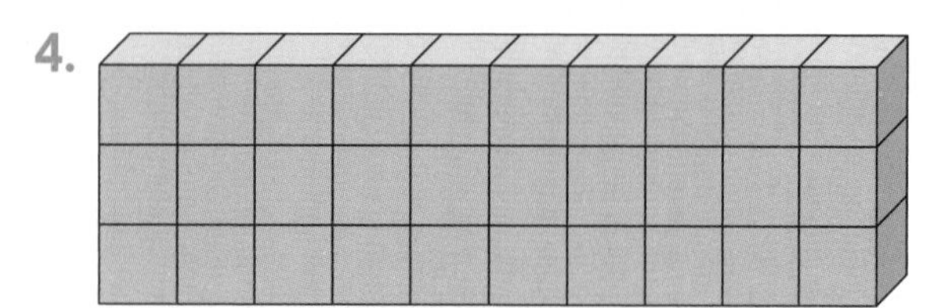

There are ____ unit cubes.

The volume is ____ cubic units.

5. This figure is made from centimeter cubes. Find the volume of the figure by following the instructions given in a–d.

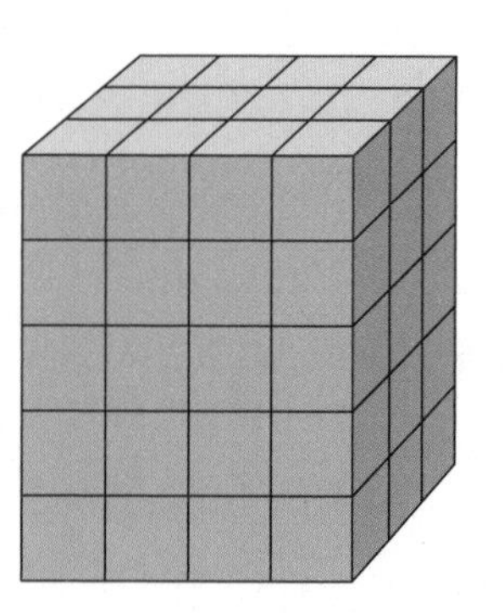

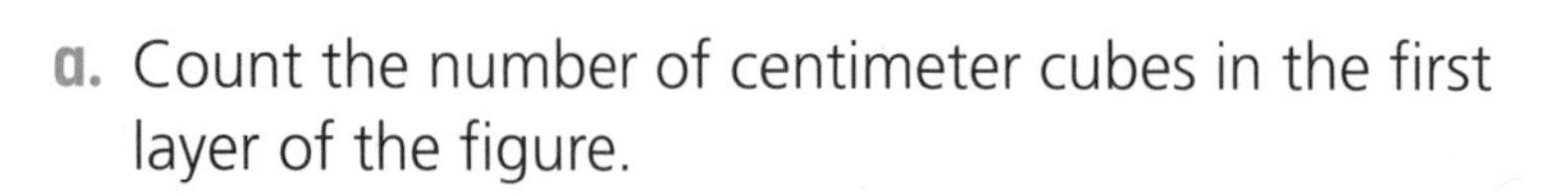

a. Count the number of centimeter cubes in the first layer of the figure.

There are ____ centimeter cubes in the first layer.

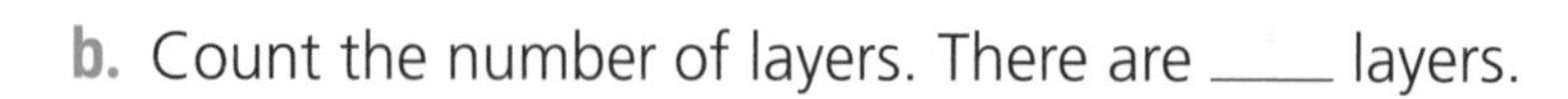

b. Count the number of layers. There are ____ layers.

c. Add the cubes in each layer to find the total number of cubes.

____ + ____ + ____ + ____ + ____ = ____

d. The volume of the figure is ____ cubic centimeters.

Independent Practice

6. This figure is made from meter cubes. Find the volume of the figure by following the instructions given in a–d.

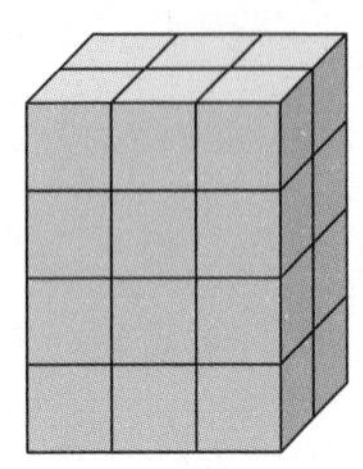

a. How many meter cubes are in the first layer of the figure?

____ meter cubes

b. How many layers of cubes are there? There are ____ layers.

c. What is the volume of the figure?

____ + ____ + ____ + ____ = ____

d. The volume of the figure is ____ cubic meters.

Find the volume of the figures using any method.

7.

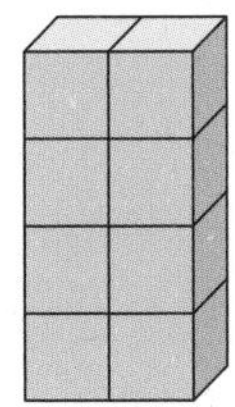

____ cubic units

8.

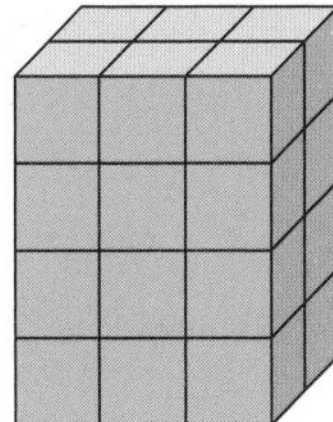

____ cubic units

9.

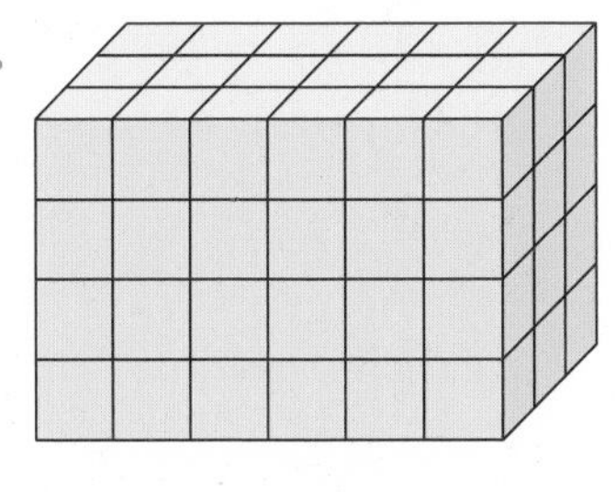

____ cubic units

10.

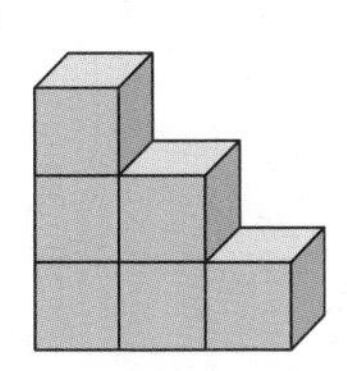

____ cubic units

Independent Practice

11. Find the volume of the figure below. Express your answer in cubic units. Explain the method you used.

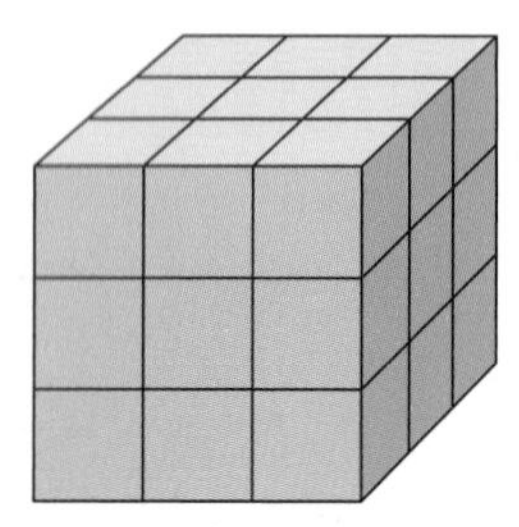

12. Amy said, "There are 3 cubic feet in a cubic yard." Explain why Amy is incorrect.

Circle the correct answer.

13. A solid figure has 6 layers of cubes. Each layer has 8 inch cubes. What is the volume of the figure?

a. 6 cubic inches

b. 8 cubic inches

c. 14 cubic inches

d. 48 cubic inches

Solve the problems.

MP1 **14.** A solid figure has a volume of 18 cubic centimeters. The figure has 3 layers of centimeter cubes. If each layer has the same number of centimeter cubes, how many centimeter cubes are in each layer?

Show your work.

Answer ______________________

Independent Practice

MP1 **15.** Carmella is making a model using centimeter cubes. She uses 4 cubes to build the first layer as shown below. How many more layers of 4 cubes must Carmella build so her model will have a volume of 60 cubic centimeters?

Show your work.

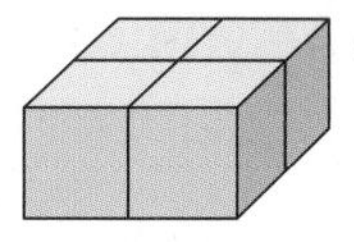

Answer ______________________________

MP7 **16.** Below is one possible rectangular prism that can be made from 16 unit cubes. Describe two different rectangular prisms you could make from 16 unit cubes.

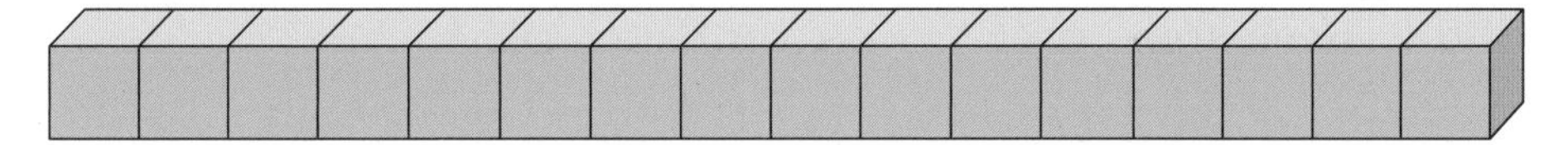

Answer ______________________________

Justify your answer using words, drawings, or numbers.

MP7 **17.** Each cube in the figure below measures 1 cubic meter. What is the total volume of the figure?

Answer ______________________________

Justify your answer using words, drawings, or numbers.

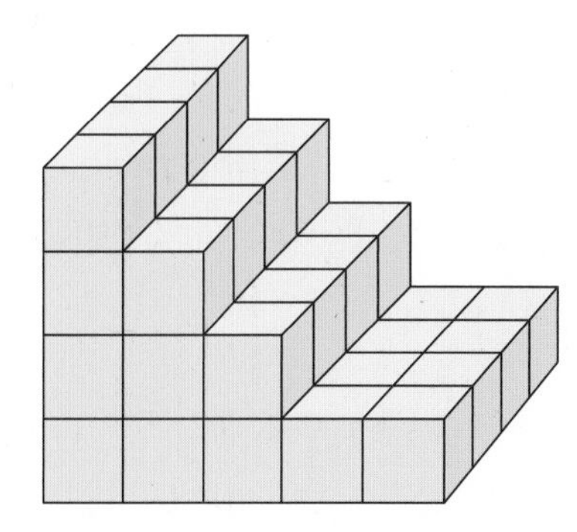

Lesson 30

Find Volume: Relate Packing of Unit Cubes to Multiplying

Essential Question:
How can you multiply to find the volume of a right rectangular prism?
5.MD.5a

Guided Instruction

In this lesson you will learn how counting unit cubes to find the volume of a right rectangular prism is related to multiplying side lengths of the prism.

Understand: How to find the volume of a right rectangular prism by packing it with unit cubes

A jewelry box is shaped like a right rectangular prism with the dimensions shown. Use unit cubes to find the volume of the jewelry box.

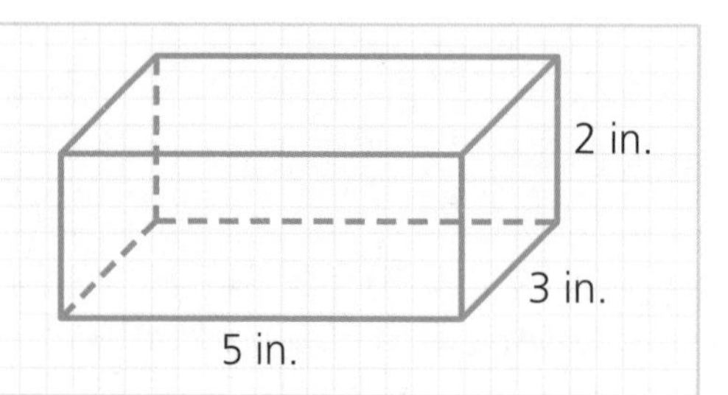

To find the volume of the jewelry box, pack the box with inch cubes.

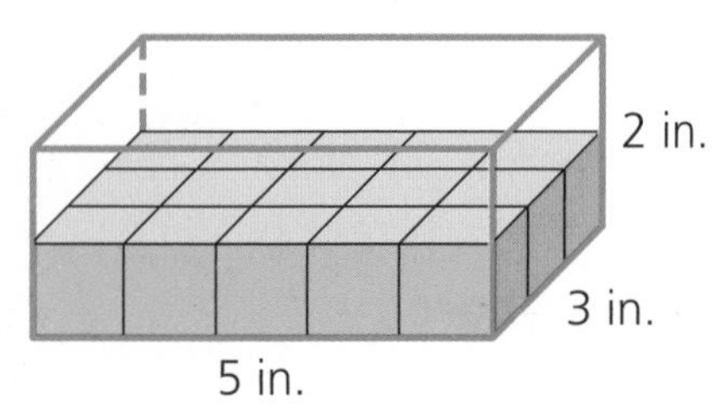

$3 \times 5 = 15$ inch cubes

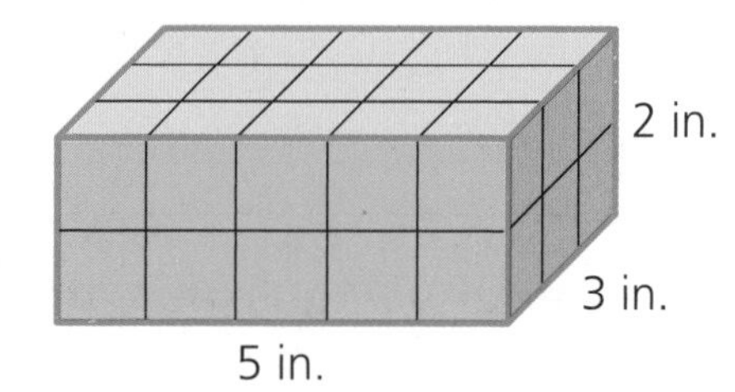

$2 \times 15 = 30$ inch cubes

The bottom layer of inch cubes has 3 rows of 5 cubes, or 15 cubes. Two layers of cubes can be packed into the jewelry box, so there are 2×15, or 30, inch cubes in the box.

➡ The volume of the jewelry box is 30 cubic inches.

Luke solved the problem above by visualizing 5 vertical columns of inch cubes, instead of 2 horizontal layers. What do you think Luke did?

Guided Instruction

Understand: How to find the volume of a right rectangular prism using multiplication

Find the volume of the right rectangular prism by packing it with unit cubes. Then explain why you can find the volume simply by multiplying the dimensions of the prism.

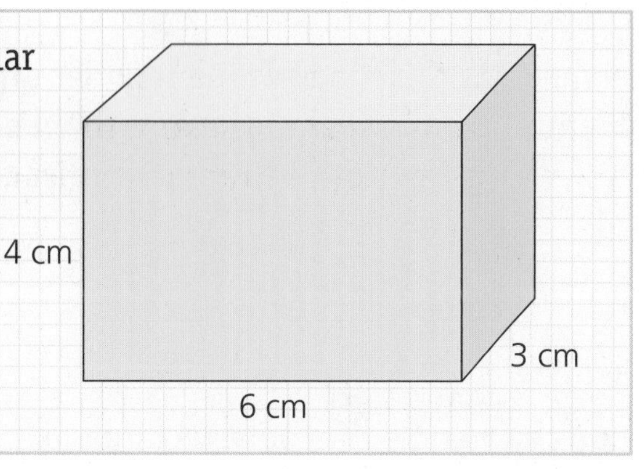

Visualize packing the right rectangular prism with centimeter cubes.

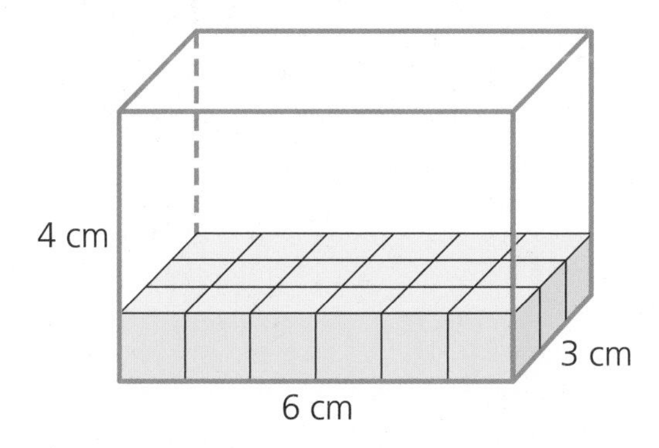

$3 \times 6 = 18$ centimeter cubes

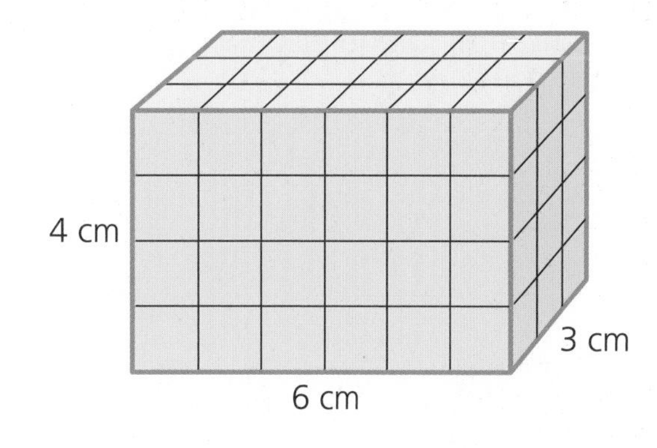

$4 \times 18 = 72$ centimeter cubes

The bottom layer has 3 rows of 6 centimeter cubes, or 18 centimeter cubes. Four layers of cubes can be packed into the prism. So, there are a total of 4×18, or 72 centimeter cubes.

➡ The volume of the right rectangular prism is 72 cm^3.

The product of the length and the width, 3×6, is the number of cubes in each layer. The height is the number of layers. So, you can find the volume by multiplying the dimensions.

volume = length × width × height

$3 \times 6 \times 4$

(3×6: number of cubes in each layer; 4: number of layers)

Guided Instruction

Connect: Multiplying dimensions to multiplying base area times height

A right rectangular prism has whole number dimensions. The area of the base of the prism is 16 square feet, and the height of the prism is 3 feet. Find the volume of the right rectangular prism.

Step 1

Plan the solution.

You can find the volume of a right rectangular prism by multiplying the dimensions. However, in this problem, you are not given the length or the width only the height of 3 feet. Since the area of the base of the right rectangular prism is 16 square feet, you know that length × width = 16 square feet.

You can try listing all the possible lengths and widths and finding the volume for each possibility.

Step 2

Make a table and calculate the volume of each possible prism.

length (ft)	width (ft)	height (ft)	volume (ft^3)
1	16	3	$(1 \times 16) \times 3 = 48$
2	8	3	$(2 \times 8) \times 3 = 48$
4	4	3	$(4 \times 4) \times 3 = 48$
8	2	3	$(8 \times 2) \times 3 = 48$
16	1	3	$(16 \times 1) \times 3 = 48$

The volume of each possible right rectangular prism is 48 cubic feet. The specific length and width do not matter.

➡ The volume of the right rectangular prism is 48 cubic feet.

Use the idea of packing with unit cubes to explain why the volume of a right rectangular prism is the area of the base times the height.

Guided Practice

The diagrams below show a right rectangular prism being packed with foot cubes. Complete exercises 1–2 using the prism.

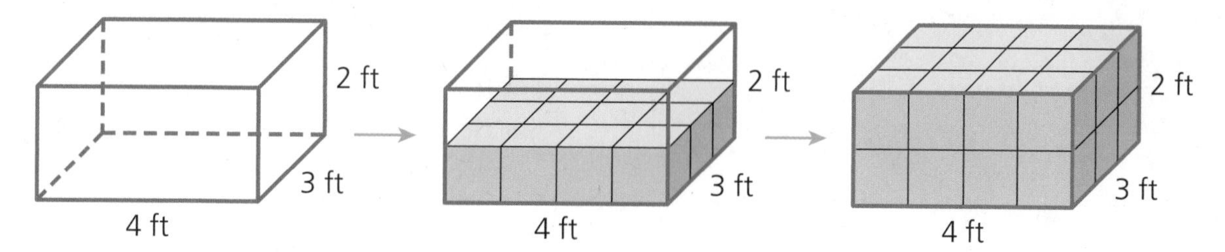

1. Cubes in one layer: ______ Number of layers: ______

2. Find the product below to determine the number of unit cubes that can be packed in the prism. This is the volume of the prism.

   $2 \times$ ______ $=$ ______; The volume of the prism is ______.

For exercises 3–4, use this right rectangular prism given below. Each cube that the prism is packed with has a side length of 1 inch.

3. Multiply to find the number of cubes in the prism.

   cubes in one layer × number of layers = number of cubes

   (______ × ______) × ______ = ______

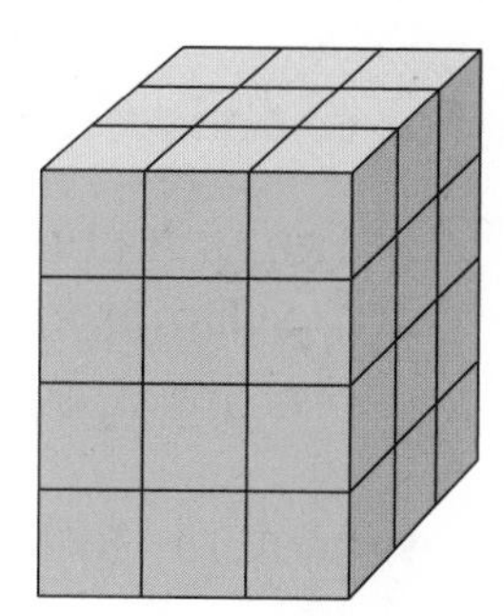

4. What is the volume of the prism? ______

Think • Pair • Share

MP3 5. Preeti says that the volume of the right rectangular prism shown can be found by multiplying the unit cubes in the front layer by the number of layers from front to back.

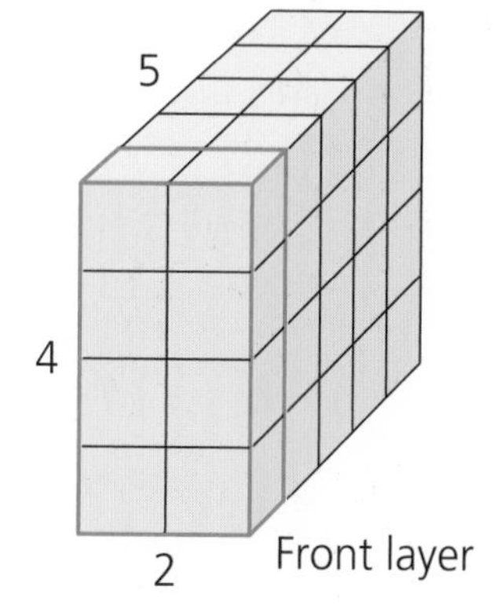

   a. Use her method to find the volume of the prism.

   ____

   b. Explain how you can check your answer without having to count any unit cubes.

   ____

Independent Practice

Each right rectangular prism is packed with unit cubes. Find the volume of each prism by counting the unit cubes.

1. 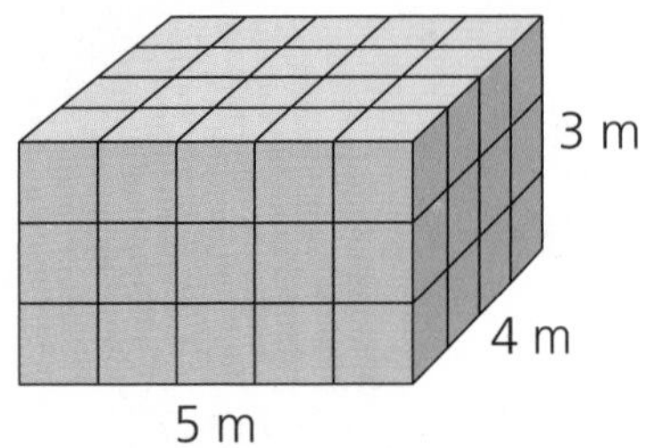

Cubes in one layer: ____

Number of layers: ____

Total number of cubes:

3 × ____ = ____

Volume of prism: __________

2. 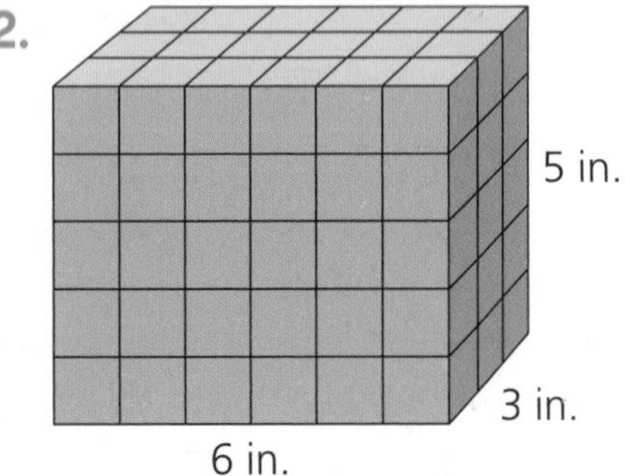

Cubes in one layer: ____

Number of layers: ____

Total number of cubes:

____ × ____ = ____

Volume of prism: __________

For exercises 3–6, use the right rectangular prism given below.

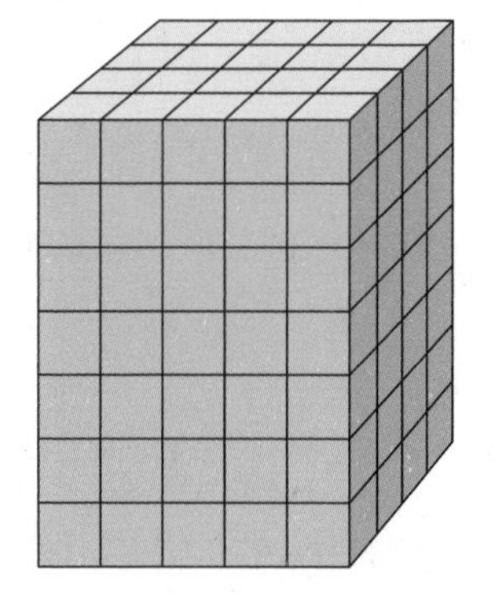

3. The unit cubes in the prism have a side length of 1 millimeter. Label the length, width, and height of the prism, using the appropriate units.

4. Multiply to find the number of unit cubes in the prism.

____

5. What is the volume of the prism? __________

6. Which expression does not represent the total number of unit cubes in the prism?

   a. 20 + 20 + 20 + 20 + 20 + 20 + 20

   b. (5 × 4) + (5 × 4) + (5 × 4) + (5 × 4) + (5 × 4) + (5 × 4) + (5 × 4)

   c. 5 × 4

   d. 7 × (5 × 4)

Independent Practice

For exercises 7–9, use the given right rectangular prism.

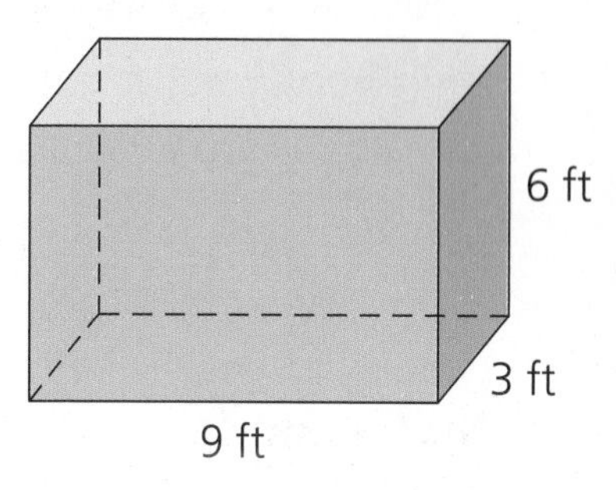

7. Multiply the length and width.

 ____ × ____ = ________

8. Multiply your answer to exercise 7 by the height to find the volume of the prism.

 ____ × ____ = ________

9. Explain how you would use the number of unit cubes to check your answer to exercise 8. Is your answer correct?

For exercises 10–11, find the volume of each box. Each box below is a right rectangular prism.

10.

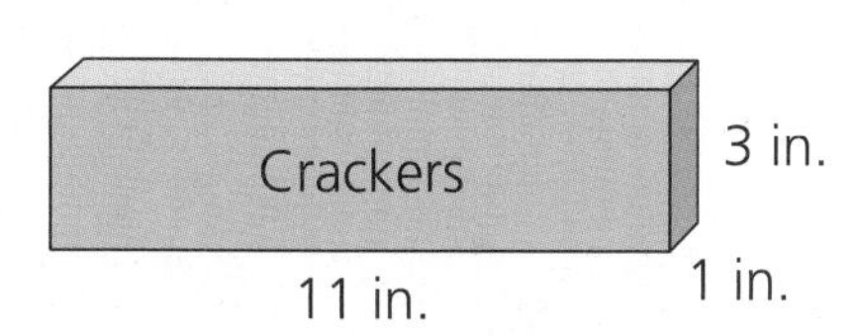

Show your work.

Answer ____________________

11.

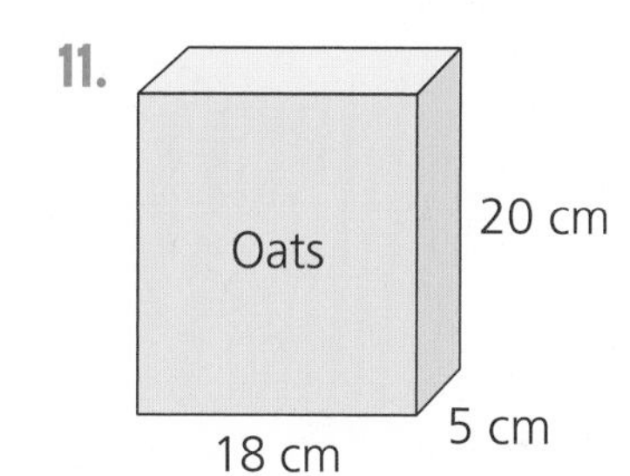

Show your work.

Answer ____________________

Independent Practice

12. Describe two methods you can use to find the volume of this right rectangular prism shown at the right.

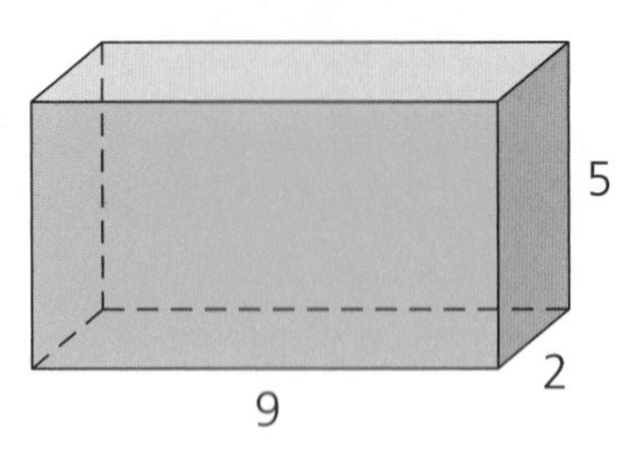

Method 1 ______________________________

Method 2 ______________________________

13. A raised planting bed in the shape of a right rectangular prism has a volume of 30 cubic feet. A large bag of potting soil contains 2 cubic feet of soil. Explain how to determine the number of bags of soil that are needed to fill the planting bed.

Solve the problems.

14. A water tank is shaped like a right rectangular prism and has the dimensions shown. Find the volume of the tank.

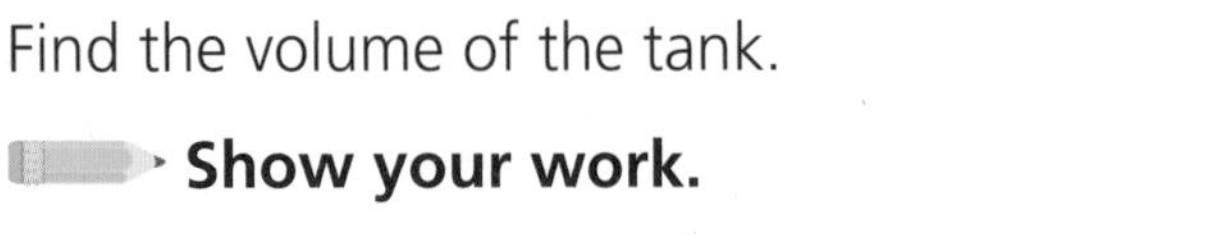
Show your work.

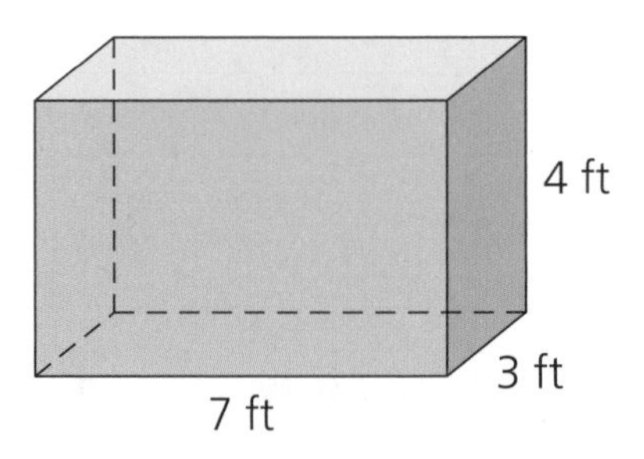

Answer ______________________________

15. The tank in exercise 14 is filled with water. A cubic foot of water weighs about 62 pounds. Explain how to determine the weight of the water in the tank, and then find it.

Independent Practice

MP1 **16.** There is a landing pit shaped like a right rectangular prism at the end of a ramp in an indoor skate park as shown. The pit is filled with foam cubes that have a side length of 1 foot.

5 ft
6 ft
10 ft

The number of foam cubes in the landing pit is equal to $\frac{3}{4}$ of the volume of the landing pit. How many foam cubes are in the landing pit?

Show your work.

Answer ______________________________

MP7 **17.** Zachary uses the expression $10 + 10 + 10$ to find the volume of a right rectangular prism. Mia uses the expression $3 \times (5 \times 2)$ to find the volume of a right rectangular prism. Is it possible that they are finding the volume of the same right rectangular prism?

Answer ______________________________

Justify your answer using words, drawings, or numbers.

MP3 **18.** Suppose that the dimensions of a right rectangular prism are doubled. Is the volume of the larger prism double the volume of the smaller prism?

Answer ______________________________

Justify your answer using words, drawings, or numbers.

Lesson

31 Find Volume: Use the Associate Property

Essential Question:
How is the Associative Property of Multiplication related to calculating volumes of right rectangular prisms?

5.MD.5a

Words to Know:
Associative Property of Multiplication

Guided Instruction

In this lesson, you will relate the Associative Property of Multiplication to finding volumes of right rectangular prisms.

Understand: How to relate the Associative Property of Multiplication to the volume of a right rectangular prism

Explain why $(5 \times 7) \times 9 = 5 \times (7 \times 9)$ by considering the factors to be the edge lengths of a right rectangular prism.

To find the volume of a right rectangular prism, you can multiply the area of the base by the height. Any face of the prism can be considered to be the base.

➡ Consider a right rectangular prism with edge lengths of 5 units, 7 units, and 9 units.

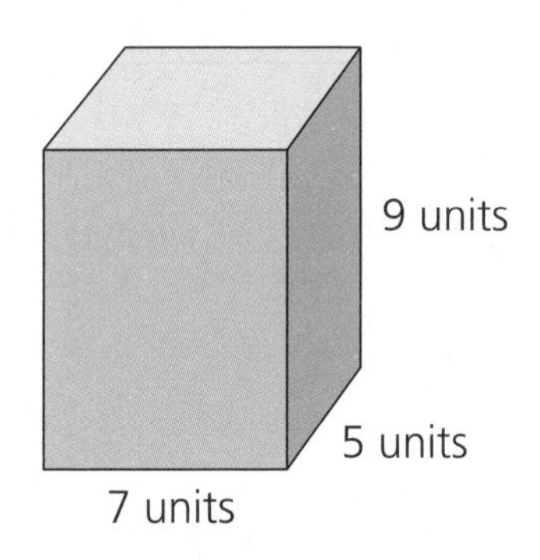

If you think of a 5 unit by 7 unit face as the base, then multiply 5×7 first to find the area of the base and then multiply the product by the height, 9. This can be represented as:

$$(5 \times 7) \times 9$$

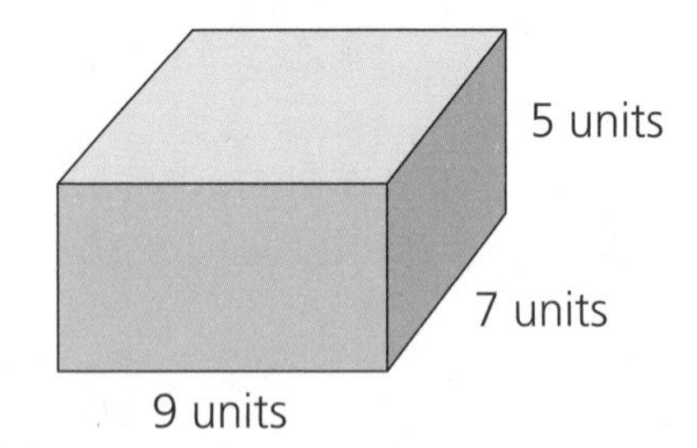

If you think of a 7 unit by 9 unit face as the base, then multiply 7×9 first to find the area of the base and then multiply the product by the height, 5. This can be represented as:

$$5 \times (7 \times 9)$$

Because the volumes are the same in both cases, $(5 \times 7) \times 9 = 5 \times (7 \times 9)$.

This equation $(5 \times 7) \times 9 = 5 \times (7 \times 9)$ is an example of the Associative Property of Multiplication. The property states that changing the grouping of the factors in a multiplication expression does not change the product. Thinking about a right rectangular prism can help you visualize this property.

Connect: What you know about the Associative Property of Multiplication to help you find the volume of a right rectangular prism

Carmen's new laptop computer was shipped in this box, which is a right rectangular prism.

Find the volume of the box using the Associative Property of Multiplication.

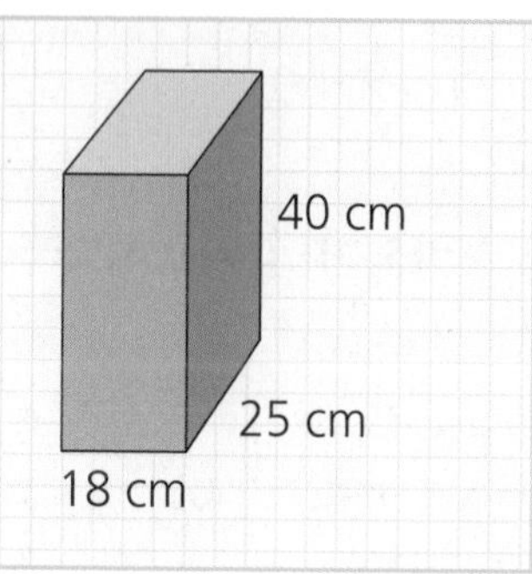

Step 1

Plan a solution

To find the volume of the box, first write an equation that determines the volume. Then, use the Associative Property of Multiplication and mental math to solve.

Step 2

Write an equation for the volume of a right rectangular prism.

The volume is the area of the base times the height:

$$\underbrace{(18 \times 25)}_{\text{area of base}} \times \underset{\text{height}}{40} = \blacksquare$$

Step 3

Multiply to calculate the volume.

Notice that if you regroup the factors to multiply 25 × 40 first, you can use mental math.

$(18 \times 25) \times 40 = 18 \times (25 \times 40)$ ← Use the Associative Property to regroup.
$= 18 \times 1000$ ← Multiply in parentheses.
$= 18{,}000$ ← Multiply.

➡ The volume of the box is 18,000 cubic centimeters.

Guided Practice

1. Which equation *best* illustrates the Associative Property of Multiplication?

   a. $(9 \times 7) \times 10 = (10 \times 7) \times 9$
   b. $(9 \times 7) \times 10 = 9 \times (7 \times 10)$
   c. $(9 + 7) \times 10 = 16 \times 10$
   d. $(9 \times 7) \times 10 = 63 \times 10$

Evaluate the expressions on both sides of the equation to show they are equivalent.

2. $(13 \times 5) \times 3 = 13 \times (5 \times 3)$
   $65 \times 3 = 13 \times 15$
   ______ = ______

3. $(5 \times 6) \times 9 = 5 \times (6 \times 9)$
   ______ $\times 9 = 5 \times$ ______
   ______ = ______

4. $(3 \times 13) \times 7 = 3 \times (13 \times 7)$
   ______ $\times 7 = 3 \times$ ______
   ______ = ______

5. $(3 \times 6) \times 7 = 3 \times (6 \times 7)$
   ______ $\times 7 = 3 \times$ ______
   ______ = ______

Use parentheses to show two ways of grouping the factors in the expression. Do not evaluate.

6. $3 \times 19 \times 6$
   ____

7. $13 \times 4 \times 2$
   ____

8. $9 \times 10 \times 5$
   ____

9. $1 \times 8 \times 21 \times 4$
   ____

10. A model of a school ring box is shown. One expression that represents the volume of the box is $(8 \times 4) \times 12$.

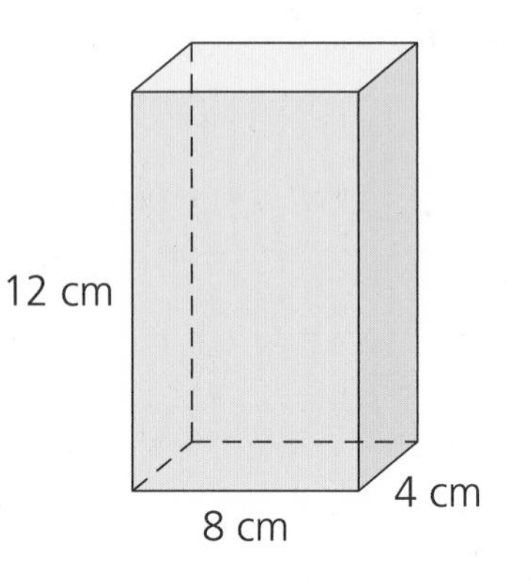

   a. Use the Associative Property of Multiplication to write a second expression for the volume of the box.
   ____

   b. Find the volume of the box.
   ____

Guided Practice

Use the Associative Property of Multiplication to write a second expression for the volume of each right rectangular prism. Then, find the volume of each prism.

11.

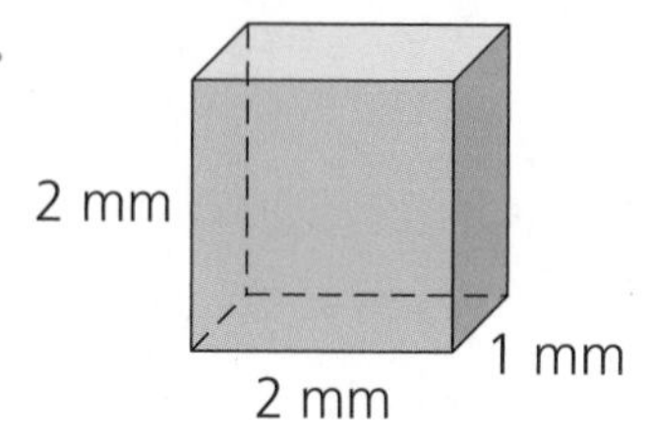

(1 × 2) × 2

12.

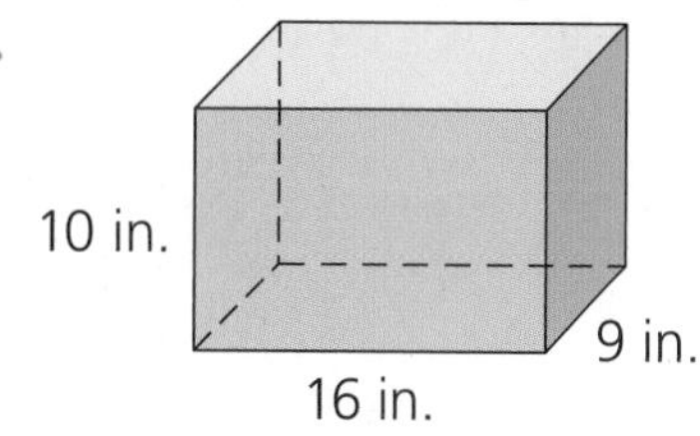

(9 × 16) × 10

13.

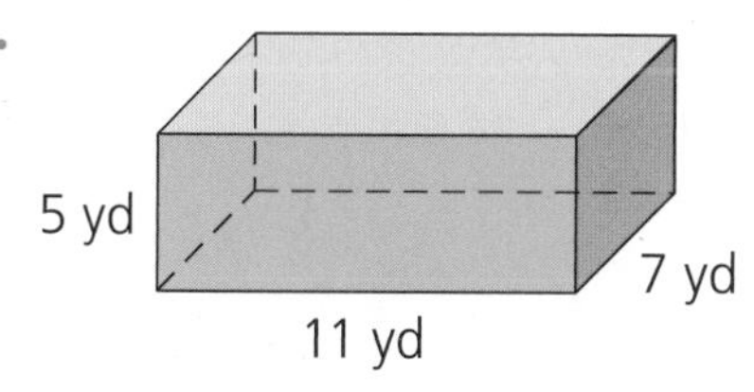

(7 × 11) × 5

14.

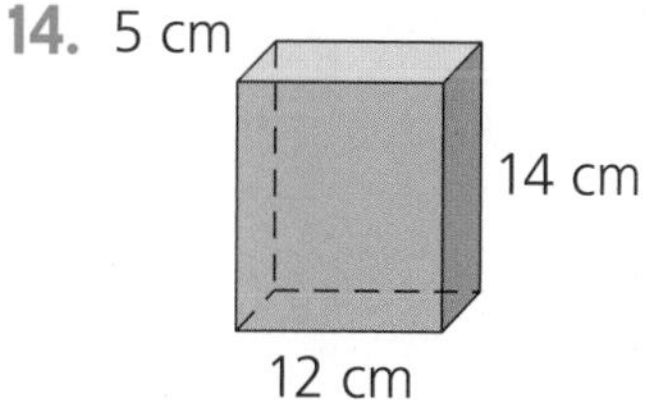

(12 × 5) × 14

Think • Pair • Share

MP2 **15.** Find the volume of each box with the dimensions in the table below. Then, use the Associative Property of Multiplication to explain why the volumes of the two boxes are equivalent.

	Box 1	Box 2
Length	3.5 cm	2 cm
Height	2 cm	5 cm
Width	5 cm	3.5 cm

Independent Practice

Evaluate the expressions on both sides of the equation to show they are equivalent.

1. $(8 \times 2) \times 9 = 8 \times (2 \times 9)$
   $16 \times 9 = 8 \times 18$
   _____ = _____

2. $(7 \times 8) \times 6 = 7 \times (8 \times 6)$
   _____ × 6 = 7 × _____
   _____ = _____

3. $(20 \times 6) \times 3 = 20 \times (6 \times 3)$
   _____ × 3 = 20 × _____
   _____ = _____

4. $(6 \times 3) \times 4 = 6 \times (3 \times 4)$
   _____ × 4 = 6 × _____
   _____ = _____

5. $12 \times (27 \times 10) = (12 \times 27) \times 10$
   12 × _____ = _____ × 10
   _____ = _____

6. $5 \times (11 \times 7) = (5 \times 11) \times 7$
   5 × _____ = _____ × 7
   _____ = _____

For exercises 7–10, show an equivalent expression using the Associative Property of Multiplication.

7. (9 × 5) × 10 = 9 × (____ × ____)

8. 9 × (12 × 4) = (____ × ____) × ____

9. (31 × 7) × 18 = ____ × (____ × ____)

10. (8 × 13) × 15 = ____ × (____ × ____)

Use parentheses to show two ways of grouping the factors in the expression. Do not evaluate.

11. $8 \times 25 \times 2$

12. $\frac{7}{11} \times 5\frac{1}{4} \times 4$

13. $0.65 \times 20 \times 2.2$

14. $19 \times 8\frac{2}{7} \times 2 \times 24$

Independent Practice

Use the Associative Property of Multiplication to write a second expression for the volume of each right rectangular prism. Then, find the volume of each prism.

15.

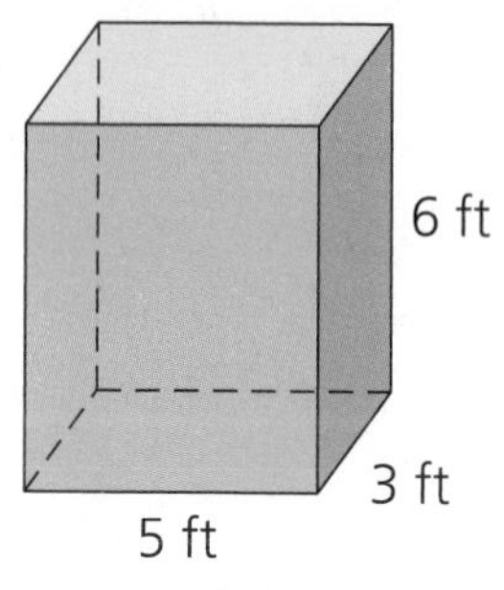

$(5 \times 3) \times 6$

16.

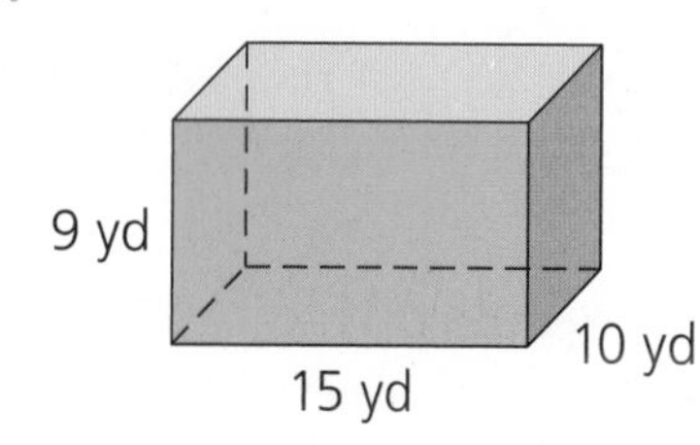

$(10 \times 15) \times 9$

17.

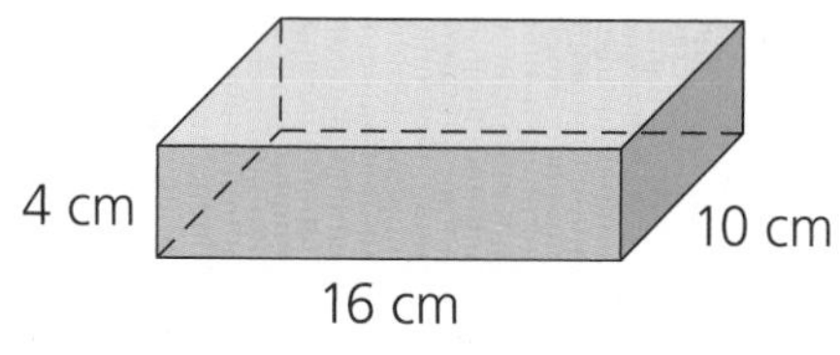

$(16 \times 10) \times 4$

18.

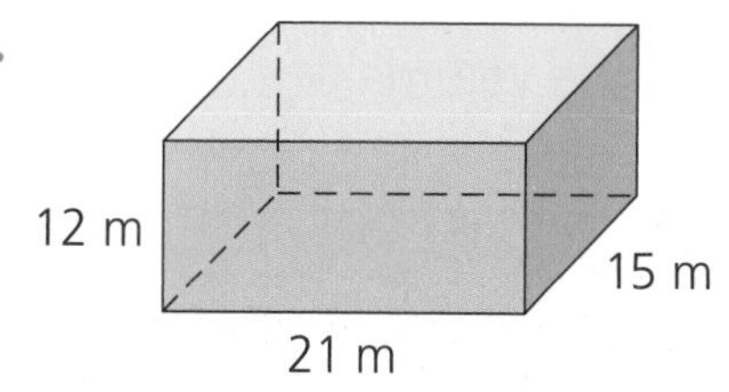

$12 \times (21 \times 15)$

Solve.

19. A sign at a commuter train station states that no passenger can bring suitcases any larger than 28 inches by 22 inches by 14 inches on a train.

a. Apply the Associative Property of Multiplication to write two expressions for the volume of the largest suitcase a train passenger can bring.

b. Find the volume of the suitcase.

Independent Practice

MP3 **20.** A box has a volume of 56 cubic inches, and each dimension is a whole number of inches. If one dimension of the box is 8 inches, explain how you can find the other two dimensions.

MP2 **21.** Write two expressions to represent the volume of a storage unit with a length of 14 feet, a width of 18 feet, and a height of 10 feet.

Circle the correct answer.

22. What is the volume of the right rectangular prism below?

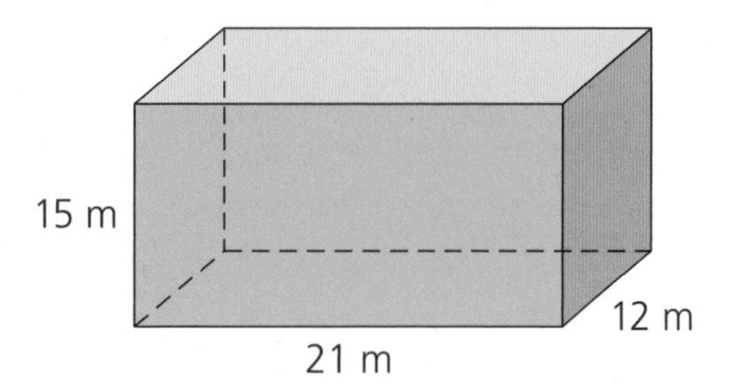

a. 180 m^3

b. 252 m^3

c. 3600 m^3

d. 3780 m^3

23. What is the volume of a walk-in refrigerator that is 13 feet long, 11 feet wide, and 10 feet high?

a. 143 cubic feet

b. 153 cubic feet

c. 260 cubic feet

d. 1,430 cubic feet

Independent Practice

Solve the problems.

MP3 **24.** Logan says he wrote three equivalent expressions to represent the volume of a right rectangular prism with a length and width of 17 cm and a height of 4 cm. Are his expressions all correct?

a. $17 \times (17 \times 4)$

b. $2 \times (17) \times 4$

c. $17 \times 17 \times 4$

MP1 **25.** Multiply the factors 12, 4, 8, and 7. Because of the Associative and Commutative Properties of Multiplication, you can multiply the factors in any order. Explain in which order you multiplied the factors, and why.

Show your work.

Answer ______________________________

MP3 **26.** Tyrone says he used the Associative Property of Multiplication to write two expressions equivalent to $8 \times 1.25 \times 9 - 5$. Evaluate all three expressions to see if they are equivalent. If they are not equivalent, explain the error Tyrone made.

a. $8 \times (1.25 \times 9) - 5$

b. $8 \times 1.25 \times (9 - 5)$

Show your work.

Answer ______________________________

Lesson

32 Problem Solving: Apply Volume Formulas for Prisms

Essential Question:
How do you find volume using a formula?
5.MD.5b

Guided Instruction

In this lesson you will solve real-world problems using formulas for volume.

Understand: How to solve problems using formulas for volume

Mr. Bower's new post office mailbox is 12 inches tall, 9 inches long, and 6 inches wide. What is the volume of the mailbox?

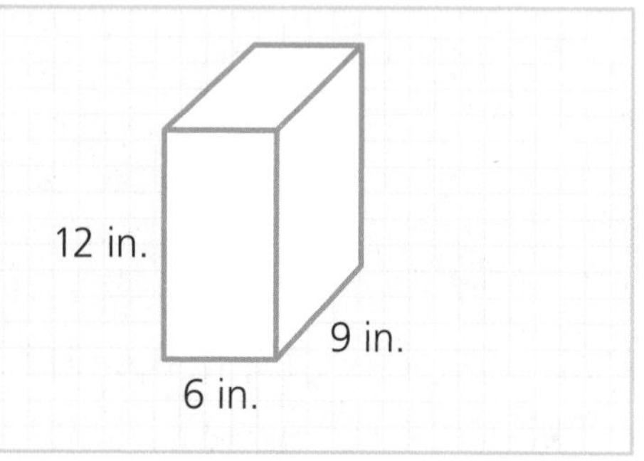

To find the volume of the mailbox, you can use a formula for the volume of a right rectangular prism. There are two equivalent volume formulas.

In this formula, V is the volume, ℓ is the length, w is the width, and h is the height:

$$V = \ell \times w \times h$$

In this formula, V is the volume, B is the area of the base, and h is the height:

$$V = B \times h$$

You know all three dimensions, so you can use the formula $V = \ell \times w \times h$. In this case, $\ell = 9$ in., $w = 6$ in., and $h = 12$ in.

$V = \ell \times w \times h$ ← Start with the formula.
$V = 9 \times 6 \times 12$ ← Substitute values for ℓ, w, and h.
$V = 648$ ← Multiply to find the value of V.

➡ The volume of Mr. Bower's post office mailbox is 648 in.^{3}

✏ How would you find the volume of the mailbox using the formula $V = B \times h$?

Guided Instruction

Connect: What you know about formulas for volume to solve problems

There are two empty sandboxes on a school playground. Sandbox 1 has a base with dimensions 4 feet by 6 feet and is 2 feet high. Sandbox 2 has a base area of 35 square feet and is 1 foot high. The school maintenance crew has 90 cubic feet of sand. Is this enough to fill both sandboxes?

Step 1

Plan a solution.

Find the volume of each sandbox and then add to find the total volume. Compare this volume to 90 cubic feet to see if the crew has enough sand to fill both sandboxes.

Step 2

Use formulas to calculate the volumes.

Sandbox 1: You know all three dimensions, so you can use the formula $V = \ell \times w \times h$.

$V = \ell \times w \times h$
$V = 4 \times 6 \times 2$
$V = 48$

The volume is 48 ft^3.

Sandbox 2: You know the base area and the height, so you can use the formula $V = B \times h$.

$V = B \times h$
$V = 35 \times 1$
$V = 35$

The volume is 35 ft^3.

Step 3

Find the total volume and compare to 90 cubic feet.

$48\ ft^3 + 35\ ft^3 = 83\ ft^3$

The total is less than 90 cubic feet.

➤ 90 cubic feet of sand is enough to fill both sandboxes.

Guided Practice

Use the formulas to find the volume of the right rectangular prisms.

1.

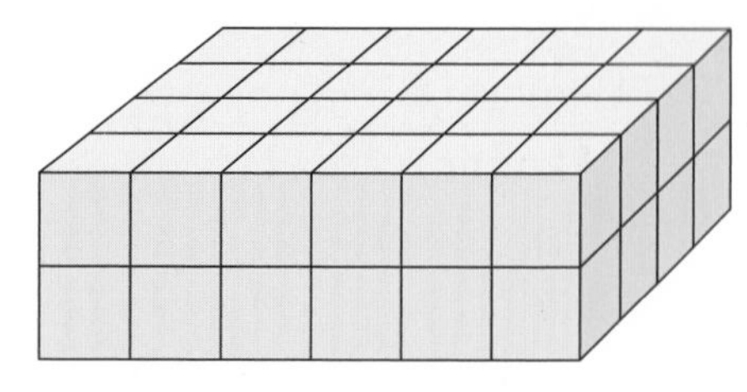

$V = \ell \times w \times h$

$= 6$ units × ____ units × ____ units

$=$ ____ cubic units

2.

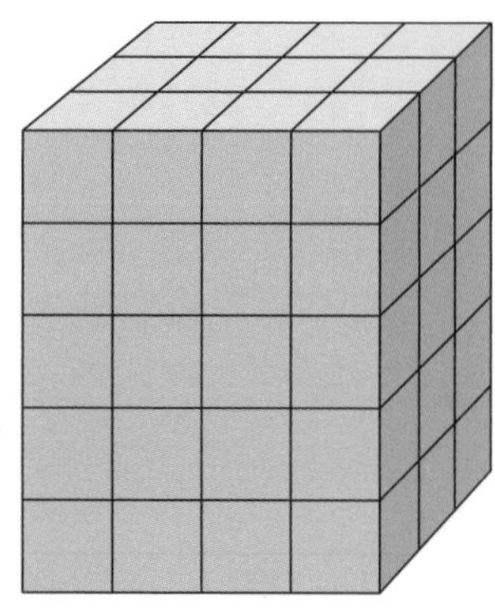

$V = \ell \times w \times h$

$= 4$ units × ____ units × ____ units

$=$ ____ cubic units

3. Anna builds a spice drawer that is 40 cm long, 15 cm wide, and 10 cm tall. What is the volume of the spice drawer that Anna built?

$V = \ell \times w \times h$

$= 40 \times 15 \times$ ______

$=$ ______ cm^3

The volume of the spice drawer is ______ cm^3.

4. Skye is mailing a present and needs a box that has a volume of at least 200 cubic inches. Is this box big enough? Explain.

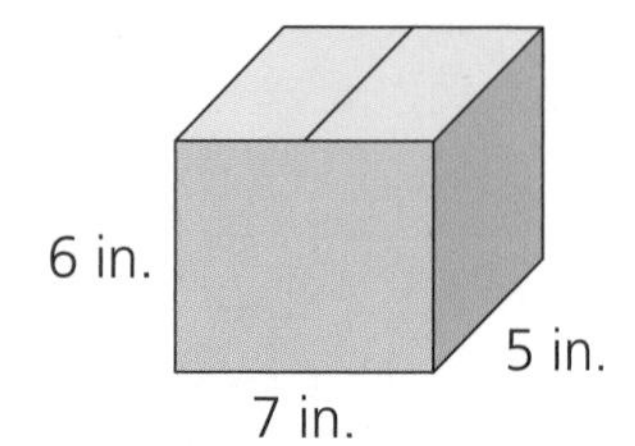

$V = B \times h$

$= (7 \times 5) \times$ ____

$=$ ____ $in.^3$

Guided Practice

Find the volume of each figure.

5.

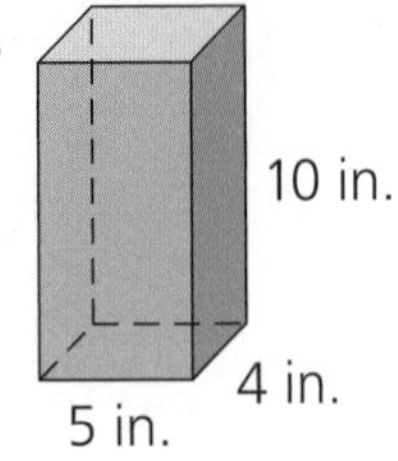

______

6.

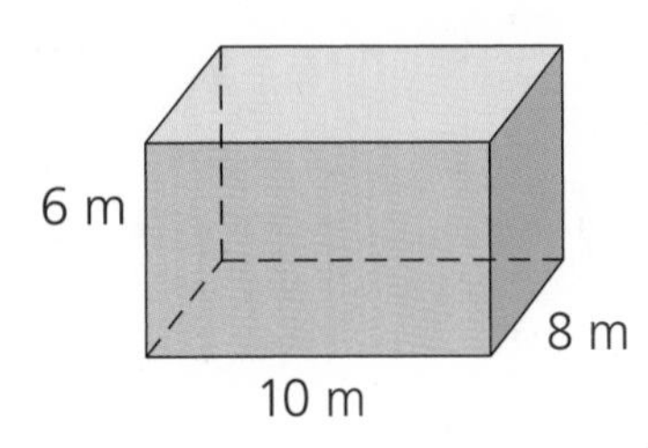

______

Solve.

7. Todd wants to use organic soil to fill his flower boxes. Each box is a right rectangular prism that has a base area of 3 ft^2 and a height of 2 ft. How many cubic feet of organic soil does Todd need to fill one of the flower boxes?

Todd needs ______ of organic soil to fill one of the flower boxes.

8. Which box has the greater volume?

Box A

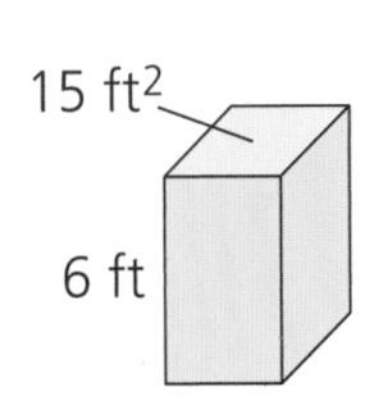

$V = B \times h$

$V =$ ____ $ft^2 \times$ ____ ft

$V =$ ____ ft^3

Box B

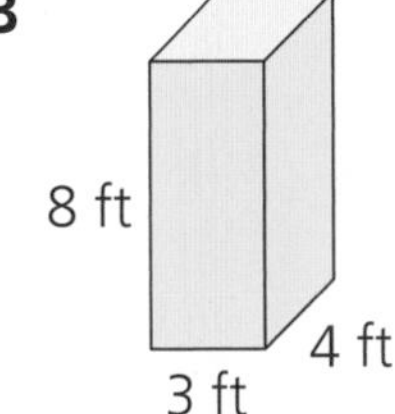

$V = \ell \times w \times h$

$V =$ ____ $\times$ ____ $\times$ ____

$V =$ ____ ft^3

Box ____ has the greater volume.

Think•Pair•Share

MP4 **9.** Joy needs a container. The container has to have a volume between 600 cubic inches and 800 cubic inches. It has to be longer than it is tall. What could the dimensions of her container be?

Independent Practice

Use formulas to find the volume of the right rectangular prisms.

1.

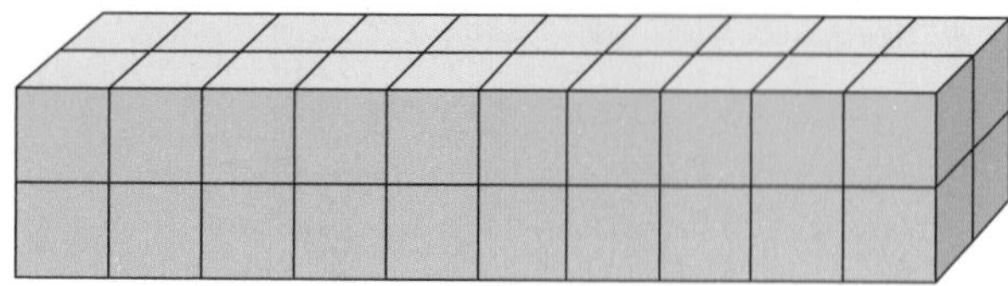

$V = \ell \times w \times h$

$= 10$ units $\times$ ____ units $\times$ ____ units

$=$ ____ cubic units

2.

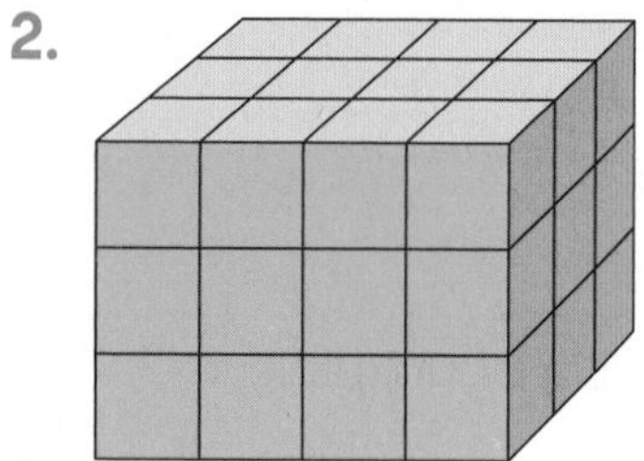

$V = \ell \times w \times h$

$= 4$ units $\times$ ____ units $\times$ ____ units

$=$ ____ cubic units

3. Each of the containers, labeled A and B, has a base with an area of 12 m^2. Find the volume of each. Then find the difference in the volumes of the two containers.

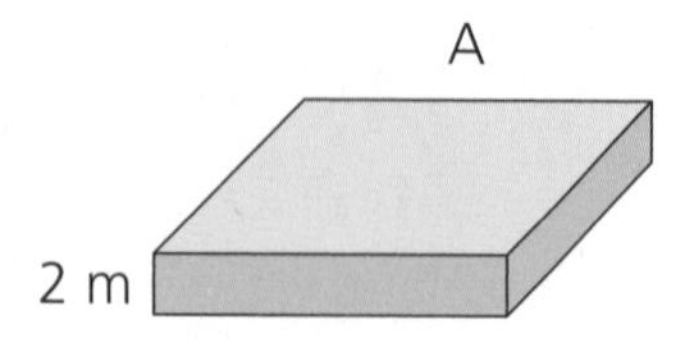

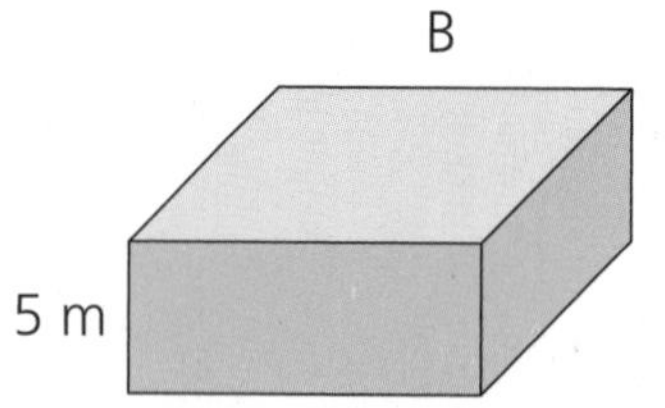

The volume of container A is ____________.

The volume of container B is ____________.

The difference in volumes is ____________.

Independent Practice

For exercises 4–7, circle the correct answer.

4. Erin built the box shown. What is its volume?

a. 42 m^3 b. 72 m^3

c. 108 m^3 d. 144 m^3

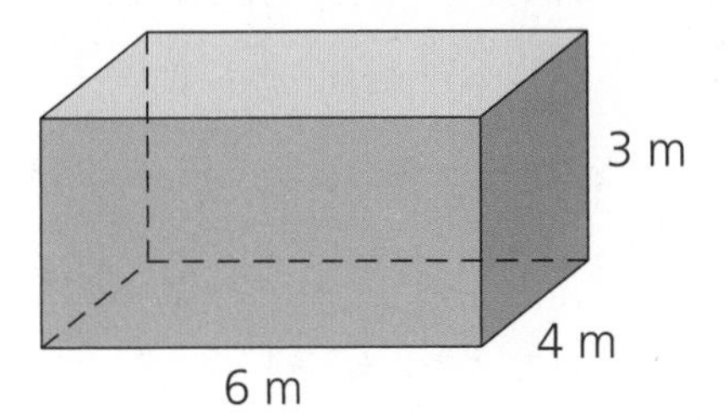

5. Luke bought the reptile tank shown. What is the volume of the tank?

a. 440 $in.^3$ b. 1,200 $in.^3$

c. 2,000 $in.^3$ d. 2,400 $in.^3$

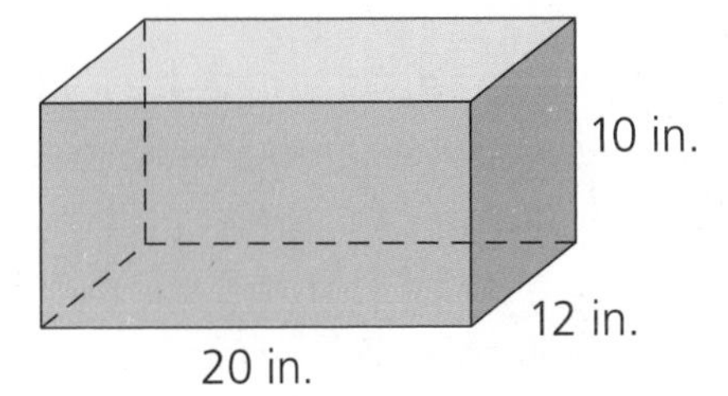

6. A storage chest has a base with an area of 25 square feet and is 5 feet tall. What is the volume of the bin?

a. 15 ft^3 b. 25 ft^3

c. 125 ft^3 d. 125 ft^2

7. Shelley has a pencil case that is 30 cm long, 4 cm wide, and 3 cm deep. What is the volume of Shelley's pencil case?

a. 210 cm^3 b. 360 cm^3

c. 720 cm^3 d. 1200 cm^3

Solve.

8. Mr. Kim has a man-made pond that is shaped like a right rectangular prism with a base area of 72 square meters. The pond has a volume 72 cubic meters. What is the pond's depth?

The pond has a depth of ___________.

Independent Practice

MP2 **9.** Leonard is packing boxes that are cubes with 6-inch sides into a crate. The crate is 2 feet wide by 3 feet long by 2 feet tall. How many cubes can Leonard pack into the crate? Show your work.

Leonard can pack ____ cubes into the crate.

MP1 **10.** Alexandra's house has a backyard patio that is 4 yards long by 5 yards wide. Alexandra's mother is building a rectangular storage shed with a volume of 1,080 cubic feet and with the entire patio as its base. What is the height of the shed Alexandra's mother is building? Give your answer in feet and then in yards. Show your work.

The height of the shed is ____ feet or ____ yards.

In exercise 11, the chart shows various dimensions and volumes of right rectangular prisms. Complete the chart, then answer the question below.

11.

Length	Width	Height	Volume
50 in.	10 in.	10 in.	
50 in.	8 in.	10 in.	
50 in.		10 in.	2,500 $in.^3$
50 in.	3 in.		1,500 $in.^3$

Describe what happens to the volume of the right rectangular prisms above as the base area changes.

Independent Practice

Solve. Use the figure.

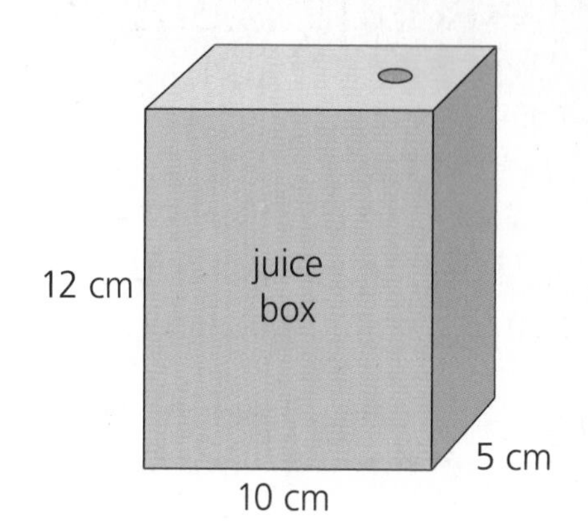

MP6 **12.** A manufacturer makes juice boxes that are 12 cm tall, 10 cm wide, and 5 cm deep. What is the volume of each juice box in cubic centimeters?

The volume of each juice box is ________.

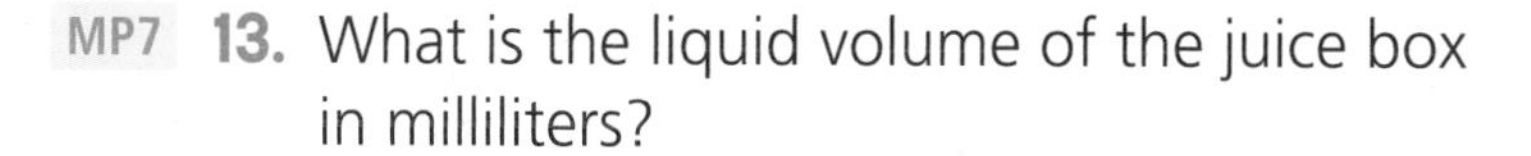

MP7 **13.** What is the liquid volume of the juice box in milliliters?

The liquid volume of each juice box is ________.

MP4 **14.** The juice box company decides to make three different juice box sizes. They want to have a mini juice box, a regular sized juice box, and a large sized juice box. Use the rules given below to choose the new dimensions of each box and find its liquid volume in milliliters.

Rules: The mini box should hold no more than 300 mL. The regular sized box should hold between 450 and 550 mL. The large sized box must hold at least 800 mL.

Sketch each new box, showing the dimensions and volume. Explain your choices.

a. Mini juice box

b. Regular sized juice box

c. Large sized juice box

Lesson

33 Problem Solving: Decompose Figures to Find Volume

Essential Question:
How do you find the volume of a composite figure?

5.MD.5c

Guided Instruction

In this lesson you will find volumes of three-dimensional figures by breaking them into right rectangular prisms.

Understand: Breaking apart a figure made from unit cubes into right rectangular prisms to find volume

Jason uses cubes to construct a model of a building with two sections. Each cube is 1 cubic meter. What is the volume of the model?

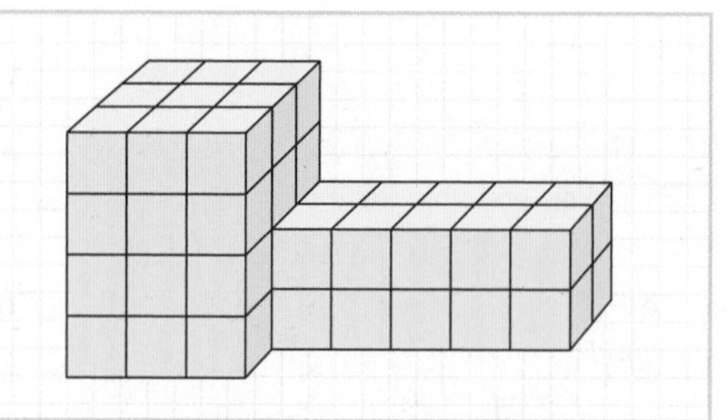

To find the volume of the model, break apart the figure into two separate right rectangular prisms and find the volume of each. Count the cubes to determine each prism's length, width, and height.

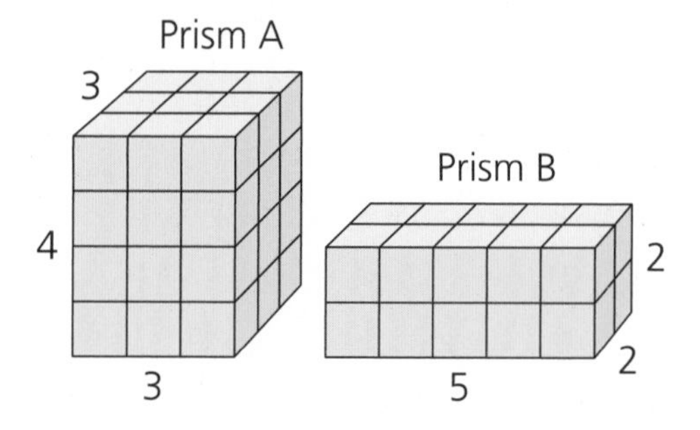

Use the formula for the volume of a right rectangular prism $V = \ell \times w \times h$.

Volume of Prism A

$V = \ell \times w \times h$
$= 3 \times 3 \times 4$
$= 36 \text{ m}^3$

Volume of Prism B

$V = \ell \times w \times h$
$= 5 \times 2 \times 2$
$= 20 \text{ m}^3$

Add to find the total volume: $36 \text{ m}^3 + 20 \text{ m}^3 = 56 \text{ m}^3$.

The volume of the model is 56 m^3.

Find the volumes of Prisms A and B using the formula $V = B \times h$.

Guided Instruction

Understand: How to find the volume of a figure composed of two right rectangular prisms

What is the volume of the figure?

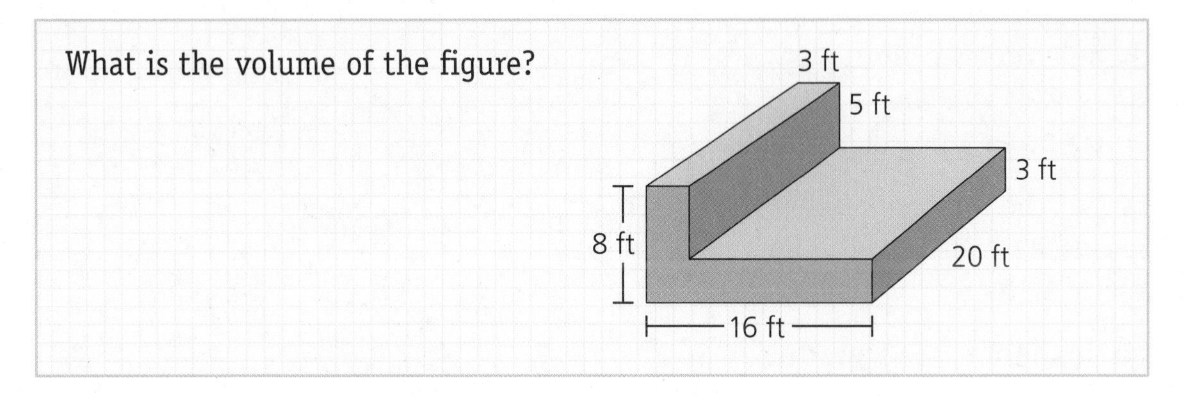

To find the volume of the figure, you can break it into right rectangular prisms. Be sure the prisms do not overlap. One way to break up the figure is shown at the right.

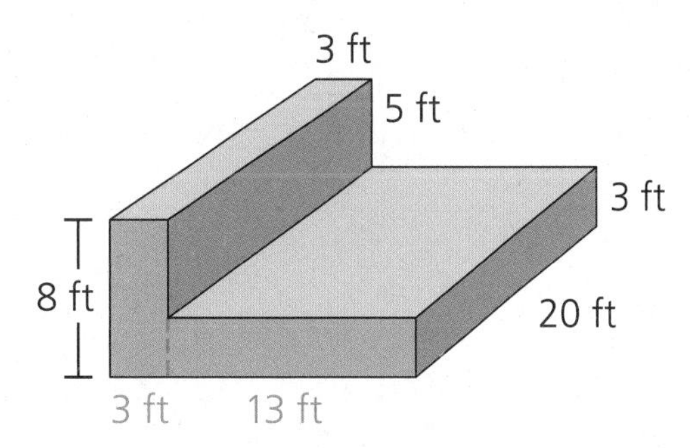

Find the volume of each prism using the volume formula.

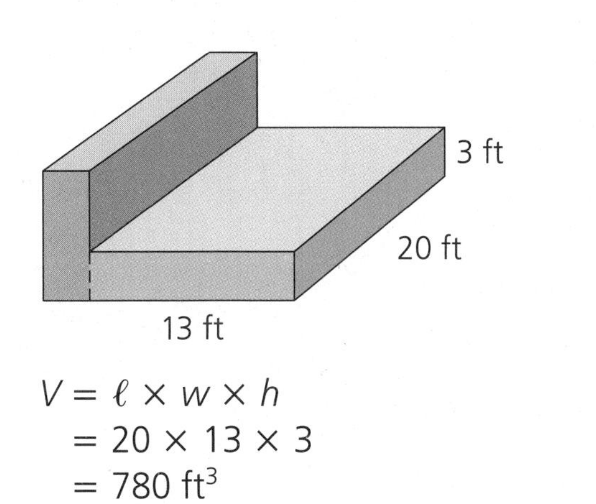

$V = \ell \times w \times h$
$= 20 \times 13 \times 3$
$= 780 \text{ ft}^3$

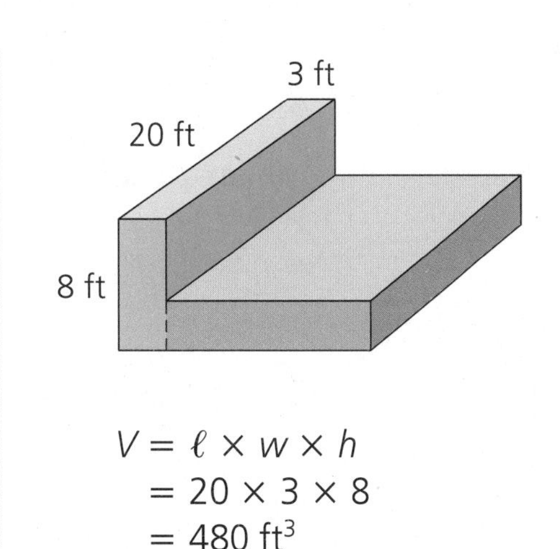

$V = \ell \times w \times h$
$= 20 \times 3 \times 8$
$= 480 \text{ ft}^3$

Add the two volumes to find the volume of the composite figure.
$780 \text{ ft}^3 + 480 \text{ ft}^3 = 1,260 \text{ ft}^3$

➡ The volume of the composite figure is 1,260 cubic feet.

Guided Instruction

Connect: What you know about finding the volume of composite figures

Nan just bought an air conditioner. The manual says it will cool a space with a volume up to 1,000 cubic feet.

The diagram at the right represents the floor plan of Nan's bedroom. The height of the room is 12 feet.

Will the air conditioner be powerful enough to cool Nan's room?

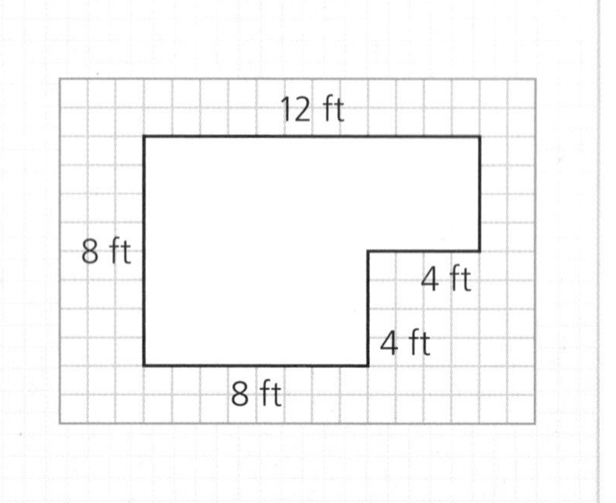

To solve this problem, find the volume of Nan's room and compare it to 1,000 cubic feet.

Step 1

Break apart the bedroom into two right rectangular prisms and find the volume of each one.

Separate the diagram into two squares as shown. Each square is the base of a prism with a height of 12 feet. Find the volume of each prism.

Larger prism	**Smaller prism**
$V = \ell \times w \times h$	$V = \ell \times w \times h$
$V = 8 \times 8 \times 12$	$V = 4 \times 4 \times 12$
$V = 768\ \text{ft}^3$	$V = 192\ \text{ft}^3$

The two prisms have volumes of $768\ \text{ft}^3$ and $192\ \text{ft}^3$.

Step 2

Add the volumes of the prisms to find the volume of the bedroom.

Volume of Nan's bedroom $= 768\ \text{ft}^3 + 192\ \text{ft}^3 = 960\ \text{ft}^3$.

Step 3

Compare the volume to $1{,}000\ \text{ft}^3$. The volume, $960\ \text{ft}^3$, is less than $1{,}000\ \text{ft}^3$.

➡ Yes, the air conditioner will be powerful enough to cool Nan's bedroom.

Guided Practice

For exercises 1–3, use the figure shown at the right, which is made from centimeter cubes.

1. volume of top prism
   $V = \ell \times w \times h$

   $V = 2 \times 2 \times$ ____

   $V =$ ____ cm^3

2. volume of bottom prism
   $V = \ell \times w \times h$

   $V = 5 \times 6 \times$ ____

   $V =$ ____ cm^3

3. volume of composite figure

   ____ cm^3 + ____ cm^3 = ____ cm^3

For exercises 4–7, use the figure shown at the right.

4. volume of bottom prism

   $14 \times 12 \times 2 =$ ________

5. volume of top prism

   $2 \times 4 \times 12 =$ ________

6. total volume

   ________ + ________ = ________

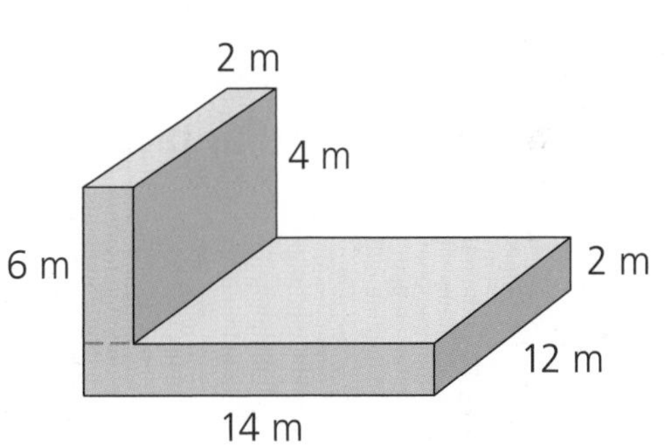

MP4 7. Find the volume of the figure in exercises 4–6 by separating it into two different prisms. Describe the dimensions of the new prisms. What is the volume of the figure? Is it the same? Explain.

Independent Practice

Find the volume of the green figure, which is made from centimeter cubes. Use the figure at the right to help you.

1. top prism: $V =$ ________

2. bottom prism: $V =$ ________

3. volume of composite figure:

________ + ________ = ________

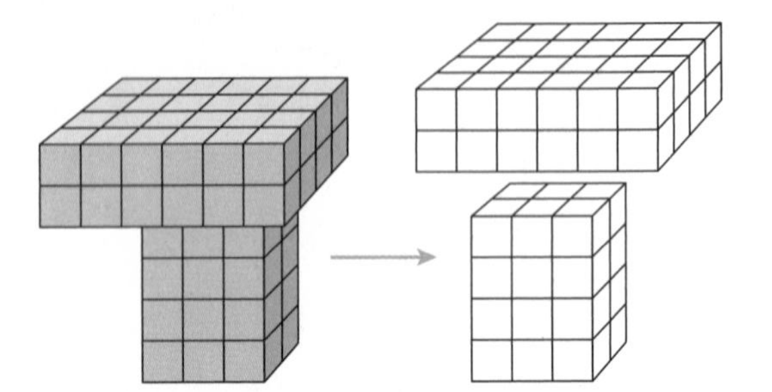

Find the volume of the blue figure, which is made from centimeter cubes. Use the figure at the right to help you.

4. top prism: $V =$ ________

5. bottom prism: $V =$ ________

6. volume of composite figure:

________ + ________ = ________

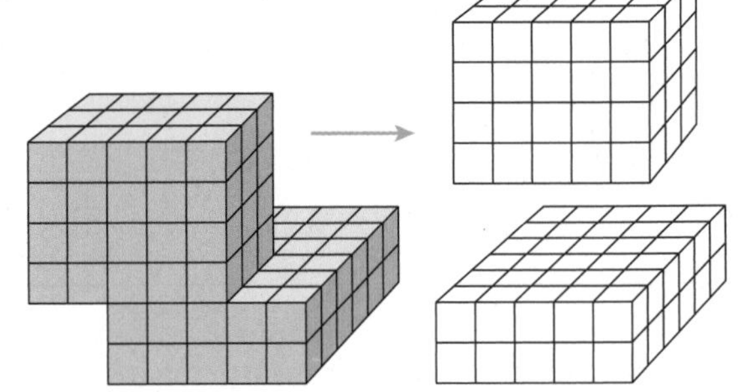

Find the volume of the figure by adding the volumes of the two right rectangular prisms. The measures are in inches.

7. white prism: $V =$ ________

8. red prism: $V =$ ________

9. total volume:

________ + ________ = ________

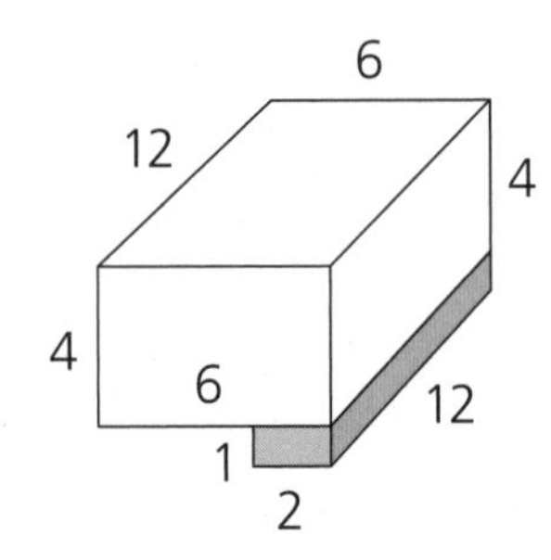

Find the volume of the figure by adding the volumes of the two right rectangular prisms. The measures are in inches.

10. white prism: $V =$ ________

11. purple prism: $V =$ ________

12. total volume:

________ + ________ = ________

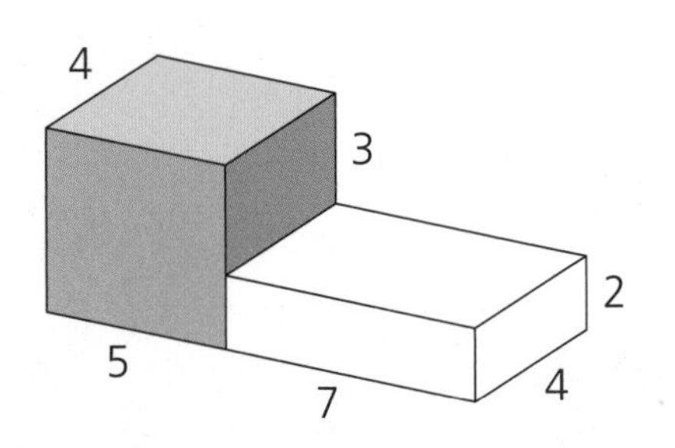

Independent Practice

For exercises 13–14, draw the base of each figure on the grid provided. Separate the base into rectangles to represent the bases of two right rectangular prisms. Find the volume of the figure by finding and adding the volumes of the two right rectangular prisms.

13. This box has an open top. Lengths are in inches.

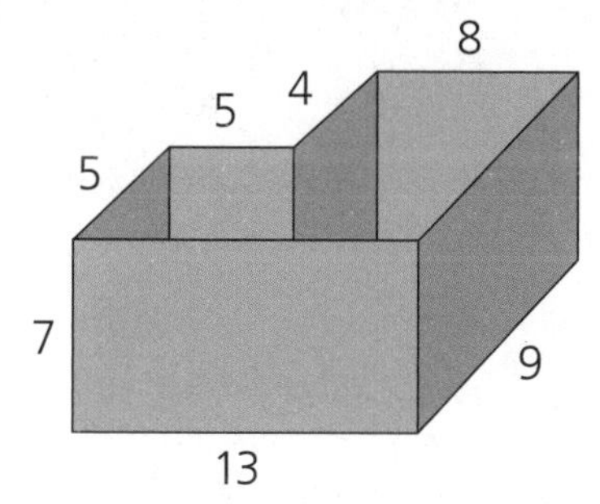

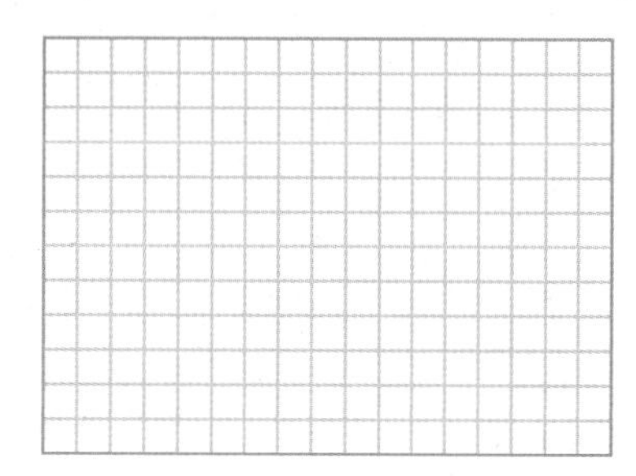

14. This figure is a solid piece of wood. Lengths are in centimeters.

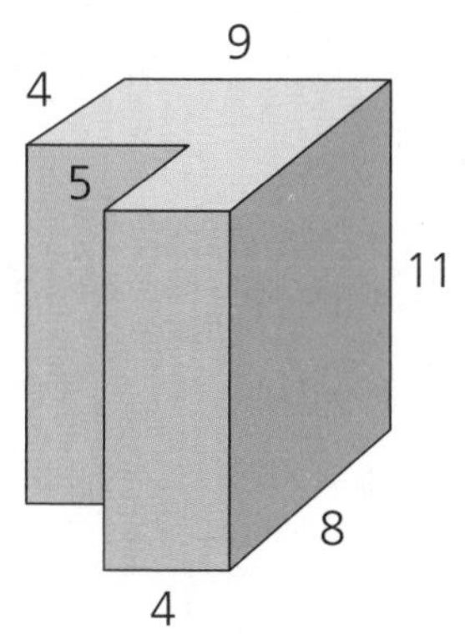

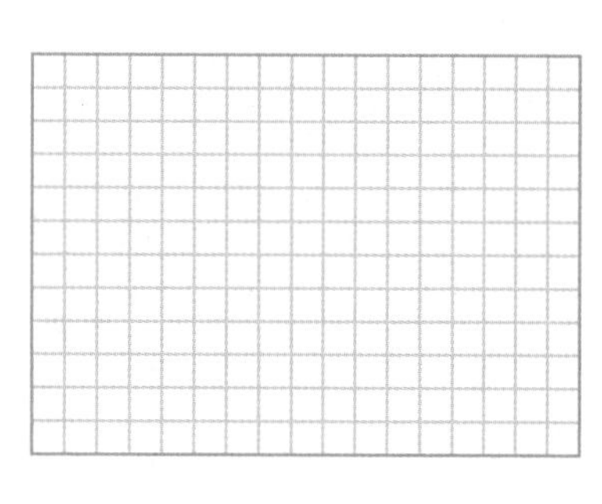

Independent Practice

Use figure to solve.

MP2 **15.** Mr. Arthur dug this foundation for a building. Describe two different ways to find the volume of this figure by breaking it apart into two prisms.

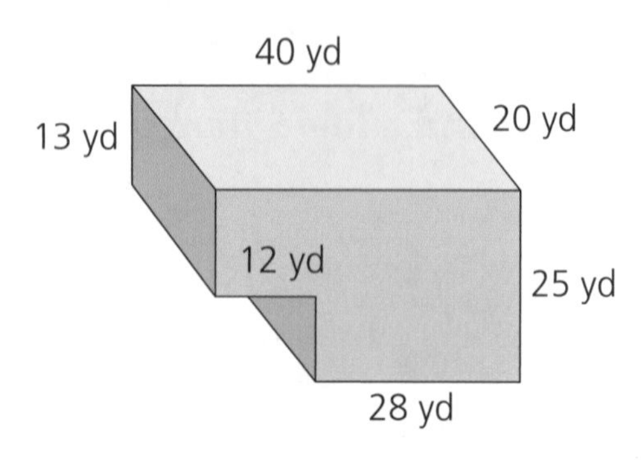

MP1 **16.** What is the volume of soil removed to pour this foundation?

Show your work.

Answer ______________________________

For exercise 17, find the missing lengths to solve.

MP2 **17.** The shaded face of the figure is square. Lengths are in feet. Find the volume of the figure.

Label the figure to show missing lengths. Show how you divide it into two prisms.

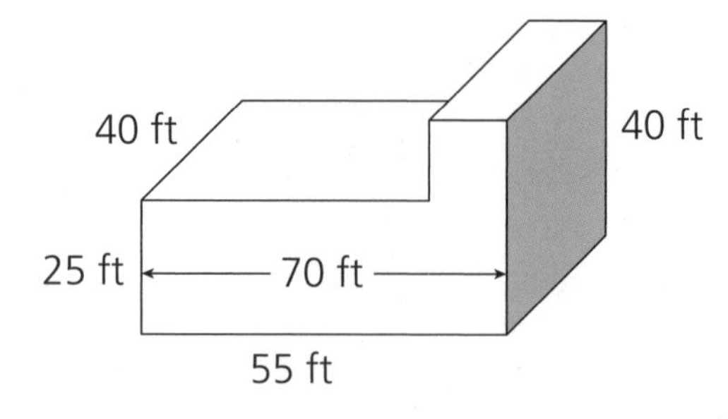

Answer ______________________________

MP3 **18.** Explain how you used the given information to solve the problem.

Independent Practice

Solve. Use the figure.

MP2 **19.** A purple cube that measures 4 cm on each edge sits on top of a green right rectangular prism with an edge of length 11 cm as shown. The volume of the green prism is 88 cm^3. Find the total height of the figure.

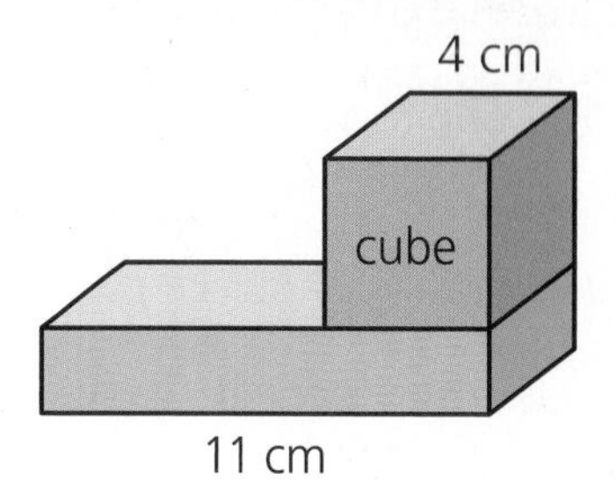

Answer ______________________

Justify your answer using words, drawings, or numbers.

MP6 **20.** Show how to break apart the figure from exercise 19 into two right rectangular prisms so that neither prism is a cube. Make a drawing and mark the dimensions or lengths of each prism.

Solve.

MP1 **21.** The drawing shows the floor plan of a 7-story building. Each story is 11 ft. How many cubic feet are in this building?

Label the drawing to show the missing dimensions. Show the steps in your solution.

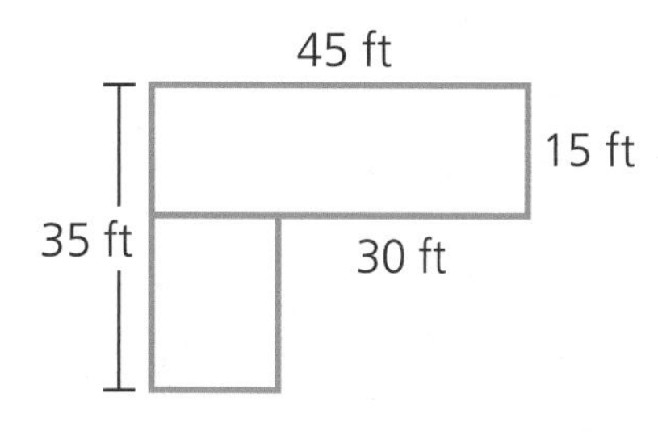

Show your work.

Answer ____

Convert the measurements from one metric unit to another.

1. 1.6 kilograms = ■ grams

   ________ grams

2. 32,000 centimeters = ■ kilometers

   ________ kilometers

Circle the correct answer.

3. Which of the following is more than 2 gallons?

   a. 8 quarts b. 25 cups c. 20 pints d. 200 fluid ounces

4. Which of the following is a unit cube?

   a. 2 in. / 2 in. / 2 in.

   b. 1 cm / 1 cm / 1 cm

   c.

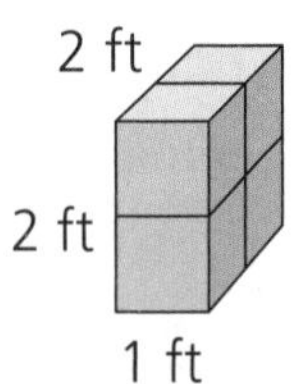

   d.

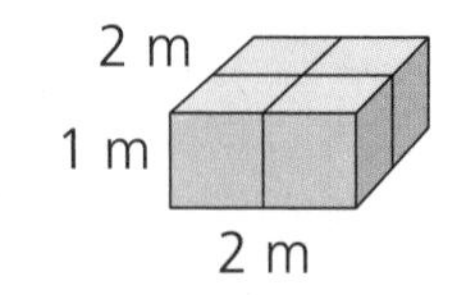

Count the unit cubes to find the volume of each figure.

5.

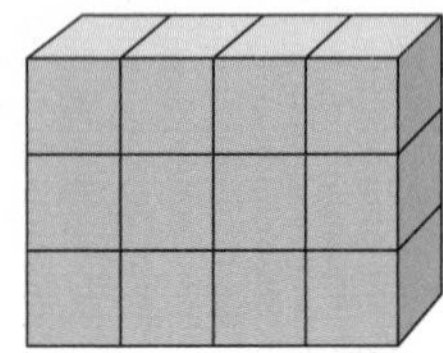

There are ____ unit cubes.

The volume is ____ cubic units.

6.

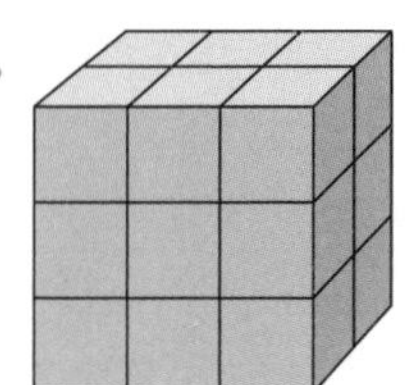

There are ____ unit cubes.

The volume is ____ cubic units.

Show how to use the formula $V = \ell \times w \times h$ to find the volume of each figure.

7.

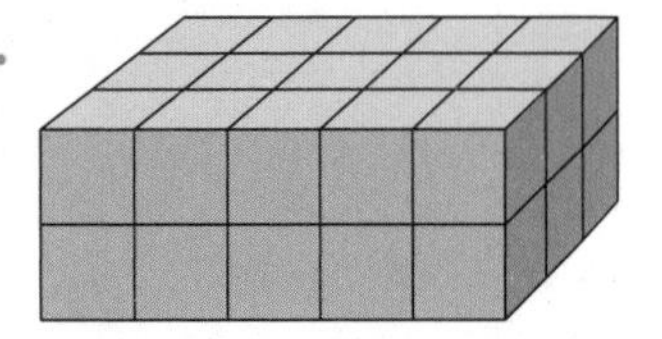

$V =$ ____ × ____ × ____

Volume ____ cubic units

8.

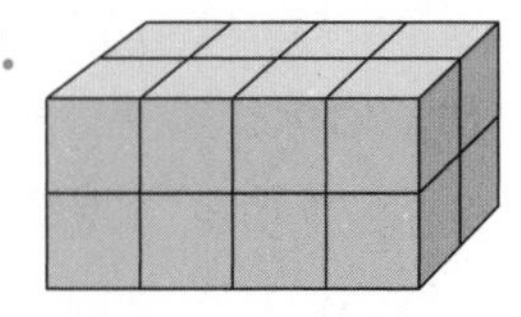

$V =$ ____ × ____ × ____

Volume ____ cubic units

Solve.

MP1 **9.** Jamil needs 200 inches of beaded braid for a craft project. The braid is sold in 2-yard spools that cost $6.50 each, or by the foot at $1.25 per foot. Find the least amount Jamil can spend to get the braid he needs.

Answer ______________________________

Justify your answer using words, drawings, or numbers.

10. Ruth's grandfather kept track of how far he walked on each of the past 24 days. Ruth made the line plot below to show these distances. On how many days did Ruth's grandfather walk more than $\frac{1}{2}$ mile?

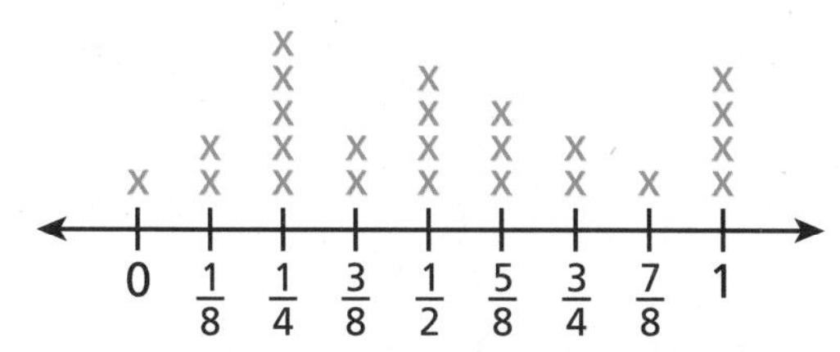

Distance Walked (miles)

Answer ______________________________

11. Matt kept track of how long it took to get home from school on 10 days. His data is shown below in fractional parts of an hour.

$\frac{5}{6}, \frac{1}{3}, \frac{1}{6}, \frac{1}{2}, \frac{1}{3}, \frac{1}{2}, \frac{2}{3}, \frac{1}{2}, \frac{5}{6}, \frac{1}{2}$

a. Make a line plot for the data. Plot an X to represent each value.

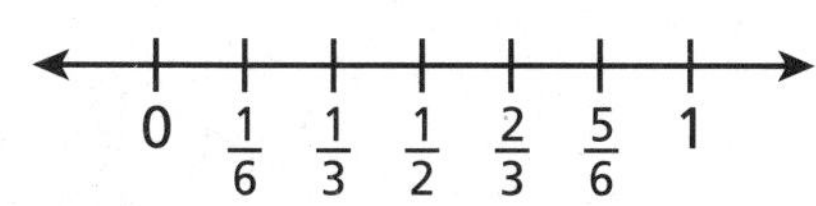

Time to Get Home (hours)

b. On how many days did it take Matt more than 30 minutes to get home from school?

MP6 **12.** Jerry built a flower box 30 inches long, 8 inches wide, and 10 inches deep. How many cubic inches of soil does Jerry need to fill the box halfway?

MP5 **13.** A wooden storage chest is 4 feet long, 2 feet deep, and 2 feet high. Explain how these unit cubes can be used to find the volume of the chest.

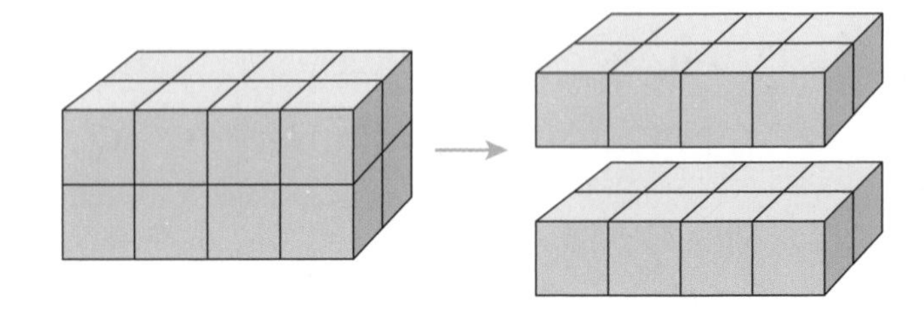

MP4 **14.** Explain how to use this figure to represent the Associative Property of Multiplication.

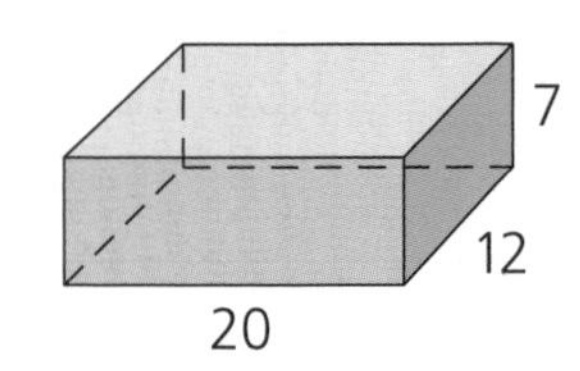

MP5 **15.** Use the model to find the volume of a rectangular prism that is 4 units long, 2 units wide and 6 units tall. Explain your steps.

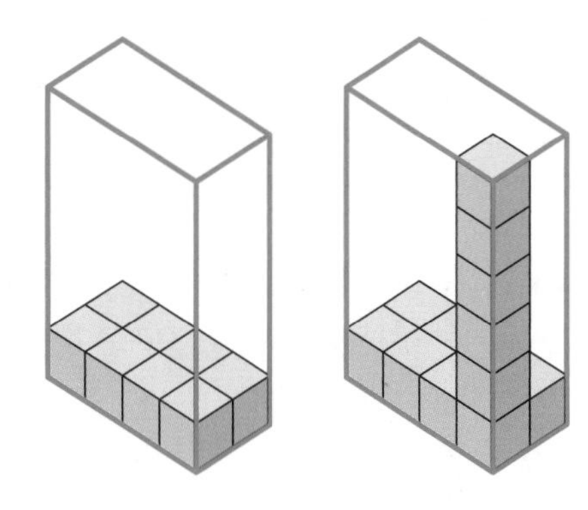

MP1 **16.** Find the volume of this composite figure.

 **Show your work.**

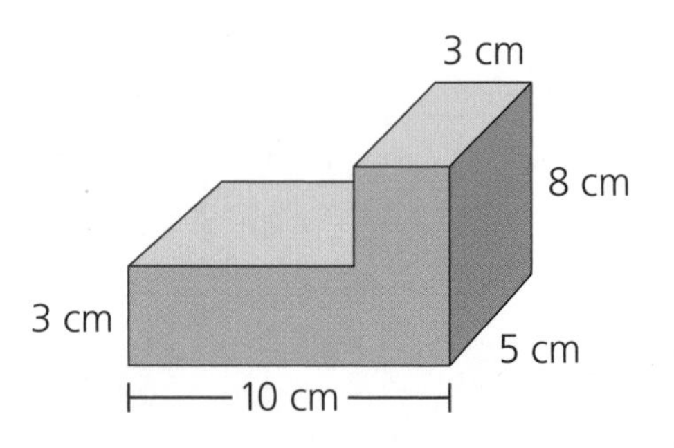

Answer ______________________________

Look at how the Common Core standards you have learned and will learn connect.

It is very important for you to understand the standards from the prior grade level so that you will be able to develop an understanding of geometry in this unit and be prepared for next year. To practice your skills, go to sadlierconnect.com.

GRADE 4 I Can...	Before Unit 5	GRADE 5 Can I ?	After Unit 5	GRADE 6 I Will...
4.G.1 Draw points, lines, line segments, rays, and angles Draw parallel and perpendicular lines	☐	**5.G.1** Understand the concept and representation of the coordinate plane	☐	**6.NS.6** Identify the quadrant an ordered pair is located in Plot ordered pairs on the coordinate plane
	☐	**5.G.2** Represent real-world and mathematical problems by graphing points on the coordinate plane	☐	**6.G.3** Draw polygons in the coordinate plane and find the lengths of their sides **6.RP.3** Given a table of equivalent ratios, plot the pairs of values on the coordinate plane **6.NS.8** Solve real-world and mathematical problems by graphing points in all four quadrants of the coordinate plane
4.G.2 Classify shapes by properties of their lines and angles Recognize right triangles as a category	☐	**5.G.3** Understand relationships among categories of figures	☐	
4.G.2 Classify shapes by properties of their lines and angles Recognize right triangles as a category	☐	**5.G.4** Classify two-dimensional figures in a hierarchy based on properties	☐	

HOME ✦ CONNECT...

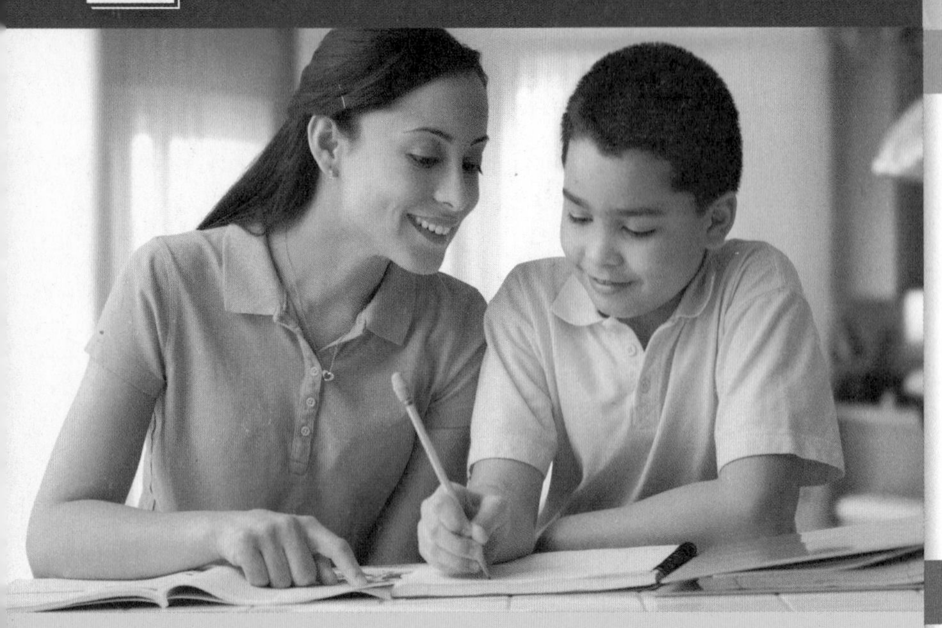

Your child will learn to use a coordinate plane to represent and solve real world problems.

You can graph a point on the coordinate plane using an ordered pair or coordinates (x, y). The x-coordinate tells how far to travel from the origin in the direction of the x-axis. The y-coordinate tells how far to travel from the origin in the direction of the y-axis.

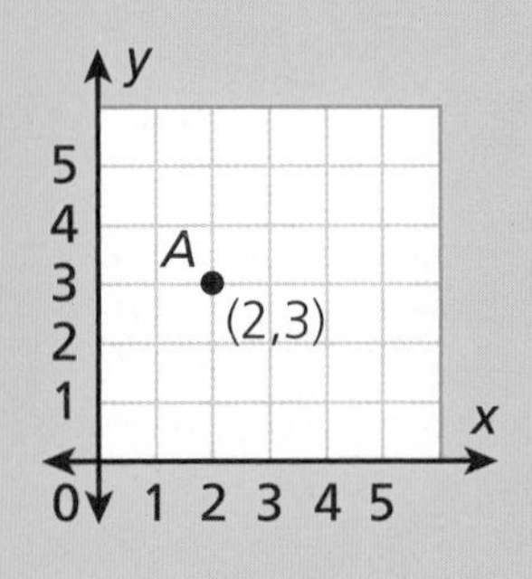

On this coordinate plane the ordered pair (2,3) is graphed and labeled point A.

Activity: Ask your child to think about designing an amusement park. Have your child draw a map of the amusement park using a coordinate plane. Ask them to use ordered pairs to identify the location of rides, games, entrances, waterfalls, and eating areas. Additionally, there are many age-appropriate interactive games available that can reinforce graphing on a coordinate plane. Take the time to play those games with your child.

In this unit your child will:

- Understand points on the coordinate plane.
- Graph points to represent problem situations.
- Analyze properties to classify two-dimensional figures.

NOTE: All of these learning goals for your child are based on the Grade 5 Common Core State Standards for Mathematics.

Ways to Help Your Child

As your child nears middle school, they will need to become more independent when it comes to completing assignments and projects. Check in with your child regularly, but avoid becoming too involved. Your support will show you are interested, but take the time to chronically reinforce that they must be responsible for their learning.

ONLINE

For more Home Connect activities, continue online at sadlierconnect.com

Focus on Geometry

UNIT 5

Essential Question:
How can you represent and analyze data on a coordinate plane?

Lesson

34 Understand Points on the Coordinate Plane

Essential Question:
How do you use ordered pairs to locate points and draw figures on the coordinate plane?

5.G.1

Guided Instruction

In this lesson you will learn how to locate and graph points on the coordinate plane.

Understand: Points on a coordinate plane

> Rosa randomly puts points on a coordinate plane. She labels them *A*, *B*, and *C*. How can Rosa describe the location of each point?

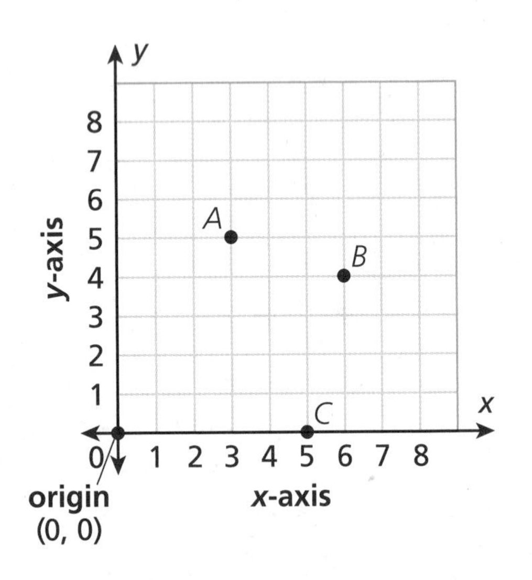

Rosa can describe the location of points *A*, *B*, and *C* using an ordered pair of numbers, called the coordinates of the point. Each ordered pair, (x, y), consists of an *x*-coordinate and a *y*-coordinate. The ordered pairs for points *A*, *B*, and *C* are all in the first quadrant, or top right quarter, of the coordinate plane.

To find the ordered pair for points *A*, *B*, and *C*, begin at the origin, (0, 0). Move right and then up until you reach the point. If you start at the origin and move 3 units to the right and 5 units up, you will be at point *A*. So, the *x*-coordinate of point *A* is 3 and the *y*-coordinate is 5. Write the ordered pair as (3, 5).

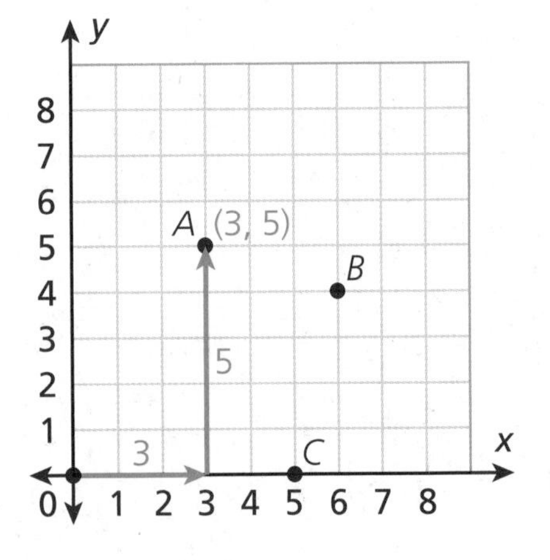

The ordered pair for point *B* is (6, 4).
The ordered pair for point *C* is (5, 0).

Rosa can describe the location of the points using these ordered pairs.
point *A*: (3, 5)   point *B*: (6, 4)   point *C*: (5, 0)

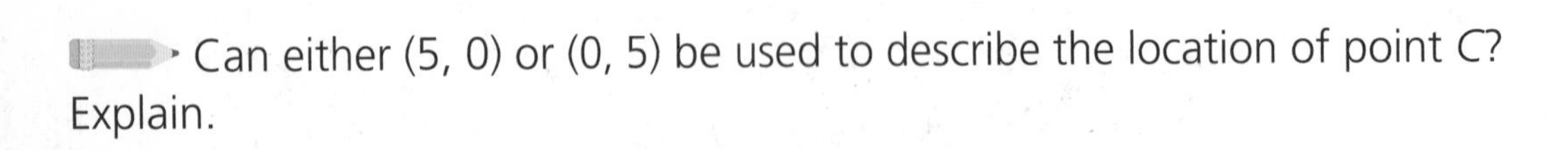

Can either (5, 0) or (0, 5) be used to describe the location of point *C*? Explain.

Understand: Using ordered pairs to graph a figure on a coordinate plane

Ethan graphs these points on a coordinate plane.
point *A*: (1, 2) **point *B*:** (2, 5) **point *C*:** (7, 5) **point *D*:** (6, 2)

He connects the points in order, and then connects point *D* back to point *A*. What geometric figure does Ethan graph?

To find the geometric figure Ethan graphs using points *A*, *B*, *C*, and *D*, plot and label each point on the coordinate plane.

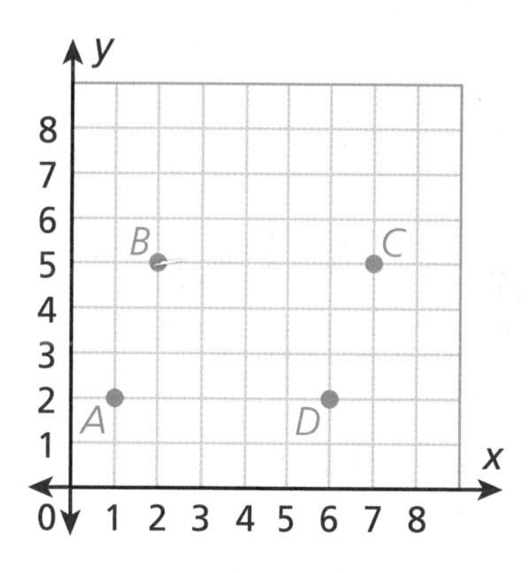

Connect the points *A*, *B*, *C*, and *D* in order and then connect point D back to point *A*.

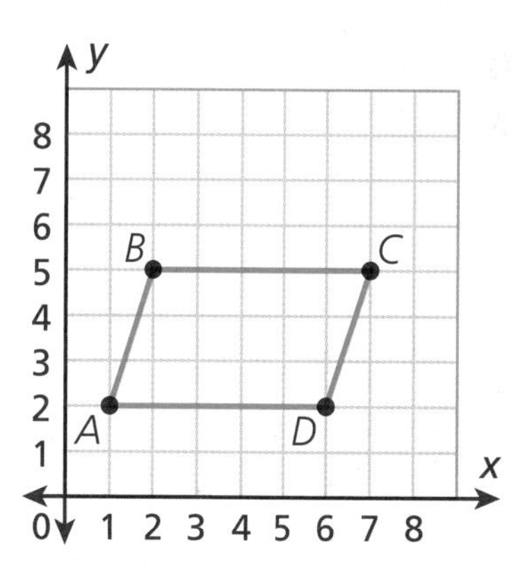

You can see that line segments *AB* and *DC* are always the same distance apart. Line segments *AD* and *BC* are also always the same distance apart. The figure is a quadrilateral with two pairs of parallel sides, so it is a parallelogram.

➡ Ethan graphs parallelogram *ABCD*.

Draw another quadrilateral that is a parallelogram. Explain how you know that it is a parallelogram.

Guided Instruction

Connect: What you know about points on a coordinate plane

Rajia uses a coordinate plane to graph the points for the ordered pairs given in the table. She then connects them in order.

What letter does Rajia form?

x	y	(x, y)
1	3	(1, 3)
1	8	(1, 8)
5	3	(5, 3)
5	8	(5, 8)

Step 1

Graph the point for (1, 3).
Then graph the point for (1, 8).
Next graph the point for (5, 3).
Finally graph the point for (5, 8).

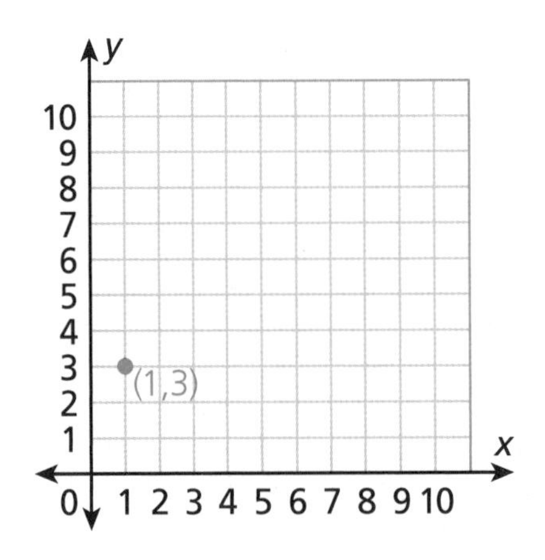

Remember!
Start at the origin for each point. Then move x units to the right and y units up on the coordinate plane to graph the point.

Step 2

Connect the points in the order they were graphed above.

Draw a line segment to connect the point for (1, 3) and the point for (1, 8).
Then draw a line segment to connect the point for (1, 8) and the point for (5, 3).
Finally draw a line segment to connect the point for (5, 3) and the point for (5, 8).
The line segments form a letter of the alphabet.

What is the letter? ____

Rajia connects the points to form the letter ____.

Graph the points for (2, 2), (2, 6), (4, 2), (6, 6), and (6, 2) on a coordinate plane. Then connect the points in the order they are given above. What letter do you form?

Guided Practice

For exercises 1–4, use the coordinate plane.

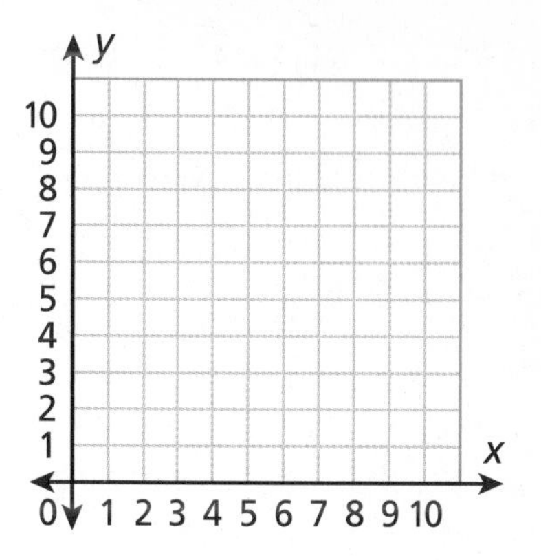

1. Graph the following points.
   point A: (3, 1) point B: (3, 6) point C: (5, 8)
   point D: (8, 5) point E: (8, 1)

   Connect points A through E in alphabetical order. Then connect point E back to point A.

   What polygon do you form when the points are connected?___________

2. Which pair of sides of the polygon are parallel? ___________

3. Which pairs of sides of the polygon are perpendicular?

   ____

4. How do you know when a pair of sides is perpendicular?

   ____

   ____

Solve the problem.

5. Garrett graphs the points for the ordered pairs (4, 6) and (4, 9) on a coordinate plane. Then he connects the points to form a line segment. Is the line segment parallel to the x-axis or parallel to the y-axis?

   Answer ___________

Think•Pair•Share

MP2 6. Elena graphs the point for the ordered pair (5, 2) on a coordinate plane. She says that the x-coordinate of the ordered pair, 5, means that the point is a distance of 5 units from the y-axis and the y-coordinate of the ordered pair, 2, means that the point is a distance of 2 units from the x-axis. Is Elena correct? Explain your reasoning.

Independent Practice

For exercises 1–3, use the coordinate plane.

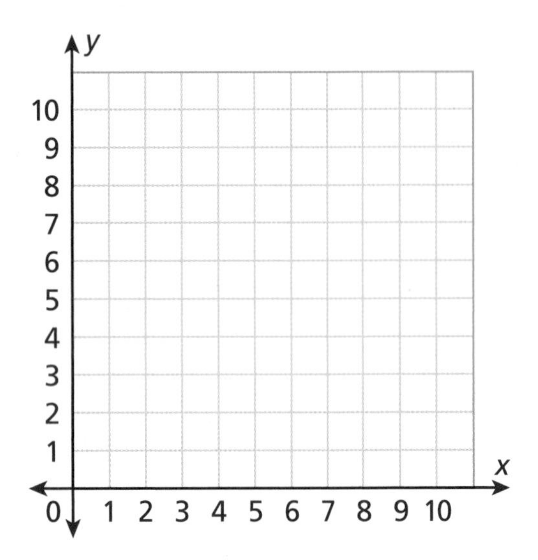

1. Graph the following points.
   point C: (2, 8) point D: (3, 3) point E: (5, 6)
   point F: (7, 3) point G: (8, 8)

   Connect points C through G in alphabetical order.

   What letter is formed when the points are connected? ____

2. Are any pairs of line segments that form the letter parallel? ____

3. Are any pairs of line segments that form the letter perpendicular? ____

For exercises 4–5, use the coordinate plane.

4. Graph the following points.
   point J: (1, 1)
   point K: (1, 4)
   point L: (3, 4)

5. Connect points J, K, and L in alphabetical order. Then connect point L back to point J.

   What polygon is formed when the points are connected? ________________

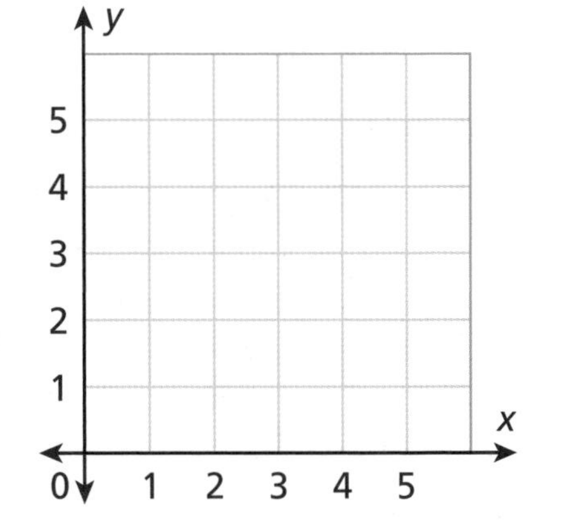

Independent Practice

For exercises 6–8, use the coordinate plane.

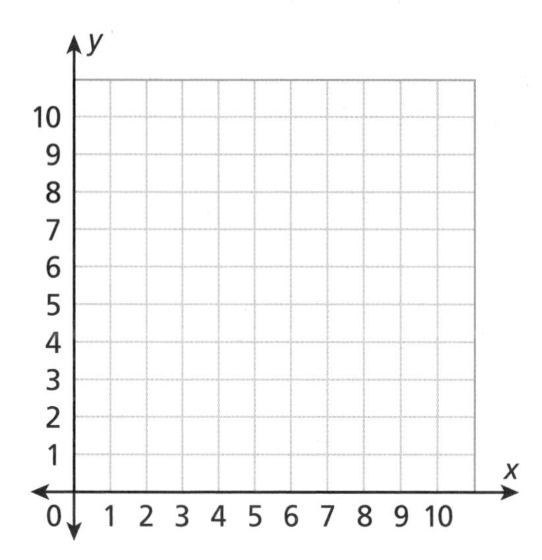

6. Graph the points for the following ordered pairs. Connect them in order.
   (7, 9) (7, 4) (10, 4)

   What letter do you form? ____

7. Graph the points for the following ordered pairs. Connect them in order.
   (1, 5) (3, 0) (5, 5)

   What letter do you form? ____

8. Graph the points for the following ordered pairs. Connect them in order.
   (2, 10) (4, 10) (2, 7) (4, 7)

   What letter do you form? ____

For exercises 9–10, use the coordinate plane.

9. Graph the following points.
   point Q: (1, 5) point R: (5, 5)
   point S: (4, 2) point T: (2, 2)

10. Connect points Q, R, S, and T in alphabetical order. Then connect point T back to point Q.

    What polygon is formed when the points are connected? ________________

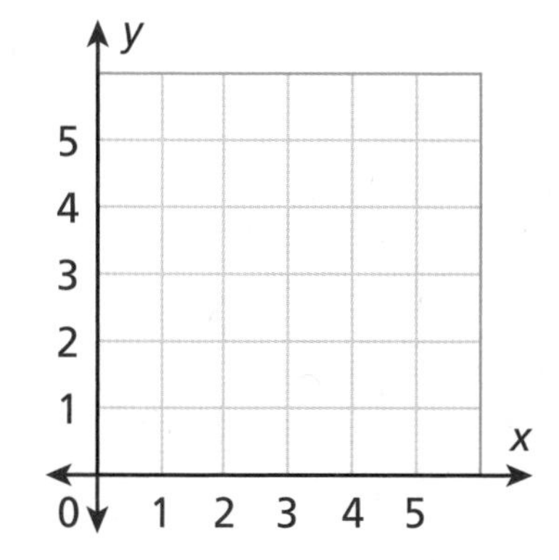

Independent Practice

11. Graph the following points on the coordinate plane.
point L: (2, 0)
point M: (0, 4)

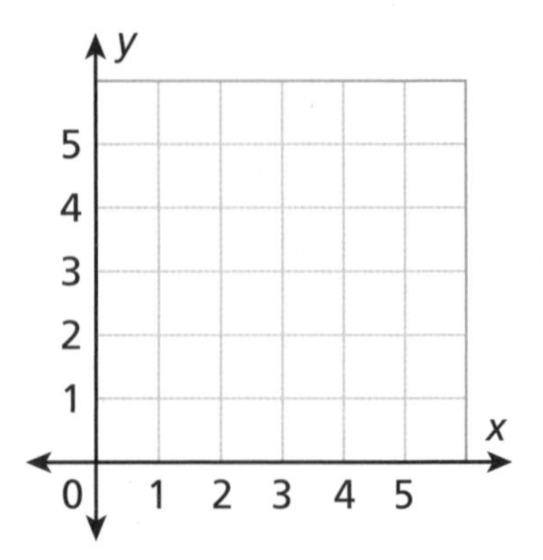

When a point is located on the x-axis on a coordinate plane, what is the y-coordinate of the point? When a point is located on the y-axis on a coordinate plane, what is the x-coordinate of the point? Explain your thinking.

Answer ______________________________

Solve the problems.

MP5 **12.** Hong Kun graphs a quadrilateral on a coordinate plane. The vertices of the quadrilateral are (1, 1), (3, 6), (6, 6), and (8, 1). What quadrilateral does Hong Kun draw when he connects the points? How do you know?

Answer ______________________________

MP6 **13.** A designer graphs the model of a window on a coordinate plane. The vertices on this model are represented by the following points: A (2, 2), B (2, 5), C (3, 7), D (6, 7), E (7, 5), and F (7, 2). Connect the points in order to find the shape of the window. What attributes did you use to identify the shape? Does the window have any pairs of sides that are parallel or perpendicular? If so, which pairs are they?

Answer ______________________________

Independent Practice

MP8 **14.** Draw three different vertical line segments on the coordinate plane.

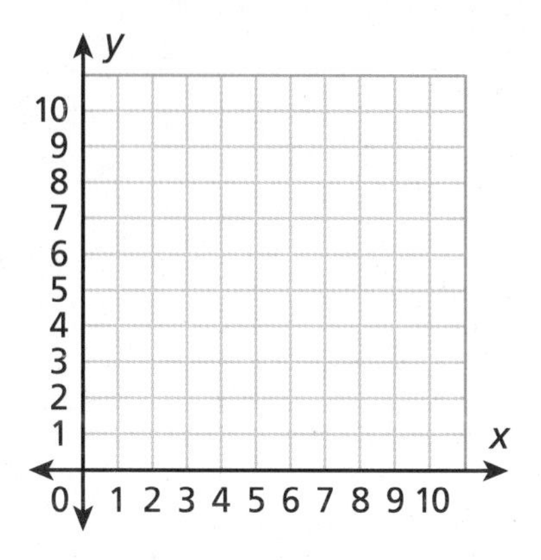

For each vertical line segment, what conclusion can you draw about the *x*-coordinates of the ordered pairs that represent the endpoints? For horizontal line segments, can you draw a similar conclusion about the *y*-coordinates of the ordered pairs that represent the endpoints? If so, explain.

Answer ____

MP4 **15.** Gaia draws a line segment to connect the points at (2, 1) and (7, 4). She draws a second line segment that is parallel to the first one by connecting the points at (2, 3) and (7, 6). If she wants to draw a third line segment parallel to the ones she has already drawn, what ordered pairs could she use?

Answer ____

Justify your answer using words, drawings, or numbers.

MP7 **16.** Jules draws a line segment to connect the points at (3, 6) and (8, 6). Then he graphs two more points that he connects to form a second line segment that is perpendicular to the first line segment. What could be the ordered pairs of the points he graphs?

Answer ____

Justify your answer using words, drawings, or numbers.

Lesson 35

Graph Points to Represent Problem Situations

Essential Question:
How do you use a coordinate plane to represent real-world and mathematical problems?

5.G.2

Words to Know:
scale

Guided Instruction

In this lesson you will learn how to use a coordinate plane to represent real-world and mathematical problems.

Understand: Locating points on a coordinate plane

Ms. Linton's class uses a coordinate plane to make a map of the area near their school. Each unit on the map, or grid, represents 1 block.

Which ordered pair represents the location of each place included on the map? Describe a possible route from the School to the Deli and from the School to the Park.

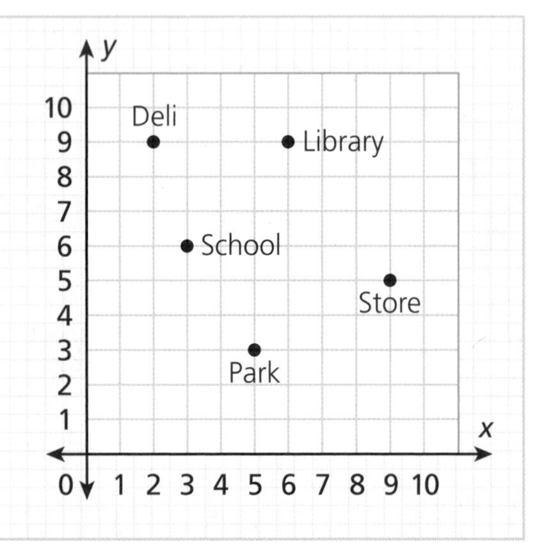

To locate the ordered pair for the Deli, start at the origin, (0, 0). Move along the *x*-axis 2 units. Then move up the vertical line parallel to the *y*-axis until you reach the point that represents the Deli at (2, 9).

Repeat the process to find the ordered pairs for all the other locations.

School: ______ **Park:** ______ **Library:** ______ **Store:** ______

To find a possible route from one point to another, try to find a route by moving horizontally right or left first and then vertically up or down.

To go from the School to the Deli, start at the School. You can go 1 block left and 3 blocks up. To go from the School to the Park, you can go 2 blocks right and 3 blocks down.

➡ The ordered pairs for the locations are: Deli (2, 9), School (3, 6), Park (5, 3), Library (6, 9), and Store (9, 5). A possible route from the School to the Deli is 1 block left and 3 blocks up. A possible route from the School to the Park is 2 blocks right and 3 blocks down.

Guided Instruction

Understand: **Drawing a line graph to represent a real-life situation**

Andy buys a pound of cheese for $5. He needs to buy more of the same kind of cheese. What will be the total cost of all of the cheese if Andy buys two more pounds? Four more pounds? Draw a line segment on a coordinate plane to show the relationship between the number of additional pounds of cheese Andy buys and the total cost of the cheese in dollars.

To find the total cost of the cheese, make a table. In the table (0, 5) represents the original pound of cheese Andy bought for $5. Use the rule + 1 for each additional pound of cheese he buys, and + 5 for the corresponding total cost in dollars.

Cost of Cheese					
Additional Pounds of Cheese	0	1	2	3	4
Total Cost (dollars)	5	10	15	20	25

Next, use the table and a coordinate plane to draw a line segment that represents the relationship between the number of additional pounds of cheese and the total cost in dollars for all of the cheese. Include a title above the grid: "Cost of Cheese."

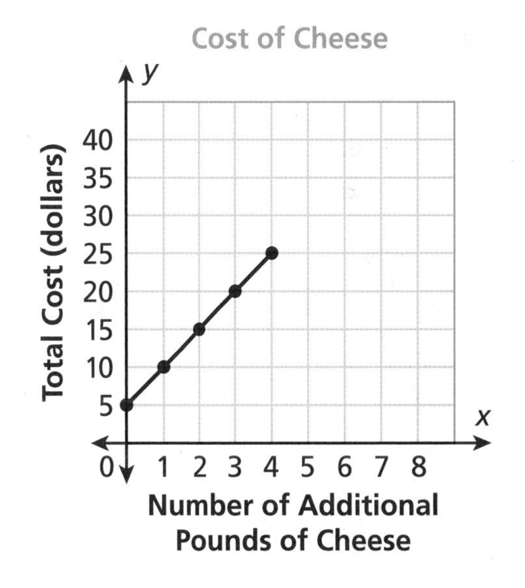

Label the horizontal axis "Number of Additional Pounds of Cheese." Label the vertical axis "Total Cost (dollars)." Since the cheese costs $5 per pound, use a scale of 5 to label the units of the vertical axis.

Plot the points for the ordered pairs in the table: (0, 5), (1, 10), (2, 15), (3, 20), and (4, 25).Then draw a line segment to connect the points on the graph.

The graph shows the relationship between the number of additional pounds of cheese Andy buys and the total cost in dollars for all of the cheese. He will spend a total of $15 if he buys two more pounds and a total of $25 if he buys four more pounds.

How can you use the graph to find the amount Andy will spend if he buys five more pounds of cheese? Seven more pounds of cheese?

Guided Instruction

Connect: What you know about real-life situations represented on a coordinate plane

Leia makes a line graph on a coordinate plane to show the weight of her dog Nelson over his lifetime. How much did Nelson weigh when Leia first brought him home? How much did he weigh when he was 4 years old? What was Nelson's greatest weight and how old was he?

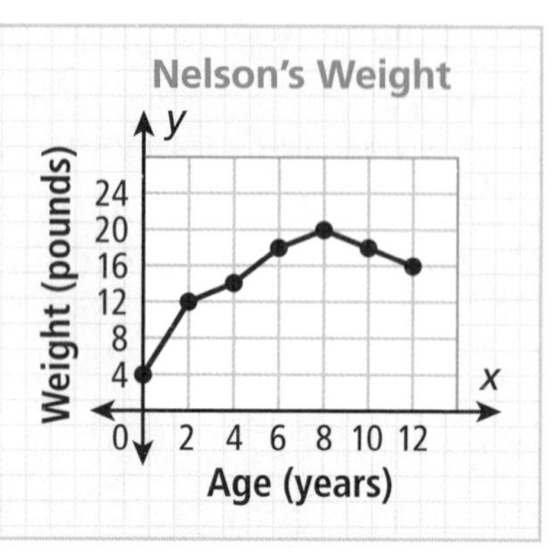

Step 1

The ordered pair for the first point is (0, 4) and it represents Nelson's weight when Leia first brought him home. How much did Nelson weigh?

____ pounds

Step 2

To find Nelson's weight when he was 4 years old, find 4 on the x-axis, or the horizontal axis. Move up the vertical line parallel to the y-axis until you reach the point that lies on the graph. The point is exactly between 12 and 16 on the y-axis. The ordered pair for the point is __________.

How much did Nelson weigh when he was 4 years old? ____ pounds

Step 3

To find Nelson's greatest weight, look for the highest point on the graph.

The ordered pair for the highest point is __________.

What was Nelson's greatest weight? ____ pounds

How old was he? ____ years old

Nelson weighed ____ pounds when Leia first brought him home. He weighed ____ pounds when he was 4 years old. His greatest weight was ____ pounds at ____ years old.

Describe how Nelson's weight changed over his lifetime.

Guided Practice

For exercises 1–6, use the coordinate plane. The coordinate plane shows the location of some landmarks in Cynthia's town.

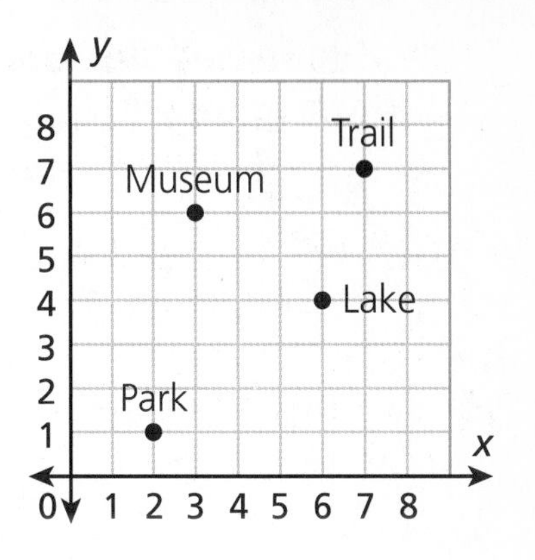

1. Which ordered pair represents the location of the Park? ____________

2. Which ordered pair represents the location of the Museum? ____________

3. Which ordered pair represents the location of the Lake? ____________

4. Which ordered pair represents the location of the Trail? ____________

5. Describe a possible path from the Museum to the Lake.

____

6. Describe a possible path from the Park to the Trail.

____

Solve the problem.

7. Rajeev has $12 saved for a vacation. He adds $4 to his savings each week. How much money will he have after 5 weeks? Use the coordinate plane to make a line segment that shows the relationship between the numbers of weeks he adds $4 and the amount of money Rajeev has saved.

Answer ______________________________

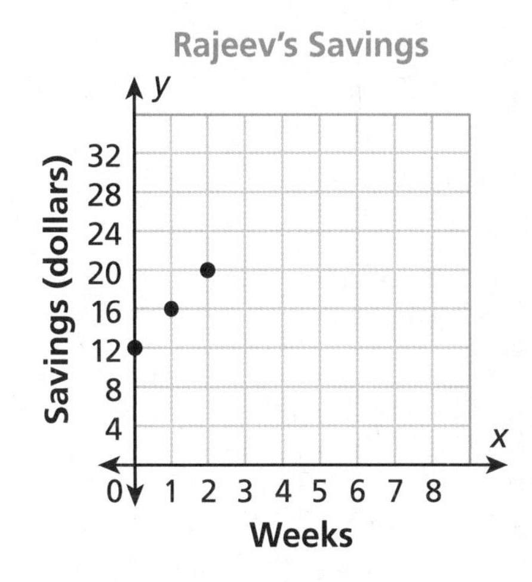

Think•Pair•Share

MP7 8. Look back at the graph of the line segment you made to show Rajeev's savings. How is the graph useful in analyzing the data?

Independent Practice

For exercises 1–5, use the coordinate plane. The coordinate plane shows where Trisha and her friends live. Each unit on the coordinate plane represents 1 block.

1. Write the ordered pair that identifies where each friend lives.

   Tricia ____________

   Ugo ____________

   Asia ____________

   Kyle ____________

   Ross ____________

   Barbara ____________

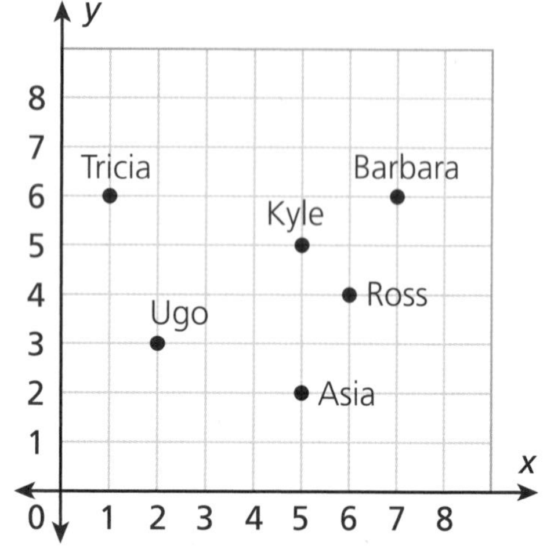

2. Describe a possible path from Tricia's home to Barbara's home.

   ____

3. Describe a possible path from Kyle's home to Asia's home.

   ____

4. Describe a possible path from Barbara's home to Ugo's home.

   ____

5. Describe a possible path from Ugo's home to Kyle's home.

   ____

6. Three of the vertices of rectangle *JKLM* are shown below.
   point *J*: (2, 3)
   point *K*: (2, 7)
   point *L*: (7, 7)

   What is the ordered pair for the missing vertex, point *M*?

   ____

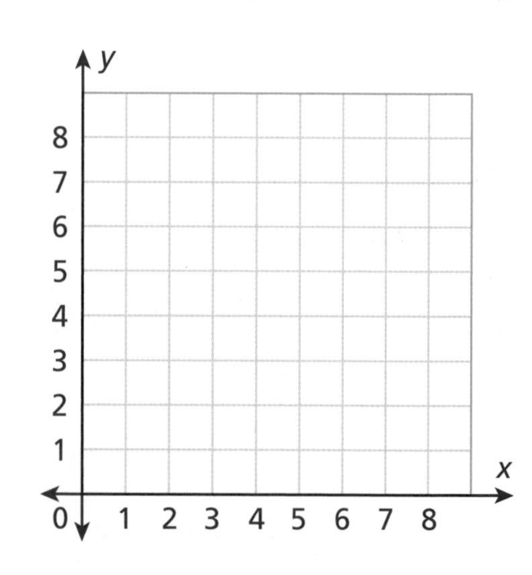

Independent Practice

7. Three of the vertices of square *QRST* are shown below.
point *R*: (7, 6)
point *S*: (7, 3)
point *T*: (4, 3)
What is the ordered pair for the missing vertex, point *Q*?

____

8. Three of the vertices of parallelogram *ABCD* are shown below.
point *A*: (2, 7)
point *C*: (5, 3)
point *D*: (2, 2)
What is the ordered pair for the missing vertex, point *B*?

____

For exercises 9–12, use the graph. The graph shows the relationship between the number of hours Hannah works and the amount she earns.

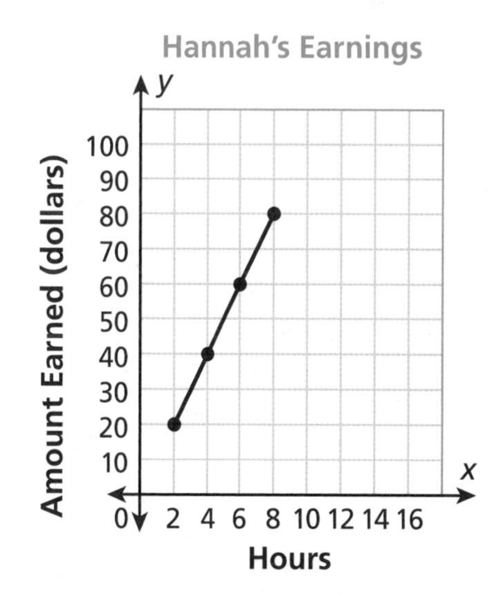

9. How much money does Hannah earn after working for 2 hours? __________

10. How much money does Hannah earn after working for 6 hours? __________

11. How much money does Hannah earn after working for 5 hours? __________

12. How much money does Hannah earn for each hour she works? __________

13. How much money will Hannah earn after working 10 hours? __________

Independent Practice

Solve the problems.

MP3 **14.** The table shows the temperature of a liquid as it cools. Draw a line segment on the coordinate plane below to show the relationship between the temperature and the number of minutes the liquid cools.

Liquid Temperature Change					
Time (minutes)	0	2	4	6	8
Temperature (degrees Celsius)	32	28	24	20	16

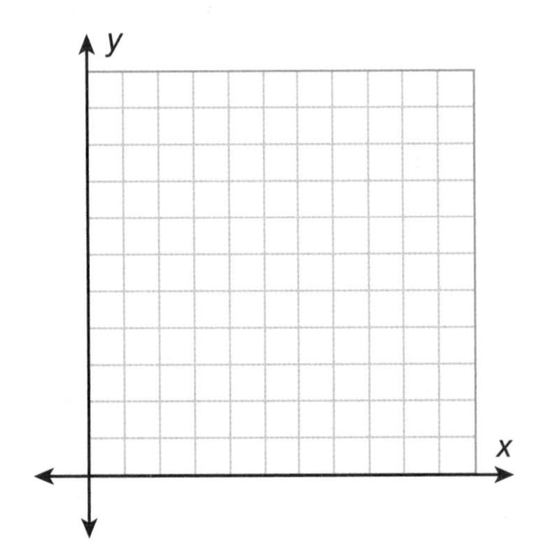

Use your graph to find the temperature of the liquid after

5 minutes. ______________

What information about the temperature change does the graph show?

Answer ______________

MP5 **15.** Sammy graphs a rectangle on a coordinate plane. Three vertices of the rectangle are at (2, 2), (2, 7), and (6, 2). What is the ordered pair for the remaining vertex of the rectangle? How do you know?

Answer ______________

Independent Practice

MP6 **16.** Draw a square with an area of 25 square units on the coordinate plane. Label the vertices of the square *A*, *B*, *C*, and *D*. Then, starting with vertex *A*, describe how to travel from one vertex to the next on the coordinate plane.

y
10 9 8 7 6 5 4 3 2 1
x
0 1 2 3 4 5 6 7 8 9 10

Answer ______________________________

Justify your answer using words, drawings, or numbers.

MP2 **17.** Today Claire cycles 5 miles to meet her friends. Then they go for a long bike ride together. The group of riders cycle 15 miles each hour for 6 hours. What is the total distance Claire cycles today after 3 hours of cycling with her friends? After 5 hours of cycling with her friends? Draw a line segment on the coordinate plane below to show the relationship between the number of hours Claire rides with her friends and her total cycling distance in miles. What does the graph show about the relationship?

Answer ______________________________

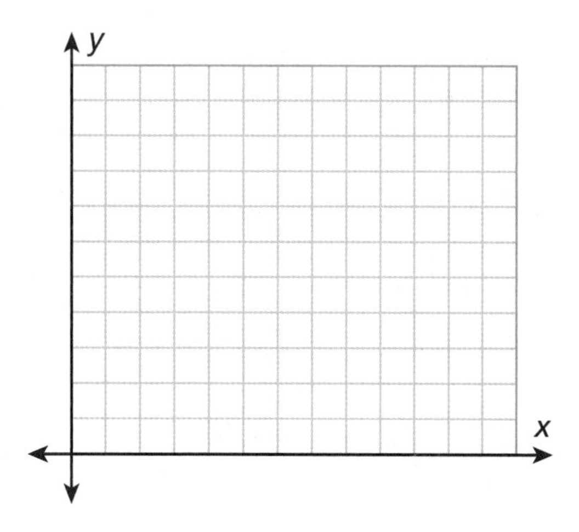

Justify your answer using words, drawings, or numbers.

Lesson

36 Analyze Properties to Classify Two-Dimensional Figures

Essential Question:
How do you use properties to classify two-dimensional figures?

5.G.3; 5.G.4

Words to Know:
- scalene triangle
- isosceles triangle
- equilateral triangle
- acute triangle
- right triangle
- obtuse triangle
- trapezoid
- kite
- adjacent sides
- hierarchy diagram

Guided Instruction

In this lesson you will learn how to use properties to classify two-dimensional figures.

Understand: Using properties to classify triangles

Renzo draws a triangle with two sides that are the same length. The triangle has one obtuse angle. How can Renzo classify the triangle?

A triangle can be classified by the lengths of its sides.

A triangle with no sides that are the same length is a scalene triangle.

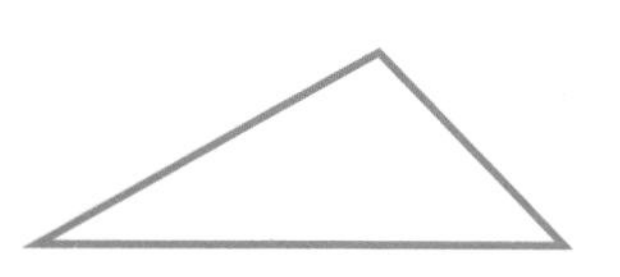

A triangle with at least two sides that are the same length is an isosceles triangle.

A triangle with three sides that are the same length is an equilateral triangle.

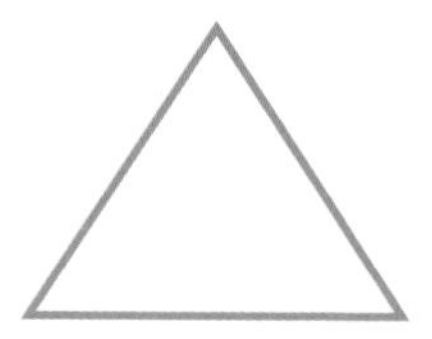

A triangle can also be classified by the measures of its angles.

A triangle with three acute angles is an acute triangle.

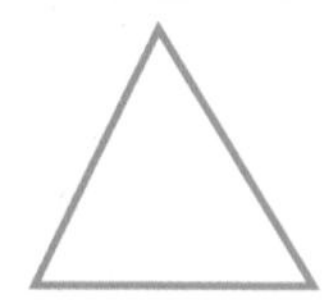

A triangle with a right angle is a right triangle.

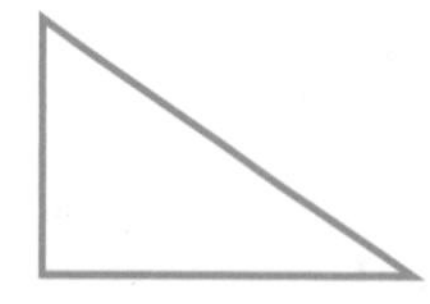

A triangle with an obtuse angle is an obtuse triangle.

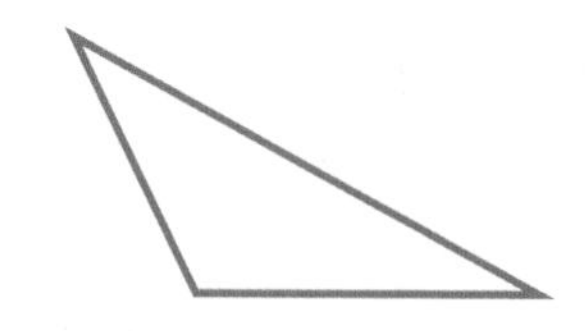

Renzo's triangle is an isosceles triangle because two sides are the same length.

Renzo's triangle is an obtuse triangle because it has one obtuse angle.

➡ Renzo's triangle is an isosceles obtuse triangle.

Understand: Using properties to classify quadrilaterals

Natalie wants to cut out a parallelogram to use in her collage. What types of quadrilaterals can Natalie use?

Examine the properties of these quadrilaterals below to decide which are parallelograms.

Remember!
A quadrilateral is a polygon with 4 sides and 4 angles.

Special Quadrilaterals

A trapezoid has
- at least 1 pair of parallel sides

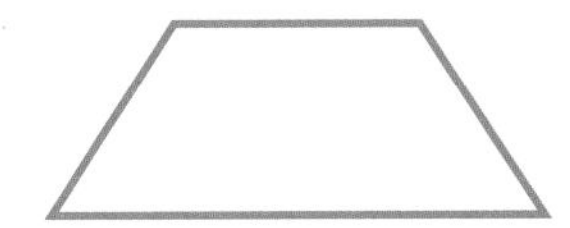

A kite has
- 2 pairs of adjacent sides that are the same length

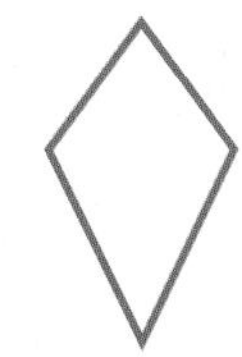

A parallelogram has
- 2 pairs of parallel sides
- 2 pairs of opposite sides that are the same length

A rectangle has
- 2 pairs of parallel sides
- 2 pairs of opposite sides that are the same length
- 4 right angles

A rhombus has
- 2 pairs of parallel sides
- 4 sides that are the same length

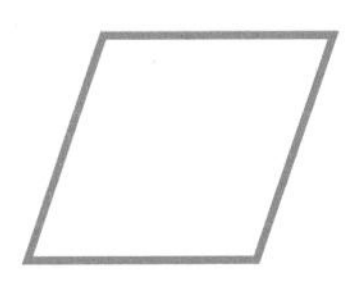

A square has
- 2 pairs of parallel sides
- 4 sides that are the same length
- 4 right angles

Look at the properties given for a parallelogram. Which other special quadrilaterals above also have those properties?

_______________, _______________, and _______________

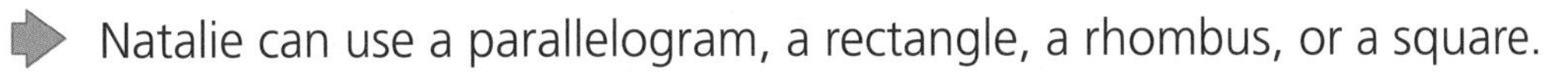

➡ Natalie can use a parallelogram, a rectangle, a rhombus, or a square.

What if Natalie wants a parallelogram with no right angles? What types of quadrilaterals are parallelograms that Natalie can use?

Guided Instruction

Connect: What you know about properties of two-dimensional figures

Make a hierarchy diagram using these two-dimensional figures: quadrilaterals, trapezoids, parallelograms, rectangles, rhombi, and squares.

A hierarchy diagram uses the properties of figures to relate them from the most general category to the most specific category.

Step 1

Start by choosing the most general category.

Which name in the list can be applied to all of the figures? ______________

Step 2

Decide how the other quadrilaterals are related.

Is a trapezoid a parallelogram? ______ Is a parallelogram a trapezoid? ______
Each of these will be on a separate line in the diagram. Trapezoid will be above parallelogram.

Rectangles, rhombi, and squares are parallelograms.

Is a rectangle a square? ______ Is a square a rectangle? ______

Is a rhombus a square? ______ Is a square a rhombus? ______

Step 3

Use your answers to complete the hierarchy diagram.

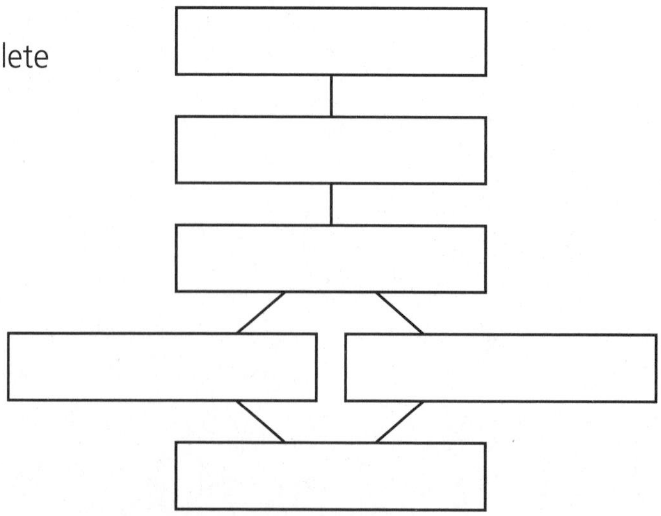

➡ A possible hierarchy diagram is shown above.

Guided Practice

For exercises 1–6, write the most specific classification of the two-dimensional figure.

1. A polygon with three sides has an angle that measures 135°. The sides of the polygon are different lengths. ____________

2. A polygon with four sides has one pair of adjacent sides, each of which measure 8 inches. It has a second pair of adjacent sides, each of which measure 15 inches. None of the sides are parallel.

   ____

3. A polygon with five sides has three sides that are the same length.

   ____

4. A polygon with four sides has one pair of parallel sides that are 6 inches long. It has a second pair of parallel sides that are 9 inches long.

   ____

5. A polygon with four sides has four right angles. All the sides of the polygon are the same length. ____________

6. A polygon with four sides has one right angle. None of the sides of the polygon are the same length. No pairs of sides are parallel. ____________

Solve the problem.

MP7 7. Colter earned a polygonal community service badge. The badge has three sides that are each the same length. Each angle in the triangle measures 60 degrees. What is the shape of Colter's badge?

Answer ____________

Think•Pair•Share

MP5 8. Olivia has a puzzle piece that is shaped like a quadrilateral. The puzzle piece has two right angles and one pair of parallel sides. What type of quadrilateral is the puzzle piece? Draw a diagram to support your answer.

Independent Practice

For exercises 1–5, write the most specific classification of the two-dimensional figure.

1. A polygon with six sides has two sides that are the same length. ______________

2. A triangle has one right angle. Two of the sides of the triangle are the same length. ______________

3. A quadrilateral has exactly one pair of parallel sides. ______________

4. A polygon with four sides that are the same length. ______________

5. A polygon with four sides and four right angles. ______________

For exercises 6–11, write all of the possible classifications of the two-dimensional figure.

6. A two-dimensional figure has five sides and five angles.

____

7. A two-dimensional figure has four sides that are the same length and two lines of symmetry.

____

8. A two-dimensional figure has two pairs of opposite sides that are parallel and the same length.

____

9. A two-dimensional figure that has no straight sides and an infinite number of lines of symmetry. Each point on this figure is the same distance from its center.

____

10. A two-dimensional figure that has three sides and three acute angles.

____

11. A two-dimensional 4-sided figure that has two pairs of adjacent sides that are the same length.

____

Independent Practice

Decide whether each statement is true or false. Draw an example or a counterexample to support your answer.

12. A triangle with at least two sides that are the same length has at least one line of symmetry.

    ____

13. A quadrilateral with two right angles must be a rectangle.

    ____

14. A pentagon always has at least one line of symmetry.

    ____

15. A quadrilateral with two pairs of opposite sides that are the same length is a parallelogram.

    ____

16. A parallelogram may have no lines of symmetry so a rhombus has no lines of symmetry.

    ____

17. A hexagon with sides that are the same length has six lines of symmetry.

    ____

Independent Practice

For exercises 18–24, write *sometimes, always,* or *never.*

18. A quadrilateral is a polygon. ____________

19. A triangle has at least two acute angles. ____________

20. A triangle has exactly one line of symmetry. ____________

21. A rectangle is a kite. ____________

22. A rhombus has four right angles. ____________

23. A polygon with six sides is a pentagon. ____________

24. A trapezoid is a square. ____________

Solve the problems.

MP6 25. The window in Keisha's room is a quadrilateral with four right angles and four lines of symmetry. Is this enough information to determine the shape of the window in Keisha's room? Explain.

Answer ____

MP3 26. LeVar says that a right triangle can be acute, scalene, or isosceles. Is he correct? Explain.

Answer ____

Independent Practice

MP8 **27.** What three and four sided polygons have all sides equal in length, and all angles equal in measure?

Answer ______________________________

Justify your answer using words, drawings, or numbers.

MP3 **28.** What are the similarities among a parallelogram, a trapezoid, and a square? What are the differences?

Answer ______________________________

Justify your answer using words, drawings, or numbers.

MP7 **29.** Make a hierarchy diagram for the following two-dimensional figures: quadrilaterals, triangles, parallelograms, polygons, rhombi, right triangles, and rectangles.

For exercises 1–4, draw an example of the following.

1. right isosceles triangle
2. rhombus
3. hexagon
4. obtuse scalene triangle

For exercises 5–8, use the coordinate plane.

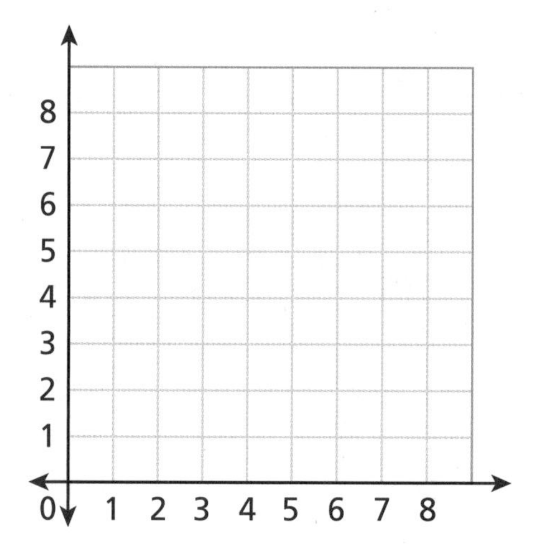

5. Label the x-axis and y-axis.
6. Graph the following points on the coordinate plane.
   point A: (1, 4)   point B: (2, 7)
   point C: (5, 7)   point D: (5, 2)
   point E: (2, 2)

   Connect points A through E in order. Complete the figure by connecting point E to point A. What polygon did you make?

   ____
7. Which line segments are parallel? ____________________
8. Which line segments are perpendicular? ____________________

Circle the correct answer.

9. Which is *not* an example of a parallelogram?
   a. rectangle
   b. rhombus
   c. trapezoid
   d. square

For exercises 10–12, use the map. Each unit on the map represents one block.

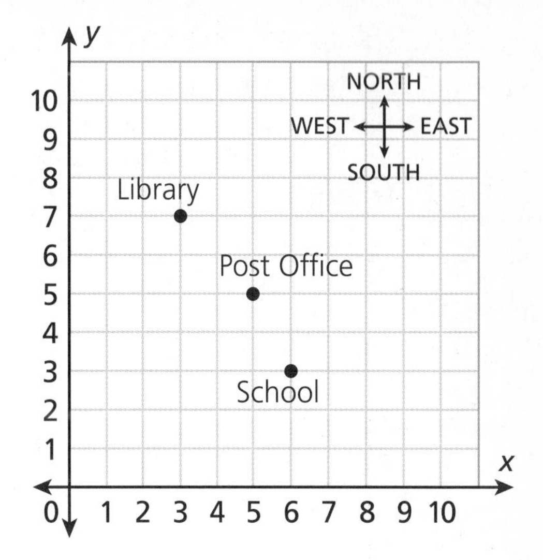

10. Which ordered pair represents the location of the Library?

 ____

11. The Park is located at (3, 4). Graph the location of the Park on the map.

12. Melanie wants to walk from School to the Post Office and then to the Library. Describe a possible path she can take.

For exercises 13–17, write *sometimes*, *always*, or *never*.

13. A kite is a square. ____________

14. A quadrilateral is a trapezoid. ____________

15. A square is a rectangle. ____________

16. A triangle has two obtuse angles. ____________

17. A rhombus is a parallelogram. ____________

Solve the problems.

MP4 18. Owen has saved $15. He earns $9 for each hour he works. If Owen saves all of his money, how much will he have after working 2 hours? 4 hours?10 hours? Make a graph to show the relationship between the hours Owen works and the amount of money he has saved.

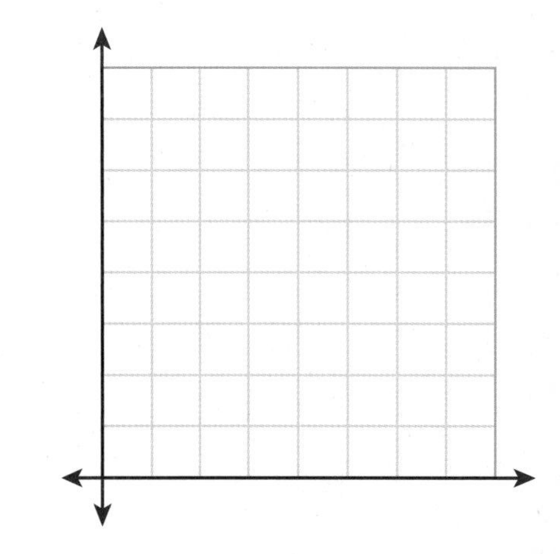

Answer ________________________________

MP7 **19.** Sal draws a line segment from (1, 4) to (5, 8). He then draws another segment from (2, 3) to (6, 7). If Sal wants to draw another line segment that is parallel to those two segments, what points can he use?

Answer ______________________________

Justify your answer using words, drawings, or numbers.

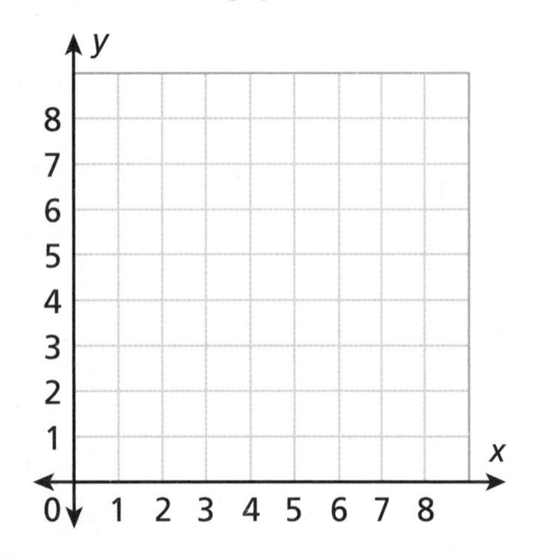

MP3 **20.** Layla drew this hierarchy diagram to classify quadrilaterals. There are two errors in the diagram. Find the errors and explain how to correct them.

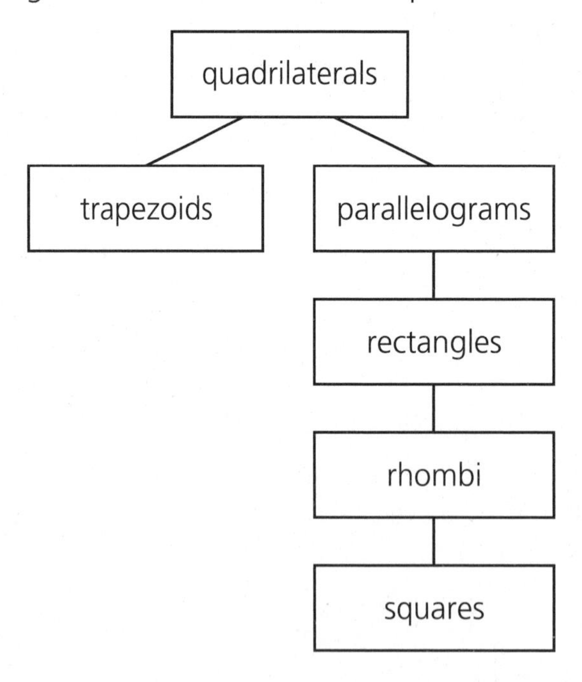

Answer ______________________________

5.NF.1, 5.NF.2, 5.NF.3, 5.NF.6, 5.MD.1, 5.MD.2, 5.MD.4, 5.MD.5b, 5.MD.5c, 5.G.1, 5.G.3

Performance Tasks

Performance Tasks show your understanding of the Math that you have learned. You will be doing various Performance Tasks as you complete your work in this text, ***Common Core Progress Mathematics***.

Beginning This Task

The next five pages provide you with the beginning of a Performance Task. You will be given 5 items to complete, and each item will have two or more parts. As you complete these items you will:

I Demonstrate that you have mastered mathematical skills and concepts

II Reason through a problem to a solution, and explain your reasoning

III Use models and apply them to real-world situations.

Extending This Task

Your teacher may extend this Performance Task with additional items provided in our online resources at sadlierconnect.com.

Scoring This Task

Your response to each item will be assessed against a rubric, or scoring guide. Some items will be worth 1 or 2 points, and others will be worth more. In each item you will show your work or explain your reasoning.

Performance Task 2

Modeling an Underground Parking Garage

1. The students in Harold's art class are making drawings and models. Harold makes a model of an underground parking garage.

a. Harold uses sandbags to make his model. The data set at the right shows the weights of the sandbags in pounds.

Make a line plot of the data shown.

Sandbag Weights (in pounds)

2	$1\frac{3}{4}$	$1\frac{3}{4}$	1
$1\frac{3}{4}$	$1\frac{1}{2}$	$1\frac{1}{2}$	$1\frac{3}{4}$

____

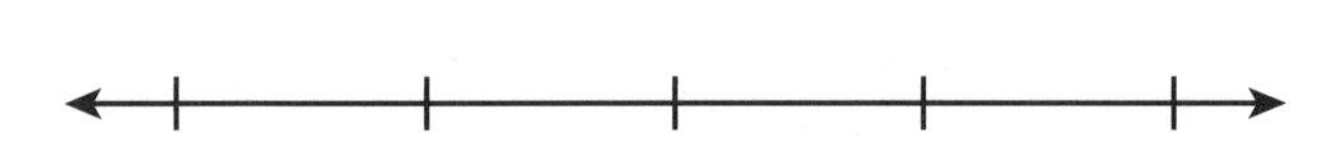

b. What is the total weight of the sandbags?

c. Suppose the sandbags were re-filled so that each of the sandbags weighed the same. How many pounds would each bag weigh?

d. Use your answer to item 1.c. above. How many ounces would each bag weigh?

Modeling an Apartment Building

2. Rebecca builds a model of an apartment building.

a. Rebecca plans to use foot cubes to make the model. She begins by making the sketch below. Draw cubes in this sketch to help Rebecca find the total number of foot cubes she needs.

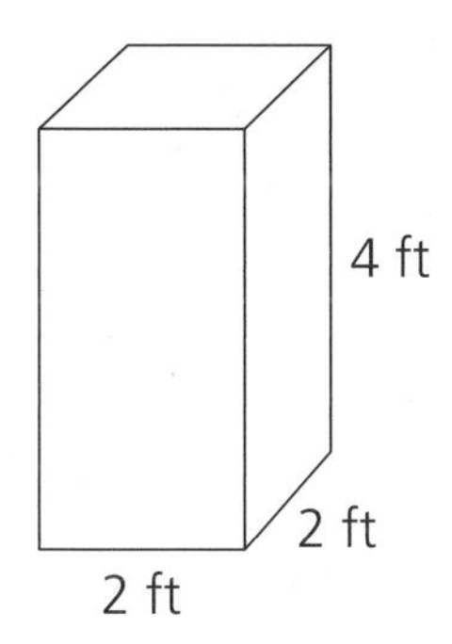

b. How many foot cubes will Rebecca need?

c. Multiply to find the volume of Rebecca's apartment building model.

d. Jarred also makes a model of an apartment building. His model is a cube with edge lengths of 1 yard. Whose model has the greater volume, Rebecca's or Jarred's? How much greater?

Performance Task 2

Modeling an Office Building

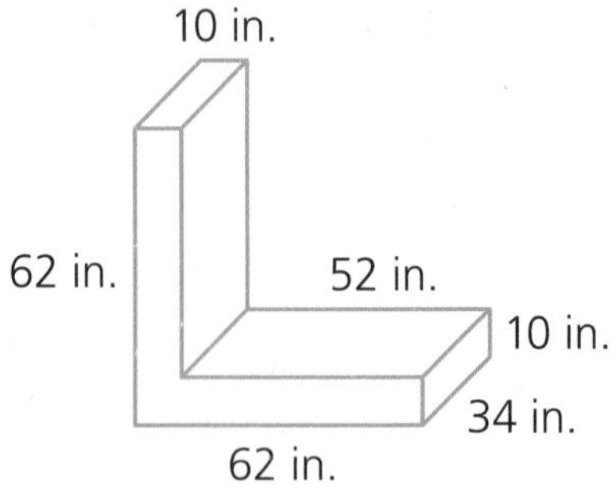

3. Jorge makes the model shown at the right of an office building.

10 in.

62 in.

52 in.

10 in.

34 in.

62 in.

a. Jorge says that he can use the formula $V = \ell \times w \times h$ to find the volume of his model. He says he will multiply $62 \times 34 \times 62$, because the length is 62 inches, the width is 34 inches, and the height is 62 inches. He says his answer will be in cubic inches. What error is Jorge making?

b. Draw a line segment on Jorge's model to show how you can break apart the model into two right rectangular prisms.

c. Explain how you can use the formula $V = \ell \times w \times h$ to find the volume of Jorge's model.

d. Find the volume of Jorge's model.

Modeling a Vacation Home

4. Hua makes a chart of clues for drawing her dream vacation home on a coordinate plane.

a. Complete Hua's chart.

Point	Directions from the Origin	Ordered Pair
A	2 units to the right, 1 unit up	
B	2 units to the right, ____ units up	(2, 5)
C	____ units to the right, 5 units up	(4, 5)
D	____ units to the right, ____ units up	(4, 7)
E	5 units to the right, 8 units up	
F	____ units to the right, ____ units up	(7, 7)
G	7 units to the right, 1 unit up	

b. What is the meaning of the origin on a coordinate plane?

c. On the coordinate plane to the right, plot and label the points for the ordered pairs from the chart.

d. Make the outline of Hua's dream vacation home. Use the coordinate plane at the right. Draw line segments to connect the points in order. Then connect the last point to the first point.

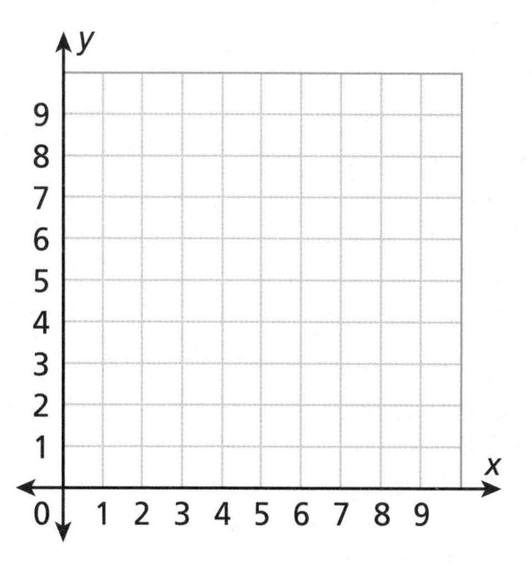

Performance Task 2

Triangular Doors

5. Ilya is designing doors for her model of an amusement park's fun house. She wants each door to have the shape of an isosceles triangle.

a. Describe the attributes of an isosceles triangle.

b. Ilya wants one door to have the shape of an acute triangle. Draw an example of an acute triangle that is also an isosceles triangle. Explain how your triangle is both acute and isosceles.

c. Ilya wants another door to have the shape of a right triangle. Draw an example of a right triangle that is also an isosceles triangle. Explain how your triangle is both a right triangle and an isosceles triangle.

d. Ilya wants the third door of her model to have the shape of an obtuse triangle. Draw an example of an obtuse triangle that is also an isosceles triangle. Explain how your triangle is both an obtuse triangle and an isosceles triangle.

A review of prerequisite mathematics needed to understand the concepts and skills of Grade 5.

A. Understand: Comparing with an unknown factor

Tyler waits 21 minutes for the school bus. Tyler's waiting time is 3 times as long as Grace's waiting time. How long does Grace wait for the bus?

To find how long Grace waits for the bus, first model the problem. Then write and solve an equation. Use g to represent the unknown quantity, Grace's waiting time.

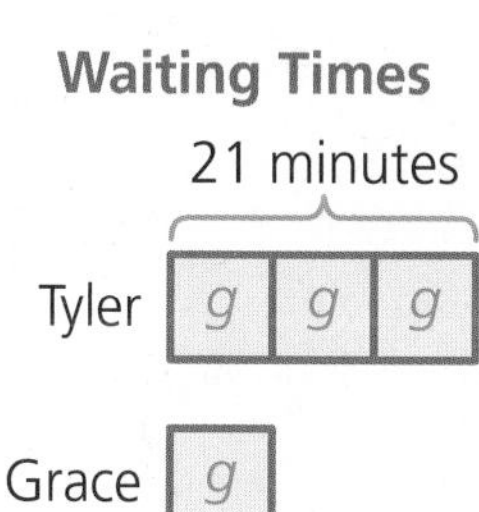

Grace's waiting time is the amount being multiplied, or the size of each group in the model.

Write a multiplication equation for the comparison.
21 = 3 times as long as Grace's waiting time
$21 = 3 \times g$

Write and solve a related division equation to find g, the unknown factor.
$21 \div 3 = g$
$7 = g$

Grace waits 7 minutes for the bus.

Remember! Multiplication and division are opposite, or *inverse*, operations.

B. Understand: Number patterns and pattern rules

To solve some problems, you can make a number pattern. A number pattern is an ordered list of numbers that follow a rule and repeat or change in some way. The pattern rule tells you how the pattern works.

Suppose you start with $10 and save $5 each week. To generate the pattern for the amount you will save in 5 weeks, start at 10 and follow the rule *add* 5. Each number in a number pattern is called a term. This pattern tells you that each new term *increases* by 5, so this is a growing pattern. **Rule:** Start at 10 and add 5.

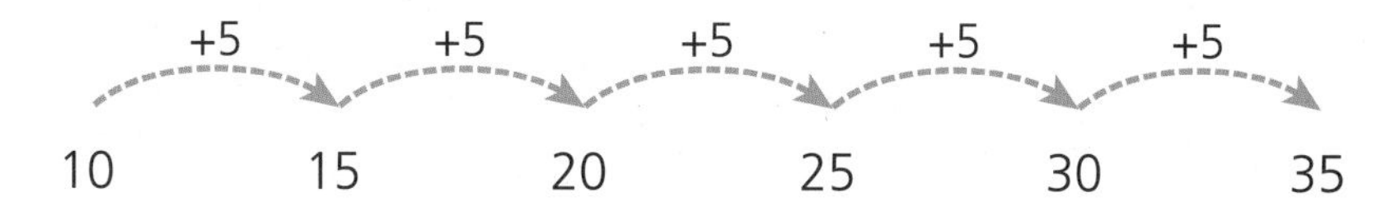

In 5 weeks, you will save $35.

C. Understand: Quotients of tens, hundreds, and thousands

Find the quotient of $200 \div 5$.

In this division 200 represents the dividend, the number you divide; 5 represents the divisor, the number you divide by in the division to find a quotient, the unknown number that is the answer to the problem.

200	÷	5	=	n
dividend		divisor		quotient

Now use the fact $20 \div 5 = 4$ and the pattern of zeros to solve.

$20 \div 5 = 4$

20 tens ÷ 5 = 4 tens ⟶ $200 \div 5 = 40$, so $n = 40$.

You can use a number line to show a model of $200 \div 5 = 40$.

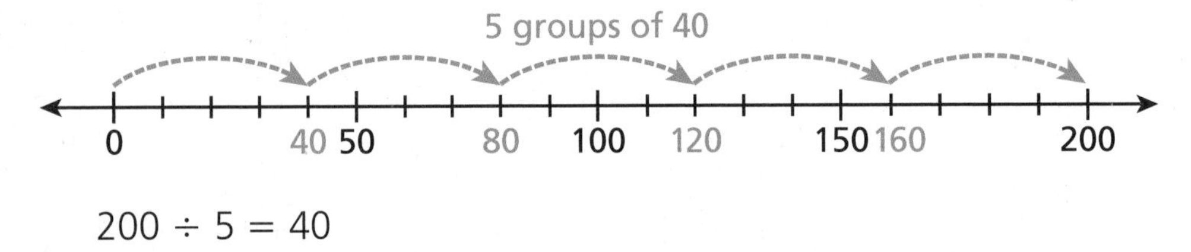

$200 \div 5 = 40$

D. Understand: Division and the Distributive Property

$2{,}280 \div 5 = ■$

To solve the division equation, break apart 2,280.

Choose a hundreds number that when multiplied by 5 would be close to 2,280. $5 \times 400 = 2{,}000$. Subtract.

Next choose a tens number that when multiplied by 5 would be close to 280. $5 \times 50 = 250$. Subtract.

Now choose a ones number that when multiplied by 5 would be close to 30. $5 \times 6 = 30$. Subtract.

$$\begin{array}{r l} 2{,}280 & \\ -2{,}000 & \leftarrow 5 \times 400 \\ \hline 280 & \\ -250 & \leftarrow 5 \times 50 \\ \hline 30 & \\ -30 & \leftarrow 5 \times 6 \\ \hline 0 & \end{array}$$

Write 2,280 as a sum of $2{,}000 + 250 + 30$.

You can distribute the divisor 5 the same way you distributed a factor when using the Distributive Property of Multipliction.

When dividing 2,280, each addend is divided by 5. Add these partial quotients to find the answer.

$$\begin{aligned} 2{,}280 \div 5 &= (2{,}000 \div 5) + (250 \div 5) + (30 \div 5) \\ &= 400 + 50 + 6 \leftarrow \text{partial quotients} \\ &= 456 \end{aligned}$$

$2{,}280 \div 5 = 456$

E. Understand: Place value and partial products

$924 \times 6 = \blacksquare$

To find the product, multiply 6 times the value of each digit in 924. Partial products are formed by multiplying the value of each digit by a factor.

Find the partial products.
Multiply the ones first.
Then multiply the tens and the hundreds.

$$\begin{array}{rl} 924 & \\ \times \quad 6 & \\ \hline 24 & \leftarrow 6 \times 4 \text{ ones} \\ 120 & \leftarrow 6 \times 2 \text{ tens} \\ 5{,}400 & \leftarrow 6 \times 9 \text{ hundreds} \end{array}$$

Add all the partial products.

$924 \times 6 = 24 + 120 + 5{,}400$

$924 \times 6 = 5{,}544$

$$\begin{array}{r} 924 \\ \times \quad 6 \\ \hline 24 \\ 120 \\ +5{,}400 \\ \hline 5{,}544 \end{array}$$

F. Understand: Fractions and mixed numbers

A mixed number shows the sum of a whole number and a fraction but does not have a plus (+) sign. You can write fractions as mixed numbers and you can write mixed numbers as fractions.

Write $\frac{9}{4}$ as a mixed number.

$\frac{9}{4} = \frac{4}{4} + \frac{4}{4} + \frac{1}{4}$ ← Write $\frac{9}{4}$ as a sum of fractions.

$= 1 + 1 + \frac{1}{4}$ ← Write $\frac{4}{4}$ as 1.

$= 2 + \frac{1}{4}$ ← Add the whole numbers.

$= 2\frac{1}{4}$ ← Write the sum as a mixed number.

Remember!
$\frac{4}{4} = 1$

Write $4\frac{1}{2}$ as a fraction.

$4\frac{1}{2} = 4 + \frac{1}{2}$ ← Write $4\frac{1}{2}$ as a sum of 4 plus $\frac{1}{2}$.

$= 1 + 1 + 1 + 1 + \frac{1}{2}$ ← Write 4 as a sum of 1s.

$= \frac{2}{2} + \frac{2}{2} + \frac{2}{2} + \frac{2}{2} + \frac{1}{2}$ ← Write 1 as a fraction with the denominator 2.

$= \frac{2 + 2 + 2 + 2 + 1}{2}$ ← Add the numerators.

$= \frac{9}{2}$

G. Understand: Multiplication as repeated addition

Multiply $6 \times \frac{2}{3}$.

Draw a model to show 6 groups of $\frac{2}{3}$. The model shows that multiplying $6 \times \frac{2}{3}$ is the same as adding $\frac{2}{3} + \frac{2}{3} + \frac{2}{3} + \frac{2}{3} + \frac{2}{3} + \frac{2}{3}$.

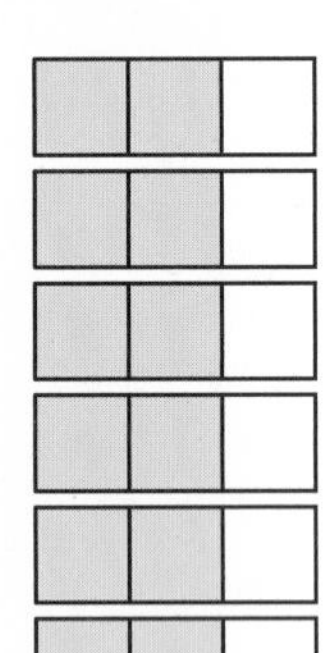

6 addends

$$6 \times \frac{2}{3} = \frac{2}{3} + \frac{2}{3} + \frac{2}{3} + \frac{2}{3} + \frac{2}{3} + \frac{2}{3}$$
$$= \frac{2+2+2+2+2+2}{3}$$
$$= \frac{6 \times 2}{3}$$
$$= \frac{12}{3}$$

Write the product $\frac{12}{3}$ as a whole number. You can use the fact $12 = 4 \times 3$ to help you find the whole number.

$$\frac{12}{3} = \frac{4 \times 3}{3} = \frac{3}{3} + \frac{3}{3} + \frac{3}{3} + \frac{3}{3} = 4$$

$6 \times \frac{2}{3} = 4$.

Remember!
You can break apart the numerator of a fraction in the same way as a whole number.

H. Understand: Multiplying a fraction by a whole number

Multiply $6 \times \frac{2}{3}$.

To multiply any fraction by a whole number, you can multiply the numerator of the fraction by the whole number. Then write the product over the denominator.

$$6 \times \frac{2}{3} = \frac{6 \times 2}{3} = \frac{12}{3} = 4$$

$6 \times \frac{2}{3} = 4$.

I. Understand: Reading and using line plots

A line plot shows measurement data in order from least to greatest.

Maple Leaf Lengths (in inches)

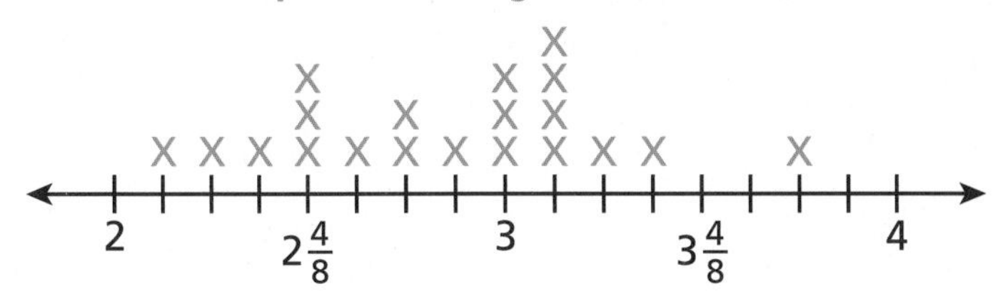

Maple Leaf Lengths (in inches)

$3\frac{1}{8}$	$2\frac{5}{8}$	$2\frac{1}{4}$	$2\frac{6}{8}$	$2\frac{1}{2}$	3	$3\frac{1}{4}$
3	$2\frac{1}{2}$	$2\frac{4}{8}$	$2\frac{6}{8}$	$3\frac{3}{8}$	$2\frac{7}{8}$	3
$3\frac{1}{8}$	$3\frac{1}{8}$	$3\frac{1}{8}$	$3\frac{3}{4}$	$2\frac{1}{8}$	$2\frac{3}{8}$	

A line plot can help you summarize data. For example:

- There are 20 X's so there are 20 measurements altogether.
- All of the leaves are between $2\frac{1}{8}$ and $3\frac{3}{4}$ inches long.
- Most leaves are between $2\frac{1}{8}$ and $3\frac{3}{8}$ inches long.
- Four leaves are $3\frac{1}{8}$ inches long.
- No leaves are $3\frac{4}{8}$ or $3\frac{5}{8}$ inches long.

J. Understand: Area formula for rectangles

To find the area of a rectangle, multiply its length by its width.

Area of rectangle = 6 in. × 4 in.
Area of rectangle = 24 in.^{2}

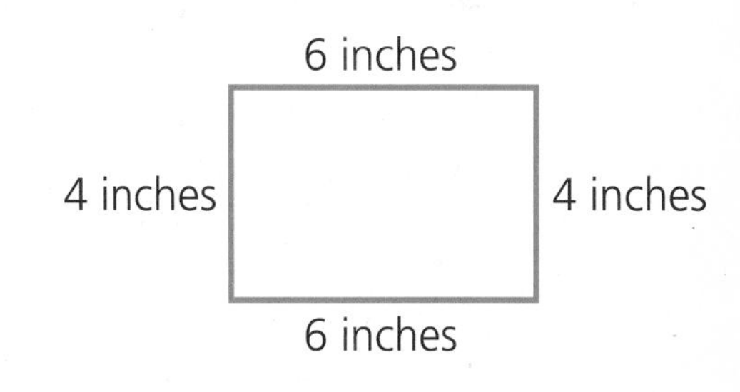

The formula for the area of a rectangle is:

$A = \ell \times w$

You can use the formula to find the area of any rectangle, including squares.

If you know the area of a rectangle, you can also use the formula to find an unknown side length.

The area of the rectangle at the right is 15 cm^2. If it has a width of 3 cm, what is its length?

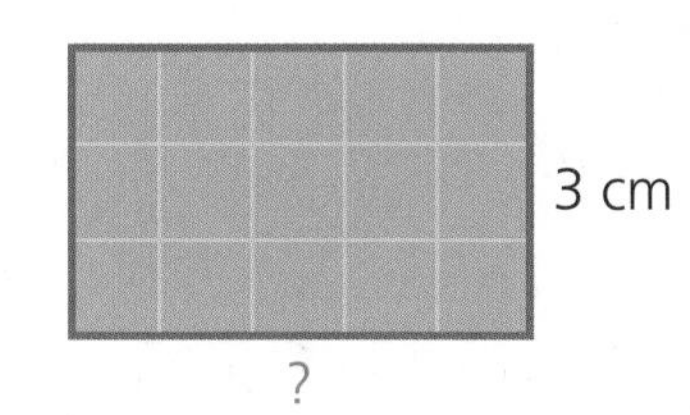

$A = \ell \times w$
$15 = ? \times 3$
$15 = 5 \times 3$

The length of the rectangle is 5 cm.

K. Understand: Identifying right, acute, obtuse, and straight angles

An angle is named by its vertex, the point from which the two sides of an angle begin.

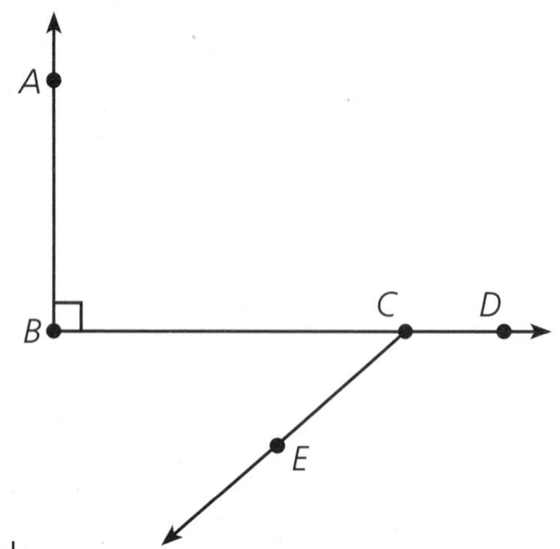

Look at the figure.

- The angle at *B* is marked by the symbol ∟ so it is a right angle and measures 90°. It can also be named as angle *ABC*, or angle *CBA*. The letter naming the vertex names the angle. In a three letter angle name, the vertex is the middle letter.
- An angle that is less than a right angle is an acute angle. It measures less than 90°. Angle *BCE* is an acute angle.
- An angle that is greater than a right angle is an obtuse angle. It measures more than 90° and less than 180°. Angle *DCE* is an obtuse angle.
- An angle that forms a straight line is a straight angle. It measures 180°. Angle *BCD* is a straight angle.

Remember!
An angle is formed when two rays share the same endpoint, called the vertex. The two rays form the sides of the angle.

L. Understand: Using angle measurement to classify two-dimensional figures

You can use angle measurement to classify two-dimensional figures such as triangles.

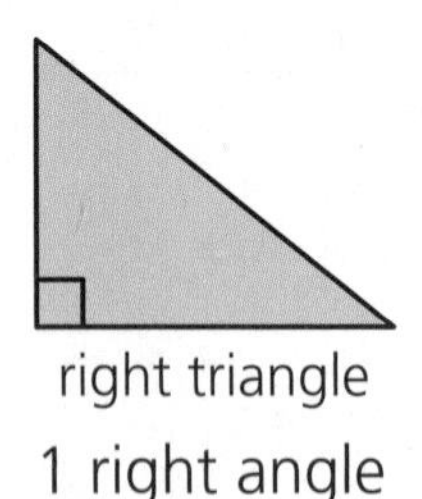

right triangle
1 right angle

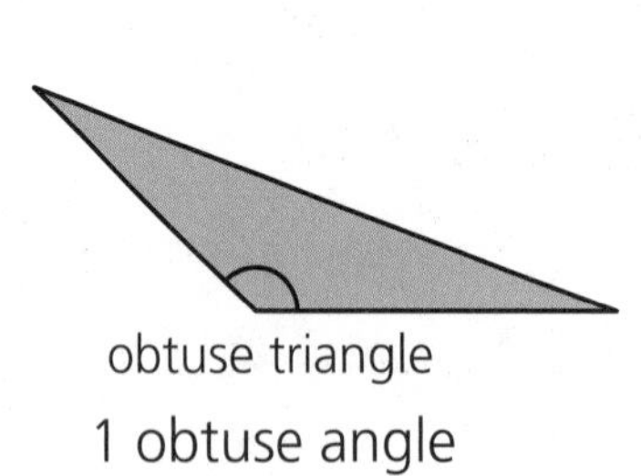

obtuse triangle
1 obtuse angle

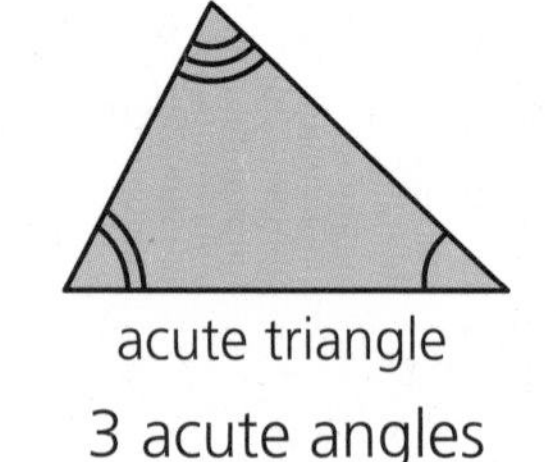

acute triangle
3 acute angles

You can use this model to solve problems.

Read

Read the problem.
Focus on the facts and the questions.

- What facts do you know?
- What do you need to find out?

Plan

Outline a plan.
Plan how to solve the problem.

- What operation will you use?
- Do I need to use 1 step or 2 steps?
- Will you draw a picture?
- How have you solved similar problems?

Solve

Follow your plan to solve the problem.

- Did you answer the question?
- Did you label your answer?

Check

Test that the solution is reasonable.

- Does your answer make sense? If not, review and revise your plan.
- How can you solve the problem a different way? Is the answer the same?
- How can you estimate to check your answer?

A Multiplication Problem

Rory multiplied a two-digit number by a one-digit number greater than 1. The product was between 40 and 45. What were the factors?

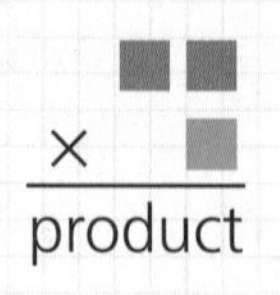

Read

Visualize the problem as you reread it.

Focus on the facts and the question.

Facts: The factors were a two-digit number and a one-digit number greater than 1. The product was between 40 and 45.

Question: What were the factors?

Plan

Make a table to record the factors and products.

To find the factors, list:

- one-digit numbers greater than 1. (2, 3, 4, . . .)
- two-digit numbers. (10, 11, 12, . . .)

Not all problems have just one solution.

Since the least two-digit number is 10 and $5 \times 10 = 50$, the one-digit number must be less than 5.

Multiply the factors to find the products that equal 41, 42, 43, or 44.

Solve

Factors	21 × 2	22 × 2	23 × 2	13 × 3	14 × 3	15 × 3	11 × 4
Product	**42**	**44**	46	39	**42**	45	**44**

There is *more than one solution*.

Look at the table. The factors for a product between 40 and 45 are: 2×21, 2×22, 3×14, and 4×11.

Check

Go back to the problem. Reread it. Compare the completed table to the facts given in the problem.

Are all the solutions reasonable? Yes.

A Book Problem

Marvin is reading a 341-page book. He has already read 128 pages of the book and skipped reading the forward containing 19 pages. How many more pages does Marvin have left to read to finish the book?

Read

Visualize the problem as you reread it.

Focus on the facts and the question.

Facts: The book has 341 pages.
Marvin has read 128 pages.
Marvin skipped 19 pages.

Question: How many more pages does Marvin have left to read?

Plan

Do you need more than one step to solve this problem? Yes.

Step 1: Add the number of pages Marvin read and skipped.

Step 2: Subtract that sum from the total number of book pages.

Solve

Step 1: Add

```
   1
  128 ← pages read
+  19 ← pages skipped
  ---
  147
```

Step 2: Subtract

```
     13
   12 3̸ 11
   3̸ 4̸ 1̸ ← total number of book pages
 − 1 4 7 ← pages read and skipped
   -----
   1 9 4 ← pages left to read
```

Marvin has 194 pages left to read.

Check

Use the Commutative Property and addition to check your answer.

```
   1
   19 ← pages skipped
+ 128 ← pages read
  ---
  147
```

```
   11
  194 ← pages left to read
+ 147 ← pages skipped and read
  ---
  341 ← total number of book pages
```

The answer is correct.

Common Core State Standards for Mathematical Practice

The Standards for Mathematical Practice, identified here, are an important part of learning mathematics. They are covered in every lesson in this book.

MP1 Make sense of problems and persevere in solving them.

- Analyze and plan a solution
- Relate to a similar problem
- Assess progress
- Use concrete objects or pictures
- Check solutions

MP2 Reason abstractly and quantitatively.

- Pay attention to all mathematical language
- Represent problems using symbols
- Consider units in problem solving
- Use properties of operations and objects

MP3 Construct viable arguments and critique the reasoning of others.

- Analyze a problem situation
- Share reasoning with others
- Explain an approach to a problem
- Construct arguments by using drawings or concrete objects

MP4 Model with mathematics.

- Relate mathematics to everyday problems
- Make assumptions and estimations
- Explain the relationship of quantities
- Use concrete tools to explain operations
- Interpret the solution in the context of a situation

MP5 Use appropriate tools strategically.

- Consider the range of available tools (e.g., place-value charts, graphs, clocks, etc.)
- Decide on appropriate tools to use for each situation
- Use tools carefully and strategically

MP6 Attend to precision.

- Communicate with precision
- Identify the meaning of symbols
- Use measurement units appropriately
- Calculate accurately
- Carefully formulate full explanations

MP7 Look for and make use of structure.

- Search for patterns or structure
- Evaluate the structure or design of a problem
- Discuss geometric shapes in terms of their similarities and differences

MP8 Look for and express regularity in repeated reasoning.

- Make generalizations in computation
- Obtain fluency using patterns
- Look for patterns with shapes and designs
- Use patterns to relate operations
- Evaluate reasonableness of answers

Key: MP = Mathematical Practice

A

acute triangle A triangle with three acute angles.

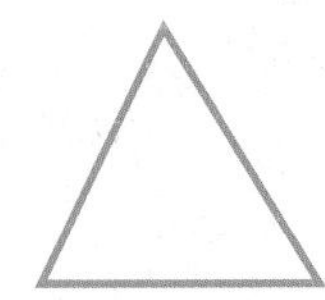

adjacent sides Sides of a polygon that are next to each other.

Associative Property of Multiplication Changing the grouping of the factors in a multiplication expression does not change the product.

For example, $(5 \times 7) \times 9 = 5 \times (7 \times 9)$

B

base The number used as a factor in exponential form.

For example, 10^2: 10 is the base.

base unit The standard unit of measurement for length, liquid volume, and mass in the metric measurement system. The base units are meter, liter, and kilogram.

braces { } Symbols used to group terms within expressions and equations.

For example, $\{\frac{2}{6} + [4 \times (\frac{5}{6} + \frac{2}{6})]\} \div 5$

brackets [ ] Symbols used to group terms within expressions and equations.

For example, $[634 - (350 + 275)] \times 5$

C

common denominator The common multiple of two or more fractions.

For example, in the addition expression $\frac{1}{8} + \frac{3}{8}$, both fractions contain the common denominator 8.

coordinate plane A grid formed by intersecting perpendicular number lines.

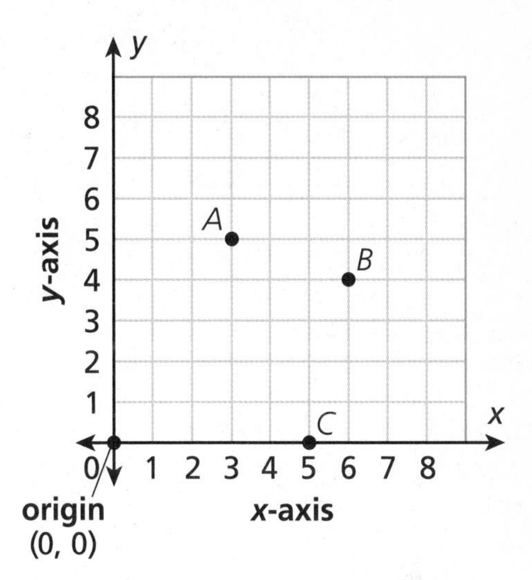

coordinates The numbers in an ordered pair used to locate a point on a coordinate plane.

For example, (3, 5): 3 is the *x*-coordinate, and 5 is the *y*-coordinate.

corresponding terms Terms that are in the same position in two patterns.

For example, pairs of corresponding terms are circled in green below.

1, 2, 3, 4, 5
3, 6, 9, 12, 15

cubic unit The volume of a unit cube.

customary units of length Units of length measure used in the customary system of measurement.

For example, inch, foot, yard, and mile

customary units of liquid volume Units of liquid volume measure used in the customary system of measurement.

For example, cup, pint, quart, and gallon.

customary units of weight Units of weight measure used in the customary system of measurement.

For example, ounce, pound, and ton.

E

equilateral triangle A triangle with three sides that are the same length.

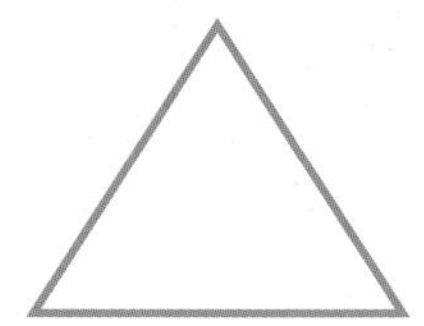

evaluate To find the value of an expression.

For example, evaluate $4 \times (9 - 3)$. The value of the expression is 24.

exponent The number of times the base is used as a factor.

For example, 10^2: 2 is the exponent.

G

grouping symbols Parentheses, brackets, and braces are examples. These symbols group parts of a mathematical expression together to show which part to evaluate first.

For example, $\{\frac{2}{6} + [4 \times (\frac{5}{6} + \frac{2}{6})]\} \div 5$

H

hierarchy diagram A diagram that uses the property of figures to relate them from the most general category to the most specific category.

I

isosceles triangle A triangle with at least two sides that are the same length.

K

kite A quadrilateral that has two pairs of adjacent sides that are the same length.

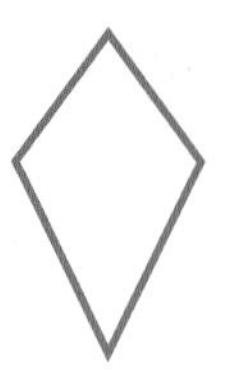

L

line plot A display of data that uses a number line and Xs symbols.

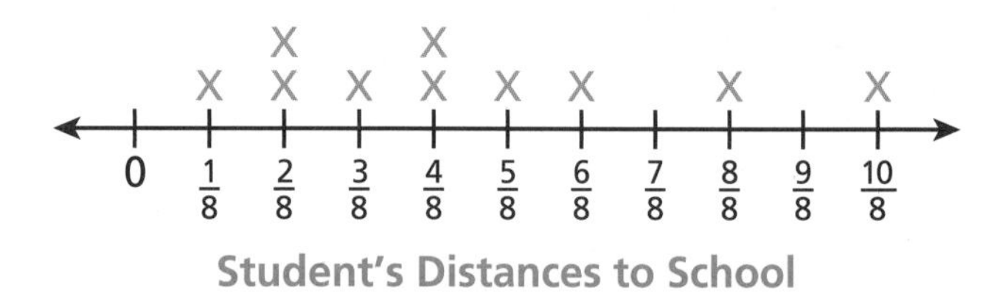

Student's Distances to School

M

metric units of length Units of length measure used in the metric system of measurement.

For example, millimeter, centimeter, meter, and kilometer.

metric units of liquid volume Units of liquid volume measure used in the metric system of measurement.

For example, milliliter, liter, and kiloliter.

metric units of mass Units of mass or weight measure used in the metric system of measurement.

For example, milligram, gram, and kilogram.

N

numerical expression A mathematical phrase containing only numbers and one or more operation symbols.

For example, "twice the sum of five and seven" or $(5 + 7) \times 2$.

numerical pattern A list of numbers that follows a constant rule.

+3 +3 +3 +3

3, 6, 9, 12, 15, . . .

O

obtuse triangle A triangle with an obtuse angle.

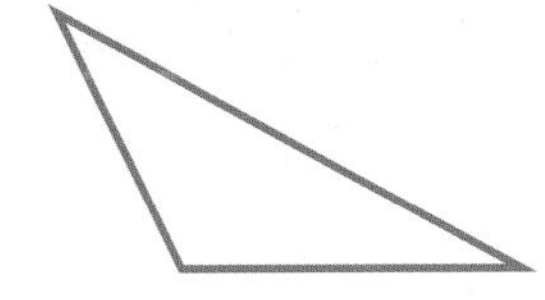

ordered pair Pairs of numbers in the form (x, y) used to locate a point on a coordinate plane.

For example, (2, 6): 2 is the x-coordinate, and 6 is the y-coordinate.

origin The point at which the x-axis and y-axis of a coordinate plane intersect. The coordinates of the origin are (0, 0).

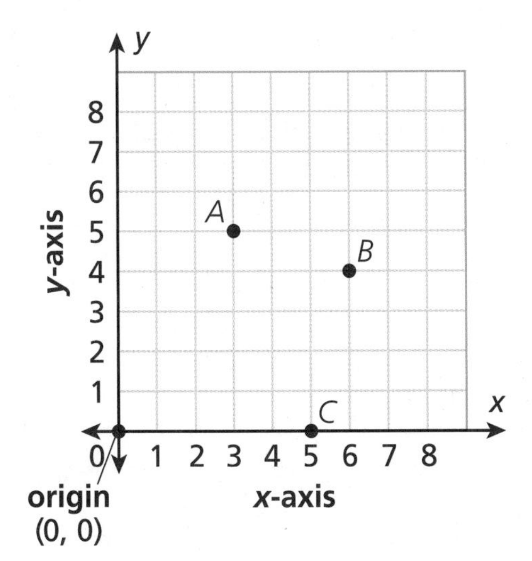

P

parentheses ( ) Symbols used to group terms within expressions and equations.

For example, $(6 + 9) \div 5$

partial product Numbers that are formed by multiplying the value of each digit by a factor.

For example, the partial products are in red.

```
      3
      2
     24
  ×  86
  -----
    144 ← 6 × 24
 +1,920 ← 80 × 24
  -----
  2,064
```

partial quotient Numbers that are formed by dividing the value of each digit by the divisor.

For example, the partial quotients are in red.

```
          4
         50
        300
    ________
 24)8,496
   -7,200
    -----
    1,296
  - 1,200
    -----
       96
      -96
      ---
        0
```

power of 10 A number with a base number of 10 and an exponent.

For example, 10^2

R

right triangle A triangle with a right angle.

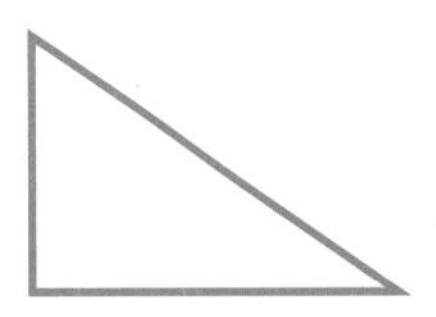

S

scale The intervals on each axis on a coordinate plane.

For example, on the coordinate plane below the *x*-axis shows a scale of 1, and the *y*-axis shows a scale of 5.

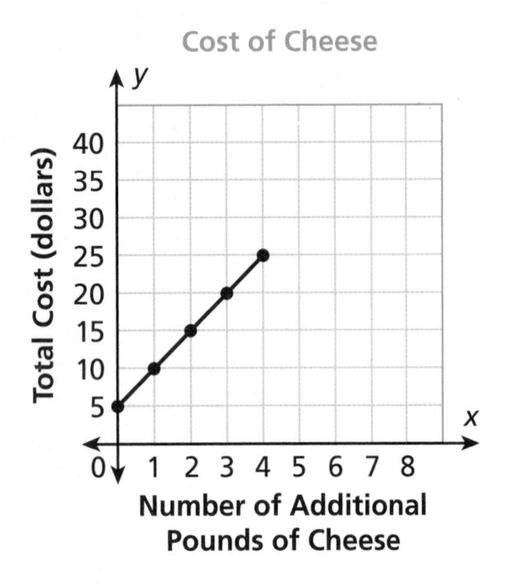

scalene triangle A triangle with no sides that are the same length.

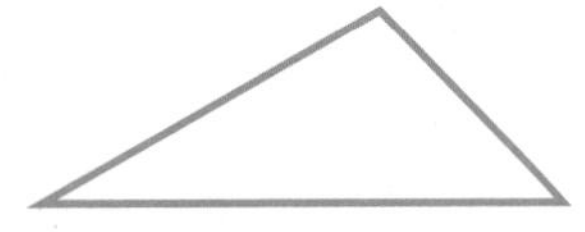

scaling Resizing a number by using multiplication.

T

trapezoid A quadrilateral that has at least one pair of parallel sides.

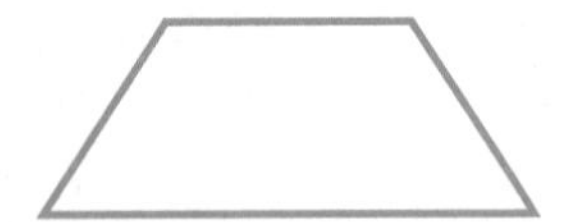

U

unit cube A cube that has edge lengths of 1 unit.

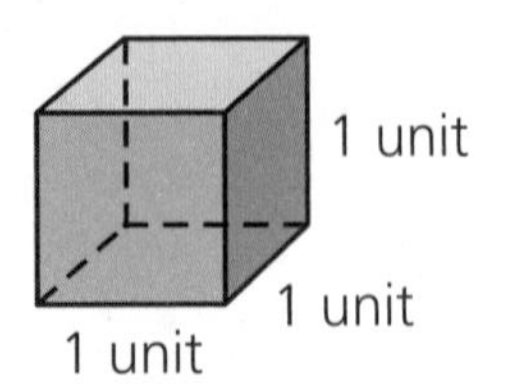

unlike denominators The denominators of two or more fractions that are different.

For example, in the subtraction expression $\frac{5}{6} - \frac{2}{3}$, each fraction has a different denominator.

V

volume A measure of the amount of space a three-dimensional figure occupies or contains.

For example, the volume of the figure below is 6 cubic units.

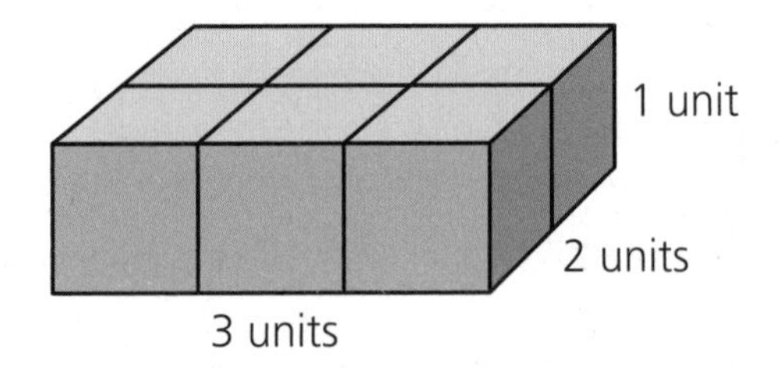

X

***x*-axis** The horizontal number line on the coordinate plane.

***x*-coordinate** The first number in an ordered pair.

For example, (3, 8): 3 is the *x*-coordinate.

Y

***y*-axis** The vertical number line on the coordinate plane.

***y*-coordinate** The second number in an ordered pair.

For example, (3, 8): 8 is the *y*-coordinate.

A

Area
of rectangles, 166–173
square units, 166–173
use tiling, 166–173

C

Common Core Review, 34–36, 128–130, 214–216, 298–300, 328–330

Common Core State Standards for Mathematical Practice, 346

Coordinate plane, 26–33, 304–311

D

Decimal
addition and subtraction of, 104–111
as quantities, 56–63
compare, 64–71
division of, 120–127
expanded form, 56–33
multiplication of, 112–119
related to fractions, 56–33
rounding, 72–79
word form, 56–33

Division
of decimals, 120–127
Distributive Property, 96–103
dividend, divisor, quotient, 88–95
equations, 96–103
methods, 88–95, 96–103, 120–127
quotients, 88–95
by unit fractions, 198–205
of unit fractions, 190–197
of whole numbers, 88–95, 96–103

E

Equations
division, 96–103
multiplication, 96–103

Equivalent fractions, 134–141, 142–149

Essential Questions—Unit, 9, 39, 133, 225, 303

Evaluate
with grouping symbols, 10–17
numerical expressions, 10–17

Expressions
evaluate, 10–17
write and interpret, 18–25

Exponent, 48–55

F

Foundational Skills Handbook
area of rectangles, 341
classifying angles, 342
classifying figures, 342
division and the Distributive Property, 338
fractions, 339
line plots, 341
multiplying fractions, 340
number patterns, 337
partial products, 339
quotients, 338
unknown factor, 337

Fractions
addition and subtraction of, 134–141
division by unit fractions, whole numbers, 198–205, 190–197
equivalent fractions, 134–141, 142–149
multiplication of, 158–165, 166–173
relation to division, 150–157
relation to scaling, 174–181
unit fractions, 190–197

G

Geometry
coordinate plane, 304–311, 312–319
hierarchy diagram, 320–327
shapes and attributes, 320–327

Grouping Symbols
braces, brackets, parentheses, 10–17

H

Home Connect, 8, 38, 132, 224, 302

L

Line plot
represent data, 242–249

Liquid volume, 226–233

M

Measurement and Data
area, 166–173
customary units, 226–233
graphing, 242–249
length, 226–233, 234–241
liquid volumes, 226–233, 234–241
mass, 234–241
metric units, 234–241
volume, 250–257, 258–265, 266–273, 274–281
weight, 226–233

Multiplication
Associative Property of, 274–281
finding unknown factors in, 96–103
fractions, 182–189
methods, 80–87, 158–165
of decimals, 112–119
of fractions, 158–165, 166–173
of whole numbers, 80–87
partial products, 80–87
power of 10, 48–55

N

Number and Operations—Decimals
addition and subtraction of, 104–111
as quantities, 56–63
comparing, 64–71
division of, 120–127
expanded form, 56–33
multiplication of, 112–119
related to fractions, 56–33
rounding, 72–79
word form, 56–33

Number and Operations—Fractions
addition and subtraction of, 134–141
division, 190–197, 198–205
multiplication, 158–165, 166–173
related to division, 150–157
related to scaling, 174–181

Number and Operations in Base Ten
add and subtract decimals, 104–111
divide decimals, 120–127
divide whole numbers, 88–95, 96–103
multiply decimals, 112–119
multiply multi-digit numbers, 80–87
round decimals, 72–79
place value, 40–47

Numerical patterns, 26–33

O

Operations and Algebraic Thinking
expressions, 10–17, 18–25
grouping symbols, 10–17
patterns, 26–33

Ordered pair, 26–33, 304–311

Order of Operations, 10–17

Origin, 26–33, 304–311

P

Partial products, 80–87

Partial quotients, 88–95

Patterns
numerical, 26–33
powers of 10, 48–55

Performance Task, 217–222, 331–336

Power of 10, 48–55

Problem solving
add and subtract fractions, 142–149
decompose to find volume, 290–297
divide unit fractions and whole numbers, 206–213
line plots, 242–249
multiply fractions, 182–189
volume formula, 282–289

Problem–Solving Model, 343–345

Progress Check, 7, 37, 131, 223, 301

Properties
Associative Property, 274–281
Distributive Property, 96–103

Q

Quadrilateral
kite, parallelogram, rectangle, rhombus, square, trapezoid, 320–327

S

Scaling by multiplying fractions, 174–181

T

Triangle
acute, equilateral, isosceles, right, scalene, 320–327

U

Unit cube, 250–257

V

Volume
use Associative Property to find, 274–281
comparison to area, 250
cubic units, 250–257
decompose to find, 290–297
use formula to find, 266–273
problem solving, 282–289, 290–297
of prisms, 250–257, 258–265
relate packing of unit cubes to multiplying, 266–273
relation to liquid volume, 250–257
understand concepts of, 250–257
units of, 250–257, 258–265

X

***x*-axis,** 26–33, 304–311

***x*-coordinate,** 26–33, 304–311

Y

***y*-axis,** 26–33, 304–311

***y*-coordinate,** 26–33, 304–311